Lettuce Wars

Lettuce Wars
Ten Years of Work and Struggle in the Fields of California

BRUCE NEUBURGER

MONTHLY REVIEW PRESS

New York

Library of Congress Cataloging-in-Publication Data

Neuburger, Bruce.
  Lettuce wars : ten years of work and struggle in the fields of California
/ Bruce Neuburger.
    p. cm.
  Includes bibliographical references and index.
  ISBN 978-1-58367-333-1 (cloth : alk. paper) — ISBN 978-1-58367-332-4
(pbk. : alk. paper) 1. Agricultural laborers—Labor unions—California. 2.
Strikes and lockouts—Agricultural laborers—California. 3. Agricultural
laborers—California—Anecdotes. I. Title. II. Title: Ten years of work and
struggle in the fields of California.
  HD1527.C2N47 2013
  331.892'835520979409047—dc23
                        2012049446

Monthly Review Press
146 West 29th Street, Suite 6W
New York, New York 10001

www.monthlyreview.org

5 4 3 2 1

Contents

To all those rightfully discontent with the stunted present.
To those who recognize a greater potential for humankind.
And especially to those who dare to dream and work, live and die,
for a world without *exploitation and oppression.*

To a future when our grandchildren and the generations that follow
will ask incredulously, "Was there once *really* a system that allowed
some people to live off the exploited labor of other people?
How could that have been?"

ACKNOWLEDGMENTS

As I was privileged to be a participant in one of the great social movements of our time, it is to the farmworkers and all those who struggled with them that I owe this acknowledgment first and foremost. I can only hope that this book will serve in some small way as such an acknowledgement.

As to the many, many people who contributed to this book, I shall only mention a few by name. One is my nephew, Steven Stoll, whose prodding encouragement and timely, insightful advice moved me into and over the humps of this project. Another is Mickey Hewitt, whose friendship extends decades and who gave of his time and knowledge to read, discuss, offer advice, and share experience. A third is Rafael Lemus, one of those "ordinary" farmworker leaders without whom there is no movement; I'm grateful for the hours spent hearing his stories, a few brief segments of which appear in this book. Rafael passed away in May 2010. Finally, Aristeo Zambrano and Mario Bustamente are among the Salinas area rank-and-file farmworker union leaders who have given, in my humble view, the movement its most important legacy. This book benefited greatly from their experience, insights, and contagious passion for social justice.

I extend my gratitude to the many other veteran farmworkers of the 1970s who shared stories and insights in homes, on the streets, at various locations, such as Kristy's donut shop near the Salinas shapeup, and at the De Anza Hotel in Calexico, where I was the beneficiary of the stories and critical observations from those with lifetimes of farm work experience. Gratitude also to the dozens of farmworkers in Salinas, Huron, Coachella, and Calexico who took the time to share their perceptions, experiences, anger, and at times, humorous dissections of life in the fields of today with that curious stranger holding a notebook. And to them I owe a vivid realization that the struggle against this monstrously exploitive apartheid system continues.

I owe a debt to many teacher colleagues and friends who read the manuscript in various stages and offered suggestions, advice, and encouragement. Their enthusiastic assurances often served as timely antidotes to the paralytic doubts that surfaced from time to time. I owe a debt as well to historian Sid Valledor, in whose long conversations I learned much about the Filipino contribution to movement of the 1970s.

William LeFevre at the Reuther Library at Wayne State, home of the UFW archive, gave valuable assistance whenever I asked for it, and librarians up and down California's Central Valley smoothed my way into many a microfilm archive. And I want to acknowledge my old friend and former colleague, Maria Roddy, and the staff at the Salinas Steinbeck library, whose struggle has kept those library doors open and whose care and conscientious work have maintained a valuable and well-organized collection of materials on those lettuce war years of the 1970s.

Frank Bardacke's hunger for tacos got the whole story rolling for me in 1971. Bardacke's insights on farm work and his great research and writing on farmworker history has enriched my own understanding, as have the writings of Ann Aurelia Lopez, Miriam Pawel, and others

Bob Avakian, in his life's work, has audaciously upheld revolution and dared to advance revolutionary theory, maintaining confidence in our battered and maligned humankind to build a new and transformed future. To his vision and steadfastness, I owe a great deal.

I cannot end this without acknowledging women such as Guillermina, Angelina, and Juanita, whose spirits have been the powerful, if largely unacknowledged, motor of farmworker struggles. They inspired me then, and they inspire me still today. No genuine movement for social justice or liberation in the fields or in the world is thinkable without the participation and liberating energy of such women.

SAN FRANCISCO, 1984

IT WAS EARLY EVENING, a few hours before my shift's end. In the cab line at the St. Francis Hotel in San Francisco it was the regular crapshoot. Sit in line and take your chances or cruise the streets for fares in hope of being bounced around the city like a pinball. You got in line because, like the people who work slot machines, there's always the chance of a jackpot. Here you invest your minutes, not your money, but the anticipation is similar. It was airport action that represented the most likely bonanza. Better odds here than cruising or taking your chances on radio calls—of a rigged radio at that—though at the St. Francis you could easily end up waiting fifteen or twenty minutes for a $5 ride to the Wharf.

This is one of the pains and attractions of cab driving—the dice are always rolling. In an hourly job there's the security of knowing what you'll take home at the end of the day. A cabby never knows. No matter how bad your day or even your week, the chance of scoring the *big ride* lurks behind every call and every "flag."

San Francisco cab companies put the allure of the gamble squarely in the drivers' job description when, in 1978, they backed a ballot proposition that won voter favor. It set up a lease arrangement. Cab company employees were suddenly "independent contractors." Independence! One of those alluring terms that hides less alluring realities: the end of company health benefits, retirement benefits—any benefits. Independence, ya right, you're on your own, good luck!

As the line at the St. Francis crept forward and my cab inched toward the front of the pack, I kept a close eye on the guests leaving the front door. This one with baggage, airport; that one, in casual clothes, probably heading for the Wharf; just behind them a well-dressed woman with a big Macy's bag, maybe heading home to the Marina or Russian Hill.

When a man in his forties, wearing a business suit with a suit bag and small suitcase left the door, my anticipation rose. And when I pulled forward and heard the doorman's flat-handed whack on the trunk of my blue and white Desoto Cab, I felt grateful—an airport! My annoyance at the doorman's outstretched and grasping hand (done surreptitiously for the sake of the clientele) as he tossed the luggage in the trunk, was mollified by the security of a $30 trip. I immediately began to calculate my best odds: playing the airport roulette or deadheading back to town.

As my passenger settled into the back, we headed down Powell to Ellis and then down to Stockton, across Market to the 4th Street entrance to the freeway. I looked in the rearview at my benefactor. "What airline?" "United." He had the fleshy face of someone who was no stranger to a dinner table. His brown hair was short, but long enough to comb to the side. No facial hair. A businessman or a lawyer, I guessed. This was no tourist—too deliberate and matter-of-fact for that.

I was still in my early years of cab driving, which meant I still relished conversations with the anticipation of gleaning some noteworthy exchange or story to pass on to cabby friends at the cab lot, where we waited to turn in our waybills, gates, and dispatcher bribes (tips) for the shift. The appreciation, the enthusiasm for this, which characterized the first few years on the job, and perhaps for some retains its attraction longer, was gradually wearing away, like the tread on cab tires, by the relentless bounding of traffic, the tyranny of repetition.

Perhaps it's true that every person who steps into a cab is a potential story, but like any kind of mining it takes energy and effort to retrieve the nugget from among the slag of normal chatter. My energy had spiked a bit then, juiced by the good fortune of an airport ride. I dug.

I found my passenger was returning to Chicago, or perhaps it was New York, after several days of meetings. "I enjoy your city," he said, as many visitors do, "but I didn't see much this time—too many long meetings." What kind of meetings were those? "Lawyer business, man, legal strategies and all that." A lawyer, as I'd guessed, but the "man" in there spoke of something less straight than his appearance conveyed. I was searching for another handle for the conversation when he offered, "I was meeting with some of your local growers' people. Well, maybe not exactly local—Salinas, that's not that far from here, am I right?" "Not too far," I said. "What kind of growers?" "Lettuce, vegetable growers," he said, "looking to get out from under their union contracts." "And you're part of that?" I asked. "Legal advice, strategies, that sort of thing. Those contracts are legally binding agreements. You can't just drop them. There are issues that need to be considered." He paused and patted his breast pocket as though he was making sure of something, an airline ticket maybe?

"And if the companies go out of business, then return to operation under a different name, they're no longer bound by the legal commitments of the previous company?" I asked. In the rearview I saw the passenger look up. "Sounds like you have a legal mind. You might be in the wrong business." He laughed. "Well, I've heard about that kind of thing happening in Salinas," I said. "Read about it?" he asked. "Ya, I guess so. Don't remember where."

Actually I knew a fair amount about Salinas, unions, and lettuce growers. I'd spent most of the previous decade working in the lettuce fields, and I knew people working in the fields there. And I knew things were going in a bad direction for them. But I didn't feel like explaining that. I wanted to hear what my rider had to say.

The lawyer was frank. He discussed dumping unions as another of his profession might explain the writing of a will or the drawing up of a contract. He was interested in technical, legal questions, like an architect consumed by the design and engineering details of a building, not how it will affect the neighborhood in which it is built. Or like the technocrat designing a bomb, oblivious, numbed, or just removed from the deadly consequences of *its* architecture. But there was also a hint of the cynical there, as though he understood there was something foul in this business.

The conversation had taken an unexpected turn, and I found the trip, which I'd sought to make as quickly as possible, too short to fill my curiosity. I eased my foot slightly off the pedal as the names Hanson, Sun Harvest, Cal Coastal, Salinas Lettuce Farmers Co-op, and others rolled out in my passenger's description. He saw bored lawyers scratching notes on legal pads and well-dressed growers' representatives discussing legal strategies; I saw farm labor buses, their sides freshly repainted, and lettuce workers with knives sticking out their back pockets standing in the chill of a morning street trying to catch a job, with the trepidations of soldiers defeated in battle, hoping for lenient treatment from their captors.

When we hit the curb at United, I popped the trunk and set his bags by the curb. Then I said what I felt I had to say, if only to relieve the pressure that was building during the conversation. "You know, when the growers drop their union contracts the workers lose their seniority, their health benefits, even their jobs. This causes real suffering to them, their families, their children—everyone is affected. And these contracts were won through long, tough struggle." The lawyer looked up from his bags. He handed me two twenties. "No one said life was fair." And, I thought, glibness is a lot easier when it's not *your* ass being ground into the dirt. The lawyer gave a hint of a shrug as he looked at me. It seemed he was about to stop and say something more, but he picked up his bags and all that came out was, "Keep the change, bud." He headed off to his flight.

1. THE THINNING CREW, OR "LOS AGACHADOS"

Seaside, California, Spring 1971

DESPITE THE SERIOUSNESS OF THE ISSUE at hand, I had to keep from laughing. "You want me to burn this place down?" Ben didn't look at me but at the wall next to the refrigerator room, stacked with bags of beans and rice and cans of chile for making chile rellenos. There was weariness in his eyes and a sense of desperation in his voice. "Rosa," he said, "she almost killed herself two nights ago. The bullet was just this close to her heart." He held his fingers apart an inch, about level with his face. "You know, we're having a hard time here in this location." I knew about that. But Rosa, with a gun to her heart . . . the image was unreal to me.

I knew that the situation was difficult. The Highway 1 freeway now bypassed Seaside, so that traffic no longer flowed through the business district as it had when Ben and Rosa had opened up their small restaurant on Fremont Boulevard several years before. Their first restaurant had been displaced from its location when urban renewal wiped out an entire neighborhood and turned it into a huge ugly auto mall in the middle of the city. And now it appeared they were going to lose this new place as well. Rosa, despondent about their money problems, and perhaps other things I had no inkling of, had put a gun to her chest, breathed deep, and sent a bullet through her body within a whisper of ending her breath forever.

Ben looked toward the door that led from the kitchen to the takeout area adjacent to a small parking lot, and spoke without looking at me, "With the insurance money I could start over. I could give you several thousand dollars." His large hands rested in his lap on the kitchen apron he wore when he was cooking.

"Ben," I said, "Margaret lives upstairs. Other people live upstairs. What if somebody dies?" Margaret, a single mother and the restaurant's waitress, had worked there since the move to Fremont Boulevard. Her apartment was right above the restaurant. Not that I would have considered Ben's scheme even if that wasn't the case.

Ben looked at me for the first time since the subject came up and then he looked away. "You're right, Bruce, it's a crazy idea."

You don't know how crazy, Ben. I thought about the day several weeks before when I rode to work lying in the back seat of the CRLA attorney's car to avoid the police who'd come to my house looking for me. I hadn't told Ben about it, and I wasn't sure if I should tell him now. Nor about being put in a Seaside jail, for a fix-it ticket. Or about that tiny barred room in the jailhouse where I yelled obscenities at a cop who seemed to find it all amusing. Or the FBI agent who *happened* to conveniently appear soon after my incarceration and who *only* wanted me to answer a few "simple" questions about my "political associations." I mocked his questions and gave him wise-ass replies, too young and foolish to keep quiet, too naive to understand just how much my privileges of birth protected me from the reality he represented. But not so naïve that I didn't notice that someone was keeping tabs on me.

I didn't tell Ben any of this. He had enough to think about with a wife in the hospital and a business about to go under. And anyway I had my youthful mistrust of older people.

"You know, I can't keep you on anymore," Ben said. "Maybe two more weeks and that's it." "I'm sorry," I said. And I was. I liked Ben and Rosa and enjoyed cooking in their restaurant, even when, or perhaps especially when, it was busy and it was a challenge to keep up with the orders—rolling enchiladas and frying rellenos, preparing the beans and rice, then assembling everything on the plate, covering it with the grated cheese from a large stainless steel pot, pulling the hot plates from the stove, and setting them out on the pick-up table with the order tucked underneath, and, with the same motion, making another plate disappear into that dark hot cave.

Even doing the dishes and mopping were like a game at times. I loved it when little Zoraida, the daughter in whose name Ben and Rosa christened their restaurant, was around. If it wasn't too busy I'd pick up the mop and dance around the kitchen with it until she laughed so hard she'd fall down from the delight of seeing an adult act so screwy. I also liked the times when friends came around the takeout window and I could give them freebie tacos and chips, though I wasn't going to mention that to Ben either.

There were times when I felt really bothered. Not by the work or the hot kitchen, or anything like that, but by the music drifting in on Friday and Saturday nights from the Okie bar next door. What really got me was Merle Haggard's "Fightin' Side of Me" blasting from the bar like some anthem, an anthem for ignoramuses. And the ignoramuses would play it over and over again until I wanted to throw a frying pan at the wall that allowed the sound to penetrate.

My days as a cook were quickly coming to an end when FJ showed up at the takeout window. Enrique, my kitchen associate, and his girlfriend were at a table in the little fast-food area, and I didn't want to give any food away in front of Enrique. I was also beginning to feel guilty about the plight of Ben and Rosa, so I had to charge FJ full price for the tacos. But he didn't seem to mind. In fact, he was in a really good mood, not at all rare for FJ who loved to joke around. He was aware of our woes at the restaurant and that I'd be soon hunting for a job.

Both of us were refugees from the radical movement in Berkeley. I'd come to Seaside in the late winter of 1969 to work in an antiwar GI coffeehouse project. FJ, an antiwar movement veteran, moved south to the Monterey Peninsula months later with visions of combining his passions for writing, baseball, and political activism. We'd met some time after the coffeehouse opened, early 1970.

"I think I have a proposition you're gonna like," he said. "I picked up a guy hitchhiking the other day near Ord and took him to Monterey, and we talked on the way and he told me something pretty interesting. You remember the strike last year in Salinas?" I knew about César Chávez. Rosa had an article about him up on the wall of the takeout area. And the Salinas Valley, a major farming area, was just up the road from Seaside. The previous spring I'd gone with GIs and civilian activists from Fort Ord to Salinas, one of the few times I'd been there, to act as security at a farmworker rally where Chávez had spoken. We were part of a group that called itself MDM, the Movement for a Democratic Military, which began among the Marines at Camp Pendleton and spread rapidly to Fort Ord and beyond. Someone in the group had arranged for us to help out the farmworkers. We showed up at the rally site, the GIs in their civilian clothes with MDM t-shirts and armbands, and were sent around the college field to keep a lookout for troublemakers. The growers in the area were threatening to disrupt the rally. We stood guard around the rally and on the roof of a nearby building, though we weren't really sure who we should be watching for. As it turned out, the rally was pretty uneventful, at least as far as any disruption was concerned.

But otherwise I was unaware of what was going on in the fields of Salinas. Our focus that spring was on the student actions that had broken out all over the country in response to the invasion of Cambodia. MDM soldiers and civilians like myself had gone to the Greek theater at the UC Berkeley campus at the invitation of striking students. Malik Shabazz, one of the GI leaders at Ord, had addressed thousands of students packed into the theater thanking them for rebelling against a war that pitted poor and oppressed people in the United States against people they had no business or interest in fighting.

We'd also gone to Stanford a few days later just as the pot was boiling over on that campus. In one of the school's auditoriums the conservative students, who by that time were arguing a pacifist point of view, were debating the more radical students about steps to take in response to Nixon's invasion of Cambodia, proposing a sit-in or something like that. The radical students were not in the mood. They wanted to take more decisive action to get ROTC off their campus.

There was outrage in the air and it struck to the bone. The war was now being escalated despite Nixon's pledge to pull out the troops. People were outraged at the secret bombings of Cambodia, whose scope and deadliness were just beginning to come to light. The radical students, the majority present at that meeting, were boiling, but they wanted to hear what GIs in their midst had to say about the situation. The GIs were also bitterly unhappy. Nearly all were Vietnam vets, angry that what they had fought for was a lie and drawn to the outraged spirit of the students and a radical analysis of the system that sent them there.

The year 1968 had been a turning point. The Tet Offensive in January had extinguished the "light at the end of the tunnel" that U.S. President Lyndon Johnson insisted he kept seeing. The assassination of Martin Luther King Jr. in April and the uprising that followed set the fires of rebellion burning in the hearts of youths in and out of uniform. Many were becoming convinced that the old order was no longer worth defending. In fact, many GIs were concluding that they'd been pointing their weapons in the wrong direction; their real enemies were the ones who had been giving the orders. In any case, what the GIs said in that Stanford auditorium stoked the outrage. As the temperature rose, we were told by one of the faculty that it was prudent for us to leave before the shit hit the fan. We left. And it did.

Not long after we returned to Seaside, news came that Stanford students had set the ROTC building on fire![1] Things were very hectic around the coffeehouse and on the base. That whole summer we faced numerous efforts to sabotage and break up the GI organization that had so dramatically and rapidly grown. For us, the farmworkers' strike of that August of 1970 was a distant rumble.

"So what'd the hitchhiker have to say?" I asked FJ. "He told me he'd just spent a few weeks in Salinas working the fields. There's a union hiring hall that was set up after the strike, part of the contract. You can get work there through the union—in the fields!" FJ laughed, almost doubling over. "That's great, isn't it!" Even if I didn't quite see it that way at the moment, there's no way I'd admit it. FJ was far too happy to contradict. I had no idea what this meant. But I needed a job, and the idea of working in the fields, among farmworkers, seemed pretty damn interesting. Great, actually.

When I told Ben about my decision to work in the lettuce fields he gave me a fatherly look. "I guess a few weeks out there won't hurt." I got the impression that he thought I wouldn't last very long. As to that, I had no idea. I just knew that with the GI coffeehouse shut down and most of the active-duty organizers now returned home, there was nothing holding me in Seaside.

Dispatched

So, on a Monday in April, FJ and I headed south and east from Seaside along the Monterey-Salinas Road, Highway 68, that runs through a narrow valley skirting the Laguna Seca raceway and Fort Ord and the rolling hills of the Santa Lucia Mountains, which form the eastern edge of the Carmel Valley. At River Road the highway crosses into a broad fertile valley that stretches from Monterey Bay at its northern end eighty miles south past San Ardo.

Salinas sits at the northern end of the Salinas Valley a few miles from the Bay, close enough to be regularly swaddled by its cool, damp breezes. The city straddles Highway 101, the modern offspring of the Spanish-colonial El Camino Real.

We found the farmworkers' union office on Wood Street, in a building that was once a post office, half a block from Alisal Street in the district by that name. The hall was not much more than a large room with chairs and benches placed haphazardly along its edges. A dozen or so men and women in work clothes sat in small clusters along the perimeter. Fluorescent light fixtures attached by long metal poles hung from the ceiling. On the far wall a large, hand-painted sign proclaimed "Viva La Huelga!" and a magazine rack against a wall held a collection of newspapers and leaflets in English and Spanish.

At the far end of the hall were several makeshift teller windows. They looked as though they had been recently hammered together with pine and plywood. Above one of the rectangular openings was a handwritten sign: "Dispachos."

FJ and I waited in the short line that crept toward one of the windows. An animated woman in her thirties greeted us at the window. "Are you here for work?" she asked. We nodded. She looked at us for a few seconds, maybe to see if we just might realize we'd made a mistake. "We have jobs in the thinning—thinning and hoeing, is that okay?" We nodded.

"I'm Gloria," the woman said as she filled out the work dispatch. "Welcome to our new union. You know that the hourly wage with the new contract is $2.10?—that's the highest in the valley." Gloria smiled as she handed us our copies. "We ask you to pay union dues in advance." "How much is that?" FJ asked, digging in a pocket for his wallet. "It's $10.50, that's three months. We ask everyone to pay in advance. Then you won't get bothered for three months," she said cheerfully. Neither of us said what we both were thinking—what if we don't make it that long? As it was we only had enough to pay for the first month. "You can pay after your first check. But don't forget. We can't run this struggle without funds." We nodded again.

Gloria asked if we knew the address she'd written on the dispatch, and then, in our silence, proceeded to draw us a map. "This is where you'll meet your bus. You've got to be there about 5:15." At that, my excitement was challenged by a new sensation, dread, as I thought of getting up at four the next morning to make it to work. As we turned to leave Gloria said, "I don't think you've worked in the fields before?" We shook our heads. "Well, good luck."

It was still dark when we entered the large parking lot Gloria had mapped out. The *corralón*, as it was called by the farmworkers, was off Market Street adjacent to a building housing a California State Farm Labor office. At the far side of the parking lot was a row of white buses, their sides emblazoned with letters. Yellow parking lot lights played off the bus windows amplifying a glow that contrasted with darkened buildings surrounding the lot.

As we got closer we could make out the letters on the buses: Interharvest, in green letters, was written on the majority of them. This we discovered was one of the main gathering points for farm labor buses of recently unionized companies. Companies that had not signed with the union, or rather, the United Farmworkers' Organizing Committee as it was called, chose to gather their crews elsewhere.

Perhaps a dozen of these white and green Interharvest buses were here at the corralón. There were also a smattering of buses from other companies like Fresh Pict and D'Arrigo Brothers.

Workers streamed in from side streets breaking the early morning stillness. The women were dressed in jackets and sweatshirts, most of them wearing baseball caps emblazoned with the names of companies or towns, "Mexico," or the stylized black eagle symbol of the union. Most of the women had scarves under the caps that covered their foreheads, and in some cases their faces, though for most the scarves were open and dangled by their cheeks as they walked. The men wore baseball caps, wide-brimmed cowboy hats, and straw hats. A few wore knit caps. Like the women many men carried sturdy, plastic tote bags of various colors filled with containers and wide-mouth thermoses. Some workers came in clutching cups of coffee.

Shouts of greetings pierced the otherwise quiet, heavy morning air, and there was some laughter and what we could only assume was friendly banter animated by arm waving and handshaking.

This was the first year of union organization in the vegetable fields, the first season since the big strike the previous summer. And perhaps the oddness of a couple of young gringos asking awkwardly for such and such a crew matched the oddness of this new time. Something dramatic had changed, and now we were, in a sense, a part of that. Groups of people gathered near the buses and in one of them I recognized Gloria from the union hall, clipboard in hand, taking notes it seemed and discussing something that engaged the attention of the small crowd around her.

We finally found our assigned bus and stood at its open door. The driver looked puzzled as we stepped on. The dispatches we thrust at him did not seem to alleviate his confusion, but he motioned us to get in.

Since it was still dark outside the bus's internal lights were on. We were greeted by amused and curious looks from the passengers waiting to leave for the fields. They varied from girls in their late teens to women in their forties, and a few well past that age. Most of the men were also teenagers or older men. Later we found out that a lot of the men in their middle years worked the better-paid but more physically demanding piece-rate jobs.

We walked toward the back of the bus passing pairs of young women, a few male-female couples, what looked to be women with their teenage daughters, a few single men of various ages, including one who greeted us in English, and who, we later learned, was the union rep. At the very back of the bus was a silent figure, dressed in dark clothing with a baseball cap pushed back on his head, smoking a pipe. He stood out as the only person reading a newspaper, holding it at an angle to catch the light.

FJ and I found a seat near the back and sat together. I nervously looked around and then settled back, with my knees propped up against the seat in front of me with its metal backing.

The driver pulled the door lever, cranked the engine awake, and set the gear with a brief sharp grind. The bus lurched out of the lot onto Market Street and south toward the fields. Our trip lasted thirty minutes or so, including stops to pick up several people from street corners along the way. The sound of the bus engine rose and fell as it accelerated and decelerated, gears clanging into place; the rattling of windows, and who knows what bus bolts and rivets; the clatter of a chain that secured the portable toilets the bus towed behind it. There was little, if any, conversation. Occasionally someone turned in their seats to see if the two phantoms were still there. We made an odd-looking pair with our lighter hair and skin and our Anglo mannerisms. That neither of us wore a hat, well, that alone made us stand out.

We headed south out of the city on 101. Traffic was light, but there were other buses of various colors, some being trailed by lines of cars. Our bus turned off the highway just passed a sign that said "Chualar," and then onto a dirt road.

The sun now began to peek above the Gabilan Mountains on the eastern rim of the valley, sending a spray of light across the valley to the hills that ascend above River Road. The air was moist from coastal fog. The ground was wet, but only superficially from the dew. The smell of the fields, of soil and vegetables, hung in the air. It would become a familiar smell. Gradually, from the pale light emerged the outlines and patterns of fields, some brown and flat, others sprouting bands of green in various thicknesses amid rows of dark soil. From the higher spots in the road you could see the patchwork of fields carpeting the valley and angling up the gentle slopes of distant hills.

Finally the bus came to a stop on a road lined on one side with a ditch and on the other by a broad flat field with its rows of small green plants radiating out into the distance. Emerging from the haze, other farm labor buses appeared, pulling up to fields, some halting near large, dark, motionless figures that we found out later were lettuce machines. Felix, our foreman, pulled open the back door of the bus and began sliding tools that were piled behind the back seat, onto the ground, as we slowly left the bus.

Puerto Rico, the union shop steward, introduced himself in English and asked if we had ever thinned before. "No, never. This is our first day in the fields," we answered, surveying the damp ground and the crew slowly making their way down the dirt road from the corner where the bus had stopped. FJ and I both laughed as the foreman handed us hoes long enough to maybe touch our knees. The foreman and Puerto Rico exchanged some words. "The foreman wants to know if you know the work. I told him you guys are new. He'll show you what to do. You'll get the idea. And don't worry, the company has to give you time to learn." While the union rep turned and walked down the road to his row, the foreman, a short man in his early forties, wearing a tan broad-brimmed hat, a tan suede jacket, dark cotton pants, and leather boots, led FJ and I to the edge of the field, to rows of young lettuce we were there to thin—*desaijar*, we learned, was the word in Spanish. The foreman demonstrated while we watched, leaning down over the young lettuce plants, his body bent at the waist at a 90-degree angle, his two feet set in the trough between the rows of plants. With his right hand holding the short hoe, he hit at the ground with swift sure blows, sending a spray of dirt and infant lettuce plants, leaving behind, at eleven-inch intervals, tiny plants looking frail and vulnerable in their new singularities. He then set the hoe blade down on the row to demonstrate the distance between the lettuce plants. He swept his hand around several of the plants to clear the row of any weeds that remained. There were none, but he said, "Quita la yerba," and picked up a weed and tossed it to illustrate what he meant. After several minutes he stood up and motioned for us to begin.

Our backs began to hurt after the first few minutes, By the time we'd worked half an hour, the morning had barely established itself, the air was still cool and damp, and we were sweating and struggling, watching the rest of the crew glide silently off in the distance. The foreman, Felix, did sections of our rows for us, and then sent other crew members to boost us forward. We staggered ahead, awkwardly flaying at the earth, pushed forward by a stubborn determination not to give up.

Around ten o'clock we heard cries from several directions, "Quebrada! Quebrada!" followed by laughter. We stood up to see the crew lying or sitting in the rows, some in small circles, a few laughing at the sight of us working after break had begun, and then, in free fall to the dirt on realizing it was break time.

We lay motionless next to the row of lettuce shoots. Who would have thought lying in the dirt could feel so good? After a few moments I pulled myself up on my knees. "Fuck, this is hard!" FJ said. "What the hell did we get ourselves into here?" "That's the last time I'm listening to suggestions from a hitchhiker," I answered back. "How do you think that guy did out here?" I asked. "Why do you think he was leaving town?" FJ replied. We both laughed so hard we almost choked. Puerto Rico came over to see how we were doing. "This is great, I'm enjoying every minute of it," I said. "When does the real work begin?" FJ asked. Puerto Rico laughed. "They always give us the easy fields in the morning," he said. "Great," I said, laughing, "but when does it stop hurting?" "When you stop working," he said, as he turned and walked toward his row.

After break we staggered on. We tried to talk while working, but the pain was such that it was hard to think. Every few minutes we stood up to survey where we were, but we still couldn't see the end of the row. Some time after noon we reached the end of the row with a lot of help from the crew. The foreman had moved the bus from where we began at the beginning of the rows to the end of the rows and waited until everyone had emerged from that first pass to call for a lunch break. Some of the crew sat on the ground at the edge of the road with their tote bags, preparing to eat. FJ and I lunged our way up into the bus where we'd left our lunches. While we sat eating, Domi, a good-natured woman whom I guessed was in her early forties, handed each of us a styrofoam cup with a thick white liquid. "Have this," she said, "for your energy." The cup was warm; the thick liquid was rice pudding with cinnamon. It was fantastic. As we stood up to leave the bus, I thanked her, "Gracias, muchas gracias." "Por nada, mijo" (You're welcome, my son), she said, using a term of endearment I would later learn the meaning of.

We somehow made it through the rest of the day, barely noticing the movement of the sun as it crossed from one set of hills toward another. The sheer pleasure of tossing our hoes in the back of the bus and flopping in our seats for the ride home was indescribable. We watched the fields glide by on the trip back to the corralón, noticing the trucks stacked with boxes of lettuce racing toward town. We got in my car, a '54 Ford with a tiny steering wheel and a missing back window, and drove back to Seaside. By the time we arrived, evening was already coming on. We ate and slept.

At 4 a.m. we were up again, slapping together sandwiches and then making our way back to Salinas. It was a damp morning and the headlights reflected off the floating droplets of fog. We compared our body pains and concluded that there were areas of pain in places we had never experienced it before, in places we didn't know we *had* before. There are many pains one experiences in life, and we comforted ourselves that, on balance, these pains were good pains, not the pain that comes with illness or sadness, but the pain that comes with doing new things—the pains of growth, to put it another way.

We arrived at the corralón and were greeted by our fellow crew members, some, I suspect, surprised to see us back. Felix seemed both surprised and disappointed.

It wasn't long before we received our first Spanish lessons in commentaries on work—"Mucho trabajo, poco dinero!" A lot of work for little money—a phrase that more than one crew member thought it important for us to know. And there were jokes and insults, usually directed at the foreman and the company. "El mayordomo es un cabrón" (The foreman's an ass.), said Reuben while he and his sister Maggie laughed. Reuben stood straight and tall as he instructed us in that important phrase, and we stood to look him in the eye, as it would be improper for a student to remain bent over during a lesson. Reuben was one of the few young men on the crew and was thinning while he waited for his harvest crew to begin.

Like many people, Reuben felt more confident and less intimidated this first year of a union foothold. "El es un pinche barbero," he informed us, referring once again to the foreman, and it had nothing to do with his ability to cut hair. A *barbero*, we learned, was a company man (or woman), a kiss-ass, anyone who curried favors from the company. Often this judgment was reserved for workers who worked faster than thought reasonable for the money that the job paid or who sought the protection or favors from the company while deriding efforts to unite the crew.

El Cortito

After lettuce, broccoli, cauliflower, celery, or beets are planted, usually in a thick long patch, they must be thinned out to allow enough space between the plants for growth. At the same time weeds are also removed. This work was done by a hoe called the "West Coast shorty" by the English-speaking workers, "*el cortito*" by everyone else. El cortito had a long and infamous history in the annals of farm work, I would later find out. How many backs it wrecked is anyone's guess, but who was counting? It had been popular in the fields for perhaps a hundred years, from the time the Chinese came to California fields to work the sugar beets—popular, that is, among the growers. There were reports of protests and even work stoppages going back to at least the 1920s by workers fed up with the short hoe. The Salinas Valley strike the previous year brought calls to end its use. César Chávez had declared its elimination one of the goals of the union. But the growers vigorously defended its use.

El cortito can only be used bent over and with one hand, and as such it leaves one hand free to pull weeds or any "doubles," extra lettuce plants, that the scrape of the hoe leaves behind. Properly used the hoe called for two swipes to knock away the excess plants and leave a space between the remaining plants of about one and a half widths of the hoe blade. Conveniently, any foreman could instantly survey his crew of *agachados*—people bent over—and see who was working and who was not. The labor contractor or company supervisor, with many crews working at once, could, by one glance from the road, be assured of labor efficiency, measured in bent bodies. Working bent over for hours at a time causes intense pain, and the only relief was to stand up. Often the only time a worker could stand up without risk of reprimand or worse was at the end of the row, when for a few precious moments you could "legitimately" walk with your back straight until you reached your next row. So this

brief reward served as an inducement to work faster to finish up a row—
an efficient instrument of production, an effective means of control and
subjugation. It was to capitalist farm labor what the whip was to slavery,
an instrument, and a symbol as well.

The Crew

Pain and fatigue were constant companions in the thinning. But as days
and weeks went by their dominance over our every thought and conversation dissipated, dulling into a persistent background noise. As we got
better at clearing weeds and spacing plants we gained space to connect
with the broader life of the crew. Our initial efforts to use the language
of our co-workers brought amusement, and at times hysterical laughter
from our teachers for the awkward way we repeated phrases in Spanish.
Finding us two eager parrots, seemingly impervious to embarrassment,
some of the crew, especially the younger women, could not restrain their
teasing. They tried out their arsenals of puns and tongue twisters on us.
One day, as I was bent down, pounding my hoe among baby lettuce plants
and weeds, a young campesina several rows over, her face covered with
the bandana most women wore as protection from the sun, caught my
attention and asked sweetly, "Que hora son, corazón?" amid the laughter
of her friends. Evelia Hernandez, a shy girl of seventeen or eighteen who
always worked alongside her mother, assailed me, over a period of time
with a dazzling array of tongue twisters so seemingly complex and yet
spoken with such rapid fluidity that it left me speechless. Well, not quite.
I tried to repeat them but never got beyond the first few words—"El que
poco coco compra, poco coco come . . ."

As the days went by, we began to feel more comfortable on the crew,
warmed by the generosity and friendliness we experienced, to say nothing
of the food we were handed without a chance of refusal. The spicy stews,
the pozole, the pinto beans with chunks of ham, the rice with vegetables, the meat and salsa tacos, all kept warm in the workers' wide-mouth
thermoses, put to shame our limp sandwiches, made bleary-eyed in our
dimly lit Seaside shack, and motivated us to change our own culinary
habits. I especially appreciated the rice pudding that Domi continued to
offer me on those occasions when we were near each other in the field
when the foreman yelled "quebrada!" or "lonche!" (both words had first
come to life north of the Mexican border as they were based on a cross-
pollination of English and Spanish). Domi usually worked alongside her
teenage daughter Carmen. They'd come north together from Michoacan,
the state of origin of many of those on the crew. Domi made no secret

of being on the lookout for a suitable prospect for Carmen. And I think she may have placed me on her list of considerations at one point, having found I was *soltero*, single and unattached.

Little by little, by patching together various combinations of Spanish, English, and sign language, and with the help of the shop steward Puerto Rico, who spoke both languages fluently, we were able to learn some things about the life and feelings of our fellow workers. This was a crew of people that in these years began calling themselves "Chavistas." They were the backbone of the union. Most were Mexicanos, a good number of them with many years in the vegetable fields. Over time low wages and uncontrolled harassment had deepened and hardened their disgust for the growers, and the whole apartheid-like system that surrounds farm labor. It nurtured a rebelliousness that the 1970 strike had just begun to unleash.

For some of the workers, working at Interharvest was itself a statement, as they had purposely chosen to work in the first company that signed with the union. Some workers came to work for Interharvest after the strike, having been blacklisted for organizing activities in other companies.

Of all the workers that the union struggle touched in the late 1960s and early 1970s, it was among these vegetable workers that it struck the firmest roots and developed its strongest base. This had much to do with the nature of the work itself. Work in vegetables, in contrast to grapes, where the United Farmworkers Organizing Committee (UFWOC) began, is year-round and requires a stable work force. Lettuce, broccoli, cauliflower, and celery workers often worked year after year on the same crews and developed both unity and the confidence of familiarity. The work stability was important in terms of waging the kind of protracted struggle that the farmworker movement would require to maintain momentum.

Up until 1964 much of the work in the lettuce fields was done by contracted workers, *braceros*. Bracero wages, working, and living conditions were set by mutual agreement between the U.S. and Mexican governments. The bracero was little more than an indentured servant, barred from actions such as strikes or protests to influence their conditions, under threat of immediate deportation.

Braceros were concentrated more in some crops than others. For example, braceros were hardly used for table grapes. In the vegetable crops they were concentrated on the very crews where the most effective protests could be waged, the harvesting crews.

When the Bracero Program ended, in 1964, growers scrambled to replace their bracero crews. With authority granted them by the immigration service, growers converted many of their former braceros into green carders through the issuance of special letters. Growers and the immigration service worked together to maintain a supply of workers sufficient to work the crops and keep down wages. The border gates were opened to allow a flow of workers to the fields. Labor contractors, hired by growers to supply labor, competed among themselves to deliver field tasks at the lowest price, adding further downward pressure to wages.

Abuses to which farmworkers had long been exposed continued in the new post- bracero conditions. Callous disregard for the workers was the order of the day as contractors, supervisors, and foremen tried to squeeze out the product with a minimum cost. Workers who couldn't keep up with the fast pace of work, because of sickness, pregnancy, or age, were pushed out. Those working were run like beasts of burden under the threat of being told not to report the next day. Survival often depended on keeping in the good graces of foremen and contractors. And good graces came at a price. While favors took various forms, it was from the women workers on our crew that I would occasionally hear references to pressures for sexual favors in exchange for "job security."

The strike of 1970 had turned whispered resentment into shouts of defiance. And though workers, after years of intimidation, had just begun to break out of their timidity, in the wake of the strike it was, by and large, the growers and their foremen who now began to find themselves on the defensive. The changes were not limited to the unionized companies. Non-union companies also felt the pressure of the movement. They raised wages and eased up on working conditions to keep up with changes forced by the union struggle. For the first time some growers began paying benefits. They became more sensitive to worker grievances. This was their security wall to protect themselves from unionization.

FJ and I had come into the fields without knowledge or understanding of this history, and also without any feeling of intimidation. Our defiant attitudes, nurtured in other struggles, flourished in this new post-strike atmosphere where the bewildered foreman could do little but keep his resentment of us to himself, and where our gestures of disrespect for authority were popular on the crew. Our background in the student and GI movements, and in the larger rebellious landscape of the day, gave us a context for the struggle in the fields. The rebellious spirit we found there heightened our sense of the righteousness of our convictions.

Yet, as newcomers, we could hardly appreciate the change that had taken place during the strike and its aftermath. Many of us, who came of age in the upsurge of the 1960s, came to regard the rebellious spirit of the times as natural and normal, rather than a relatively rare anomaly. Like newborns, brought into a world populated by people with a feisty disrespect for authority, we believed on some level that this was the way things had always been.

By the end of our first month of thinning, FJ and I were beginning to get into the rhythm of the work and were generally strong enough to hold our own, and even, on occasion lend a hand to some other crew member.

One day I brought a Spanish edition of the *Little Red Book* of quotations from Mao Tse-tung. This book was popular among the politicized GIs I'd worked with at Fort Ord, and I began showing it around to the crew. I even began reading sections of it aloud on the bus. The workers listened politely, occasionally laughing when a phrase like "overthrowing the landlords" was substituted with "overthrowing the foremen," or some other quotes likely to cause discomfort to the unfortunate *mayordomo* who happened to be the most immediate representative of the force people felt was oppressing them.

This was a period in which national liberation and independence movements and anti-colonial struggles were prominent around the world. Mao's ideas and the overt support for these movements by China were fairly well known, so that Mao's name was linked with anti-colonial and revolutionary aspirations. When I began wearing a Mao button to work, some of the crew asked for buttons of their own.

The Open-Air Classroom

The thinning crew became a classroom. There were Spanish lessons intermingled with discussions ranging from the strike and field conditions to the war in Vietnam, student and GI movements, women's liberation, the Black Panthers, Cuba, China, and revolution. The fact that the political terms we were familiar with in English were similar in Spanish made political discussion in Spanish possible within a far shorter time than would have been the case with another language. Occasionally we'd stop and talk in the field, our cortitos resting on our shoulders in defiance of the foreman, and launch into some discussion or continue one that had begun in our break. These conversations were usually carried on in Spanish, and my understanding of what people were saying was often shaky. Sometimes I'd state an opinion in my very tentative Spanish only to have a response I could only just guess the meaning of.

The urge to talk about world events was sustained by the intensity of the times, a deep disdain for the "world situation" as we saw it, and a passionate interest in whatever actions might indicate resistance to the established capitalist order or hint at a striving for something better. In these often one-sided conversations I became adept at reacting to responses by measuring tones and gestures, by smiling and nodding, "Si, está bien, está bien"—that's good, that's good—at what sounded like a comment that deserved a positive reply, taking on faith that I hadn't just been politely compared to the rear end of a diseased cow.

It would not be surprising to find that my weakness with Spanish led me to presume more agreement than was really the case, as there were many nuances lost in the haze. But I was not dismayed by disagreements. I eagerly pursued political arguments when they arose. I recall one that took place within earshot of much of the crew during a lunch break. Jose, an older Chicano who was in the fields after years of working at Gerber Foods in Oakland, hotly expressed his disdain for student activists who, in his view, were "running crazy when they should be keeping to their studies." "I guess you're talking about me," I said, laughing. Jose was undeterred. It was the Russian and Cuban communists, he insisted, that were getting all the students in Mexico out protesting when they should stick to their studies. "Well," I said, "considering all the people who come here to work because they can't make a living in their own country, Mexican students might have a point or two, don't you think?" Would he rather see students silent in the face of a brutal war waged behind a veil of lies like in Vietnam? "Lies? Defending democracy is not a lie," Jose said with conviction. "Do you want the North Vietnamese communists to take over?" "Take over? Isn't Vietnam their country, divided by occupying powers against their will?" I was not going to change Jose's mind, nor he mine. We would spar on occasion on the bus or during breaks. Eventually his acerbic comments about the union and his tendency to cozy up to the company made him unpopular with a large part of the crew.

Richard

FJ was hoeing when a tall, thin worker dressed in green pants and a dark green long-sleeve shirt rolled up to the elbow came up the row from behind him and said in a loud whisper, "Hey, how's the *weather*, man?" This was our first direct contact with Richard, the pipe-smoking newspaper reader from the back of the bus. He had a broad, lively, and mischievous grin. Several teeth missing on the top row gave him a strange but also strangely boyish and playful look. His question reflected his political savvy. He had figured us out, a couple of youthful activists "exiled" to the fields. His reference to the weather was a play on words, a reference to the Weatherman organization, one of the many radical groups that coalesced out of the student movement of the day, and which by 1970 had gone underground to "wage war" on the system. He was

older than FJ and I, probably in his late thirties. He carried a file in his
back pocket, which he used to sharpen his hoe, a habit he picked up from
his regular gig, cutting lettuce. Like other young and middle-aged men,
Richard was on the thinning crew until his lettuce-harvesting "ground
crew" started up, in this case with Bruce Church, one of the mainstays of
the valley growers.

Richard, his dark complexion implying some Hawaiian blood in his
ancestry, knew the farm scene and farm work well. He first entered the
fields several years after getting his engineering degree from Berkeley.
He'd begun working at an aerospace plant in Southern California when
something, a bout of depression, a broken relationship, a tiff with a bottle
he could not put down—he only made cursory references—left him sipping cheap wine on sunny L.A. park benches and downtown side streets.
His trajectory was down, but he bounced from town to town. In Stockton one summer day, a labor contractor asked him if he wanted to make
some money picking tomatoes. He needed the cash so he hopped in the
contractor's van. From the blistering tomato fields he made his way to the
cooler green vegetable fields of the coastal valleys where he worked with
the contracted laborers that were first brought in to do essential work for
a country at war in the 1940s.

Richard was one of the few non-braceros on his lettuce ground crew,
and he became one of the fastest lettuce cutters and packers around. His
work in the fields over the years made his body strong and lean and kept
his powerful thirst for beer from killing him. In the years I knew him, he
lived with an Okie woman from Salinas he referred to, either jokingly or
cynically, depending on his mood, as "La Loca" (the crazy one). She was
large in body and strong in temperament, and they had a stormy relationship. Richard, normally quite shy, would, after a few tall beers (he never
bought the normal 12-ounce size), become more expansive, jovial and
cynical, emboldened to verbal combat with his gregarious housemate,
with whom he frequently exchanged verbal punches, sometimes playful,
sometimes not. The truculent La Loca would give Richard tit for tat and
then some. And off they would go. They argued constantly when drinking, which was a good deal of the time.

Richard had developed a fatalistic view of his own life and he projected it on society. Both were unsalvageable. To Richard people were
basically selfish and out for themselves. Even if someone acted in a way
that seemed selfless or courageous, Richard would find the hidden motive
that could only prove the true baseness of their intentions. This was the
deep-seated concept that proved resistant to our arguments about the
possibility of radically changing society. Still, he was a willing partner
in discussion and debate (when sober) and had a decent knowledge of

history and politics. He had fought for the union in 1970 but didn't see any great salvation in it. He did, however, in the late 1970s and into the 1980s become an active advocate for a union contract at Bruce Church, when he saw the stability of lettuce harvesting work being undermined, and looked to the union to stave off what became a rapid, downward spiral in conditions.

Raiteros

The thinning crew and the company engaged in a running battle over working conditions. The workers struggled to enforce a slower pace on the crew. "I didn't know you were working by piece rate" (*por contrato*) was the sarcastic comment often directed at anyone deemed working too fast. The general strike brought wages up from $1.85 an hour, the wage growers pegged in 1970 to avert a strike, to $2.10. It brought into existence the dispatch hall that allowed for a more regular seniority system and increased job security. It placed the first small step toward health and other benefits. But the most powerful effect of the strike was in affecting a change in attitude. "We're paid by the hour, we'll work by the hour!" was how it was put by people vividly recalling hourly crews pushed to breakneck speed, and the distress of those workers struggling to keep up, only to be coldly told, "Don't bother to show up tomorrow."

There had always been some form of resistance to the exploitation in the fields, although nearly always sporadic and occasional. In this new moment when farmworkers were able for the first time to show a sustained organized strength, the battle over speed was, in effect, a test of that strength. The growers had had their way in the fields, and they instinctively fought to keep that control. If the crew could not keep the company from stepping up the pace, it would be in danger of being pushed back to pre-strike conditions. At the same time, the workers were determined to impose new standards on the work, and it could only do so if the crew was united in standing up to the company. Our foreman, Felix, had learned his job in the pre-union days. Since the strike, a lot of the older foremen, hated by the workers, were forced out or opted to move to non-union companies. But Felix kept on. He tried to keep the crew moving fast but was no match for the veteran workers, especially the women, like Domi, Evelia's mother, Maggie, and others who were quick to react, often with very biting remarks, at the foreman's efforts to regain control over the crew.

One method the company used to enforce a vigorous work pace was with the so-called *raitero*. The raitero was a crew member assigned by the foreman to help other workers, ostensibly those who were falling behind, to keep up. When FJ and I started out, a raitero helped us keep up with the rest of crew by doing a patch of thinning in our rows, allowing us to leapfrog to within a reasonable distance of the crew. To speed up the crew, the foreman would assign the raitero to push workers forward who were already keeping pace, causing others to feel they were lagging and therefore speed up. This could also be a form of favoritism, since being moved forward afforded one the luxury of keeping up at a less hectic pace. Thus this move could provoke or intensify divisions.

Foremen frequently used differences among the crew to their advantage. And the workers watched out for such manipulations. A worker who was being "given a ride" emerged from a row before the rest of the crew and could choose to walk to a new row and begin working, thus exerting pressure on others to catch up, or take a visit to the portables, adjust his clothing, file his *asadón* (hoe), waiting for others to catch up, or double back and help others finish their rows and thereby nullify the speed-up effect. In the first case, he might well expect further favors from the raitero, and in the second case he could well forfeit any help in the future. It could thus be a test of one's sense of solidarity.

There were times when the crew, incensed by manipulations of the foreman, would call on the shop steward to put the company in its place. In more extreme cases there would be talk of countermeasures, and even of the ultimate weapons in such circumstances, the walkout, or *la tortuga*, literally, the turtle, the slowdown. This phenomenon was hardly limited to our thinning crew. Throughout Interharvest's fields that summer battles raged over the new terms set by the strike. This struggle at Interharvest was seen by all sides, and by farmworkers across the valley, as a test of the strength of this newborn movement.

Interharvest

United Fruit (later United Brands), Interharvest's parent company, grew wealthy and powerful from its extensive Central and South American banana plantations and its rail and sea transport monopolies. When it set foot in California vegetable fields in the late 1960s, it instantly became the largest operation in the Salinas and Imperial valleys with 20 percent of the lettuce and 50 percent of the celery.[2] Shortly after Interharvest appeared, Freshpict, a subsidiary of the Purex corporation, leased 42,000 Salinas Valley acres for vegetable production. For the established local farmers, it looked like the monopolies were coming to gobble up the industry.

When the 1970 strike hit the valley, Interharvest was the first to sign with UFWOC. There were a number of factors that pushed Interharvest to sign. United Fruit had a reputation among a growing population of the politically aware for ruthless exploitation of Central American banana workers and deadly meddling in the internal affairs of countries in Central America. Its bananas were sold under the very identifiable Chiquita label, making it vulnerable to a boycott. United Fruit (or United Brands as it was known after 1970) also controlled such companies as Baskin Robbins and A & W Root Beer, whose names could well be soured by the associations an active boycott could reveal.

Interharvest, which in 1970 represented 20 percent of the valley's green vegetable production, had every reason to believe that its large size would give it a competitive edge. It had plans on the drawing board to reorder the lettuce industry using its muscular capital. But it needed labor peace to allow this machinery to function smoothly. As a big corporation run from offices in Boston, its managers were not caught up in the emotionalism or the "traditions" of the local ranchers accustomed to having things their way when it came to dealing with "their" workers.

The year before the Salinas strike, an investor named Eli Black bought up enough United Fruit stock to gain controlling interest in the company. Black, a rabbi turned speculator, liked to think of himself as a liberal, humanitarian CEO. He believed he could achieve success by changing United Fruit's loathsome image. Eli Black became friendly with César Chávez and even invited Chávez to his temple at Passover to read passages for a religious service, commenting later to a colleague that it was his "public relations." Black's desire to prettify United Brands' image cannot be discounted as a factor in Interharvest's willingness to sign a contract with the UFWOC.

Now the mighty lettuce growers saw a union gain a foothold in their midst, negotiating terms for workers who had never before had a voice in such affairs. Interharvest became a union stronghold. A complex and protracted struggle began.

Skirmishes

One afternoon a white Ford Galaxy, its long shortwave antenna flapping in the wind and dust, pulled up to the field where our crew was thinning lettuce. The company supervisor, a man in his late fifties with thin white hair and a permanently red fleshy face, walked briskly along the rows of thinned lettuce to where Felix was standing, just behind the crew. After a few minutes he came over to where FJ and I were working and stood watching us for a while. Then Felix came over and said to us, "You guys have to watch your work." We thanked him for his advice and stood up to talk, thinking it inappropriate to bend down to work in front of a supervisor. Soon the supervisor came over, his flushed face now growing even redder as he pointed to a spot on my row where two little lettuce plants stood where only one should have been. By this time the whole crew had stood up to look at what was going on. The supervisor told Puerto Rico that it was up to the union to make sure the work was done properly. Puerto Rico nodded as the supervisor walked out of the field after threatening to fire people who "refuse to do a good job." While the field boss aimed his remarks at FJ and me, the whole crew took this as an attack on them.

The previous few days Felix had been pushier than usual, checking up on work, goading people to work faster. The crew now felt even more upset and some people proposed we walk out right then and there. FJ and I did not want to be at the center of a walkout, and we sided with crew members who wanted to wait until after work to report the incident to the union. This is what we did.

That afternoon the crew showed up at the union hall on Wood Street to discuss the situation. Ours was not the only crew there. The efforts by the company to assert its control had sparked conflicts on crews all over the valley. The big hall was abuzz with activity, workers and crews arriving after work, checking up on union rules, reporting on conflicts, discussing, debating, arguing.

It was a summer of continuous unrest in the fields, with frequent skirmishes on one crew or another. On one occasion, several hundred workers from the lettuce harvesting ground crews left work and marched directly on the company offices with their grievances, causing panic among the company administrators and phone calls to the union officials asking for help to calm down irate workers. In those days, the company could expect little sympathy from local union officials who generally supported the militant stand taken by workers. The growers in the valley pointed with alarm at these actions and stiffened their opposition to what they disparagingly called the "social movement" in the fields.

On another political level efforts were being made by growers to cope with these changes. In Sacramento, that summer of 1971, pro-grower legislators pushed measures to make harvest-time strikes illegal. In response, the union mobilized farmworkers to rally at the state capital. About 2,000 workers from crews throughout the union companies took off work to protest the proposed law. Some of us went from our thinning crew. When we returned, we found the company had hired a number of workers off the street in violation of the contract. The company argued that the contract allowed them to hire workers when the union was unable to meet their needs, which they claimed was the case on the day of the exodus to

Sacramento. The union demanded that the workers hired off the street be laid off. Most left, but three remained on our crew and the company refused to fire them. Eventually they were given dispatches to "legalize" their status on the crew.

The company handed out letters to workers who'd taken the day off to demonstrate, warning they'd be fired if they took off work again without approval. In the midst of this controversy a shop steward on a harvesting crew was fired, and the crew, which worked by contract, began a protracted *tortuga* in protest, pretty much crippling production.

To add to the turmoil of the moment, the union field office, in an exquisite act of bad timing, sent a letter to UFWOC members warning of punitive action for workers who were in arrears on their union dues, setting off anger and dissension at the very moment when tension was mounting with the company.

At the union hall we sat around, talked, joked, and waited for the head of the field office to talk to us. Finally he appeared, a slightly built man with a thin mustache named Juan Huerta, who only a short time before had been a field supervisor for a grower in King City. Huerta worked for the growers but developed a keen hatred for the paternalistic, exploitive system whose hand of oppression reached into every aspect of farmworker life. As with so many people around the valley, the general strike turned Huerta's sentiments into a determination to act. As the union was hastily setting up new offices in the wake of the strike, Huerta came forward to run UFWOC's Salinas field office, and later the office in King City.

On that day, as our crew sat waiting to see him, Huerta looked harried and tired. He had been besieged by a continuous eruption of activities in the fields, pressured on the one side by the company to calm things down, and by the workers seeking advice and support in conducting their struggle. It seemed evident that the strength demonstrated by the workers had a powerful influence on the atmosphere, so much so that the cynical felt hopeful and those who'd convinced themselves that farmworkers were too weak and intimidated to ever triumph now felt the drug of militancy coursing through their veins. Never before in anyone's memory had the arrogance of the growers been given such a blow. The most pragmatic UFWOC officials in those heady days felt the possibilities and saw the need to consolidate the reforms being wrested from the growers to serve as a base to win over workers in the other companies, to spread the union, and perhaps much more. People had begun believing that they were part of a transformation, a larger cause. People had begun to believe in themselves and the cause, including the Juan Huertas among them.

Huerta listened to our concerns and assured us that the union supported efforts to stand up to the company's pressures. But he also counseled against actions that might stiffen opposition to the union. We have bigger battles to wage, he said. We have just begun here.

Vicente

Vicente was the oldest worker on the thinning crew. He'd been in the fields since the days before Mexican workers became the big force there. It was Vicente who was often assigned as the crew's raitero. This afforded him a chance to stand up and stretch as he moved from row to row. I'd had little contact with Vicente until one afternoon when we both finished our rows about the same time and he struck up a conversation.

Vicente was also the crew's unofficial hoe sharpener. He grabbed my cortito as we were about to step into a new row and yanking a file from his back pocket went to work on the edge. He crouched bent over the hoe, one knee resting on the ground. "I like to keep my hoe sharp, then I don't have to hit the ground so hard. I don't mind hitting the ground, I just don't want it to hit me," he said, laughing. "You know this company Interharvest, it's part of something bigger, they have land all over the world, also in my country, the Philippines. That's how they become big and rich, the banana and the pineapple. And also the Dole company"—a name I was hearing about in Salinas lettuce—"in the Philippines these companies control millions of acres of pineapples. We are not an independent country; we have these people controlling us, United Fruit and Dole and other companies. They are imperialists, that means they control other countries." This frank use of the word *imperialist* struck me, because despite the fact that this was a period of intense struggle against the war in Vietnam, imperialism was a controversial word. I had known people active in political movements of the time who strongly objected to using imperialism in connection with the United States, as though the country with all its "democracy" could never be such a thing. But for Vicente the character of the United States was rather clear. It had invaded the Philippines in 1898, and under the pretext of freeing the islands from Spanish colonialism, became its new colonial master, slaughtering tens of thousands of Filipinos in the process. After that, the Philippines was laid open to exploitation by U.S. corporations, much of its land gobbled up by agribusiness like Dole, Standard Fruit, and United Fruit.

I felt honored that Vicente began to talk to me about his views and his life, and took it as a sign that I was becoming regarded as an equal, not just some young, foolish outsider. On other occasions Vicente spoke of his experiences as a youthful immigrant in the 1930s and his years of work and struggle in the fields. "I never saw a union get this far before," he said as we moved down our rows, our backs bent low. "The growers were able to beat us down when we tried to organize."

Vicente began working at a time when Filipinos did most of the lettuce harvesting. Lettuce was cut in the fields and sent to sheds to be iced down and packed into wooden crates before being shipped to market. Neither the shed workers, who were mainly Okies, nor the Filipino harvesters were unionized. But the shed workers made roughly double what the harvesting crews were paid.

The Depression had given the grower shippers cause to knock wages down further. In 1934, Salinas shed workers struck to win back lost wages and improve conditions, demanding union recognition. The previous few years saw field wages slashed even more dramatically, from forty cents to fifteen cents an hour! Angered by these deep cuts, Filipinos also struck. They demanded twenty cents an hour, still well below the thirty cents being paid to Anglo shed workers. The Filipino lettuce workers also demanded recognition for their farmworker association. They struggled tenaciously but failed to win their demands. The growers used violent means to suppress the strike, and Vicente had found himself in the middle of all that.

Vicente's vivid stories aroused my curiosity. But it wasn't until some time later that I learned from a veteran shed worker from the vegetable packers' union and some research in local papers more details of the bitter story of the Filipino farmworkers and the Okie shed workers in the Salinas strikes of the 1930s. The shed workers and the field workers were out on strike in 1934, and the growers felt threatened and vulnerable. Not only was the strike creating pressure to raise wages, but a long-standing division among workers was being broken down by pledges of mutual support among field and shed worker representatives. Confronted with a strike at two critical points of production, the shipper growers announced their willingness to settle with the *shed* workers. They offered them a raise and union recognition. The shed workers accepted the agreement and returned to work under contract with the newly recognized Fruit and Vegetable Packers Union. The Filipino field workers were left to fend for themselves.

With the Filipinos thus isolated, the growers went after their leaders. Goons were sent to the Filipino camps to intimidate and brutalize them. Vigilantes set fire to a large Filipino labor camp in Chualar. Their organization was shattered. Many activist lettuce workers were driven out of the area, and the Filipinos were forced back to work without recognition.[3]

Two years later, in 1936, the growers, now more united in an association of their own, went after the shed workers. When the shed contract expired, the shipper growers locked the workers out of their workplaces. They contracted with a retired national guard officer named Colonel Sanborn, whose name now graces one of Salinas's main streets, to organize a vigilante force to crush resistance. The Colonel and Salinas Sheriff Abbott (another immortalized on a Salinas street) raised a vigilante "army" of 2,000. Colonel Sanborn's force went after shed strikers with bats and guns, breaking up their picket lines and gatherings.

One day during the strike a pitched battle erupted between strikers and Sanborn's forces after striking workers attacked and dumped a load of scab lettuce from a truck brazenly moving through downtown Salinas. The incident attracted attention well beyond the valley.

Barricaded packing sheds strung with barbed wire, guarded with armed men, in some cases with machine guns, came to symbolize the conflict. Strikebreakers were recruited from around the state. To arouse locals and justify extreme measures against the strike, the local paper and some local politicians whipped up a kind of war hysteria with the claim that Salinas was under siege by radicals. They said extreme measures were needed in face of an imminent invasion—from San Francisco. In 1934 a bitterly fought longshoremen's strike broadened into a general strike and shut down San Francisco. Such labor actions earned the city a reputation among conservative rural Californians as a stronghold of leftist insurrectionists. When red flags were spotted near lettuce fields bordering Highway 101, rumors rippled through the area that the flags marked the assembly point for a march of San Francisco communists intent on overthrowing the local Salinas government. Emergency measures proposed to protect the town from the Bolshevik hordes added to the general climate of fear.[4]

The growers succeeded in crushing the shed strike, and shed workers were forced back to work under humiliating conditions. Calls by the Packers' union for support from the Filipino field workers went largely unanswered as the Filipino workers bitterly recalled how they'd been abandoned two years before.

Vicente had been encouraged as a youth to come to the United States by recruitment campaigns that sought vigorous, young workers for California's economy, even as Filipino women were prohibited from entering the United States. At the same time, anti-miscegenation laws prohibited Filipino men from having relations with white women. These laws descended directly from anti-miscegenation laws in the post-slavery South meant to keep blacks from developing any kind of family relationships with whites. This southern law was adopted in California and applied to the different racial mixes in the state. It was racism intended to ensure a workforce that was low-paid, isolated, migratory, and unable to settle down to raise families and form communities. In that sense, the Filipino farmworkers were, for a time, a kind of ideal workforce. But Filipino strikes and organizing in the lettuce and other crops also brought disfavor on that group and encouraged growers to begin looking elsewhere for their "ideal" source of labor.

Settling in Salinas

During our first few months in the fields FJ and I lived in a makeshift cabin in the middle of a large Seaside lot overrun with tall weeds. FJ had taken over the cabin when its previous occupant, Kai (Steve Coyle), a Marine and Vietnam vet, a survivor of one of the most bitter and bloody extended battles of that immensely brutal war, Khe Sanh, moved out. Kai had been one of the key activists in the GI coffeehouse. He was a person of great gentleness and creativity, who found in his antiwar activism some respite from the torment of his horrific recollections of war.

In that little cabin FJ and I talked about our work in the fields and dreamed about struggles present and future. One night we both happened to have similar dreams of some kind of great upheaval. In my dream hundreds of farmworkers were rushing forward, coming off buses, fists and flags in the air, storming into some battle while I moved in the crowd among them. FJ dreamed about a struggle also, but in his dream he was leading the action. After we finished relating our dreams, it was FJ who remarked on the contrast, which he interpreted as the collective versus the individual.

I don't know how long I'd have continued to live in Seaside and commute to Salinas for work if FJ hadn't decided one day that we needed to move. FJ wanted a place where he could live with his girlfriend, Julie Miller. Before summer officially began, we exchanged the one-bedroom cabin for a three-bedroom in a middle-class Salinas suburb off North Main Street. Our new Salinas neighborhood sat at what was then the northern edge of town, abutting fields that stretched in their patchwork and slightly undulating grace to the Gabilans. Four of us lived there: FJ, Julie, Aggie Rose, a friend of Julie's, and myself. Aggie came to Salinas after the 1970 strike to be part of the farmworkers' movement. She was from a Portuguese family and grew up in the Central Valley where Portuguese workers from the Azores were a significant part of the workforce in the vineyards. Aggie spoke fluent Portuguese as well as Spanish. In Salinas she found a job in a social welfare agency working with farmworkers, and she used the opportunity to organize gatherings where she showed films like *Salt of the Earth*.

Aggie was very independent in her thinking and hated the idea of being subservient to a man, a prospect she believed inevitable in any relationship. At the same time she was torn by guilt and felt strong social pressure to settle down with someone, get married, and have a family. This ambivalence tore her up, and threw her into periods of depression. Although she was only twenty-five at the time, she insisted that she had "missed the train" and was doomed to be an "old maid." Ironically, she always had plenty of prospects. It seemed that as soon as anyone made advances toward her, she became nervous and anxious. She once confessed to me that she only felt comfortable around men who were already committed to a relationship. The fact that I was a single man in the same residence added considerable strain to our living arrangement and in fact contributed to my leaving the following winter.

Political differences also created strains in our household. We shared, like most of the youth in those days, an intense interest in politics and disgust for the prevailing political order, the war, racism, and the exploitation the system was based on. Yet sharp differences arose any time we ventured beyond this common ground and tread on the terrain of solutions. I had lost faith in the system to do anything but create more injustice and inequality, war, and other disasters. I did not see this injustice as a blemish on an imperfect system but as an essential part of the economic and political order. Aggie believed in reform and change from within and rejected revolutionary ideas as ideology imposed from the "outside."

Not many months after our Salinas household formed, Aggie began working directly with the farmworkers' union. She was then assigned to Livingston, a small San Joaquin Valley town, not far from where she grew up, where she ran a union local of Gallo winery workers, applying tireless energy to a very challenging job. Every union meeting of Gallo workers had to be conducted in three languages to accommodate the Portuguese, Mexican, and Anglo workers who were under a UFWOC contract won after the grape boycott in 1970. She thus applied herself to creating those changes she believed could be accomplished from within.

Crew Rep

When Puerto Rico left thinning to work on a harvesting crew, there was need for a new shop steward. Many of the crew decided that FJ or I should take the job, arguing that since we spoke English and "understood the laws" we could better handle affairs with the company. We opposed this, arguing that the crew should be represented by someone with more experience in the fields and a greater familiarity with the majority of the people. But when other likely candidates for the job came up with one or another reason why they couldn't accept it, we gave in. With FJ planning to leave thinning to try his hand at harvesting celery, a harder but better-paying job, the task fell to me. I was the crew rep when the union called for the mobilization to Sacramento.

As shop steward I felt the responsibility to oppose the company's efforts to trash the contract when they saw it in their interest to do so. This put me at odds with Felix and company supervisors.

The contract with Interharvest specified that water be available to crews at all times, including cold water on hot days. Weather in the Salinas area, even in midsummer, is normally mild. It is this summer coolness, with the moist ocean air, that makes for a climate suitable to green vegetables like lettuce. But hot spells do occur. During one it was stifling in the fields and workers wanted cold water. The question of cold drinking water may seem trivial, but incredibly enough, the lack of drinking water in the fields and even the lack of toilet facilities had long been a source of grievances between workers and the companies. And it continued to be so even after laws on the state level mandated things like portable toilets in the fields.

During this particular hot spell we'd gone several days with warm drinking water. When the field boss arrived in his white Galaxy and stood near the bus talking to the foreman, I walked over to let him know that we were unhappy with his warm water. His pink face turned red. "I haven't heard anyone complain but you," he said. "It's not their job to complain," I said. "It's my job since I'm the rep on this crew." "If they want ice let them bring their own," he replied, and he turned to walk toward the bus where Felix now awaited him. I followed him to the bus door. "You're always talking about us observing work rules and following the contract, but what about you? The contract calls for cold water on hot days!" I was getting hotter than the outside temperature. He was pretty livid as well and said, "Oh, to hell with your contract!" Apparently uninterested in further discussion, he got up on the bus with the foreman and slammed the door while I stood outside screaming and swearing, ready to fight. Later, the company tried to make an issue of this and threatened to fire me, but their effort never got very far. For his part, the field boss denied ever having said anything about workers bringing ice or denouncing the contract, but the company ended up relieving him of his position over the thinning crews, in part because of these remarks.

Showdown with the Company—Chávez Comes to Town

The conflicts in the fields provoked the company to appeal to the union to impose discipline. They complained that production and quality were being affected by the disruptions on the crew and that this was hurting them in a competitive market. It was midsummer when the Salinas UFW field office called union reps to a meeting to discuss the company's allegations. The union had agreed to meet with the company, but it insisted that field reps be there. Hence this meeting to prepare.

The reps spoke their minds about various issues. They denounced what they saw as undue harassment from the company around quality-of-work issues, the firing of reps such as happened on a harvesting crew after the trip to Sacramento, the hiring off the street in violation of the contract, the lack of respect accorded union reps and the union by various company men, and a litany of other grievances.

The meeting with the company was planned for a weekday. Since the company called the meeting, all the reps got a day off with pay. The meeting was held in the conference room of a hotel just north of downtown Salinas. At one side of the room, behind long tables, were a row of well-groomed, middle-aged men, mainly white, but some Mexicanos as well. Among them sat a well-dressed, graying man by the name of Lauer, United Fruit's vice president of labor relations from Boston. On the other side of the room, and behind other long tables, were farmworkers of various ages, many wearing baseball caps and sombreros.

I was there that day and recall the moment César Chávez walked into the room, accompanied by a number of other union officials and volunteers, including Juan Huerta and Roberto Garcia, whom I knew from the union hall as the union coordinator for the Interharvest "lechugueros." César Chávez was shorter than all of them, certainly one of the shortest people in the room. He had abundant black hair combed back. Despite his small stature he had a presence; he clearly commanded respect and exuded confidence. I was standing around talking to other reps, when he came in the room, and one of them brought me to where Chávez was standing and introduced me to him. I was nervous and didn't have much to say except, "Good to meet you." I was surprised at the smallness of his hands.

Soon everyone settled down, and Chávez opened the meeting, greeting the representatives of the company and the workers and thanking them for their presence. He then related the communication he had received from the company regarding their concerns and their request for the meeting. He ran down some of the charges the company had made regarding poor quality of work, insubordination, violations of the contract, and so on. Chávez also related how he had requested that the union reps be present so they could participate and hear the complaints being lodged by the company and be allowed to respond to them. Then Mr. Lauer began to speak. He hadn't spoken more than a few words when one of the ground crew reps got up and, taking several steps toward the company table, said, "Cal Watkins es un perro racista" (a racist dog). If his words were not enough, he stood and pointed to a tall man who was the company's head of personnel in Salinas. A company man, who appeared at first ready to translate his remarks for his colleagues, just sat back in astonishment. Another worker arose to make a statement concerning treatment by a foreman he found unacceptable. He then translated his own remarks, briefly, with emotional but unsteady English. Then a woman from one of the lettuce machines spoke up about an incident on her crew. She had hardly finished when someone else spoke up, not bothering to translate and then was interrupted by another worker, and so on until a crowd of workers were on their feet, either talking or raising their hands to speak. They were edging their way toward the company table when Chávez raised his hand and called for quiet. "Thank you, compañeros and compañeras." He turned to the company men. "I think we can see that the workers have some complaints to discuss as well." It was theater at its best.

This confirmed for me Chávez's tactical wit. He had responded to the concerns of the company, but, with the help of the workers, had turned the meeting on its head. The accusation about racism at the beginning of the meeting, whether by design or spontaneously—and certainly not without merit—put the company on the defensive. The meeting continued but with an atmosphere quite different from what the company had expected or hoped. After more discussion the meeting broke down into smaller meetings, with committees from the union and company discussing particulars of the grievances from both sides. The meeting adjourned with the decision for company-union working meetings to come up with recommendations based on their respective concerns. The workers were pleased with the outcome, for the tone of the meeting, if nothing else. I imagine the company was somewhat less pleased.

The grievances were negotiated over a period of three weeks of meetings. At the union hall an office staffer who'd been attending the sessions pulled me aside to relate an incident with the company. Trying to regain the initiative in the meeting, the company sternly brought up the subject of a pamphlet they said had been passed out to a crew by a union rep. "That was your crew," the staffer told me with some amusement. The pamphlet was in support of steelworkers who were then embroiled in a battle over speed-ups and layoffs. Placing the pamphlet with great deliberation on the conference table, an incensed company man had declared, "We won't put up with communist propaganda on our crews!" The union side dismissed the issue, I was assured, by pointing out a non-discrimination clause in the contract. The union staffer took some delight in the company's discomfort. But this stand by the union would prove, in time to come, to be rather ironic.

In the end, a compromise was worked out. The workers were counseled in meetings at the union hall, or through their reps or field office workers, to be more careful with quality, and in exchange the company agreed to make concessions, the most visible of which was the change of foremen on some crews and the firing or transfer of several supervisors, including the supervisor in the thinning crew who'd argued about the cold water. Within a short time Felix was gone, and in his place we had a new foreman by the name of Geronimo, a man in his early thirties with a strong build and a wide face, with a shy smile that revealed a row of gold-capped teeth. Geronimo was both quieter and shyer than Felix. He also had less taste for confrontation.

By their job actions the workers were beginning to exercise a right that had long been denied them, the right to influence their conditions of work, to be more than uncomplaining tools at the mercy of market conditions and the thirst for profit. And exactly because of this, the determination of the growers to crush the union and the spirit it had begun to give expression to grew in intensity.

The Migra

Conflicts with the company were not the only source of problems for the workers. More hated than the companies themselves, and that's saying a lot, was *la migra*. You did not have to be around Salinas or the fields long to hear about them. And it was rare to hear any mention of the INS from the workers without a tone of intense bitterness and disgust. I had seen their green and white vans around town on occasion, but I hadn't had any contact with them, and as an "Anglo," I had no cause to fear them.

One day in late July we saw the INS vans approaching the field we were working. Field raids at the end of the harvest season were common. Raids during the height of the season were rare, though not unheard of. Yet there was some suspicion that they were targeting the union companies. As was their practice, they converged on the field from different directions to head off any escape. In this case the only side of the field they did not enter was lined with an irrigation ditch. Anyone seeking to avoid them by running out of the field would have to jump into that ditch.

After checking the crew for green cards or other forms of ID, they took away one of the workers, a youth named Carlos. We were working near the road and when they handcuffed Carlos and walked him off the field, I followed. I went over to where they had parked their van to find out what was going on. I did not know Carlos's legal status, and frankly, I didn't care. The idea that he could be hauled away in handcuffs for doing nothing but working seemed absurd and criminal. I asked them why they were taking Carlos, and they answered, "None of your fucking business." I felt the heat rising in the back of my neck, and I yelled over to Carlos to ask him what was going on. He said that he had left his papers at home. I thought for a second about going over and trying to grab him back. But it didn't seem like an idea destined for success. Still, I wasn't about to just turn and walk away, so I yelled to the migra, "Let him go. He's a union member, you got no right to take him!" One of the migra who was leading Carlos to a car took several steps back and turning toward me yelled, "Fuck your goddamn union!" "Fuck you, you migra pigs!" was my response, the heat now having risen to my ears.

When I turned to walk back toward the crew, one of migra grabbed me from behind and threw me on the ground. I was handcuffed and thrown into the back of their car. The Immigration car was like a police car and had a metal grate between the front and back seats. Now handcuffed, I sat on the wide backseat. The van with Carlos aboard headed off. The car I was in headed in a different direction down one of the dirt roads that skirted the fields. Several times the driver abruptly applied the brakes. With my hands securely behind me I was unable to stop the momentum of my body as it headed toward the metal divider that separated us. It was all I could do to twist so that the blows landed on my shoulder and not my face. I was driven around the fields for maybe twenty minutes while the two agents took turns insulting me and discussing which means they would use to leave me torn and bloody.

At one point the driver made a sharp turn and screeched to a halt in front of an irrigation ditch. His partner jumped out of the car and went to the passenger door, while he yelled to his buddy, "Let's beat the crap out of this asshole and dump him in the ditch." He pulled the door open, took hold of my arm, began pulling me toward the door, then let go. He got back in the car, and we drove some more until they had fully amused themselves. Finally, we drove back to the field where the migra agents had grabbed me, and while they took me out of the car and unlocked the handcuffs, they assured me the next time I ever called one of them a "pig" I could look forward to a trip to the hospital.

Later, when I related this story I was assured that, as it was, I was lucky. If I had been an immigrant, I might not be around to discuss it with anyone. And furthermore, I was fortunate not to have been arrested for interfering with a federal officer in the line of duty.

The confrontation with the migra had an impact both within the crew and throughout a wider circle of people, where the idea of an Anglo tangling with the migra was surprising, if not shocking. What I didn't know at the time was that Carlos was our foreman Geronimo's brother, and the incident would have an impact on our relationship on the crew and after. Our conflict over the company and union affairs was altered by our shared dislike for the migra. For years to come, whenever I'd see Geronimo on different crews and different companies, he'd smile his broad gold-crowned grin and remind me of the time I'd "fought the *migración*."

2. FALL AND WINTER

THE LAST LETTUCE CROP in the long Salinas growing season peaks in late August, and diminishes rapidly in the shorter and cooler days of October and early November. As the days grow short, a deciduous valley "sheds" its seasonal workers. Few jobs were to be had over the winter and without unemployment insurance, unavailable to farmworkers until years later, and with almost all the labor camps closing down until spring, most vegetable workers had to hit the road. They had to live out the winter in Mexico, or more likely, join *la corrida*, the crop circuit, and, like the swallows of the north coast beach cliffs, make their way south with the sun. Many migrants were green carders, who called the border towns of Mexicali and San Luis, Rio Colorado their home. Winter brought their homes and workplaces into closer geographical harmony—or at least, proximity in the winter "salad bowls" of the Imperial Valley and Yuma.

Winter transformed Salinas's farmworker district. It disbanded the early morning crowds of vegetable workers who gathered along the railroad tracks that crossed Market Street just yards from the old Chinatown, or wandered into the cafes and breakfast joints in the original Salinas downtown that had, by the 1970s, become its skid row. Gone for the winter were the labor contractor pickups and El Caminos that trolled the streets for the hands to fill out crews. Gone as well was the morning movement around the many labor camps that dotted the city and its outskirts, and at the *corralón* day haul center and supermarket parking lots, where, in season, farm labor buses and vans exhaled morning steam and smoke as workers huddled in the chill nearby. Gone too the scene on many street corners of Salinas's Alisal district where quiet figures scanned the streets for their rides, clapping hands to slap out the cold. Lost to all these places were the pre-dawn energy and vibrancy, the bustle of early morning streets, where the hangover of sleep gives way to hoarse calls of greeting and banter about jobs and family, complaints about work and other aches and pains, debates about the union movement, and worried comments about immigration raids. All this driven away, swept out by the wind and pounded into silence by the onset of cool fall and winter rains.

By late September I'd begun looking for work with an eye on the better-paid contract work. FJ had left the thinning crew in the middle of the summer to try his hand at harvesting celery by piece rate. When I asked him how things were going in his new job, he said, "If I'm still alive, don't blame the work for it. It's done its best to kill me!" "Let me tell you about piece-rate celery," I remember him saying one evening after work. "The hardest physical challenge I ever endured was high school football practice. Celery is like eight hours of football practice, eight hours of fucking football practice." Thus encouraged, I looked for a way to break into contract work. I was interested in the better money but, I admit, I was also interested in the challenge.

Broccoli

Long ago, farmers in the Mediterranean region and parts of Asia domesticated wild native plants from the genus *Brassica*. The plants showed promise. Through selection these farmers derived an amazing variety of cultivars that we know today as cabbage, kale, turnips, kohlrabi, cauliflower, Brussels sprouts, and a green flower with a thick stem surrounded by dark green leaves called broccoli. The Etruscan precursors of the Roman Empire purportedly relished the plant, which was fortunate for its survival because for a long time it found little favor outside the Italian peninsula.

Broccoli was introduced to the United States in the early 1800s but didn't gain popularity until the 1920s. It was the D'Arrigo family that first put the plant in production on a ranch in San Jose. When broccoli was introduced to Salinas, it took a great liking to this cool, damp coastal valley where it grew well virtually throughout the year. By the 1970s, the great majority of the U.S. broccoli crop was being grown in Salinas.

The word *broccoli* is of Italian origin and comes from the Latin word for arms, *bracchium*, presumably due to the way the broccoli flower extends arm-like from its stalk. Thus it has the same root as the Spanish word *bracero*. So, curiously, for many years, arms (braceros) harvested arms (broccoli).

I got a dispatch on a cool October day from a staffer at the union hall relieved to find someone to help fill out a D'Arrigo broccoli crew. And so I got my chance at contract work in a vegetable adored by mothers and hated by children, charged up with enough vitamin C, soluble fibers, and other nutrients to be considered one of the healthiest vegetables, with anti-cancer properties among its bountiful virtues.

But the health is in the eating, not the harvesting. Broccoli cutting may not have required the skill or the endurance that piece-rate lettuce and celery demanded, but the work was exhausting. That I had a shot at making it on the crew owed much to the experience and stamina I'd acquired in thinning.

In the Salinas Valley and elsewhere in California, broccoli is cut with the help of a machine, a long conveyor belt on wheels that moves ploddingly through the fields. In the 1970s, before broccoli was packed in cardboard boxes in the field, this machine, with a neck that stuck upward, carried the cut vegetables to large bins on a flatbed truck that moved in pace with the machine. Cutters followed the moving conveyor, standing in the troughs between rows of plants, wearing yellow "impermeables"—raingear—thick waterproof pants and jackets and knee-high rubber boots, to shield against the dampness. We carried sharp knives with ten-inch blades and wore hats to ward off the sun. Broccoli crews with men and women workers were not uncommon, but there were no women on this one.

Some broccoli varieties grow waist-high, which allows for cutting standing up. That was a great relief from the pains of *el cortito*. Still, cutting with a piece-rate crew of experienced "*brocoleros*" was no Sunday stroll. I spent much of those first days in broccoli on the edge of panic. In those fields heavy with plants, the green broccoli heads moved furiously from under the lumbering machine. I forced my hands and body to move faster than I thought possible, through fields that seemed to stretch to the horizon. I watched the technique of other workers and, pushed by the necessity of the moment, learned to grab the heads and slash the stems at the same time, flipping them forward toward the belt with a snapping motion of the wrist and, with vegetables still in flight, turn to the flowers speeding by on various sides—grabbing, cutting, flipping them forward, before turning once again—back and forth, in frantic motion, while stumbling clumsily and painfully over uneven and slippery ground. It was only the slowing of the machine at the end of a pass that allowed my attention to turn to clothes soaked in sweat, and driblets of liquid running down my neck and back, that salty anointment into the world of contract work.

In those first days, crew partners on either side would sometimes reach over and, without a word, pluck plants I wasn't fast enough to grab. Later, when more used to the work, I tried to return these favors to others near me.

In contract broccoli, wages were not calculated by the ticking clock, but by the revving and rattling of the heavy flatbeds as they accelerated out of the field. The crew needed no other authority to push it; it willingly transformed itself into a harvesting mechanism that commanded every individual muscle to strain to the limits of its collective pace. As an individual, you submitted, or you left. And you submitted for as long as the machine moved through the field, suppressing pain and fatigue, postponing relief to a point in space and time that, with the energy to think of such things, could only be approximated but was always anticipated.

Only at the end of a row, while the machine awkwardly pivoted in a wide arc to head back down the field in the opposite direction, was there time to move at a normal rhythm, momentarily untethered to that invisible line that pulled us through the field. These were precious moments to re-gather strength or to molt the skin of heavy raingear, which, with the passage of morning, had become insufferably hot, something like a mobile steam room.

Growers plant various broccoli varieties, depending on the time of year, field soil conditions, microclimates, and the all-important commercial viability (how it looks in the supermarket). For the farmworker harvesting the stuff, what mattered most was that some broccoli grew on short stocks, others on taller ones; some had small, puny heads, others thick, heavy ones.

In a good field with heavy broccoli, while the sweat beaded its way down the sides of your face and your arms and your feet sent you regular updates on their state of fatigue and discomfort, you could at least take solace in the running count in your head of bins filled with product bouncing its way out of the fields and calculate its worth in dollars per hour. But when the broccoli was small, or sparse, or both, or when it was knee- or shin-high and required more bending and walking and stretching to reach and cut, it could seem at times like the bins just lingered forever beneath a shower of broccoli. At such times, there was little to offset the discomfort. As moods grew darker, patience grew shorter.

D'Arrigo had been in the valley many years and was an entrenched part of the local grower oligarchy, so it came as some surprise when, in late November of 1970, D'Arrigo signed with UFWOC, the first non-conglomerate vegetable company to do so. This was taken as a measure of the strength of the 1970 general strike and the union movement, and the fear engendered by the threat of a boycott.

Whatever factors brought D'Arrigo to the union bargaining table, it was evident, at least from the vantage point of the broccoli crew, that the workers were not as solidly united around the union at D'Arrigo as they were at Interharvest. I believe this was, at least in part, owing to the fact that after the 1970 strike union activists, blackballed by non-union companies, had gone to work at Interharvest. Such was less of a factor at D'Arrigo. Nevertheless, everywhere the union raised its flag there was conflict and controversy, and this broccoli crew was no exception. Whereas in other harvesting crews, like in lettuce, conflicts over quality led to repeated explosions of struggle in the fields, broccoli battles turned over quantity. This is because broccoli requires less skill in selection and cutting and is less susceptible to damage. Meanwhile, calculating the quantity of broccoli harvested is less than exacting.

Of the twenty or so cutters on the crew, one was assigned to stand on the truck to direct the vegetables tumbling off the belt into the bins. As one bin filled, the "bin watcher" pushed the mouth of the conveyor toward an empty bin, and so on until all the bins were filled and the truck rumbled off to the packing shed. Prior to the union's entry into the fields, the company foreman and supervisors were free to pick a crew member to direct the mouth of the machine. The companies would see to it that the bins were filled to the brim and then some. Choosing the person to do this job, privileged because it was easier than cutting, gave the company leverage. Those chosen had incentive to remain in the company's good graces and bend to the company's will. With the union, however, workers suddenly had the potential to challenge the company control of the bin watcher.

It was easy to feel cheated when the bins were filled like steep hills above the rims. The company insisted this overfilling was necessary because the movement of the bins to the packing shed caused the broccoli to settle. The workers countered, "We're being paid by the bin *in the field* what happens to it after it leaves the field is no concern of ours."

The D'Arrigo crew was union, but it was not united. Among us were workers who had chafed under the semi-slave conditions of the bracero years and who now felt they had to have a say in the work if they were not going to be constantly and forever trampled by the company. They welcomed the space the movement was wrenching open, ready now to fight for something better. There were workers, like our union rep Enrique, whose fathers or grandfathers were peasant union members or leaders in Mexico, or who had socialist or communist influences in their lives and who saw things in class terms, who could no more side with the company than boycott breathing. But there were others who identified their interests with the company. Some were former braceros who had grower help with their green cards and felt an obligation to the company. As the union movement spread, the "paternalistic instincts" of the growers grew in proportion. There were workers who felt alienated from the union or lacked confidence in it. Some reasoned that the union may stay or go, but the growers would always be there. The company tried to take advantage of these sentiments and divisions to maintain the near total control over production they insisted they had to have to survive the rough and tumble of farm competition.

The majority of the crew were Mexicanos, men of different ages, and most had come originally from Michoacan. But there was also a group of black workers who had been with D'Arrigo for some years. They had very little faith that the union would do anything good for them. They did not, of course, share in the nationalist sentiments of a union strongly identified with Mexico and its national symbols, such as the Virgin of Guadalupe, and its close ties to the Catholic Church. Several of these workers were open in their ridicule of the union, and they declared they wanted no part of it. There was one exception among them, a worker I got to know as a friend in those days, Clarence.

Clarence

Clarence was a veteran of the Longshoremen's union in San Francisco, where he had spent the better part of his working life. He had come to Salinas after the breakup of his marriage and other circumstances he chose not to talk about. During the 1970 general strike he walked out of D'Arrigo's field and was recruited by the UFWOC for lettuce boycott work in Cleveland, where he stayed for that first winter after the strike. The following summer he returned to the fields.

Clarence and I became co-conspirators on the crew and friends off the job. I relied on his experience for advice when issues arose on the crew. Clarence would consult with me about things he observed or felt because his limited Spanish isolated him to a degree from the non-English speakers, and though my Spanish was no great shakes, it was better than his. Sometimes when there was controversy on the crew, Clarence would come over to me and ask, "What are them guys hasslin' about?" If I understood, I'd tell Clarence and then we'd talk about it. Our relationship was welded by our common support of the union movement and our common language. As time went on, our views on other matters drew us together.

Clarence lived near downtown Salinas. Sometimes I'd see him on the street there, and we'd go to a little Chinese-owned restaurant that served American food, the Rodeo Café. We'd order something like meat loaf and lima beans or string beans and a healthy little pile of mashed potatoes buried in a thick brown meat gravy or liver with onions, carrots and peas, and mashed or baked potatoes. And then sit and talk over cups of watery coffee.

When off work Clarence liked to dress in slacks, a long-sleeve shirt, a jacket, and a dark suede hat with a hat band. In those clothes he hardly resembled the broccoli-cutting creature in a baseball cap, blue work shirt rolled up to the elbows, yellow rain pants with gray suspenders, and high rain boots, he was during the weekdays.

Clarence was even-tempered, and generally fairly quiet, soft-spoken, and shy, not one to joke around much. But he had an intensity centered around a disposition toward justice. Clarence believed in justice and kindness toward people, especially those he saw as victims of an intolerant society.

Clarence lived the single life in the area of Salinas where farmworkers, homeless people, alcoholics, prostitutes, drug addicts, and other "outcasts" shared the opprobrium of the more "cultured society." On a number of occasions, sitting at the Rodeo, denizens of the neighborhood who came to greet Clarence, sometimes asking for a favor, would visit our table. These included prostitutes who were momentarily short on cash or just hungry or just stopping to say hello. Not infrequently Clarence would invite them to sit for a while and share food and talk. Thus I would hear bits and pieces of a side of Salinas with which I otherwise had no contact.

Across from the Rodeo was the Caminos Hotel, a Salinas landmark. Opened in 1874 as the Hotel Abbott, it was the first large hotel in the early days when Salinas was little more than a dusty stop on a stagecoach line. The Abbott boasted of state-of-the-art features—telephone, telegraph, and messenger service. Through the following decades it was natural for people coming to Salinas by rail to stop in at the hotel, which stood a few hundred yards from the train station. Looking at the Caminos it was not hard to imagine that it had once been a grand place, a special night-on-the-town kind of place. During the 1930s its bar was a hangout for locals who found their way into the pages of Salinas writer John Steinbeck's works like *East of Eden*. In 1936, a Salinas newspaper writer watched, from the vantage point of the hotel, a violent battle between grower goons and lettuce strikers that raged on Main Street, and he wrote his story from there.

By the 1970s the Caminos was old, run-down, and unpleasant. Its halls were musty; its carpets raggedy and dirty; its plumbing and lighting in decay. Its walls were discolored with mildew and other assorted fungi. It was an embarrassment to the town fathers, but it was a cheap place to live and was filled with people who could not afford other arrangements, among them many farmworkers. Though there were labor camps for single men, places for unattached women were more limited. I knew single-women farmworkers who lived there and saw their children racing and shouting through the halls of that hotel. I knew crew members from various ranches who lived there. There were couples with and without children, single men, and retirees. For the low-income residents of the area it was an affordable place to hang their hat. For the local establishment it was a symbol of decay, a boil to be lanced, and it would be finally demolished in 1989, despite its connections with the once reviled and now revered John Steinbeck and over the loud objections of local preservationists.

Over time and over plates of roast beef or ham, Clarence and I would kick things around. Clarence was not of the generation or of the militant disposition of the Black GIs I'd known at Fort Ord. He did not relate to the Black Panthers, for example. Nor was he much into storytelling. But I learned enough being around him to realize that his course through life left him with some painful moments and memories. Even though his Spanish was limited he regularly attended union meetings and took an interest in the union's affairs. He sympathized with the Mexicanos and felt a commonality with them based on having suffered at the hands of the same forces—that of a white "power structure." He visualized, in the hysterical anger directed at the farmworkers by the local powers in Salinas, the segregationist and lynch mob mentality of his youth. He saw no justification for siding with the growers against the Mexicans, and he would sometimes poke the air angrily when talking about some of the black workers on the crew who swore at the union because it "ain't nothing for us." "They're fools, man, they're goddamn fools. They think the company's gonna protect them! The company'd shake them off like fleas. Like fleas off a dog, you wait," he'd say, poking the air in front of him for emphasis. "Whaddaya mean, Mexican union? Ain't them Mexican fellows out there working like us? Better get your head screwed on right, man." He'd say things like that to me, though I knew he was talking to some broccoli cutters in absentia since he knew I agreed with him.

Battle of the Bins

Controversy sometimes erupted when the person assigned by the company to work on the truck would, under pressure from the foreman, fill the broccoli bins well above the rim. Depending on the mood of things at that moment someone might yell out, "No seas barbero, la compañía no es tu madre!" (Don't be a kiss-ass, the company ain't your mother!).

We "malcontents," which Clarence and I estimated at more than half the crew, sympathized with this sentiment, and would complain to the crew rep, who would instruct the bin watcher to fill broccoli level to the rim, no more. The foreman, whom everyone called La Coneja, would instruct that same person to fill the bin higher, and so on. There were occasions when these protests erupted in fits of anger, but the company managed to keep control over the bin watcher, a power they used to their advantage. The crew was not united enough to force the issue.

One day, working in a field full of big heads growing waist-high, the crew was feeling frisky, and we burned up the field with hot knives. In the early afternoon, as the machine was approaching the end of a pass, but still a long way from finishing the field, the foreman suddenly ordered us to grab harvesting bags, which we slung over our shoulders. While the machine sped up and rolled out of the row, we stayed behind cutting broccoli, tossing it into the bags we wore like backpacks. Once filled, we walked unsteadily to the flatbed where the bin watcher grabbed our filled bags and hoisted them into the bins. We finished out the row that way, sheathed our knives and stepped up into the bus. We sped off to another field nearby, bumping and thumping down the dirt road scarred by tractor, truck, and cat tracks, the rattling bus trailing a screen of dust as it moved. We arrived at the field just as the broccoli machine was entering a row of a large field of low-standing broccoli.

Once we got close we could see this was a second or third cutting, with relatively small scraggly heads that under some circumstances might have just been disked under. All I could figure was that the market for broccoli was hot and we were going to pick every scrap we could from this sorry-looking field. As the machine began its trek, its big tires plodding down the row, we bent and stooped to snatch the little heads of broccoli that sometimes stood feet and even yards apart from each other. Many of the heads looked anemic, barely wider than the stems. We worked later than usual that day. By the time we got back to town it was nearly dark and we were cold and tired.

The next day the routine was similar. Only we finished off the good field before noon and headed off to the field from hell for the afternoon. Once again we worked late. My back ached from the constant up-and-down movement; my legs felt as if I had strapped weights to them. The good-humored joking that went on in the morning evaporated like the morning mist, and we marched in silence through the broken wreckage of the field. We watched with wary and weary eyes as the bins were slowly filling, watched for the first sign of a leaf, a blotch of green to show above the rim. Then the calls would start, "Ya está lleno cabrón. Muévelo, muévelo, ya." (It's full. Move it, move it). The "cabróns" and the "yas" got louder and more insistent. But the bin watcher was more sensitive to the foreman's cries of "llénalo más, más mis babies. Mueven las nalgas. Métense la verga." (Move your asses! Stick your dick into it!) We were hurting, but La Coneja was having a happy-go-lucky time being the company's stooge.

La Coneja was notorious for his foul mouth and loud and lewd manner. How and why he got such a nickname (*apodo*) like La Coneja (a female rabbit), I never found out, perhaps because he was so quick to do the company's bidding. There were cruder interpretations. In later years I ran into an old union friend from those days who had a more favorable view of La Coneja, but I was disgusted by his manner and by the cynical way he dealt with us with his orders from above. Foremen frequently thought of themselves as better than the other workers and acted the part. Sometimes the tyranny of those who have "risen above their peers" is greater than that of someone outside the community, and La Coneja, whatever else he was, could act the petty tyrant. Perhaps it was fear of being knocked down to the ranks like the rest of us that made him a hound for the company's interest. His lewd and stupid behavior had a negative influence on the crew. He was not above talking about women in a demeaning way and bragging about his manly physical attribute, which he even on occasion felt compelled to put on full display, eliciting derisive laughs, hoots, and expressions of disgust. He reveled in bringing out the more *machista* sentiments among the crew. And he seemed to enjoy the attention.

We finished up that day exhausted. When we heard that there were no new fields ready and that we were returning to that same field the next morning, my bones grew in weight.

The next morning a fall chill was in the air and it was damper than usual. The hills surrounding the valley were obscured by a morning fog that lifted slowly as the day wore on. When it did, by late morning, it left the sky clear with only a line of gray-bellied clouds, balanced on the tips of the Gabilan Mountains to the east.

We plodded on through that immense field of scraggly broccoli, sometimes hitting thicker patches, most times walking distances with only a few scattered, low growing broccoli. To add to the discomfort, the field was heavy with weeds, poised to take over the field entirely. This included a prickly plant the Mexicanos called *dormilona* that resembled mint, but stung when it rubbed against a bare arm. All the while it was hard to keep my mind and eyes off the bins.

At the noon break some of the crew sat in small groups talking; others were stretched out on the ground, soaking up weak sunlight and rest. Nearly everyone still wore their rain pants because it was cool and the ground was still damp.

We were only weeks away from the end of the harvest season. Thoughts drifted to the money we were making and how that would affect our lives after the crew ended. Some would be heading out to winter in their villages in Mexico. Others would stay in the Salinas area. Another group would roll down to the Imperial Valley to pick up a broccoli crew there.

Twice that morning we had complained to our rep Enrique that the bins were being overfilled, and there was some discussion of this at lunch. Enrique was with a group engaged in agitated discussion at the edge of the field. Nearby sat a large array of metal disks on a heavy metal frame. It would soon be hitched to a tractor and pulled over this field to bury the remains of the massacred plants that stood forlornly around us.

Among the group with Enrique was Ubaldo, a stocky worker with a huge, thick mustache that curved down the sides of his mouth and provoked some people to call him *"bigotes."* He wore blue coveralls under his rain gear and a green D'Arrigo "Andy Boy" hat that was faded and frayed from use. Next to him was Mauricio, more rounded in body, who, as a youthful-looking thirty-something already had fifteen years coming north. He and his father, who sat next to him, were corn farmers from Michoacan, where they would be heading in another month or so to tend their *milpa* (small field) in the little town people called Santa Clara de Cobre, a town famous for its amazing copper artistry.

Mauricio and his father were partisans of the union. Jesus, who also sat with the group, was more in the union's camp, but pretty cynical about both sides. Ubaldo had many years at D'Arrigo and felt his interest lay more in keeping in the company's favor than throwing in his lot with the union.

Clarence and I wandered over to the group, and I tried to get the gist of the conversation with my primitive Spanish. Ubaldo was complaining to Enrique that things were now worse under the union than before since the company men seemed more hostile and pushy than ever. Enrique argued that the company's strategy was to demoralize the workers, make the union look bad, and inoculate the workers against ever organizing. The others were nodding in agreement. Ubaldo remained argumentative, tossing his head and shrugging in a display of disgust at the whole situation.

When lunch was over, I went to Enrique to double-check that I understood what was going on. Then I relayed it to Clarence. The pressure of the strike and boycott had pushed D'Arrigo to sign with the union, but it didn't slacken their resolve to strangle the new organization. If the workers could not manage to improve conditions with the union, the logic is that they would reject it. The union movement would be discredited. This is the idea that Clarence and I discussed as we watched the crew rise crankily to their feet.

At the foreman's prodding we made our way slowly to where the machine stood about to start a new row. After eating I felt better, but work seemed difficult, sluggish, and unrewarding. And it wasn't long before someone at the far end of the machine called out, "Pinche fil, como me chingas" (This fucking field's screwing me over) and other expressions of discomfort, to a ripple of laughter up and down the line. Others picked this up, and more expressions of discontent punctured the air above the din of the broccoli machine. Even some of the black cutters started getting into the act, using "pinche" in other creative ways mixed with English and smatterings of Spanish, "Pinche broccoli motherfucker, cabrón." And the Mexican crew picked up on the English as well, and soon there were rounds of bilingual swearing up and down the line, laughter, shouts, cries.

It was late afternoon and we were coming to the last rows of the field and looking forward to the ride back to town when La Coneja broke out the harvesting bags again as the machine clattered off down the dirt road toward another field. "Thought you said there were no new fields ready," Clarence said accusingly. "Wun more fil tode," said La Coneja, "jus wun more. C'mon, amigo, jus wun more." After a short bus ride we reached another well-chewed field, about as inviting as the one we'd come from. "Vamos a la casa," Chuy, a tall worker in a orange baseball cap flipped backwards called out as we filed out of the bus. "Vámonos!"—let's get out of here!—but he got no reply.

When the first bin was nearly filled, shouts went up to the bin watcher, "Ya, basta, muevelo" (That's enough, move it) to get him to move the mouth to a new bin. "Yo mando aqui" (I call the shots), shouted the foreman and he raced over from behind the machine to stand beside the truck. We could see the field boss's pickup in the distance heading toward our machine. The foreman was going on about how he was the "*mero, mero*" (big shot) in his exaggerated, clownish manner. As he did so the flow of broccoli into the bin became a trickle. La Coneja began shouting, but his voice was muted. The machine had moved forward, but most of the crew was no longer behind it. Of the twenty cutters maybe fifteen were now standing still in a line in the field, watching the machine amble away. La Coneja looked around and called the machine operator to stop. "Que chingados muchachos, vamanos." (What the fuck, fellows! Let's get moving!)

The field supervisor pulled up in his white pickup and headed toward the now standing and unmoving crew. The union rep and the foreman were talking loudly. La Coneja was arguing that the union could not stop the crew, and Enrique was arguing that the crew had stopped on their own. They were joined by the field boss. Enrique was shaking his head.

La Coneja was gesticulating and stomping in some theatrical display of displeasure. The field boss, a tall Anglo in his late thirties stood passively. Finally Enrique made his way over to where we were waiting—having already decided among us that it was time to go home. "Compañeros," said Enrique, "the company wants us to finish the field." "Just an hour or so," he said. "Chale," said one of the younger workers, "ya vámonos." (Hell no, let's get out of here.) Then Clarence spoke up, "Tell him we'll work if they put one of our men on the bin. That fella," he said, referring to the bin watcher, "does just what the company wants." Clarence was not shouting, but he was clearly upset. Chuy picked up on that. "Nosotros controláramos la cajas, no la compañía." (We'll control the bin levels, not the company.) Enrique translated as best he could and asked the others what they thought. "Que piensan?" (What d'you think?). Enrique then presented the offer the crew agreed upon to La Coneja and the field boss. The field boss argued. La Coneja kicked at the dirt and waved his arms a few times. As they were talking, the crew began to migrate to the bus. The field boss, who wasn't as maniacal as La Coneja, agreed to allow the crew a say in who worked on the bins. It would be argued later whether the agreement was for that day or permanently. Enrique asked Mauricio to get up on the truck. The rep then called everyone together, and we agreed to finish the field.

We finished out the field without universal joy. Chuy muttered, "Pinche fil, aun los gusanos morirían aca." (Even the fucking worms would die in this field.) It took some back and leg pains and several tough days, but at least the crew finally agreed on something and stood together. It was a bit of a turning point. That was something to feel good about.

Day Off

Evelia Hernandez, who used to tease me with her *traba lenguas* (tongue twisters) in the thinning, lived with her family in a house just up the block from Market on Pajaro Street, and I spent a few awkward afternoons there, sitting with Evelia and her mother in the living room amid the organized chaos of a household with ten children. I think my attraction to Evelia was intertwined with the romantic image of a large Latino family, with young playful children and calm, enduring parents, a vision unencumbered by the day-to-day realities of such a life. Our brief "courtship" soon ended in the mutual realization that the large gap in our life experiences and cultures could not be crossed on the narrow bridge our shared vocabulary afforded us.

I was visiting Evelia that morning in response to an offhand invitation a week before. She and her mother were shyly polite, and we ate plates of delicious, sweet *capirotada* and quietly endured disjointed conversation patched together with bits and pieces of our two languages, while Evelia's younger brothers and sisters played climb-the-mountain with their solid and enduring father, the mountain, who sat in another corner of the living room, good-natured and smiling most of the time.

After a time, I excused myself and headed down to Market Street where I ran into Clarence. He was decked out in his weekend best. He had just picked up a file and a new sheath for his broccoli knife from Farmer Joe's, the little general store that stood near the railroad tracks and the old Chinatown.

Soledad Street, Chinatown's "main drag," had been at the commercial heart of a bustling, if modest, Chinese community in a neighborhood bordering nearby Carr Lake. The area had once been a popular eating, entertainment, and gambling area for the local working population. Earlier in the century Filipino field-workers found its establishments a respite from their hard labors. Salinas's polite society viewed Chinatown with repugnance. But if John Steinbeck is to be believed, that did not keep some of Salinas's "respectable" community from indulging in the services of its notorious cathouses.

The Chinese farmworkers who settled in Salinas helped lay the foundation for what became a thriving vegetable industry. But the passage of the Asian Exclusion Act in 1882 cut the stream of Chinese that fed the community, which dwindled and all but disappeared. By the 1970s little more than the fossil of Chinatown remained, a row of ramshackle and decaying buildings guarding the homeless in its shadows. One Chinese restaurant remained open, and its elaborate but aging interior woodwork spoke of a more ornate and prosperous past.

The building housing Farmer Joe's also had its history. Before the Second World War, it was in the heart of a thriving Japanese community. One of the Japanese-owned businesses in this area of Market Street was run by an Issei, a first-generation Japanese American. Katsuichi Yuki came to the United States as a young man at the turn of the century. In the family lore of Katsuichi's descendents, he was working at the Palace Hotel in San Francisco in 1906 when, on a fateful morning in April, the walls began to shake and the plaster began falling from its ornate ceilings. As the fire that followed the great quake closed in on the hotel to consume it, Katsuichi took off on foot and didn't stop until he reached San Jose, forty-five miles to the south.

In his early forties, Katsuichi settled in Salinas and began a modest farm operation near the town of Spreckels. He married a teenage "picture bride" (chosen by looking at photos supplied by a matchmaker) from the homeland and began raising a family with a stern hand. Later, when he and his wife developed an odd allergy to the soil in the area, he opened a store in town. The store featured fresh fish from nearby Monterey Bay. Katsuichi prided himself on having the freshest fish in town.

Katsuichi became a respected member of the Japanese-American community. This status proved a mixed blessing. In February 1942, Katsuichi was picked up by the FBI in the first round of arrests aimed at depriving the Japanese community of its leaders in the wake of Pearl Harbor.[1]

On this day, however, standing with Clarence in front of Farmer Joe's, I knew nothing of such history. I only knew that the Palestinian brothers who ran the general store had mastered English and Spanish and communicated impressively and good-naturedly with their diverse clientele.

Clarence had a newspaper tucked under his arm and a stomach that yearned to be "entertained." So we headed to the Rodeo Café.

When we sat down, he opened the paper to a front-page story on Angela Davis, the black activist who was awaiting trial on charges of supplying weapons for a prison break of sorts. I knew some of the history behind this. I'd followed the events from the time George Jackson, Fleeta Drumgo, and John Clutchette were accused of killing a guard in retaliation for the assassination of three black activist prisoners at Soledad State Prison, which stood in the middle of the valley just a few miles from Salinas.

The three "Soledad Brothers," as they came to be known, were transferred to San Quentin where they were awaiting trial. Earlier that summer, George Jackson, a member of the Black Panther Party and a revolutionary broadly respected by people both inside and outside U.S. prisons, had been gunned down by San Quentin guards during an alleged escape attempt. It was apparent to anyone who followed the case and knew of the persecution and murder of black activists that he was deliberately cut down by the authorities.

Later, George Jackson's brother Jonathan made an attempt to free the two remaining Soledad Brothers from a courtroom in Marin. Jonathan, Judge Haley, and prisoners William Christmas and James McClain were killed when the police opened fire on a van as they were fleeing. Angela Davis was now being charged with supplying the guns to Jonathan. Clarence was following the case, too, and he wanted to know what I thought about it. This opened up a long conversation, which we were to carry on for some weeks, on and off the job.

The issue of race, racial divisions, the civil rights movement, and the black liberation movement were the bone and marrow of much of what was going on in the United States in those days. These were things that had changed my life, my perspective on the world, my view of the United States. So when Clarence and I began an exchange of views and stories, it was valuable for me.

I don't think I'd ever really pondered my own background much before those talks with Clarence. They helped me understand some things about myself. I grew up in Long Beach, a city with a large black population, but I hardly knew black people lived there until I was in high school. And though one of the largest and longest established Latino populations lived in nearby San Pedro, I didn't know what a Mexican or Chicano was until college. Education, it suddenly seemed, was about sheltering people from reality. I knew little about the history of California. Less about how the division of colors and ethnicities developed in the United States.

The civil rights movement was a gigantic wake-up call for society. It certainly was for me.

I told Clarence about my own ethnic trauma—how the kids at my junior high school had a game of throwing pennies on the ground, which remained there because anyone picking up a penny was a "Jew." Seeing a penny on the ground was a frightening experience. I lived in fear of anyone finding out I was a "Jew." There was no one I felt I could turn to, so I kept this fear to myself.

Then one day my fears came crashing down on me. Some kids I knew, and I thought of as friends, threw pennies at me in the cafeteria line. When I turned around, they glared at me, "Dirty Jew!" They'd discovered my secret. I didn't react angrily. Rather, I felt a deep shame and embarrassment and a strong desire to hide. From then on I sought to avoid discussions about religion or ethnic background, anything that might lead to uncovering this secret. I didn't know then that other people suffered from far worse prejudices. And until the civil rights movement emerged into broader public conscience, I had no idea anyone would or could do anything about it.

The civil rights movement was the friend of anyone who felt the lash of discrimination. That was the origin of a kinship I felt. I was not very conscious of this, but I recall that in high school little enraged me more than the prejudice I saw being directed against black people and others. It pushed me to look for answers. I never settled for the argument that this was part of "human nature." But only as I began to get a better sense of history and the development of society was I able to gather arguments to take on such erroneous assumptions.

Clarence now added to my sense of how things worked in America. My upbringing was a million miles from Clarence's. His family had worked the sharecropping fields in one of the southern states. But making a living was difficult, and they were constantly faced with the arbitrary injustices of the Jim Crow system and the ever-present terror of lynchings, beatings, and harassment that were part of black life under segregation. I realized that Clarence's experiences with discrimination made my encounters with anti-Semitism seem like a picnic in the park.

Clarence got out of the South when blacks were being recruited for wartime jobs in the North. His family moved north in 1941, the same year the *braceros* came north to work in the fields and railyards. He'd been disqualified from the military for some reason and ended up in the shipyards in San Francisco, scraping and repairing ship bottoms on the dry docks of Hunters Point. He later got into the longshore union (ILWU) and stayed there until coming to Salinas.

During the Second World War, jobs that had been closed to non-whites began to open up. This is because their labor became essential. When people talk about that war and the "heroism" of it all, they rarely, if ever, mention that it was the hundreds of thousands of black people who came to work in the factories and shipyards and the hundreds of thousands of Mexicans who came to work the fields and railroads that made the U.S. war effort and victory possible. Like most everything else in the "proud history" of the United States, it was an accomplishment achieved on the backs of exploited and oppressed people who barely get a mention in its history.

Clarence was not a political radical. He did not see himself as someone advocating or organizing for a movement to change society. Though his personal grievances with society were by any fair judgment far deeper than my own, he was of an earlier generation, and he did not have the kind of fervor and hopefulness that marked many of the "sixties people" like myself. For us it was in the very air we breathed. It made us shake with rage at times and filled us with a restless impatience for justice. But it had nothing to do with us in any generic sense. It was the product of the convulsive world in which we were coming of age.

Just Cutting in the Rain . . .

Broccoli can be harvested in the rain. With our rubber boots and yellow "impermeables," we were prepared for the rain. But there were rainy days toward the end of the harvest season when the fields became so muddy that the machines bogged down, and we strapped bags on our backs and tossed broccoli over our heads into them. This was hard work. sloshing around slushy ground barely keeping traction. After a few hours of this, all of work's joy dissipated, and fatigue, multiplied by the interminable time it took to fill the bins, filled every spare space of conscious thought with one irrepressible preoccupation—when are we going to get the hell out of here?

Although the company paid a slight premium for cutting broccoli under these conditions, this hardly offset the disadvantage of this situation. Broccoli, like most crops, could only be left in the ground so long. But that was the company's concern, not ours. Market conditions were factored in to their decisions. But what did we care? High broccoli prices for them only meant more misery for us!

One day, a particularly heavy rain pelted the field into a marshy brew. The wind drove the rain in sheets. We now had a union-selected rotation for the job of bin watcher, having won this right from the company. When wet conditions kept the machine from running, it was the bin watcher's job to stand on the edge of the truck bed and, with one hand gripping the bin, pull the backpack bags off the crewmen and loft the broccoli into the bins. It so happened to be my turn on the truck bed that day, and I was trying as best I could to pull the bags quickly off crew members' shoulders. The crew managed to wobble through the field trailing the truck, but it was becoming more difficult to navigate with their heavy bags. A crew member named Rafael, also known variously by his *apodos*—Puerto Rico, or Chaparro for his short stature; he stood maybe 5-foot-3—was cutting behind the advancing crew when he suddenly disappeared. A voice called out sharply amid the patter of the rain, "Ayúdenme, ayúdenme cabrones!" (Help me, motherfuckers!) in an accent that was unmistakably not Mexican. Sloshing back from the truck, crew members found Puerto Rico on the ground, one rain boot stuck up to the knee in soft mud. Several people worked to pull him loose and onto more solid ground while Puerto Rico loudly denounced rain, mud, broccoli, the company, and anything else directly or indirectly culpable for his uncomfortable and embarrassing circumstances.

After a few more slips in the mud, and after Clarence delivered his backpack to the truck, he headed toward the bus. Without so much as a shout, the crew headed toward the bus behind him. It was all the foreman, La Coneja, could do to get us to finish the bins on the truck, promising that that would be it for the day. "OK, OK, no quieren trabajar más! No más, no más OK, OK!" he lamented. So we all got on the bus while he checked with his field boss. La Conejo argued that it was time to call it quits for the day, knowing full well he'd never get us back in the field in any case.

Like many physically unpleasant experiences, working broccoli in the rain had its upside—the relief of being inside, drying out!

Puerto Rican Soldiers

I worked on the D'Arrigo crew until the early part of December, and when the job ended I went off to tractor school. One morning in early January, I went down to Market Street to get breakfast from a little diner that served a great platter of huevos rancheros. Until coming to Salinas I'd rarely eaten spicy food, but now I was developing an addiction to salsa picante and jalapeños, such that I rarely had a meal without them. I was just getting into that healthy plate of refried beans and rice, alongside three eggs sunny-side up blanketed in cheese and red salsa and some soft, warm handmade tortillas, when I saw Clarence passing by the diner. He wasn't working, living off what he'd saved during the harvest season. I rapped on the window and motioned him to join me. He came in, dressed more casually than usual and without his black hat. "What'ya doin' here?" he asked in mock seriousness. I replied, "I was about to ask you the same thing. Trying to sneak around without your hat on so no one'll recognize, eh?" I said. "Hunger just chased me out the door before I could grab it," he said. "Why are you so hungry? Dream about workin' the broccoli last night?" I asked. "No. I was out dancing. Out at Maida's, you know Maida's down here on Market." He turned to the cook who stood in front of us with his discolored white apron and his order book. "I'll have this same thing," Clarence said, motioning to my plate.

Maida's Bamboo Village was a popular hangout for farmworkers. "I didn't know you liked salsa music, Clarence." I found out Clarence went there occasionally, usually just to sit, sip a few drinks, and listen to music that normally ranged from salsa to meringue or traditional ranchero/mariachi beat. Clarence was developing a taste for the music though he preferred jazz and blues, which you could only get if you traveled to Seaside or Monterey. Maida's had the advantage of being a short walk from downtown Salinas.

Clarence had met some Puerto Rican soldiers the previous night, and they ended up buying each other drinks. The young soldiers kidded around with Clarence and finally got him up dancing with a few of the farmworker women who came to hang out.

"So what did the soldiers have to say?" I asked. "Them fellas hate the army. They're all just waitin' to get out." "Are they trainees?" I asked. "No, they're back from Vietnam. Didn't I just say they were waiting to get out?" "And they're at Ord? I'm surprised," I said. "Most 'Nam vets aren't even allowed on the base, they send them down to Hunter Liggett so they won't contaminate the recruits." "Hunter Liggett?" Clarence said questioningly. "Ya, it's out down by Greenfield, in Los Padres, a testing ground for new military toys out in the forest. They send the 'Nam vets there so as to keep them off the training base. The one thing that'll ruin a trainee is putting them in contact with someone whose learned firsthand what a sham this war is and isn't afraid to acknowledge his 'superiors' with a middle-finger salute." Clarence laughed at that. "How do you know all that?" he asked. I told Clarence about how I had been working with a group of antiwar Vietnam vets, activists, and revolutionaries in a GI coffee shop near Ord.

As background I told him how the coffeehouse project got started, and about how another project, at the Marine base at Camp Pendleton, had begun to tap in to the rebelliousness of the soldiers there. The Pendleton work began when a Japanese-American woman, Pat Sumi, and an Anglo, Kent Hudson, moved near the base from Los Angeles. They started passing out leaflets against the war to the soldiers, and soon they had a group of black Marines working with them who began to organize. The word spread. Soon there were soldiers from many backgrounds organizing together. They started a group they called the Movement for a Democratic Military (MDM). It had a ten-point program modeled loosely on the program of the Black Panthers. From Pendleton it spread to Fort Ord.

One of the things that inspired me most about all this, I told Clarence, was the fact that black, Latino, and white soldiers started working closely together. For a lot of them it began in Vietnam when soldiers found their mutual hatred for the war and the military was stronger than any perceived differences between them. I saw white soldiers at Ord who'd developed an intense hatred of racism through their experiences of working together with other soldiers. That included some white soldiers from the South. They also began to understand that prejudice against soldiers of other races also harmed them. It allowed the higher-ups to keep control over everyone. So I learned a big lesson there among the soldiers, I told Clarence.

There was this soldier we worked with, a Puerto Rican named Ace. He was a happy-go-lucky guy, but also very serious. Ace had been part of MDM at Ord from the beginning. But one day he came to a few of us civilians at the coffeehouse and said, "We've been working together for a while, but that's gonna stop now. We're not going to work with the coffeehouse and MDM anymore. I'm only even telling you this cause we've been together for a while."

"What's up, Ace?" we asked. "Well, I'm gonna tell you, 'cause, like I said, we worked together, so we owe you that. Some of us guys have been talking, and we've kinda come to the conclusion that the civilians have been using us GIs." "How so?" we asked. "To build up your organization, to build yourselves up." We were stunned, really taken aback by this. "When did you come to this conclusion, what brought this on?" Eventually it came out that one of the civilians who worked with the coffeehouse had called together some of the soldiers. "He invited us to drop some acid with him," Ace said. "We were just gonna have a good time and relax and enjoy ourselves, and he had some good stuff. We all got high and were joking around, but then the conversation got serious. And he told us some things about how the civilians in these kinds of projects work, how they use soldiers, especially the minorities. He gave us examples from other bases. He made us feel paranoid about how we were being used." We argued with Ace and got him to agree to meet with us and other MDM soldiers and have a discussion. We had worked enough together that he felt that he owed the organization that much.

As it was, not all the core soldiers had been invited to this "get-together" with the volunteer from the community. None of the white soldiers were invited, and several of the main black soldier organizers were also not invited. These soldiers were outraged when they heard what had gone down at the meeting with the so-called volunteer. The uninvited black soldiers were the best political leaders in the group. Previously, when there were tensions with racial overtones among the soldiers, they took the initiative to call everyone together to discuss things.

Several days later we got word that this volunteer had gone down to Hunter Liggett where MDM had a group among the Vietnam veterans, and he was being generous with drugs and then tried to sexually assault one of the women staff members. When word got out the situation shifted sharply. The soldiers who'd been at the acid session now got very angry. And we had to calm them down. A meeting of the MDM soldiers concluded that there was something afoul with the "community person." We invited him to a meeting for an explanation of what he was doing. When he showed up, he encountered a hostile group of young soldiers with some pointed questions. A hearing of sorts was held.

He was confronted with accusations about that and about his attempted sexual assault at Hunter Liggett. He denied the accusations, but his credibility dropped to zero. He was told to leave and never come back around the coffeehouse or any other MDM activities or else he'd be dealt with in a less congenial way. "So," I said to Clarence, "I learned a lot from that experience about how people really desire to break down all these barriers but there are concerted efforts to stop this from happening. But I haven't told you the punch line. Six months or so after the incidents I just described I was driving around Seaside and I saw our community volunteer. He was in a Seaside police uniform. "'Suppose he'd just been moonlighting for the FBI?'"

Tractor School

That winter I went to tractor school as part of a government program that paid living expenses to farmworkers who wanted to be retrained for other jobs. But the program had a defect that called into question its stated purpose. It was conducted entirely in English. Needless to say, there were few farmworkers among us. Most of the students were young people who'd grown up in Salinas, some who'd dropped out of high school and were looking to get job skills.

Our curriculum consisted of classroom instruction in the morning on the mechanics of diesel and gas engines and other matters related to the equipment we were learning to use. Then we would check out a piece of equipment, a tractor with a harrow or discs, a bulldozer, an earth grader, and so on, and drive out to a big lot where we practiced moving piles of dirt. We'd bite into a pile and move it from one spot to another. Or we'd smooth a road through a pile. If we were using the tractor, we'd practice discing a harvested crop or harrow rows on a fairly level patch of land, preparing it, as it were, for planting. The things I learned were practical, but I had no real interest in pursuing that kind of work and only once, briefly, did I work driving a tractor, so most of what I learned went unused. Actually I was mainly there to make some money at a time when field work had largely ended.

I spent most of my time riding the equipment, so I didn't have much time to get to know many of my classmates. A group of student mechanics hung out in the diesel shop, which was on the road between the dozers and tractors and the classroom. During lunch break, I'd sometimes pass by the shop and stop for a little conversation. But I didn't feel comfortable around them. Not that they didn't have a good sense of humor. They could joke around with the best of them. But the attitudes of a few of the students really put me off. They were down on Mexicans for one thing. They complained a lot about the strikes and the union movement and repeated idiotic rumors as though they were god-given truths. Often these were about César Chávez who, in their view, was either a masterful manipulator set on taking control of the nation's food supply or the agent of a foreign power, most likely Russia, sent to subvert otherwise happy farmworkers. No story seemed too outrageous when it came to the menace of farmworkers. They had no great appreciation for the fact that Mexican farmworkers sustained the local economy and produced their food. As far as they were concerned, the farmworkers had it good and their rebellion was a mark of ingratitude. These were young workers talking, but growers' words were coming out of their mouths.

My own views on such matters were not regarded with great favor. When I mentioned one day that I'd spent the previous summer thinning lettuce, I got the same response I imagine I'd have received if I'd told them I'd just parked my spaceship behind the mechanic shop. They said little, but their expressions said, "You did what?"

I became friendly with one of the students, Faustino, a young Filipino. I admired his knowledge of mechanics, and mechanical things in general. He was also an avid hunter, and I hadn't known him long before he insisted I come along with him to hunt. I had mixed feelings about hunting, but I went with him for the experience. We drove up one evening on a road through the Gabilan hills to the east of the valley. The evening light slipped away as we made our way along the winding road through the hills of grass, shrubland, and scrub oak. We were into a long bend in the road when a deer entered the pavement in front of us. And true to the cliché, the deer was caught in the headlights; its eyes, large and curious, shone back at us. Faustino stopped the truck. He had his rifle on the seat between us and he grabbed it, opened his door, and with one shot brought the deer down onto the roadway. That was it. We dragged the deer behind the truck bed and with some exertion managed to get it onto the bed, covering it so as to hide it from any passing ranger. Apparently hunting in the dark, apart from being rather unsportsmanlike, was illegal. Either that or we were hunting off-season, I don't recall exactly.

I said I had mixed feelings about hunting. But I eat meat, so I suppose my misgivings are in regard to hunting for its own sake. If the hunting is done for food and not just for sport, I can go along with that even if it's not something I'm into. We did in fact bring the deer back to Faustino's garage where he skillfully skinned it and cut it up for food. I was very impressed with that. I was able to take a healthy chunk of deer meat back to the house where I was still living with FJ, Julie, and Aggie, and we enjoyed a few good meals from it.

Faustino's father had worked in the fields, so I felt comfortable talking to him about my situation and what brought me to Salinas. Faustino was a few years younger than I and had had no contact with any left political movements, but it aroused his curiosity. I told him about my own ambivalence about hunting and my experience with guns, which he found amusing. I'd joined the Coast Guard Reserve because I had no real interest in going to Vietnam. My brother-in-law and cousin had preceded me in the Guard, and my brother-in-law jokingly called it the "Jewish navy" because so many young Jews took the Coast Guard route to avoid the war. My views on the war at that time were fairly neutral. I had neither heard nor read anything about it to make me think it was noble or worthwhile. On the other hand, I didn't really know much about why it started or why the United States was there.

The Coast Guard sounds pretty benign, but it's military and its basic training was modeled after the Marines, which means it was mind-fucking bullshit. As I told Faustino, and anyone else who cared to hear my opinion, there's nothing glorious about the U.S. military. Here we were in basic training for eight weeks during a time of war, and we heard nothing about that war that would in any rational way justify it. No history, no background, no logic. At times we were told that the United States was there to stop North Vietnamese aggression against the South, but there was no substance to that assertion. Why was the United States interested in that? Instead we marched around shouting, "I want to go to Vietnam, I want to kill the Viet Cong." Inspiring. And the Vietnamese were often referred to as "gooks." If we were so concerned about them, why were we calling them derogatory names? So, it was in the Coast Guard, without any other influences, that I decided I was a pacifist.

One day our basic training unit was brought to Camp Roberts, a Reserve training base north of San Luis Obispo, for M-1 practice. I got the lowest score in marksmanship in our group. I was actually proud of this and told the others in my unit that it confirmed I was a pacifist by nature. It was something I believed at the time since I had no other explanation for why I felt the way I did. Of course, that wasn't true since social concepts are not inbred. But the idea of killing for the U.S. military held no appeal to me, and I didn't want to train for it. The other recruits found this amusing. None of them cared that I was a pacifist. There was no morale for the war. No one in our unit was gung-ho. Even the sailors who had signed up for regular duty had no morale. My bunkmate, for example, joined the Coast Guard to avoid going to jail for stealing car stereos. Certainly a part of this general lack of enthusiasm was due to the fact that we were in the Coast Guard. and I believe many of the recruits had gone there because they were low on inspiration to fight in Vietnam. And we knew we wouldn't *have to* go there to fight.

When I left basic training, I was a pacifist. But later, when I learned more about the war and the history behind it, I became convinced of the righteousness of the Vietnamese struggle. Then I had to confront a contradiction. I was a pacifist, but I could not condemn the Vietnamese for fighting against what I saw as a criminal aggression against them. So I concluded that violence for some purposes was justified. There were just wars and unjust wars. Then I read things about Malcolm X and his stand on the right of black people to defend themselves against Ku Klux Klan and police violence. And again I had to agree that they were right to do so, as were the Black Panthers who defended their right to arm themselves against the violent attacks by the police.

When I began working in the GI coffeehouse, many of our staff were Vietnam vets, and among them were combat soldiers and Marines. They were, naturally, familiar with guns. And we kept guns at the coffeehouse for protection. And this may well have saved us from a bad situation.

One day, we got word that Jane Fonda was coming to visit Fort Ord and the coffeehouse as part of a tour of antiwar projects being filmed by author and lawyer Mark Lane. We put the word out on the base for soldiers to come and join a conversation with Jane and her crew about the war. And some soldiers showed up to talk to her. As the crew was setting up their lights and equipment for the shoot, members of a local motorcycle gang, the Monterey Losers, showed up at the coffeehouse and stormed in. They came brandishing clubs, whips, and knives. They may well have had other things concealed. As soon as they entered, they began intimidating people, threatening to tear the place up. Jane and the camera crew were able to pack up and leave out the back way.

The leader of the Losers was an obnoxious sort who went by the name "German George." He liked to strut around with a large metal swastika hanging from his neck. Well, George was strutting around the coffeehouse, and he wandered to the back where we had our office, which was off-limits to non-staff, but he pushed his way in. Fortunately one of the alert staff members, a combat vet, had gone back to the office and was there when German George pushed open the door. The vet, whose name was Steve Murtaugh, pulled a shotgun out of the closet where it was kept and chambered a round. You could hear the distinctive cocking of the shotgun throughout the coffeehouse. Steve leveled the shotgun at German George's head and told him that any further steps might have negative consequences to his health, or something like that. German George decided not to test Steve's sincerity and left the office, pulling his little gang of thugs out of the coffeehouse with him.

Curiously, the police showed up shortly after the gang left, all flustered and without a clue as to what to do. The damage had been done, and perhaps the Losers had accomplished what they'd set out to do. But I was glad that Steve did what he did because things might have gotten far uglier for us.

All over the country antiwar, radical, and revolutionary organizations were being attacked physically. An antiwar Marine at Camp Pendleton north of San Diego was shot in a drive-by at a house run by MDM activists and soldiers. Black Panther offices were being attacked violently by police in many places across the country. The police were assassinating many political activists and leaders, some brazenly. This prompted people to take measures to defend themselves, and they were right to do so.

Villa Street

Late that winter I moved out of the house with FJ, Julie, and Aggie and moved into a small wooden shack on Villa Street, in a small courtyard of shacks across from a park, rooming with Kenny, a friend from the coffeehouse days in Seaside. Kenny, outgoing and intense, had joined the coffeehouse staff in the early spring of 1970 and then enlisted in the military to do organizing work from inside the army. He even got sent for training at Fort Ord and became an active member of MDM. The military was keeping tabs on their activist soldiers. The Pentagon under Nixon decided to rid the ranks of troublemakers. Within a matter of weeks, nearly every soldier who was known to relate to the MDM was summarily discharged and ordered off the base, Kenny among them.

In conducting its purge, military authorities frequently gave activist black soldiers bad conduct discharges, while white soldiers mainly got general discharges that turned honorable after a period of time, thus assuring whites yet another advantage in a world where discharge status was an important consideration in hiring.

In 1969, I'd been given a general discharge at the Coast Guard base at Government Island in Alameda. I'd had numerous run-ins with the brass for handing out antiwar literature during Reserve training sessions. I was recalled to active duty as punishment, but when I persisted in these activities after reactivation, I was told to leave the base and never return, under threat of arrest for trespass. I was given a general medical discharge, which eventually turned honorable. Meanwhile, black soldiers who had served in Vietnam but had spoken out against the war upon return were drummed out of the service with bad conduct discharges, nearly the equivalent, in practical terms, of being pegged with a criminal record.

Around the time I started working in the fields, Kenny began work at the Spreckels sugar factory near Salinas. Kenny's activist temperament led to involvement in the sugar workers' union. He was active during a rocky and wrenching time when the domestic sugar industry was dying under the pressure of cheaper imported cane sugar. He presided as the head of Sugar Workers Local 180 in the years before the aging factory was shut down in the 1980s.

Alfonso and Dolores

In our little courtyard on Villa Street, I was underneath the 1962 Volkswagen van I'd bought when my old Ford gave up on me. I was changing the oil when a face appeared next to the rear tire. It was on the youngish side of middle age, with a black knit cap pulled down to the eyebrows. "Te ayudo, amigo?" (Help you?) the face offered. "Gracias, estoy bien, pero muchas gracias" (I'm doing ok, but thanks), I replied to the face. A conversation ensued as I slipped out from under the rear of the van. Soon I was presented with an invitation to dinner at the shack across from ours.

Over dinner we learned about our neighbors. Alfonso was only in his late thirties but he'd worked in the fields nearly twenty years and he was tired. He suffered migraines and back pains. He'd worked for a time in the grueling lettuce contract crews, but when he couldn't keep up the pace he moved to hourly work in cauliflower, lettuce machine harvesting and thinning, onions, and irrigation. His physical problems made him more pensive and taciturn than he might otherwise have been. His domestic partner, and opposite in many respects, was Dolores, who worked on the Bud Antle lettuce machines as a wrapper. Dolores had the kind of spirit that could put a grin on a zombie. It was nearly impossible to be around her without flexing your good humor muscles. She had an easy and genuine laugh, an appreciation for people, lots of positive energy. I think she sustained Alfonso and, to some degree, everyone around her.

In my years in the fields I would be the fortunate recipient of much farmworker hospitality and generosity. I discovered that if you visited a farmworker family, you'd better be prepared to eat. Only a doctor's note certifying certain death upon the consumption of food would permit you to leave without first sharing a meal. But then, why would you want to?

When Kenny and I sat down to dinner with Alfonso and Dolores in their little shack, identical to ours, we took up what was the living room, dining room, and kitchen area. Over a meal of carne asada, nopales, refried beans, salsa, and tortillas, the conversation turned to their curiosity about me. They wanted to know, what in the world was I doing in the fields? This was a question I would be asked many times in the years to come. And I'm not sure my answers ever sounded comprehensible. "I'm working in the fields, well, by accident," I said, "but I am really here now because, of the struggle." When I saw a strain on their faces, I added, "Because of the movement." "Oh. So you work for the union?" I searched for an answer that I had not quite worked out yet. "I see the farmworker movement as part of the struggle to bring about a better society. I think we need to fight for a more just world. I want to be part of that." Kenny and I explained our views on society and why we believed we needed a different kind of social system, a different kind of world, which could only be brought about by revolutionary means.

What I also tried to express was a sense I had just begun to grasp, that it was a relief to be among people whose values were based on a community sense rather than individual outlook. I grew up in a middle-class environment where people were judged by what they "accomplished" or how they rose in some way above the rest. It's like this joke I heard: When does the fetus become viable for the middle-class Jewish parent? Answer: When it graduates from medical school. There are social truths entwined in this that make it funny, as well as a measure of stereotyping. But what is clear is that the joke makes no sense to a farmworker community where people are less subject to rating on some individual success scale. There seemed to be, especially in this area of farmworker movement (as well as an aspect of the broader social movement of the time), a greater value placed on people's contribution to the general effort. Farmworkers want the best for their children as other communities did, but it seemed their children were not judged as lesser if they worked in the fields, fixed cars, or cleaned offices. That's not to say that these middle-class American values with their emphasis on upward mobility have no influence among farmworkers; it's just that other values were dominant.

At one point in our conversation we got to this question: "Isn't there something seriously wrong with a society that treats the people who produce our food as inferior?" It was a question I would mull over and discuss many times. Alfonso and Dolores certainly thought there was something deeply wrong with society's disregard for workers in the fields. They, like many farmworkers I'd meet over the years, were proud of the work they did. They were also critical of the "conspicuous consumption" people from the wealthier sectors often pursued. To them it was pointless and wasteful.

But the larger society was working constantly to promote certain values, and, despite a lot of hypocritical moralizing, hard work and modest living was not among them. So there was no telling to what degree Alfonso and Dolores, like many farmworkers and people on the so-called bottom, would internalize society's judgment that if you're "down *there*," in the ranks of the poorly paid workers, there must be something wrong with *you*.

Though neither Alfonso nor Dolores worked in union-organized companies, they felt the need for organization and justice in the fields. They supported the movement and participated in union rallies and marches. Beyond that, they saw the war in Vietnam as a lie perpetrated by the rich and fought by the poor. They saw their own country, Mexico, as a victim of this predatory power to the north. "Pobre Mexico," Alfonso said laughing, reciting the famous saying from, of all people, the notorious Mexican dictator Porfirio Diaz, "tan lejos de Dios y tan cerca de Estados Unidos" (Poor Mexico, so far from God and so close to the United States). I would hear that quote again many times in the coming years.

Gustavo and the Spanish Language

Gustavo and Isabel also lived in our court on Villa Street. Gustavo, the more outgoing of the two, was an intellectual from Argentina. I don't recall the circumstances that brought him to the United States. He was a slightly built man, with receding hairline, into its graying phase, and a goatee that he trimmed so it came to a point. This alone made him stand out.

Gustavo had an interest in many things, and over time our conversations, in a kind of hybrid English-Spanish, covered a lot of ground. One day while having dinner at their shack, Gustavo got intense on the issue of language. He was deeply bothered by what he called the butchering of Castellano (he insisted this was the correct name for what most everyone called Spanish) by Mexicans. He was especially incensed by the language as spoken by the people around him, the campesinos. If he'd had his way, he might have prohibited farmworkers from speaking Castellano altogether, so offensive did he find their version of Spanish.

Here was a point of view that I immediately found narrow-minded and illogical. I objected to Gustavo's insistence that there is a "correct" way of speaking. Certain individuals may speak incorrectly, I agreed. They may use words inappropriately, and so on. (Though even here the line is not totally clear since individuals can add inventive new forms of speech. Think of Shakespeare, to whose creative use of language modern English owes scores of popular words and phrases.) There are new words and phrases that constantly emerge in any living language. *Somebody* had to be the first to use them! (One only had to be around the youth of the 1960s to be aware of the explosion of creative new words bubbling up as it were from below into the culture.) Yet, when speaking of a large grouping of people who have their own manner of communicating, in what sense can you say it is incorrect? Spanish itself began as a "bastardization" of Latin, as did French, Italian, Portuguese, and Romanian. And which languages proved to be more resilient in the long run? Certainly not Latin. I saw in Gustavo a bias not only for language but for class and perhaps ethnicity as well. Besides, I was learning the Spanish he found objectionable, with, for example, its multifaceted use of such "inappropriate" words as *chingar*. And my language was already getting peppered with such words as chinga, chingado, un chingo, chinga tu . . . , un chingazo, chingón, un chingadero, a la chingada, en chinga! to mention a few. Words such as these were part of everyday expression and carried meanings, both literal and emotional, difficult to define and therefore unique in their own ways. For example, "Hay que la chingada!" was something like "Oh, my god," or "Dios mio," but more visceral, it seemed to me. And in certain circumstances, especially used inadvertently in a public setting, could be humorous. Or "Está chingada!" was a popular way of saying, "It's all fucked up," and isn't that more satisfying in certain circumstances than the more polite, "It's really messed up," or "It's all screwed up"? Maybe it was just my own fascination with "foul" language, or maybe there was an element of *machista* influence in it all, I don't know. But I will say that I heard, on more than one occasion, women on picket lines and other places using such language that, to use a popular expression, would have made a sailor blush—and in circumstances where it seemed quite appropriate.

Gustavo's objections to Mexican Spanish echoed a controversy that arose years later with so-called ebonics and the outcry against Black English. But my thoughts on this were, and still are, expressed in the question, what is language if not a way for people to communicate ideas to each other? And if a given language does this, in what sense can you say it's *not* correct? You can say it's a different form of a language, one that is embraced by a certain distinct population. But incorrect? This implies some absolute standard, and when it comes to language, there is no such thing. But I owe to Gustavo the impetus for thinking about such an issue.

What's Your Nation?

The sixties exploded into existence in the upheaval against racism and national oppression. Perhaps no other issue most defined the radical edge of the 1960s than the rebellion against national oppression in its many forms. When the curtain of sanitized history was pulled back, we "sixties people" found that the true history of the United States was one of people of European origin dominating and enslaving other races and groups, beginning with Native Americans. In the growing radical movement, support was deepening for the struggles of people of oppressed nations both internationally and in the United States against colonialism, racism, national oppression, and against the system that promoted and sustained this oppression. But shared opposition to the way things were did not necessarily mean shared agreement as to why or what to do about it. And shared opposition to the old relationships among people did not guarantee clarity on what the new ones should look like. There were intense and wrenching struggles and, at times, bitter divisions over how to understand this history and what to do about it.

One contentious question involved the role of national minorities and nationalism in the struggle in the United States. By this time I regarded myself as an internationalist. I felt revulsion toward U.S. nationalism, the ideological hook to unite people behind the drive for domination and control over much of the world. U.S. patriotism is a virulent form of nationalism interwoven with racism and contempt for other people. But the nationalism of people oppressed by the imperialist system was and is a positive, progressive force. In that period, it was a powerful and igniting force that swept people into struggle for rights and liberation. Broadly speaking, the movements toward national independence and liberation were the most important contradictions facing the imperialist system. But nationalism as an ideology has inherent limits. Left unchallenged, nationalism becomes narrow and competitive, counter to the aims of freeing all of humanity from an oppressive and backward system. Differences over the role of nationalism in the movement led to sharp, sometimes bitter arguments and debates.

Experiences among soldiers reinforced my belief that an internationalist rather than a nationalist outlook was both necessary and possible, despite a long history of racial division. One incident in particular stood out, and I used it at that time to explain my own outlook on this and argue for what I considered to be a more correct view.

It was late summer 1970 and word got out that a rebellion had erupted inside Fort Ord in an area called SPD, Special Processing Detachment, a minimum security prison inside the perimeter of the base. SPD was the army's response to the dramatic rise on the base of insubordinate and disrespectful behavior directed at military authorities. The base's small brig was filled to overflowing and could not accommodate the burgeoning ranks of the insubordinate soldiers, so the brass fashioned a minimum security prison from a cluster of barracks and encircled it with a fence and barbed wire.

SPD lacked its own mess hall so SPD soldiers were allowed out of their confinement, but they had to carry a special ID and were subject to humiliating harassment and mistreatment. Tension and anger among the SPD soldiers exploded one night and they rioted, burning down part of their prison barracks. The coffeehouse staff and MDM soldiers saw the rebellion as a valid response to an oppressive institution and a harbinger of things to come.

Several days after the rebellion, a group of white soldiers from SPD made it off the base and showed up at the coffeehouse. They asked for help in the wake of the rebellion. The wanted to put out a special SPD newspaper. We didn't understand why these soldiers who had engaged in rebellion would now want to put out a newspaper. Wasn't the struggle moving beyond a newspaper? We were reflecting a profound ignorance. And it wasn't long before we realized why.

The SPD rebellion grew out of a shared anger and frustration of the soldiers held there, soldiers of various nationalities. But shortly after the rebellion, military authorities announced to all that if there were any further rebellions, the *black* soldiers would be severely punished and confined to the base's brig, even if it meant having to clear out the brig to accommodate them. Black soldiers at SPD told their white compatriots that there will be no more riots or demonstrations in SPD because if there is *we'll* end up paying for it!

The white soldiers who came to the coffeehouse were looking for a way to overcome these divisive tactics. So they conceived of a newspaper that would bring soldiers from all backgrounds together to produce it. Appropriately they named the paper *Unity Now*. They succeeded in putting out their paper and involving soldiers from different backgrounds in the work.

I felt foolish about my initial response and my appreciation for these soldiers grew. I saw how people awakened politically could fight for the rights of all. No nationality had a monopoly on such sentiments and even those privileged by race could come to hate racism.

A Newspaper

A torrential outpouring of print known as the alternative press was a hallmark of that stormy political time. It grew from a passion for expressing opposition to the mainstream, of resistance, of searching for a new way. Newspapers appeared everywhere, from communities large and small, on campuses, and in organizations. The GI movement gave birth to hundreds of papers that cropped up on nearly every U.S. military installation. These papers spread in relation to the growing discontent.

The alternative press was exposing things the establishment media ignored or covered up. As an example, *Ramparts*, which had morphed over several years from a religious-based literary journal to a powerful magazine of radical political exposure, reported on how the CIA transported heroin controlled by pro-U.S. Laotian generals and brought it to Vietnam, where it was being sold to GIs, to help fund covert operations. Heroin addiction became an epidemic among Vietnam GIs, and soldiers were punished for addiction to drugs their own government was pushing.

Such exposures undermined the credibility of the government and woke the population from its slumber.

It was in this atmosphere of struggle and debate in our little court on Villa Street that we talked about a newspaper that could make connections between the situation in the fields and factories and what was going on in the rest of the world: the struggle for equal rights, the anti-colonial struggles, the demands of women for equality, revolutionary movements inside the United States and in other countries, and the attempt to build a radically different kind of society. Kenny was sympathetic but his mind was moving elsewhere. Alfonso was interested. Dolores was supportive. But it remained just a topic of conversation.

Even in winter there was always something going on at the union hall. People would just hang out and chew over whatever news or gossip was making the rounds. Alfonso and I were making our way to the hall, passing a group in some kind of discussion, when someone called out to him, "Se van ir a Atwater?" Alfonso replied, "Atwater? Por qué?" (Why would we want to go to Atwater?) "You guys don't know about the shooting in a union field?" an older campesino, a sombrero pushed back on his head revealing a mat of sandy gray hair, said with a look of surprise. "Who got shot?" "The migra killed a brother in the pruning. Shot him. Shot him twice, they say." "Killed him?" "Ya, killed him. They say the fella attacked the migra with a pruning knife. He was a citizen, too." "What's going to happen?" Alfonso asked. "The funeral's tomorrow. Some people here are going up there for it." Alfonso and I didn't even need to discuss it; we knew we were going to Atwater, wherever it was.

Atwater is a small farming town in Merced County, where much of the huge Gallo company is located. It's grape and tree fruit country. Romulo Avalos was working with his two brothers pruning peach trees in a Gallo orchard when the Immigration showed up. The agent claimed that Romulo had no proof of residency, so he was taking him to the Immigration patrol car when suddenly, without provocation, Romulo attacked him with his pruning knife. The agent, Edward Nelson, claimed he shot him twice in the chest in "self- defense." Some people in the orchard told the press that after the first shot Avalos clutched his hand. They emphatically denied that Romulo attacked the agent. Witnesses also declared that Romulo's brother was prevented from administering first aid.[2] Several days after the shooting, Merced County sheriffs found a card in Avalos's clothing identifying him as a U.S. citizen. Romulo was born in Hancock, Texas, and moved to Livingston in Merced County, where he'd been working at Gallo for the previous four years.

Alfonso and I drove up to Atwater the morning of the funeral. It was a cold, damp February day. The local Atwater paper put the gathering of farmworkers at 600, but to us it looked larger. The farmworkers gathered in defiance of the chill wind and marched silently along a quiet country road, from the orchard where Romulo was shot to the cemetery. I was taken by the power of that silent march; the silence seemed in some ways to magnify its presence.[3]

People around the union were attributing the killing to the increased harassment of workers at union ranches. This may have been true, but the migra had been treating immigrants as criminals long before the union came along. After the killing UFWOC called on farmworkers to stage sit-down protests in the fields whenever the Immigration came into a union field. That seemed like a creative tactic. But I don't know if it was ever used on union-organized farms.

Alfonso and I were both inspired by the intense and moving scene we had been part of. I'd brought a camera, and we were going to take my pictures, add text, and put out a leaflet on the killing. When we got back to Villa Street, we went to Alfonso's place to continue our conversation with Dolores. Over dinner we told Dolores about our plans, and she pointed out that we'd been talking about starting a paper, so this seemed like a good time for it.

The next day we went to the union hall to talk over this idea with Richard Chávez, a former auto union official, who was heading up the Salinas office, and Gloria, who dispatched FJ and me to the thinning crew, in the little office space at the back of the hall. Richard was sitting in a beat-up armchair trying to relieve the pain of an injured back. The unrelenting spasms had him stressed out and exhausted much of the time. We laid out our concept for a paper, how we wanted something that spoke to the common interests of working people and exposed injustices like that at Atwater and brought out broader social and international issues from the perspective of the victims. Richard and Gloria were supportive. For a moment the pain left Richard's face as he spoke enthusiastically about the prospect. Gloria suggested we call the paper *El Obrero* (The Worker). We left the office with some confidence. We at least had their moral support, and it meant a lot to us.

We received a good deal of encouragement from farmworkers and activists, but we could see that when it came to the work it was going to fall on a few shoulders. For the moment our enthusiasm overshadowed our doubts, and we kept those doubts at bay. We decided if we could come out with one issue we might arouse more active interest and volunteers. So we set about writing and translating the first issue.

The paper had to be bilingual, and Alfonso and Dolores translated articles written in English. We met a graphic artist, a soldier from Fort Ord who lived up the street, and he designed the paper's logo—a farmworker bent over with a short-handled hoe on the left side of the graphic and a cluster of factory buildings on the other, with a flat strip depicting the valley in between. Below the design it read, "To the Unity of Working People." The logo appeared on subsequent issues for several years.

Our shacks were so small that we had little space to do any newspaper layout, but a union official, Roberto Garcia, gave us use of his garage. When the time came, we were able to get use of a mimeograph at UC Santa Cruz. We pooled our money and asked for contributions. By the first week of March, 1972, *El Obrero del Valle de Salinas/The Worker of the Salinas Valley* appeared. The entire first issue was devoted to farmworker stories. Strawberry workers living at the La Posada trailer camp were fighting eviction. That became the centerpiece of our first issue, along with the news about Romulo Avalos.

After that first mimeographed version we began putting out monthly issues on newsprint. On one side was Spanish, and flipping it over, the other side was English. A printer in Moss Landing, a veteran of labor struggles of the 1930s who had his own progressive local paper, agreed to print *El Obrero*.

One day, into the second edition of the paper, I ran into Jose Perez, a shop steward in the strawberries and an energetic union advocate active in the valley before the 1970 strike. "I've seen this paper you put out, why don't you distribute it more widely? It's a good thing isn't it?" "I think so," I said. "Well, then, get it out on the crews. You should get it in the fields. Get the crew reps to help." And so with Jose's help a general meeting of crew reps took up the question of distributing the paper and agreed to bring issues of *El Obrero* to their crews each month. Jose even helped work out the logistics of collecting money by putting collection cans in the union hall.

Cauliflower

At the union hall one late winter afternoon, getting out *El Obrero*, Gloria asked me if I wanted a dispatch for the cauliflower. Tractor school was over and I was waiting for the lettuce harvest with plans to work on a lettuce machine at Antle with Dolores and Alfonso. But that was still weeks away. "I've never worked cauliflower," I said. "Don't worry," said Gloria, "After thinning I'm sure you'll handle it."

The next morning I bundled up and got on a bus at the corralón, fighting drowsiness. I was out of the habit of getting up before light. I sat shivering and was glad when the foreman finally started up the bus's heater as we left for the field. The warmth would have put me to sleep if it had not been for the rattling and jolting as it wove through the Alisal, picking up crew along the way. As the field emerged from the darkness, we were enveloped in a huge gray tent of fog that gradually turned white and obscured everything but the ground immediately around us. I regretted not bringing gloves, anticipating the numbness I would feel handling the cold, wet leaves. I was not mistaken.

Cauliflower comes from the same family of plants as broccoli. But it grows much closer to the ground, like lettuce. The edible flower is surrounded by a large cluster of leaves. Once the plant reaches a certain size, workers tie the leaves together with rubber bands to keep the white flower hidden from the discoloring rays of the sun. We cut cauliflower with a knife the length of a machete; the long blade served to push back the leaves to see the size of the flower. Sometimes the flower would reveal its size by the bulge at the lower part of the leaves. And sometimes we had to reach down and grab the solid white flower to see if it had a diameter roughly the size of an open hand, the cutting size. By grabbing hold of the banded leaves, you could pull back the plant and whack the stem to separate it from the flower.

We cutters walked on either side of a truck carrying large bins, in which we tossed the cauliflower with all its leaves. I learned two methods for tossing. One was to grab the leaves at the top and sling the vegetable underhand toward the bins. This method allowed the tosser the option of giving the plant a spin and experiment with various trajectories. The other method was to put the knife under the plant and push the vegetable toward the bin using the leverage of the long blade. This method inhibited creative spinning but utilized the strength of your dominant hand. The bins were a large target, and once you got the hang of the toss, hitting the target was not difficult with either method.

The truck with its bins moved slowly, but you couldn't just dawdle without the risk of falling behind, which meant hard running and tossing in order to catch up, turning a relatively easy job into an exhausting, strenuous chore.

One day our work routine was shattered by shouts and excited scampering among the plants. People were running frantically, not in the single direction one would expect if the migra were approaching, but in random patterns toward and away from each other as though a phantom had suddenly descended on us. Amid the running and excited shouts, I heard the word *"liebre."* Only when I saw one of our crew bend down between the rows of leafy plants and emerge with a delighted grin, a brown body writhing between his dirt caked fingers, did I realize what was up. "Ya tienes para tu pozole, compadre," someone shouted—he'd found something for his rabbit stew.

Like most everyone who worked in the fields, I would occasionally take home some of the food we harvested. I had a diet heavy in vegetables! The company had no problem with that. But there was food in the fields beyond that purposely grown on these factory farms. I would pass by plants in the field with no other thought than "another weed." But one person's weed was another, more knowledgeable person's nutritious greenery. People from Mexico's countryside knew about many plants that grew wild. And they were often taking home "weeds" like *lechuga del monte*, a kind of wild lettuce that grows on stalks with tender pointy leaves, and *verdulaga*, a succulent with small, soft, down-covered leaves and thick, moist stems. On more than one occasion, I was encouraged to take a bunch of such plants from the field but declined. I had my citified prejudice against anything that had not been cultivated for the market. And, anyway, I had no idea how to prepare these greens.

Daniel

A lucky thing occurred for me on that crew. By the end of the first week in the cauliflower, I found myself working next to a fellow who kept my days from melting into tedium. He was a little older than I, with a dark ponytail that extended to the small of his back. He had a tall, slim build, sharp features, and dark expressive eyes. He spoke no Spanish, and so gravitated to the only other English speaker on the crew. I was happy to have someone to talk to, as my conversational skills in Spanish were still on the primitive side. He spoke softly with such fluency that you'd have been hard-pressed to guess English was his second language.

Daniel grew up on an Indian reservation in Southern California. In the weeks that I worked with him, I was audience to remarkable, entrancing stories, of growing up on a "rez," of the people who lived there, of their trials and errors, their triumphs and tragedies, their wisdoms and frailties. These were stories, most of all, of his brothers and sisters, parents, cousins, aunts, and uncles. Stories about a world I knew nothing about, a world inside a world where a people maintained and practiced traditions even while their culture was being stripped from them.

Daniel told me about growing up wild on the reservation, of his mischievous youth, and of worldly knowledge and wisdoms handed down to him from other generations. He told me about the ritualistic harvesting of pine nuts and acorns, describing the processes with delightful detail. He described hunting and reverence for the hunted.

He told me about the boarding schools for Indians where self-righteous teachers preached to the students about the value of learning the ways of the larger society, and of the petty punishments meted out to students who practiced their Indian ways, especially those who used the language they'd learned at home. He spoke of boarding schools that looked like prisons, where students were regarded with fear by the society at large, of being separated from his family. He spoke of relatives who descended into the abyss of alcohol or drugs or both; of corruption among the tribal authorities; of crazy self-destructive actions that would have seemed comical if not so tragic for the parties involved.

One of the stories he told was of a relative, I think an uncle, who as a youth rebelled against his family and traditions and abandoned the reservation to live in a city. The uncle felt embarrassed and ashamed of his "backward" Indian ancestry and determined to cast it off and assimilate into the society that had seemed so superior to his own. This uncle managed well in the first years of his "exile," but after a time he began to feel distant from the new society he'd adopted. He'd thought that criticism of his Indian society had been justified on the grounds that it had clung to backward, useless ways. But off the reservation, he found discrimination that had nothing to do with criticism of Native American life but related only to the way he and others looked. Modern society was powerful, he learned, but it was also blind and stupid in the way it used resources without regard to the consequences, and it was wasteful of human and animal life. Most of all, he began to question the reckless disregard for or ignorance of nature, as though nature were an adversary to be defeated rather than a wondrous reality to be understood and cared for. His disillusionment grew and so did his appreciation for his much maligned tribe and society.

Having experienced alienation in the world to which he had hoped to escape, he became determined to defend his native culture, which, with all its defects and deformities, seemed a saner alternative. Thus he returned to the tribe and began to advocate for the preservation of tribal traditions. This was an uphill battle, because the forces that had driven him from the fold were, if anything, becoming more powerful. But there were countercurrents as well. The civil rights movement and the struggles that erupted from many oppressed nationalities, Native Americans among them, strengthened his conviction that the claims of non-Indian society to its superiority were not to be believed. The stories of this uncle had a deep impression on Daniel, who had not lost sight of the value of his culture even when he was forced to leave the reservation to find work and get away from some of the self-destructive ways into which some of his people had fallen.

Listening to Daniel occupied a lot of my working hours, making them slide by with a pleasure that belied the work itself. I searched my memory for stories from my own upbringing with which to repay him in kind, but I came up empty. Or they came out so pale next to the rich textures of his narratives that I felt embarrassed by them and ceded the time to his recollections, which were plentiful and eloquent.

One morning I arrived at the corralón for work and Daniel was not there. I never saw or heard from him again.

3. THE WINDS KEEP BLOWING, 1972

FOR THE FERTILE VEGETABLE FIELDS of the Salinas Valley, winter's rest is a short nap. No sooner are the last of the year's broccoli and cauliflower chaff disced into the soil than the first of next season's crops are being prepared. By mid-December flat brown fields begin to take on new contours. Tractors, like tiny boats plying a vast brown sea, traverse the fields dragging harrows that carve long rows and furrows—*hilos y surcos*—symmetrical wrinkles in a dark, yielding flesh. Then the planters lay down their seeds on the flattened rows. Within weeks faint green lines appear, then deepening green paths as the days pass and the sun angles higher, lingering longer. By January and February thinning crews, backs bent, plod across the damp sown fields. By late March or early April the first lettuce crop is maturing—the growers' "spring deal" and for the local-bound harvest worker a first week's work after austere months of lying low.

Dolores and Alfonso were anxious to get back to work after their layoff from the Bud Antle lettuce machines, their winter funds more than exhausted. For Alfonso it was a test to see how his back would hold up, but with his migraine torments at bay he was feeling optimistic for the first time in a while. I had my mind set on breaking into lettuce or celery contract work and thought that the lettuce machines, with their slower pace, would be a good place to start. Dolores assured me that she could get me on at Antle, and I was curious about work on a non-union crew, or rather a Teamster union crew, which essentially amounted to the same thing.

Lettuce Machines

It was still dark this first day of the lettuce harvest season, when Dolores, Alfonso, and I arrived at the Antle camp, a clump of wooden barracks off Natividad Road above Carr Lake, which is a patch of rich soil smack in the center of Salinas—a "lake" in reality only during winter of a heavy rainy season. Workers were straggling out of the mess hall toward buses parked at the center of the camp. Foremen were checking the portable toilets connected to the buses or loading yellow water containers and talking with people looking for work. Dolores found a supervisor and began negotiating on my behalf while I fidgeted with the lettuce knife I'd borrowed from Alfonso. The supervisor didn't say a word to me, but nodded in the direction of a bus, taking Dolores' word that I could cut lettuce and endure, at least a day, in the fields.

It was a short bus ride from the camp to where a machine perched like an awkward bird at the edge of a field. As it started to move forward into the rows of mature lettuce, it swayed, its rectangular wings dipping and rising slightly as it settled into its pace, its wheels perfectly aligned with the carved irrigation rows.

I worked alongside Alfonso on a line of mostly male cutters trailing behind the machine. Alfonso counseled me on the technique of cutting, trimming some outer leaves and stacking the heads on a flat area on the machine for the wrappers. Alfonso did double duty for a time, cutting lettuce from my row as well as his until I got the hang of the cut. But it did not take long until I was able to handle the rows on my own.

All the wrappers who sat on perches in front and above us had their faces covered by colorful bandanas revealing little but their eyes. In smooth, quick movements they took the naked heads and stuck them in the center of a sheet of plastic (supplied by Dow Chemical, a big investor in Antle), pulling the wrap around the lettuce and sealing with a heated iron device. Wrapped lettuce moved down a conveyor to the packers supplied with boxes by the machine operator/stitcher.

Bud Antle, the founder of the company, was an innovator among lettuce growers. He is credited with bringing lettuce packing to the fields in the 1950s, a huge change that took advantage of the technical advance of vacuum cooling to replace ice packing. This all but eliminated the lettuce packing sheds. Antle also introduced the lettuce wrap machines in the early 1960s. By the end of the 1960s most major lettuce companies were using these machines for part of their production. Whereas "naked pack" lettuce ground crews operated under piece rate, machine work was mainly hourly. Far less time was required for workers to learn the slower-paced job, making machine workers easier to replace. It also allowed a greater degree of control over quality than was generally the case with ground crews. Growers got a premium price for wrapped lettuce, which was gaining popularity among market chains.

I wouldn't call the pace on the machine leisurely, but it was tolerable. There wasn't the tug of war between the workers and company I'd found on hourly crews resisting the growers' impulse to speed up. This is because the growers—Antle was a pioneer here, too—built a device into the machine to keep crews on a tighter leash. If the crew exceeded a certain number of boxes per hour, a piece rate kicked in, with a corresponding increase over the hourly wage. By this method the company got maximum production out of hourly pay as they dangled the allure of a piece rate like a carrot before a horse.

Though hardly slow, the work routine allowed for some conversation and joking around, which was the preferred mode whenever possible. A crew that included a mix of young men and women was a sure combination for flirtations, if for no other reason than relief from a deadening routine. I had been making some progress in my Spanish but was still in the novice stage. Joking around in Spanish was beyond my grasp, but I enjoyed what I understood of the banter around me when I wasn't entranced by the young women whose enticing eyes, behind those bandanas, could drive me to distraction.

One of the wrappers I'd gotten to know a bit was in her early thirties, with several small children, cared for by her mother while she worked. One day, as the morning break was called and the machine came to a halt, this wrapper turned to me and said, I thought rather seriously, "Bruce, me quieres mucho, verdad?" I knew enough Spanish to have some idea what she meant, but I wasn't totally sure. "Me quieres" translated literally is "you want me." But I thought it meant, "you love me." Then I thought, well maybe it really means "you like me," though I suspected one of the other interpretations. In this moment of indecision I stammered, and blushed. Was she just joking with me? Was this a rebuke for some semiconscious flirtation? I took the defensive way out and blurted, "No entiendo." The wrapper looked at me and said, matter-of-factly, "Si entiendes, Bruce, si entiendes"—you understand. I insisted on my ignorance and the subject was dropped.

Another time during the morning break, a group of wrappers competed among themselves to see who could get this young *güero* (light-skinned fellow) to eat one of the innocent-looking little green chiles they brought to spice their lunches. I had a pretty good idea what was in store, but not wanting to spoil their fun, nor mine, I took a healthy bite of one. With the wrappers looking on I tried to calmly endure the blowtorch that enveloped my mouth and tongue. "No es nada para mi" (This is nothing for me), I insisted, a lie that no one believed, much less when I made a run for the water cooler, leaving behind a ripple of laughter.

Antle

In 1942, Bud Antle, along with his father, Lester, founded the company that bears his name. His success, and that of other area growers, was not affected when their Japanese competitors were rounded up that year and sent off to the camps, among them some of the most successful and innovative farmers, credited with beginning what became the seasonal crop rotation from Salinas, south to the border area, what the workers call *la corrida*.[1] In fact, some Salinas growers were more than happy to see the concentration camps relieve them of competition from Japanese-American farmers and not shy about expressing this publicly.

The Second World War period was a time of cheap *bracero* labor and a rapidly growing market for lettuce. By the 1960s, Antle was a big deal, with designs on dominating the lettuce industry, one of the most lucrative and powerful sectors of California agriculture.

In 1962, much to the distaste of the local grower oligarchy, Antle negotiated a Teamster contract covering its farmworkers. That move was so unpopular among growers that they forced Antle out of the Grower Shipper Vegetable Association and he endured bitter public denunciation. It's possible that Antle foresaw the end of the Bracero Program days (bracero ranks at the end of the 1950s made up nearly 90 percent of the Salinas lettuce harvesting crews) and struggles potentially emerging from that. More likely, Antle saw business advantages in a deal with the Teamsters, with their power in the shipping and cooling operations vital to the industry. From the worker standpoint, unionization at Antle, like other Teamster companies, was noticeable only on payday in the form of paycheck deductions. There were no Teamster crew reps, no Teamster meetings, no sense of a movement to improve conditions or empower workers such as existed at that time in UFWOC companies. However, over the years Antle did keep farmworker wages slightly above those of other valley growers. Antle was also unique in offering health benefits. In this way Antle built up a kind of internal loyalty, which served to stave off the union movement that erupted in the summer of 1970.

During the 1970 general strike UFWOC set its sights on Antle, one of the three largest Salinas lettuce operators. By so doing they also targeted the Teamsters, who had scabbed on the union movement by signing contracts with lettuce growers on the eve of the strike. Chávez declared a boycott of Antle lettuce, and union organizers inside and outside Antle worked to bring the company down. Soon after UFWOC declared its boycott of Antle products, the U.S. Department of Defense discovered a great hunger for Antle lettuce among its soldiers and greatly increased the Antle lettuce it acquired for GI mess halls. According to UFWOC statistics, Department of Defense purchases increased from 8 percent to 40 percent of its total lettuce purchases.[2] In December 1970, a Salinas judge ruled UFWOC's boycott of Antle illegal and sent Chávez to jail when he refused to call it off. This was a major PR moment, with César Chávez marching solemnly into the Salinas jailhouse through a corridor of hundreds of silent workers, some of them on their knees. A visit by Ethel Kennedy, wife of Robert Kennedy, lent the moment the aura of the Kennedy name.

Bus Talk

At the end of the day Alfonso, Dolores, and I would sometimes compare notes over things we'd heard and discussed at work, with an eye on issues that might be grist for the *El Obrero* mill. Dolores worked on another crew, so she wasn't witness to a dispute that arose one day on a bus ride from work.

It was a sunny day, the kind that made the surrounding hills look like you could touch them. The crew was in a good mood. The lettuce had been heavy on a first-cut field, the ground dry, the weather clear and cool, and the machine had gone at contract speed. Now we were heading back to the camp on Natividad Road, at 1:30 in the afternoon.

It all started out innocently enough. Someone mentioned that an Antle foreman was going to Mexico to work for the company at its ranch in Culiacan. Don Felipe, who was proud of his many years with Antle and made no secret of his loyalty to the company, said he thought Antle was enlarging its operation in that Sinaloan valley. "This," he added, "would be good for the country." Emilio, a young worker who wore a red bandana that covered his hair and partially hid the ponytail that hung just below his shoulders, sat directly behind Don Felipe. He had his back to a bus window and his feet resting in front of him on the seat. "What country?" he asked dryly, his fingers playing on the seat back behind Don Felipe. "Mexico, muchacho," said Felipe, turning to look at the youth. "Cómo *bueno* para Mexico, abuelo?" (What do you mean *good* for Mexico, gramps?), said Emilio putting emphasis on "bueno" with irritation in his voice. Don Felipe was in no mood to be challenged by the youth. "I'm not your grandfather, you know! I don't think your grandfather could cut circles around you like me." At that people in the back of the bus near the action erupted in laughter. "Mexico needs companies like this one to invest and get things going there. I don't see anything wrong with them investing there," said Don Felipe.

"The gringos only come to rip us off," said Emilio, his voice now a pitch higher with agitation. "That's only because our government of rats lets them get away with things," said Felipe.

At that point a sharp voice echoed through the back of the bus: "I want to know who's training the rats!" It was Doña Carmona. "Why are we all here? Because we can't make a living in our own country! Because the best of what's there is in the hands of other people. The best land, the best water; they do better than us because they steal the water and get all the help from the *caciques y ladrones* [thieves] *en el gobierno*. In Culiacan the gringo ranchers control the best land and send all the vegetables north; we never see them in Mexico. They send all the money here. The best of everything comes here." Doña Carmona, I found out later, was from Michoacan, part of a family that had long been active in land reform movements.

"Si, como nosotros!" (Yes, like us!) said a young campesina across from Dona Carmona, to more laughter. The youth in the bandana nodded appreciatively. "Well . . ." Felipe said, but then stopped. I knew where Don Felipe was coming from because while cutting one day he'd told me he hoped the United States would seize and annex part of Mexico and make it the fifty-first state. Don Felipe was not the only one I heard express such a view, but it seemed evident to me that not only was this extremely unlikely and very unfavorable to Mexico, but it came out of intense frustration and disgust with the ineptness and corruption of the Mexican government, a perpetual theme among Mexican farmworkers. The great irony of Don Felipe's view, it seemed to me, lay in the fact that the most damaging corruption of all was in opening Mexico's economy to exploitation by foreign, especially U.S., interests.

Doña Carmona, who stood all of 5' 3", had a strong stocky build. But her most prominent features were her outspoken manner and tough spirit. She had the courage and conviction to speak her mind, and she had a power in her that you saw sometimes in other women in the fields, never quite matched by men. A romantic might say, with some justification, that it was a power fed by centuries of oppression.

Doña Carmona had played a role several weeks earlier when our machine crew was in a field off Market Street and a crop duster began spraying nearby. Use of pesticides in the fields and their effects on farmworkers had become an especially contentious issue since the summer of 1970, during the negotiations that preceded the general strike. A story broke in the press at that time of three farmworkers from North Carolina who died after returning to a field that had been sprayed several days prior with the insecticide parathion. UFWOC publicized the story and used it to back up its demand for strict contract language on pesticide spraying. But every worker in the fields was aware of the potential dangers that lurked with chemicals one could not usually even see.

On one of its passes the duster in the adjacent field let loose its spray and the stiff breeze off the bay pushed a chemical cloud in our direction. It fell short of the field we were working, but it was close enough to the machines to believe that another pass could quite possibly shower us with a toxic drizzle. It was Doña Carmona who spoke up and nearly led us off the field. She even stepped down from her seat on the machine. With Doña Carmona telling everyone in her determined voice that they needed to protect themselves from these chemicals, the machine foreman was scrambling, frantically calling on his shortwave for a supervisor. A walkout for pesticide spraying was just what the company men didn't want—concerned as they were with anything that would give UFWOC supporters leverage to rouse the crews. All the while Doña Carmona was warning people to be ready to take up and leave.

Many of the crew were standing and watching the small plane make its looping turn. It was heading toward the edge of the adjacent field that sat no more than fifty yards from our machine. With the crew at a standstill, the machine driver stopped the machine, ready to make his own dash if necessary. Whether a call had been made to the pilot or he'd considered the field covered is not clear, but the duster kept its altitude and instead of making its short, steep dive to a spraying height, it pulled up and headed away from us. After several minutes we were back at the machine.

After work, a Spanish-speaking supervisor climbed on the bus to assure everyone that the company was aware of the dangers of pesticide and doing everything it could to protect the workers. While he was talking a young woman worker from the back of the bus shouted, "Mentiras, traemos a Chávez" (You're lying and we're bringing in Chávez). The supervisor turned red, but he didn't respond and soon left the bus.

Today, as Doña Carmona ended her agitated observation, the youth in the bandana added, "That's a political problem of the country, because the government allows all these foreign companies to come in and take out what they want. Lately a lot of Japanese companies have come in. Near Morelia there are mountains and the forest is being cut, the wood hauled away, and the land is being left bare. They've contaminated a river that supplies water to the city, they're messing up the environment and looting the country."

The bus had quieted down, and we were now heading up the pitted gravel driveway to the Antle camp. "Bueno, muchachos," said Felipe after a long silence. "Mañana resolvemos todo, como no" (Tomorrow we'll resolve all of this, why not?). "Ándale, ándale" (Of course), said Carmona as she and the rest of us filed off the bus, fleeing into a day young enough to welcome us into its brilliant embrace.

When Alfonso related the story of the outburst on the bus, Dolores said, "Good. *El Obrero* should do a story about Bud Antle in Mexico." We all agreed. But in the crush of other issues and events it never happened. Before long, Dolores and Alfonso, pulled by family concerns, were heading out of Salinas into a Central Valley town. I lost contact with these friends to whom I had become so endeared.

What's Revolution Got to Do with It?

I was in my early twenties when someone first placed a book by Karl Marx in my hands and urged me to read it. At the time my disillusionment with the world around me was growing exponentially. It was fed by the daily horror of the Vietnam War; by poverty and discrimination in places that once had been invisible to me; by the shameless lying of those in government; and by powerful events that shredded my naïve and sheltered view of the world. One day, in the summer of 1968, after arriving in Berkeley to attend college, I happened on an antiwar rally on Telegraph Avenue and began listening to speeches being given on a flatbed truck. Suddenly the crowd around me began to disperse in front of a cloud of tear gas followed by a phalanx of police whipping their clubs at anything they could make contact with. Within a flash, police brutality was not a complaint in some other people's community. That moment I realized my head was as eligible a candidate for the end of that shiny stick as anyone's. Nor did I feel any more a criminal for having attended the rally.

Nothing in my education up to that point could explain all these disturbing events. It took Marx and materials influenced by his thinking to bring some clarity. And my vocabulary began to embrace new words and concepts, like exploitation, oppression, classes, and the struggle between classes, class dictatorship, and imperialism. And so, in a sense, I joined a generation that was experiencing similar epiphanies and set off on a journey to explore the terrain of resistance and revolution.

An evolution of thought was unfolding among many people drawn into impassioned opposition to the government. Among many of the young people there was a great debate over the nature of the enemy we were facing in opposing the war and racism and so on. Many young people were moving from what they saw as the need to rescue democracy (as in American Democracy) from its corruptors and defilers, to the realization that it might well be democracy itself, or the bourgeois version of it, that was the source of the corruption.

The word *system* began to take hold in our vocabulary, embracing a concept that went beyond government to describe something even more basic to the way society operated. Or, in other words, a system whose public face was Democracy, but democracy for a select group of people, meant to hide or obscure the basic, unequal, and exploitative relationships that lay at the foundation of society. It was Karl Marx who'd brought to light the "dirty secret" at the heart of capitalist society, revealing how exploited human labor was the source of capitalism's existence and growth. From this basic relationship of exploitation of some humans by others, other social evils, such as violent human conflicts, result.

Many young people began to see this democracy not as some governing system standing above and apart from the basic inequalities of the economic system, but as the representative and enforcer of that inequality. Democratic governments, like ours, were not neutral arbiters pushed and shaped by competing public interests but ultimately serving the good of all. No! Government was the enforcer of the interests of a relatively small but powerful class of people who ruled society in their own interests, themselves subservient to the system of production and exchange around which society was organized. Or as it was widely put in common terms at the time, "It's the system, and it sucks."

This was a time when a youthful generation groped for the words to describe their disaffection from this system. The Black Panther Party, coming out of Oakland in the late 1960s, clarified the issue. They called out the oppression of black people as victims of centuries of cruel exploitation and brutal repression, and linked their oppression to international colonial and imperial systems in a way that struck a chord among many people in oppressed communities, especially in the large cities. The impassioned response of many black youths from the inner cities to Black Panther politics put *revolution* into the mouths of millions more.

People like myself, who were not "under the gun" of extreme oppressive conditions like those faced by black people and other peoples, had to ask if the extreme conclusions the Panthers were advocating were valid. Only when one began to study and consider the long history of murder and betrayal of oppressed groups in the United States, and where the world as a whole seemed to be headed—such as the widening division between rich and poor countries, and wars for control and domination, such as in Vietnam, and how all this came to be—did the idea of a radical, revolutionary change seem not only valid but necessary.

Around the same time—the late 1960s—events in China began to make an impact in this new world. The Cultural Revolution, which began in China's universities, had drawn millions of Chinese youth into the revolutionary political movement. People were picking up on Mao Tse-tung's advice to the youth of China: "It's right to rebel." This was welcome encouragement but unexpected coming from the leader of a country. Encouraging people, and especially young people, to rebel seemed a far cry from political leaders we knew, such as Ronald Reagan, the California governor, who threatened to unleash a bloodbath against students who dared to protest the Vietnam War, or the likes of a Lyndon Johnson and Richard Nixon, under whose governments (we all strongly suspected) people were persecuted and murdered for threatening the status quo. The names of Martin Luther King Jr., Malcolm X, and Fred Hampton, the Chicago Panther leader murdered in his sleep by Chicago police, were much on our minds in this regard.

When people became aware of the Cultural Revolution going on in China, with its aim to bring forward a new kind of society free of the kind of social inequalities that wracked the one we were struggling against, rebellion took on a different meaning. Not only did we now feel justified in opposing the oppression of society as we knew it, but suddenly that opposition could be seen in a larger context; there was a coherent, historic effort under way to create a society on a different foundation. This prospect of a different kind of world where people did not war or prey on one another or exploit others for the sake of advancing private interests but rather sought to build society on a cooperative basis was a really powerful vision.

Awareness and understanding of the Cultural Revolution and groups like the Black Panther Party, which was also influenced by the Cultural Revolution, was uneven among this politicized sixties generation. But these revolutionary currents, by their very presence, impacted how people felt and acted. It was like a change in temperature that, though we might not be conscious of it, nonetheless affects the way we feel. A different social climate was taking hold, and outlooks and actions on all levels were influenced by it. It pushed what became known as the sixties to a different political plane.

Through the ideas and slogans it advanced, the Cultural Revolution encouraged a sense of optimism. It promoted faith in the masses of people and their ability to change the world for the better. It promoted a different sense of self with its emphasis on "serve the people." The Cultural Revolution promoted the Marxist view that human nature, when that term is applied to *social relations* among people, is not some static quality, but something in a constant state of change, according to the social conditions in which people find themselves. In embracing the bold experiment in China, one embraced a belief that humans are capable of great changes and even capable of transforming themselves into different kinds of social beings.

These ideas had some material weight behind them. China, once arguably the most miserably poor and brutalized of all the world's nations, had, through the course of its revolution and in the decades after, undergone enormous and positive changes. For example, the horrendous, feudal practice of foot-binding that grossly mutilated women, that "bound" them to the dictates of the husband and in-law family, was banned after the revolution of 1949. The equality of women and men was formally declared and became the official goal of the society. Foot-binding, it turned out, was not an immutable part of the Chinese character and culture. The revolutionary process empowered the Chinese people to deal with formerly "intractable" problems, such as feeding a huge population, raising the literacy of a rural population that had been largely illiterate for millennia, dealing with widespread drug addiction, prostitution, infant mortality, limited life expectancies, warlordism, and other social problems.[3]

For a moment in time the influence of revolutionary ideas challenged the dominant narrative in ways that were both overt and subtle. When people talk about the sixties as a more optimistic time, they are speaking, to an important degree and on a global scale, about the vision that was part of the great popular upheaval in China, and other revolutionary movements and liberation struggles at the time. It influenced the language. Even those not ideologically in agreement with the goals and values of the Cultural Revolution were influenced by its concepts and drew from its vocabulary. For example, César Chávez in a speech in the late 1960s spoke to the need to arouse the human spirit: "We need a cultural revolution. And we need a cultural revolution among ourselves not only in art but also in the realm of the spirit. As poor people and immigrants, all of us have brought to this country some very important things of the spirit. We must never forget that the human element is the most important thing we have—if we get away from this, we are certain to fail."[4] And in a letter written in 1971 to a supporter, he used expressions that had currency among those inspired by the vision of a new kind of world: "We are working toward creating the *new man*, the new man in the fields, the man who will think of the common good, as you and I do, instead of the man who thinks of himself first."[5] This is not to imply that Chávez was a revolutionary or partial to the revolution in China. But such ideas as those coming out of the Cultural Revolution had a currency that grew in proportion to the broad disaffection with the established order, whose hold over society, for a brief historical moment, was deeply shaken.

While my migration to the fields was somewhat accidental, my attitude owed much to the influence of the Cultural Revolution. The massive movement of educated Chinese youth into the countryside provided an inspiration and context within which I and others of the sixties generation could view the experience of breaking out of the bounds of the social class we were born into, to become part of the life of people broadly defined as "proletarians." The Cultural Revolution's call for China's urban youth to "unite with and learn from the masses of people," to learn from the peasants there—challenging these youths to break with urban prejudices that associated rural people with ignorance and backwardness—gave people like myself initiative to cast off preconceptions and seek out contact with the "basic masses."[6]

I shared with the Chinese youth who, contrary to popular conception, voluntarily went to the countryside, a sense of being part of a historic effort to break down the old walls that divided humanity and supported the edifice of privilege and oppression.[7] Of course, the very fact that I, and others, including the educated youths of China, could choose to take this course, could decide whether or not to live in the countryside, or in any case had other viable options, reflected the inherent inequality. Neither the masses of farmworkers here nor peasants in China had such choices easily available to them.

I had ties with middle-class friends and family in the cities, and other privileges, including the privilege of being able to leave the countryside pretty much when I wanted to. I was also living in a place that was hardly remote and distant from urban centers. But, after a time, rather than miss the urban middle-class life I had given up, I began to feel alienated from it. Rather than seeing farmworkers as isolated from mainstream middle-class life, I began to regard the urban middle class as isolated in their big cities, cut off from the reality of those who supplied their food. And because the conditions in which farmworkers labored and lived had more in common with billions of oppressed people in communities around the world, I felt that the situation in the fields more closely reflected the broad reality of the world than the privileged world I'd come from. I also began to feel in a very personal way how different social realities affect our consciousness, giving form to Marx's observation that "social being determines social consciousness" or at least strongly influences it.

That there was knowledge and valuable life experience to gain from being among rural people only became evident when you opened your mind and dared to challenge conventional wisdom that looked down on "ignorant peasants" or farmworkers. How much more refreshing, inspiring, and true seemed this notion of people and social reality than the stultified, prejudicial, and cynical views of the society I grew up in.

This view of looking down on rural people as dirty and ignorant was also deeply embedded in Chinese society among the urban elite, and breaking down the wall between the urban and the rural was one of the goals of the Cultural Revolution.[8]

In China the movement of urban youths and professionals into the countryside had a broad purpose. It was part of a long-term vision of a society where the walls that separated urban from rural people, and divided those trained to use their minds from others consigned to strain their backs in work, would be torn down in a future where people could engage their energies and creativity in solidarity to make a better world.[9] The ability of the people to emancipate the world from bitter class, ethnic, and national conflicts once they understood society and the source of these problems was a hallmark of Mao and what he and his associates in China promoted through the Cultural Revolution.[10]

By the time my own odyssey landed me in Salinas, I had been involved for several years with an organization called the Revolutionary Union. This was one of many radical groups that formed in the late 1960s, inspired by efforts by people everywhere to liberate themselves. Here in the United States, the tenacious struggle of black people was especially inspiring. Among the newly emerging radical groups, the Revolutionary Union seemed to me to take the issues raised by the Black Panthers and by Mao Tse-tung and the Cultural Revolution most seriously and most deeply, and I owed much of my own understanding of the political and social issues to that organization. One of the hallmarks of the radical point of view espoused by this and other organizations was that since the advent of classes thousands of years ago, oppressed people tried in one way or another to throw off oppression. But only in the modern era, with the development of powerful means of production and scientific knowledge of the world and of society itself, had such liberation become possible. This has allowed people to become conscious of their history, of how society functions, and of how they might radically change it. It was all about people becoming conscious. So if you really wanted to bring about a change for the better, consciousness was the key. This was yet another powerful idea that had currency. But knowing how to actually put this understanding to use in a creative way, taking into account current conditions, well, that was another matter altogether.[11]

The Union Hall

The stucco building on Wood Street which once housed a post office became the nerve center and meeting place for the young union movement. It was a plain building with a large open room in the front and small offices in the rear. Its architecture captured the democratic spirit of the time. The building was in perpetual motion in its first few years, with perpetual union meetings: ranch committees discussing contract issues, committees of workers not yet unionized discussing organizing strategies; crews arguing over field battles; workers unloading bags of broccoli, lettuce, or cauliflower for workers on strike; strikers organizing picket duties; visits by delegations from movement and labor groups presenting their views on war, racism, women's rights, and other union battles.

When a gathering outgrew the hall space, people moved outside to the parking lot. Meetings sometimes got loud and provoked complaints from neighbors, especially those not well disposed to the union, causing a flap in the local paper and condemnation from authorities and denunciations all out of proportion to the "offense" of making too much noise! But it was the disturbance to the *growers' peace* that was the real issue.

That was ferment. Angelina, an Interharvest thinner through much of the 1970s, would, years later, look back and marvel at the energy that allowed her and her compañeras to raise kids, keep house, work the fields, and attend to continual meetings and battles.

I spent time at the hall. It was my Spanish-language school, my front-row seat on the unfolding drama that was the lives of my fellow workers in the struggles of those times. I heard stories of border crossings and run-ins with the migra; of lands abandoned and families left behind, driven by necessity, sometimes disguised as the pursuit of adventure. I met ex-braceros—many now green carders—with a backlog of stories of hardships, hard work, and endurance. And there were the ambitious youths who'd come north to work "just a few years" and were now aging workers staring down the path of advancing years, their route of retreat narrowing with age. There were youths, still fresh with the triumph of a crossing, certain they'd return home in "just a few years" on firmer ground after gathering the fruits of their sacrifice.

I understood the outlines of these narratives, even when the sharper details and, frequently, the fine humorous edges that gilded them, were lost to me by the coarseness of my Spanish ear and my primitive understanding of the culture. A frustrating poverty of language did not keep me from absorbing a slant on the world from a perspective that was a far cry from my own early life experiences. Its cumulative effect changed me as profoundly in its way as my plunge into Marxism had changed my political orientation a few years before. Here was an angle on the great ship of society from the crowd that worked in its boiler room, breathed its engine fumes, and sweated at its furnaces, far from shiny passenger decks. Here was the American Dream turned inside out; here the lives of those whose labor built the ladders for *others* to climb.

Of course, farmworkers had dreams of their own and for their children. There were individual dreams, like everywhere, but there were also collective ones. There was a dream expressed in resistance and hatred of national oppression and a striving for what could only be described as liberation. It may not have been expressed often in clear political terms, but one felt the force that came from an awakening people, and it felt formidable.

El Obrero

Our newspaper, *El Obrero*, drew together people ranging from longtime Salinas residents to youthful activists to farmworkers. Organizationally the paper had ties to the Revolutionary Union (a national left-wing political organization, one of several "New Left" organizations formed in the 1960s and 1970s), and through that organization to a network of similar papers cropping up in many cities. But the views of the staff covered a broad spectrum, united by opposition to the extreme exploitation of farmworkers, imperialist war, racism, gender discrimination, and so on.

The paper began with an ambitious goal, to be a voice for the struggles of workers in the fields and to help forge unity among working people in the area by focusing on their common interests and concerns. The rage many of us felt against the system and its injustices and our sense that nothing short of revolutionary change could seriously address these did not find a consistent voice in the paper. In part this was due to our lack of understanding of how to connect day-to-day struggles to a longer-term vision, as well as a spontaneous impulse to relegate strategic questions of revolution to some indefinite time in the future. "Economism" is the seductive tendency to narrow politics to the most immediate concerns, and it was a problem that sucked the life out of many radical movements. Along with other revolutionary activists of the time, we struggled with these sorts of issues.

Distributing the paper occupied a good part of our political efforts. Sometimes we'd hawk copies in the morning before work, jumping on the company buses. It was scary at first to stand in front of a busload of people and make a speech in Spanish. After a while we got used to it, aided by the politeness and sympathy with which we were generally received. "Buenos dias compañeros y compañeras, aquí tengo *El Obrero*, un papel para hostigar a los rancheros y todos los chupa sangres" (Here's *The Worker*, a paper to harass the growers and all the bloodsuckers) For a long time I avoided using the Spanish word for newspaper, *periódico*, because I couldn't pronounce it. One time I got up on a bus and began, "Hola amigos, aquí tengo un perrodico, peridico, per—" and someone from the back yelled, "Pe-*ri-ó*-dico, güero!" "Gracias," I said, "un papel de la lucha," which drew laughter. I had to use *papel* (paper) or *noticias* (news) until I was finally able to wrap my tongue around that r-i-o combination, two syllables (pair-REE-OH-dee-co), where in English the same combination of letters is pronounced as one syllable, as in "period."

Scattered throughout the Salinas and Pajaro valleys were farm labor camps, surrounded by fields, shaded by strips of trees or, in town, sandwiched between bus yards, sheds, canneries, and factories. In 1971 the Monterey County Department of Health counted eighty-seven single men's camps housing 10,000 workers and forty-seven family camps housing 600 families in the Salinas Valley.

Camps varied in size and shape, but most were little more than warehouses for people—four wood walls, a cement slab, no insulation. Many were long open barracks without partitions, with army-style cots and no private space. Collective space was limited to the common rooms for sleeping and eating. The dining hall usually had simple wood benches and long tables. The bathrooms sometimes had partitions between toilets, sometimes not. Shower facilities were often crude, with exposed plumbing that was often not working.

Camps built for braceros now housed the green carders who migrated up from the border cities and interior states for the harvest season. The camps closed down in winter, "encouraging" migration. Many of the larger companies ran camps. Others were run by labor contractors. It was in some of these labor contractor camps that we found the most pathetic, depressing, even shocking conditions, with workers who were dehumanized and demoralized by extreme forms of exploitation that often involved alcohol and drugs. As in other aspects of farmwork life, camp conditions varied depending on the organization and morale of the workers. For example, even under the restrictive conditions of the Bracero Program resistance was sometimes effective in forcing an improvement in conditions. A former bracero told me how on one ranch the workers detested the white-bread sandwiches they were served at lunch every day and finally resolved to do something. So one day, as the lunch break began, the crew brought out their Wonder Bread sandwiches with thin slices of meat on mayonnaise and threw them at the feet of a surprised foreman. They demanded more substantial food—at least rice and beans, some meat, tortillas, salsa, "comida verdadera," they told the foreman, real food! The next day, to their surprise, the grower came to camp to talk to them. Did they know of any good Mexican cooks? After searching, he found one and the food in the camp improved.

Family camps increased in number after the Bracero Program ended. Most of these were not very pleasant either. The Monterey County Department of Health found that a majority of family camps consisted of small one- and two-room cabins containing families with eight or more people. A third of these family camps had no toilet facilities; a third had no cooking facilities.

Sometimes the very worst of the camps were hidden away or guarded to discourage outsiders from entering them. But, to be fair, the labor camps had no monopoly on poor housing. There was plenty of that to be found in Salinas and in all the other agricultural towns in the area.

Entering a camp barracks was like going into someone's bedroom, and when we distributed the paper we were careful not to take the openness for granted. We'd announce our presence and ask for permission to come in. Even with such precautions a fearful look might remind us that we were, in the view of these camp dwellers, a frightening spectacle. It was rare for a white person, or any outsiders, other than someone in authority—police, migra, ranch boss—to enter such a place. We tried to allay people's fears: "Amigos, we're from *El Obrero*, un periódico (o papel) de este area."

When women on the staff went to men's camps, we had to be very clear that we were there on political business because most women who visited the men's camps were prostitutes. Having the issue raised this way afforded *El Obrero* staff—too often it was just the women—an opportunity to discuss why the struggle for rights of women was an important part of the outlook and purpose of the paper. Nevertheless, the question of women and women's oppression was too often avoided.

Normally there wasn't a lot to do in these camps after work. There were few Spanish-language papers or media around in those days, so the paper was, just on that score, unique. The papers passed from bunk to bunk, reaching a readership well beyond the numbers sold. As the paper became known, distribution tended to get easier. Sometimes in a barracks someone would hand us a wad of change collected from around the room, and then take the papers to distribute themselves.

In the camps one could talk to people in a quiet setting. Not infrequently, out of curiosity, or because they heard a subject that aroused their interest, people would come around to listen or join in a discussion. It was a chance to engage with a group and find out what was on people's minds and about things going on in the fields and in their lives. It was a source of material for the paper.

While I certainly learned about the people we met in the camps, this was often limited by my still lagging comprehension of the spoken language, compounded by a nagging habit of speaking too much and listening too little.

The paper gained popularity because it was a partisan of those who worked the fields, and was uncompromising in opposing racism and national oppression. Mexico too was a hotbed of political activism in the early 1970s, and occasionally we met Mexican activists who came north to work in the fields. We had just begun to distribute the paper at a labor camp near Chualar one evening when a worker suddenly got up from a bunk and hastily left the room. Soon he was back with some friends. "Sientete," sit down, they invited. Tell us about your paper. What organization are you from? What is your politics? What political trend do you relate to? Our interrogators were teachers from the state of Oaxaca, active in a coalition of workers and students that was a force in that state. Working in the U.S. fields allowed them relief from politically difficult conditions, to make money to support their families and their struggles, and to investigate circumstances among their immigrant brethren.

It sometimes surprised these visitors to find radical politics surviving on U.S. soil, thought by some to be too politically sterile, too crassly materialistic, or just too happy with life in the imperial motherland to support such politics. And we spent many hours in the camps, and at times in town, exchanging views on issues such as China and the Soviet Union; Che Guevara and what was called foquismo, a strategy for revolution in Third World countries; and the prospects for revolution in the United States and Latin America.

Newspapers like *The Worker* in different parts of the country faced problems of getting good material with limited resources, so in the early 1970s a news service began providing centrally written articles. This allowed *El Obrero* to cover more of the important issues of the day. However, *El Obrero* was a Spanish-language paper and most of the articles were written in English. Translation was a big problem.

Louie Aguilar

I was distributing the paper downtown, when a passerby came up to me. He looked familiar, a thin man in his fifties, with a peculiar way of walking, slightly bow-legged, bony shoulders that slumped a bit forward. "Louie," I said, almost to myself. We'd worked together a short time on a thinning crew. We hadn't talked much. I remembered him as person who mainly kept to himself. Before I could offer him a paper he said, "I want to show you something," and he pulled a copy of *El Obrero* from his jacket pocket and unfolded it. He took reading glasses from a breast pocket of his jacket and placed them toward the front of his thin nose. "This is translated wrong, the wrong words." Louie pointed to an article on the front page.

"This says the union meeting took place in the *escuela alta*. You mean the school was up on a hill?" "I think it's trying to say 'high school,'" I said, laughing. At that Louie seemed more indignant than humored. "That's completely wrong," he said. "You should say *escuela secundaria*." "As you can see, we have problems with translation," I said. "This word here," he said, opening the paper to another page, "*actualmente*, that means *now* in Spanish, not what you think in English."

"Seems like you have a knack for language," I said. "I grew up with Spanish," he said. "You guys should work on your Spanish. People will have more faith in what you say if it's said more correctly. And those are not the only mistakes I found!" And he turned the page again. "OK, Louie, how would you like to help us? We could really use it. You could be a proofreader," I suggested. "I don't have a lot of time." "Well, how about translating an article? The paper comes out once a month. Try it one time and see." "I don't know," he said. "Maybe my politics is not like yours." He had a way of hunching his shoulders when thinking about something. "We don't have to agree on everything. Don't you like a good argument?" I said, trying to lighten the conversation . "Why don't you come by my place and we'll talk about it," he said. "I live near here, by the train station."

I went by Louie's a few days later after work. The Salinas railroad station is off Market Street, near where Main and Market meet. Louie lived in a small two-story building just yards from the station, which once was a busy hub but now seemed large for the number of people one usually found there. Louie's was the first apartment off the street; it had just enough room for a bed, a small desk, a chest of drawers, a night table, a few chairs, and a sink. The toilet and shower were down the hall. There was no kitchen, so Louie cooked a lot of his meals mostly out of a can on the hotplate next to the sink.

Louie agreed to translate articles, and later do some proofreading. In his apartment we would come to sit and talk about the fields, about articles in the paper, about Spanish, about his life previous to Salinas, and about politics. Louie had been in the fields for nearly a decade before our paths crossed. His life's path had taken him from the Texas border area where he grew up to Los Angeles, where he lived most of his adult life. Language had always been an important issue for him. "I got hit on the head for using Spanish at school," he told me one time, "but that didn't stop me from using it, just the opposite." That was in Texas. During his last stretch in L.A. he worked in a meatpacking plant where he watched over the production of cooked meats like bologna. His job was to pull the hot, freshly cooked sausages from the cooking room, and roll large trays of them to the cooler. Shuffling between scorching heat and numbing cold made his bones ache and wore down his resistance. Working inside those years made him long for the outdoors. So, after staying long enough to qualify for a small pension, he took his leave of the factory, and looked for a small town where he could plant his feet on something that could be called countryside.

His search ended in Salinas, where the mild climate suited him and the vast panorama of the valley fulfilled his yearning for open space. Still energetic and in need of money to supplement his pension, he found work in the fields.

He worked mainly by the hour, and mostly in thinning, but occasionally in cauliflower, broccoli, and mustard. He also worked the "tuna" (prickly pear) harvest, picking the sweet, seedy red fruit bulbs at D'Arrigo's cactus farm off Hecker Pass Road that connects Watsonville with Gilroy. On this cactus farm the workers wore thick gloves and the same heavy yellow raingear worn by broccoli workers. Only here it did not protect them from dampness but the prickly cactus spines whose tiny slivers could make life miserable for anyone unwise enough to touch them unprotected. Wearing baskets like backpacks Louie and his crew picked the avocado-sized fruit tossing it over their shoulders into the baskets.

Louie spent his working days walking in the fields. But apparently this wasn't enough. On weekends or when work was slow he would walk the streets of Salinas or catch a bus for Monterey and walk the wharf, cannery row, or Pacific Grove. Sometimes he'd catch a train or bus for San Francisco. From the south of Market he would walk through downtown to the Fillmore district, west toward the Haight to Golden Gate Park, and out to Ocean Beach. Then, he'd catch a bus back to the Mission district or the Tenderloin for a night in one of the city's cheap hotels. Wherever he walked it was with a style peculiar to himself, his thin shoulders slightly hunched, making his body seem slightly bent forward and giving a seriousness to his fairly rapid strides, as though he were a man in a hurry.

After work or on weekends when he wasn't out walking Louie spent time doing crossword puzzles. He was quite good at them, attested to by a chest of drawers stacked with newspapers with completed puzzles from the local paper—and the *New York Times*, even ones from the latter, harder part of the week—along with several dictionaries to assist him.

Louie had a facility with English and Spanish, loved playing with the language, and had no patience for people who were careless with language. He was very critical of the tendency of people like me, poor in Spanish, to use false cognates or assume certain words in English were the same in Spanish. For example, anyone who would call a woman in an embarrassing situation, *embarasada*, would themselves be embarrassed to discover they were spreading rumors of a nonexistent, and probably unwanted, pregnancy. Or if you thought an *éxito* was a way off the freeway, or that *suceso* is something you did right, well, you'd be wrong on both counts, because *éxito* is success and *suceso* is an event, as likely to be a failure as successful.

Sometimes, proofreading an article, Louie would get a little indignant by Spanish translations that were really just English in disguise. This was the problem of syntax, a deeper problem in language than vocabulary and grammar. Without proper syntax the language loses its rhythm and tone. Here style, or lack of it, can trump or at the very least interfere strongly with content.

Louie was equally, if not more critical of the tendency for U.S.-dwelling Spanish speakers to take English words and convert them into Spanish by adding a vowel to the end. Like *lonche* or *troque* for lunch or truck, or, his real bane, *wátchele*, which people used all the time to express "watch out!" when, as Louie would insist, they should have used *aguas* or *cuidado* or *ponte abusado!*

Sometimes at night I'd find him sitting at the small table with a glass of wine, a dictionary, and pad of lined paper on which he wrote his translations. Sometimes he'd grouse about our articles. "How can I translate clearly into Spanish if you don't write clearly in English?" Political differences were also at play in these discussions. Louie had come to dispute the present order through the discrimination and injustice he had experienced in his own life and saw all around him. But where many of us saw only demagoguery in the different rhetorical styles of the major political parties, Louie saw real differences, and in any case was more willing to give Democrats the benefit of the doubt.

Visitors, Newcomers, and Social Reality Tours

In a Kris Kristofferson song, Janis Joplin tells of Bobby McGee slipping away in Salinas. Bobby, Janice told us soulfully, was looking for a home. It was the 1970 lettuce strike that brought many of Janis's generation to Salinas, looking for a home in the struggle. Sometimes they'd show up at the union hall like FJ and I had, to get work. More often they'd come to the hall for meetings or rallies. Some came there to work with the union as office staff or in the medical clinic the union opened later on in the Alisal district. Some came to work at a peace center that opened in downtown Salinas around 1970 and sought work in the fields to support themselves. A few would just arrive at the doorstep of one of our circle of activists living in Salinas.

In those days, when most of us activists were quite young, a year at something could qualify you as a veteran. So as a veteran of several years in the area, I took it as a task to show newcomers around the Salinas-Monterey area. My interest in this lay not so much in its abundant natural beauty, but in its social contours and the sharp contrasts between different communities. For those of us weaned on the concept of a classless America, it struck me as significant to find conditions so remarkably class-like.

Thus motivated, I found occasion to crank up my green and yellow, rusting VW van, and with a few willing sightseers, strike off to explore "social reality."

The Alisal district was a logical place to begin such a tour. The Alisal began as a squatters' camp for farmers driven out of the Dust Bowl in the 1930s. It was always on the other side of the tracks both literally and figuratively from the more prosperous Salinas—a large patchwork of shacks, cottages, and low-rent apartment buildings that sat northeast of the rail line that cut across Market Street and ran through Salinas's industrial area at the southern end of town. Many Alisal residents felt marginalized by the more affluent Salinas and resisted incorporation into the larger city until 1963.

In the hierarchical order that the growers enforced in the lettuce industry of the 1930s, '40s, and '50s, Filipinos and Mexicans were "on the ground" in the fields; the Okie "immigrants" and their descendants worked the sheds where lettuce was packed and iced down for shipping. In the early 1950s when vacuum cooling replaced ice cooling, and field packing eliminated shed packing, six to eight thousand jobs melted away, devastating the Okie community. In the following years Mexican families largely replaced the Okies, but some of the old-timers were still around the Alisal, veterans of the sheds and canneries that stood on either side of the rail line.

Distributing *The Worker* in the Alisal area put us in contact with its residents. By the 1970s most were Mexicanos and field workers. People were generally poor, but poverty and unemployment wreaked a special havoc on some of these white working people, who seemed to carry a burden of shame and demoralization that I never sensed among the Mexicanos. We also met veterans of the various union struggles in cannery and sheds who were proud of their history of resistance.

The cultural influence of the Okies and Arkies was still in evidence in the Alisal district, and Okie bars and dance clubs sat along Market and Alisal Streets, shaking to their own rhythms on weekend nights, alongside the Mexican dance joints.

Heading south from the Alisal you came to an area of truck and bus yards, workshops, yards full of stacked pallets and boxes, and small factories intermingled with whitewashed camp barracks, their exteriors blistered, their surrounding asphalt parking lots bare and uninviting. Most of the dozen or so men's labor camps within the Salinas city limits were concentrated in an area around Vertin and Abbott Streets toward the southern edge of the town. During the lettuce season they held about 3,000 workers.

Just south of the industrial area the city ended abruptly, giving way to a vast living quilt of fields twenty miles wide, stretching nearly 100 miles long, with 250,000 irrigated acres (out of the 1.5 million acres of the entire valley), flanked on the east by the Gabilans and on the west by the Santa Lucia Mountains.

It was on one of the peaks of the Gabilans that explorer and colonizer John C. Frémont built a small fort in 1846 where he raised the American flag to stir patriotic enthusiasm among the American settlers. The enthusiasm was over the prospect of seizing Indian and Mexican lands. Could war be far behind? Fortunately for Frémont he was able to avoid a confrontation with the stronger forces under the Mexican governor in Monterey that year. But by 1848 the United States defeated Mexico in war and Frémont served as an interim governor of the conquered territory. Patriotic citizens in the 1970s still celebrated Frémont's flag raising on the very peak of the Gabilans, which bears his name.

Turning southwest outside of Salinas along Harris Road, a squat and ugly Firestone tire factory, the biggest industrial employer in the area at that time, sprawled to our left. The workforce was mainly white and Chicano (of Mexican descent but born in the United States), and hourly pay dwarfed what one could get by the hour in the fields. The work was hard and subject to speed-up. But in those days, a Firestone job practically guaranteed a loan to buy a house and the trappings of a middle-class existence.

Driving west meant heading toward the Santa Lucias whose rolling foothills reminded me of giant green and yellow lizards resting on their haunches. This part of the valley is said to be among the most fertile grounds on earth, surpassed, some claim, only by the fabled Nile Delta. So fabulously fertile in fact that John Steinbeck made special note of it in his novel *East of Eden*, and Salinas city leaders decreed it forever off-limits to non-farm construction.

Approaching the Santa Lucias, a building stood out among the sprawling fields around it, gradually gaining in stature, a large red-brick building huddled against a cluster of enormous concrete silos. It stood five stories high and spanned two football fields in length. In 1897, 600 workers labored for more than a year using four million bricks to make the Spreckels sugar factory a reality.

Claus Spreckels made a fortune in Hawaiian sugarcane at a time when most U.S. sugar was imported. But when political strife in cane-growing areas and high tariffs placed on imported sugar made processing sugar in the United States more attractive, Spreckels took a lead in domestic sugar production and built this monstrous sugar mill, then the largest sugar beet-processing factory in the world.[12] The new factory consumed beets grown on thousands of acres of land directly surrounding it. The first farmworkers to plant, thin, and harvest the beets were Chinese and Japanese.[13] It was Chinese laborers who prepared the grounds for the irrigation system that made large-scale cultivation of sugar beets possible.[14]

Before sugar beets, valley farmland was sown with wheat and other grains. Spreckels's mania for sugar began to change all that. Sugar beet production became, in the words of historian Carey McWilliams, the first great example of "factories in the fields," a model that would become the hallmark of California agriculture.[15]

Spreckels built more than a factory; he built a Spreckels town that spread out at the feet of his castle-factory: Spreckels fire department, Spreckels library, a plantation with peons and overseers, and, of course, a reigning monarch. But by the 1970s the dominion was fading. Its decline began in the 1920s when more profitable lettuce, broccoli, celery, and other vegetable crops pushed sugar beets to the margins.[16] Three hundred acres of lettuce planted in the Salinas Valley in 1922 became 43,000 acres by 1929, while 23,000 acres of beets in 1920 dwindled to 200 by the end of the decade. New economic mixes diluted old concentrations of wealth, and created new ones.[17]

In the early 1970s Spreckels was still among the world's largest sugar beet factories—an aging plant consuming 3,500 tons of dirt-brown sugar beets a day, disgorging a sea of white crystalline sweetness for a country on a sugar high. And there, driving along Harris Road to the factory town, we saw a mile-long line of railcars with thousands of tons of large brown beets brought from the Central Valley to feed the beast. But Spreckels's producing days were already numbered, undercut by competition from corn syrup and sugar from cane grown in places with hot climates and desperately cold wages.

Up the road from Spreckels, past a tunnel of towering black walnut trees and making a jog west along Highway 68, we found Reservation Road and the aforementioned Fort Ord, a 44-square-mile patch of land with its eastern edge resting several hundred feet above the Salinas Valley floor. At the time of our tour, in the early 1970s, Ord was the largest army training base on the West Coast.

In September 1971 national attention was focused on Ord and the trial of Vietnam vet and former Ord trainee Billy Dean Smith, who was accused of killing several officers in Vietnam with a fragmentation grenade. There were significant protests during the trial by people who saw Smith, an African American, as the scapegoat for a military that had lost not only the loyalty but the acquiescence of its soldiers.[18] If convicted he could face the death penalty.

Smith was held in solitary confinement at the Ord stockade throughout his long pretrial period. This treatment provoked considerable outrage. People compared Billy Dean's treatment with that of Lt. William Calley, a white officer who commanded a platoon that rounded up and massacred 500 Vietnamese children, women, and old men in the Vietnamese village of My Lai. Calley was personally accused of murdering 104 villagers, but he was allowed to walk free while awaiting his trial.

In the end, Billy Dean was found innocent. There was no credible evidence against him. But the not-guilty verdict also had something to do with the size and intense scale of protest during his trial.

In 1975, Ord's infantry training facility was permanently shut down. The base's commander said the decision was due to the "encroachment of civilians." For example, in the summer of 1970, thousands of antiwar protesters converged on Fort Ord, marched passed its main gate, and held a rally in the sand dunes a short way up the coast from an infantry rifle range. The day of the march, Ord soldiers were ordered locked down in their barracks. Extra guards were posted to keep the GIs in their place. But, much to the chagrin of the military, many jumped the fences surrounding the base and joined the march and rally.

It is not hard to imagine that the decision to close down the Ord training center was influenced by such events. The war in Vietnam was just about over then, but other wars to secure empire were certain to come and the brass wanted no repeat of the GI movements that emerged on their bases in the late 1960s and nearly crippled their military machine. Fort Ord's proximity to the radical ferment in San Francisco Bay area was certainly a factor on the minds of military planners.

Just to the west of the base, the city of Seaside appeared spread out over a large plain of sand that was once a Spanish land grant called Rancho Noche Buena. Seaside's growth paralleled that of Fort Ord, and many of its residents were soldiers and their families or military retirees. A significant part of Seaside was African American, making it the only large black community in Central California. Seaside's terrain was unique to the area, but the resemblance of many of its homes to those in the Alisal could hardly be missed.

Cabo de Pinos is the name the Spanish gave to the area of towering Monterey pines, coast live oak, and Monterey cypress trees on the peninsula of Monterey. The city of Monterey was once the capital of California, with Spanish-style buildings lining narrow downtown streets. This and its stunning coastline, curving along the bay in collision course with the expanse of ocean, long ago made it a tourist haunt. Going back to the 1800s, wealthy Californians had chosen this area for their turf. Charles Crocker, who made a fortune as a railroad baron, in 1880 staked out a piece of real estate on the approach to downtown Monterey where he built a hotel that became a magnet for the rich and famous,royalty, diplomats, presidents, and maharajas. The hotel remained one of the most fashionable outposts on the West Coast until 1948, when the government bought it and the land around it to make the Navy Post Graduate School.

Skirting the old downtown past Fisherman's Wharf and through Minnie's Tunnel, built by a mayor of that name, is the Cannery Row area. This was once a factory district where shift whistles called workers down steep narrow paths to the steamy, odorous fish-canning plants, and, in the early 1970s, where new boutiques and restaurants were, beginning to beckon buyers of tourist trinkets, not sellers of labor power.

The century had seen many changes to the Row. In 1910 the area had a thriving fishing industry based mainly on salmon and abalone that was run by Chinese families and single Japanese men. Out of 185 salmon fishing boats, 145 were owned and operated by Japanese. Monterey became the third largest port for fishing in the country. Japanese also worked in the canneries as fish cutters. Before it was Cannery Row it was a Chinatown. Its gambling joints, dance halls, and opium dens went down in flames like so many other such communities. By the 1920s, Sicilians and other Southern Europeans were arriving and so was anti-Chinese violence. Soon legal restrictions and town sentiment drove the Chinese from the fishing fleet and reduced the Japanese to a smaller, yet still determined part of it.

Sardines transformed the place. By 1930, sardine fishing and canning predominated. Twenty-four canneries processed thousands of tons of the little fish a year. In 1947, the same year Fort Ord became an army training center, the huge schools of sardines disappeared and overnight the canneries ground to a halt. Soon the loud clattering and whirling sounds of industry were replaced by the whispers and howls of the wind off the bay coming through the shards of broken window glass and over motionless conveyor belts and cleaning tanks. Later came the somewhat louder sounds of debates about what to do with the rusting hulks that lined the Row. Different interests weighed in on the debate, including John Steinbeck, who still bemoaned the loss of the old Chinatown and suggested, facetiously, that it might be re-created with Hollywood set designers. But commercial interests triumphed here, as they do most places. By the beginning of the 1970s Cannery Row was well on its way to its third incarnation in less than a century, as a stylish tourist trap with a historical, if somewhat fishy, flavor.

As we pass by the metamorphosing cannery area and an avenue of small shops, the road winds through the remains of the old forest of Pacific Grove. The area was discovered in the 1800s by religious groups who felt in its beauty a spiritual quality and set up campsites for their services. In 1880 it became a site of the Chautauqua Society, a religious and cultural retreat that was enormously popular in rural areas across the United States until the 1940s.

The main road, Lighthouse Avenue, passes through the grove-shaded upscale neighborhood that still retains a serene, often foggy, mystic beauty until it finally meets the lip of sand where the ocean begins and then curves around a coast of tide pools and tiny, rocky beaches to where Asilomar, a conference center retreat, sits located on higher ground over-looking the ocean. Facing the ocean here are formidable homes moored like ships in the vast rolling green sea of ice plant–covered sand.

Farther along, the coast recedes quickly and the forest appears. Up a road was the guarded entrance to the ultra-exclusive Pebble Beach. It is situated on the western edge of the Monterey Peninsula, on land once part of two Spanish land grants, which fell under control of wealthy Americans after the Mexican War—5,300 acres of woods, bound on the west by the Pacific Ocean. Samuel F. B. Morse, the grandnephew of the great inventor, and his business partner Herbert Fleishacker gained con-trol of the land in 1919 and oversaw the development of the Pebble Beach community. Their vision was always exclusive in two senses of the word. It was at once to be a small community amid the splendor of a beautiful place. And rules written under Samuel F. B.'s guidance mandated that deeds and leases for Pebble Beach properties explicitly exclude "Asians, Blacks, Arabs, Jews, Turks, Greeks, and Armenians." Later, when those overt restrictions were ruled illegal, restrictive qualifications for the local social clubs served to enforce a social exclusiveness. This was a kind of "Morse Code" that ruled Pebble Beach.

Pebble Beach has seven public and private 18-hole golf courses and a 9-hole par-three, for a population of 2,500 families. In the early 1970s a round of golf on one of Pebble Beach's courses cost the equivalent of many long hours of sweaty labor in the vegetable fields a few miles to the east.[19] You could drive into the gated Pebble Beach, which was part of a scenic 17-mile drive, but you had to pay for the privilege. Short on funds and on a desire to *pay* to see the homes of the overly wealthy, we decided to move on.

Beyond Pebble Beach is the town of Carmel, a prosperous upper-middle-class community bordered by ocean on its western edge and on its inland side by a quiet, narrow valley winding its way south toward the Los Padres forest along the western edge of the Santa Lucias.

In 1970 an incident took place in Carmel that caught the attention of the public. A group of hippies suddenly showed up at a park at the center of town on Carmel's cute and fashionable main street. They hung out, played music, smoked things, and who knows what else. The city authorities and some residents became alarmed. The walls of the fortress had been breached. What frightening reality was about to encroach on this beautiful enclave with its arms opened out to sea? There were no laws to legally drive the intruders out of the park. So the city fathers decided to turn on the sprinkler system during the day to discourage the unwanted from hanging out there.

This struck some people as mean-spirited. I was still in Seaside when this happened and was friendly with a local activist, Brady Avery, who ran a gas station and mechanic shop on Del Monte, up the street from our GI coffeehouse. Brady was constantly at odds with the Seaside authorities for his loud and insistent criticism of police harassment in the black community and other matters related to discrimination and city government. This got him into trouble, and the authorities were always looking for ways to shut him up. His shop was frequently visited by city agencies trying to find some kind of violation of city ordinances. He was always being fined or threatened with fines and in legal hot water.

One day at Brady's gas station we were talking about the sprinkler incident in Carmel, taking turns denouncing it with some of Brady's employees. Then Brady came up with an idea. "Let's get some people from Seaside together and go to the park in Carmel." So we organized a trip of some friends of Brady's from the Seaside community and some GIs and staff from the coffeehouse and caravanned there.

When our entourage arrived at the park, Brady took out the signs he and his friends had made for the occasion. Three large signs with a watermelon on each and the words, "Guess who's coming to Carmel now!" We hung out in the park, played Frisbee, and had a picnic until evening. We had fun while the local police cruised around the park. But otherwise they chose to leave us alone.

A round of laughter greeted this story as the VW rolled and rattled down Carmel's main street. The social distinctions of the Monterey Bay area revealed a complex pattern, but, like canyon walls, they had definite layers. The contrast was striking for those travelers who were looking for such things.

What was usually taken for granted had for us profound significance, perhaps because we consciously rejected the "commonsense" view that justified such polarizations of wealth and privilege as natural, inevitable, and unchangeable. For us it was all about class exploitation and national oppression and a state that existed to enforce them. Justifications for this lopsided state of affairs always came down to some form of racism or chauvinism. In America this was predominantly the ever-present white supremacy, and these wealthy areas provided a color-coded contrast to the Salinas neighborhoods and fields that were now our home ground.

Social class is not just a matter of wealth, but a relationship to the production of wealth. It is not just good versus bad, as there are people with many different qualities on the various sides of the equation. It's that the very existence of these social classes limits and shapes what society as a whole is and can be. No amount of rhetoric can change this reality or give a voice to those who, within the context of the productive system, have mainly been deprived of dignity and opportunity. Only their struggle can do that, and then, it seems, only for certain special historical moments.

Though an individual may be "free" to pass from one social level to another, classes and strata are held in place by a structure that is ultimately determined by its system of production.[20] These different social levels come with their socially imposed values. I mean, no one was paying to tour the Alisal district! But beyond the monetary issue, the human value placed on the lives of those in the Alisal and those in Pebble Beach was and still is starkly divergent.

Ironically, connections between production, labor, and wealth, so obvious to a farmworker, are often an obscure mystery to people in the upper classes. No doubt the prosperous middle class is the beneficiary of the social wealth accrued by capitalism and by the empire. But this alone does not define them. The cruel means by which this wealth is obtained also creates moral outrage and resistance. I knew residents of Pacific Grove and Monterey who took risks to provide safe havens for Vietnam-era soldiers from Fort Ord who went AWOL rather than ship out to war. The grape boycott found fertile ground among a broad section of the middle class.

No genuine movement to fundamentally change society could ever come about without the significant participation of the middle class. Yet it is also true that such movements cannot be anchored in the middle class, but only among the sections of the people most exploited and held down by the workings of the social order. Theirs is a consciousness that could flow directly from their class position, something not true for the middle class.

I still believe that though the middle class benefits to a degree from this exploitation within the context of this system, it actually loses much more in living a life alienated from much of humanity, best symbolized by walled borders and gated communities where people isolate themselves physically and psychologically from the majority of people. The United States as a whole has a gated community mentality, which leaves people spiritually poorer. Fortunately there are those who rebel at the loss this isolation causes and of the injustice of this order. Such rebellion is surely warranted and justified.

Despite the remarkable physical beauty of places like Pebble Beach, Carmel, and Monterey I was happy to return to Salinas. There I was among people whose culture I barely knew and whose language I was struggling to understand. But my heart was there. At that time in my life, it felt like home.

Rafael Lemus

On Pajaro Street near Market I saw a familiar figure working on his car in his driveway—a thin, wiry man in his forties, with a sharp nose and wry smile. "Güero," he said, looking up from under the hood of his green Oldsmobile battleship of a station wagon. "Que dices, güero," he repeated using the *apodo* that a lot people used for light-skinned people like myself. Such nicknames were widespread and usually carried no negative connotations.[21]

I didn't know him well, but I'd seen him at the union hall and at rallies. I knew that people generally just called him by his last name, Lemus. I didn't know any *apodo* for him, but if I had to make one up it would've been Flaco(skinny).

"Hola, Lemus, como ándas." (How're you doing?) I could see from the slight glaze in his look and a slight hesitation that he'd been doing some drinking. "Vivo. Pero mas que eso no puedo decir." (Alive. More than that I can't say.) Even in casual conversation he had a pronounced fatalism. After a brief description of his car's latest ills, our conversation drifted toward some recent events, such as the eviction of the Pic'n Pac workers from La Posada and the ongoing conflicts with Interharvest management. Lemus was on the D'Arrigo ranch committee and was the leader of the celery workers there. D'Arrigo workers were having their battles with management, and Lemus was part of the negotiations to untangle the various grievances in which the workers and company were enmeshed. He had his finger on a lot that was going on in all union companies. He'd heard how the Interharvest supervisors had made a big fuss about a pamphlet I'd passed out to the crew. "Todavia andas con los comunistas?" (Still hanging out with the communists?) he said in a way that seemed somewhere between joking and scolding. I think he was happy at how upset the company got with a little pamphlet denouncing a no-strike deal struck up by the union and the steel companies at a time when wages and working conditions were deteriorating. "Cómo no," I said. "We've got to give the company something to talk about at the grievance meetings." Lemus grinned. "You guys are getting a little notorious around here." "Well, we do our best," I said, not sure what he meant by that.

I always thought of Lemus as a tough fellow. Not that he was physically imposing. He wasn't much taller than I, and thin. But he had a *don't mess with me* kind of aura about him, that he would stand his ground in a fight. He'd been working the fields for more than twenty years. From practically the day he crossed into Calexico as an adventurous sixteen-year-old from Michoacan, he got to know the callousness with which a farmworker could be treated. His first job paid forty cents an hour for "topping beets," pulling beets from the ground and cutting their tops off. He slept under a tree and lived on apricot jam sandwiches. He escaped that job one day when a big car approached the fields they were working. The other workers yelled "*Pajaro,*" a word they used for the migra, and ran off. Lemus, a bit more intrepid, approached the car and found a woman who needed help on her land. Lemus quickly jumped at the chance to make twice what he was being paid.

In the years that followed he worked many different jobs, on many ranches. He picked up English fairly quickly and learned how to use it to defend himself and others. Some people choose to use savvy experience and knowledge for personal advantage. They sell their skills to the growers and become company men. Lemus didn't have the stomach for that. He hadn't lost his contempt for factory system of agriculture that degraded the workers, and he didn't want to be part of it.

In September 1963 Lemus was driving a truck, hauling celery from the field in Chualar to the cooler in Salinas. He left the field with his last load just as a Southern Pacific train loaded with sugar beets plowed into a truck carrying celery workers on their way home from the field. The collision tore the truck in two and scattered bodies up and down the track. Lemus raced back to the field to inform the company of the accident and then returned to the track, helping the injured and recovering bodies from the wreck. The flatbed truck had been outfitted with board benches running lengthwise to serve as a bus. It held more than sixty workers and its overloading may have contributed to the accident. The driver, one of the few to survive, insisted his view of the track was blocked. Thirty people died and another thirty-one were injured, the worst such accident in the history of California.[22]

Lemus worked through the bracero days, though not as a bracero himself, and like all the workers during that period had to sit tight with little hope of redressing grievances or making a serious protest of conditions. For some, years of enduring the indignities of injustice can wear down the sharp pangs of outrage until they become dulled aches of resignation, but not for Lemus. His years of work in the fields gave him a sharp eye for what went on there and he knew well the various tricks that were used to cheat the workers. When working by piece rate, he'd count the trucks leaving the field, knowing how much each one would mean to each worker on the ground. He kept track of the numbers and noted when paychecks did not add up. Frequently, contractors, supervisors, and foremen shorted the workers by making out checks to "los muertos" (the dead), fictional workers on the payroll, and then pocketing these checks themselves.

There were other tricks. Crew bosses offered advances to new workers or workers short on funds for expenses. Cash up front, "la tira," would come out of the next check. Such debts mysteriously ballooned with inflated interest. It was often difficult to redress these grievances when your job was on the line. But Lemus, and others like him, waited for the moment to come.

As the end of the 1960s approached, these lettuce workers, most of them braceros until 1964, had reason to believe their time had come. Small groups of volunteers leafleted the Salinas and Santa Maria valleys and distributed the UFWOC newspaper.[23] The workers, many of them dispossessed farmers and farmworkers, including among them workers who were no strangers to struggles for land and rights in Mexico, were watching events unfold in the grape growing areas.[24]

By 1968 a number of wine companies, fearing a boycott of their easily identifiable labels, came to terms with UFWOC. This included Almaden and Paul Masson in the southern Salinas Valley. Then, on July 29, 1970, Delano grape growers, battered by the nationwide boycott, met UFWOC officials in Delano and reluctantly signed union recognition contracts, putting an end to an epic five-year grape strike and boycott.

Workers in the coastal valleys appealed to UFWOC that their time had come. Chávez, who was feeling somewhat overwhelmed by the new responsibilities of the union to set up dispatch services and enforce contracts to 85 percent of the table grape industry, wanted the Salinas and Santa Maria Valley workers to hold off on a strike.

Sensing an approaching groundswell, the growers set out to erect a wall of protection. So while Delano grape growers were concluding that agreements with UFWOC were inevitable, Teamster union officials were counting bundles of cash delivered to them by vegetable growers to sweeten a deal the growers desperately wanted. On July 27, 1970, the day before the Delano signings, came the stunning news: thirty-two Salinas, Watsonville, and Santa Maria growers signed contracts with the

International Brotherhood of Teamsters to represent their workers. The Teamsters declared that farmworkers had approached them about union representation, but it was the lettuce growers, not the workers, who had done so.[25]

The Teamster deal provided growers with a valuable legal argument. In the event of a strike they could claim they were the victims of a union jurisdictional dispute and plead for legal relief. To undermine a boycott they could claim that their lettuce was already union label, a tactic sure to confuse at least part of the public. This was strike and boycott insurance financed out of the union dues now being deducted from farmworkers' paychecks. And as an additional bonus, the Teamsters got 2 percent of each worker's check for their "retirement fund."[26]

When the Teamsters announced they were moving into the vegetable fields the anger of many Salinas Valley workers headed toward a breaking point. When workers on Salinas ranches refused to sign with the Teamsters and were fired, it was spark hitting tinder. Sporadic, unorganized walkouts began and were spreading. If UFWOC didn't call a strike, it might just happen anyway. There were intense, heated meetings, with members packed shoulder to shoulder in the union hall on Wood Street, where the UFWOC leadership argued with the workers to delay a strike while the union tried to bargain with United Fruit negotiators and placate Church allies who feared the consequences of a big strike. There were delays as the growers and union leaders jockeyed. But the determination of the workers to strike was palpable. Chávez came to Salinas and called for all the union staffers and volunteers from around the country to head to Salinas and Watsonville. The flame ignited.

Lemus was at the union hall in August 1970 when union staffers put out signs for different ranches and asked workers from these ranches to claim them. Lemus picked up the D'Arrigo sign and held it up over his head. With that he became an organizer. Word got back to the company. The next day at work a supervisor approached Lemus and offered him a foreman's job. "Do I look like a dog to you?" Lemus asked the smiling supervisor. "What do you mean?" the supervisor replied. Lemus said coolly, "You must think I'm a dog. You just offered me a bone. I don't take bones."

This defiant attitude was expressed in a mass way on August 24, 1970, when 7,000 workers in dozens of companies from Watsonville, Salinas, and Santa Maria walked out and joined long caravans that wove their way through the valleys. Production stopped in the middle of the year's biggest harvest. For days no lettuce market figures were being quoted out of Salinas because, as one grower spokesperson understated, there was a "scarcity of the product."

Production of strawberries, celery, carrots, and tomatoes was also hit. In the days leading up to the signing of union grape contracts, representatives chosen by strawberry workers at Pic 'n Pac had gone to farmworker rallies in the Central Valley to seek out UFWOC leaders. "We're awaiting your arrival in Salinas," they told the union people. "We're ready to strike. We've waited a long time for something like this." As strike fever mounted a group of Pic 'n Pac workers and their families were gathered near the entrance to the La Posada trailer camp at the edge of the Alisal, near Salinas's old Chinatown. When a union sound truck passed by La Posada announcing the decision of Freshpict workers to strike, someone in the camp misunderstood the message and yelled out, "Ya ha llegado el momento. Nos estan llamando en huelga!" (The time has come. They're calling us out on strike!) The residents of La Posada formed a car caravan and went to the Pic 'n Pac fields and called the pickers out on strike! They'd misunderstood the message, but the strike was on.

It did not take long for Pic 'n Pac's losses to mount up. After losing 500 acres of berries, the company signed with the union, one among ten strawberry companies to do so.

The wall the growers erected to keep out the flood they feared did not hold. Grower unity broke down when Interharvest renounced its agreement with the Teamsters and signed a UFWOC contract on the last day of August. Local growers, already disturbed and worried about the entry of conglomerates like United Fruit into vegetable farming, were furious. They formed the Citizens' Committee for Agriculture, announced a boycott of Interharvest products, and set up a blockade of an Interharvest yard to keep trucks from leaving. Salinas police and sheriffs, normally quite adept at keeping traffic flowing at struck firms, were somehow unable to this time. The Interharvest blockade ended after a little more than a week, but it provided tactical advantages to the growers. By keeping Interharvest, the largest Salinas Valley grower, with about 20 percent of the valley's production of lettuce, out of the fields for a crucial week of the strike, lettuce prices were driven skyward, aiding some struck firms to recoup through high prices at least some of what they'd lost in volume.

The strike gave weight to the threat of a boycott. By October, Freshpict, another giant with 40,000 acres of vegetables, and a subsidiary of the Purex Corporation, signed with UFWOC. In November, D'Arrigo, a long-established, family-owned grower, also gave in. By then, UFWOC had companies representing nearly 20 percent of vegetable production under contract. But others held firm and fought wickedly to keep the union out.

By forcing some of the most powerful growers and agribusiness corporations to recognize a union of farmworkers and negotiate wages and working conditions, the general strike accomplished what no other farm strike had previously achieved. Most crucially it put initiative in the hands of workers as a collective organization.

These accomplishments did not come easily. Many striking workers were evicted from the labor camps and forced to sleep in the fields or on the concrete floors of those camps that remained open. Families of strikers endured intimidation and harassment from police and eviction from company housing. Striking workers faced forces mustered by the growers and the state—police, private guards, and bands of armed vigilantes, some of them directly employed by the Teamsters Union, which partnered with the growers to suppress the strike.

The strike met with unrelenting hostility from the Salinas establishment. Bumper stickers proliferated around the Salinas community with the message, "Reds, Lettuce Alone" and "Get César Out of Our Salad." Early in the strike the local Salinas paper, *The Californian*, published front-page stories and pictures featuring growers and their families bravely taking to the lettuce fields determined to save their rotting crops. A look at the news photos was enough to cause sidesplitting laughter from Lemus and his fellow workers. In none of the photos are the hardworking growers even bent over. Either they were unable to bend down as their workers did for hours at a time, or they felt it was beneath their dignity, so standing up, head of lettuce in one hand and knife in the other, they smilingly carried out the harvest work. Such pleasant work, the photos seemed to say: only a misled ingrate would choose to strike over this!

Numerous articles in the local paper pleaded the growers' case: They could not survive on the $2.10 an hour demanded, or a union hiring hall the new contract would force on them, or the new rules that guided the use of pesticides in the fields. Economic disaster was on the horizon, and furthermore, the American way of life was now under siege. To dramatize this, growers flew U.S. flags from non-union trucks and buses and field equipment. Even the celery *burros* (work tables) of the strikebreakers were propped with U.S. flags. (Indeed, there was more truth to this threat than perhaps the growers themselves realized, since the American Way of Life was, and is, only possible because the intense, cruel exploitation of some sustains the privileged lives of others.)

Growers organized rallies denouncing the intrusion that now threatened the well-being of California's farms. Anne Merrill, from one of the prominent local grower families, became a star at these gatherings. Acclaimed as the growers' answer to the union's Dolores Huerta, Merrill spoke in defense of farmworkers who now faced an evil form of unionism. She and other grower representatives became champions of the workers' right not to be forced to join a union. Suddenly secret ballot union elections in the fields became a growers' cause célèbre.

By the end of the 1970 Salinas harvest season, UFWOC had contracts with Interharvest, D'Arrigo, and Freshpict, major vegetable growers; Meyers and Brown and Hill tomato packers in the King City area; Delfino, the largest artichoke grower; and Pic 'n Pac and other strawberry firms in the Salinas-Watsonville area. In addition, it had contracts previously won at Almaden and Paul Masson wineries in the San Ardo area south of King City. In all, by 1972, UFWOC could count 147 contracts in the grapes and vegetables covering more than 50,000 jobs, thirty-three boycott centers in major cities, and more than 600 volunteers on its staff.

The strike was a life-changing event, sending some workers on a path of activism they had never imagined for themselves. Something "immutable" had been suddenly flung in the air, and no one could tell how it would come back down to earth, nor what things would look like when it did.

The growers feared their old autocratic control over workers would never be the same. Farm unions may be inevitable, one grower conceded after the strike. Although this reflected the direction things were going at the time, it did not signal any general resignation. Whereas growers gave ground in wages and working conditions, this was only a tactical retreat. They remained hostile to unionism but even more so to the dangerous elements they saw lurking in the shadows of the picket lines.

When clergy and religious activists joined the Delano grape strike, a hue and cry went up of "outside interference." When students, fresh from the civil rights, antiwar, and Free Speech movements, turned their energies toward supporting farmworkers, the criticisms intensified. The struggle of farmworkers for better conditions hit up against the racism and chauvinism they faced as Mexicans, Filipinos, and so on, raising issues that struck deeper than workplace conditions, issues that hit on a central feature of a society built on national oppression. This drew in politically awakened sections of people with a broader critique of U.S. society, which in turn provoked denunciations that drifted across the political landscape like a smoky cloud after an explosion. UFWOC was accused of leading, not a union, but a "social movement."

In the wake of the Salinas general strike these accusations grew more persistent. "Movement" became a dirty word. In the discourse of the day, unions, as long as they stuck strictly to bread-and-butter issues, were judged in the court of public opinion makers as respectable and responsible. Movements, on the other hand, were political, social, and reckless. For the growers and a growing chorus from other defenders of the system, including, as we shall see, powerful trade union leaders, there was no place in the fields for a social movement.

There was, for sure, an element of truth to the charge that UFWOC was part of something more than a union struggle, but this was one of its great strengths. The farmworker struggle gained in vitality to the degree to which it came to represent the rebellion against the two-fold oppression of farmworkers: as highly exploited workers with low wages, few benefits, poor housing, and so on, and as Mexicans, subject to intense forms of repression and discrimination in nearly every aspect of social and civil life (or as some farmworkers considered themselves with ample justification, a lower caste). To many campesinos these early years of the 1970s brought a newfound strength and optimism. It seemed only a matter of time before the storm that swept the valley the summer of 1970 would reshape the landscape. The other valley growers would fall one day to the union. The balance of power was shifting, all this in the context of other changes going on in society and the world. It was possible for farmworkers to sense their struggle was part of something larger, contributing to bigger changes taking place. Not to oversimplify the matter, individual outlooks varied greatly. Many farmworkers were, after all, displaced peasants, that is, small owners who maintained entrepreneurial ambitions. And some still ran small farms or aspired to return with money made in the United States to begin their own businesses. Visions and aspirations thus varied greatly. This does not contradict the notion that the struggle had opened up the field to new potential and new aspirations, including radical ones, as farmworkers sought to struggle against exploitation and the oppression they faced.

After the general strike, Lemus had gone east to work on the lettuce boycott. When the windows of his family's home in Salinas were smashed late one night, he asked to return to Salinas. Now he was the leader of a celery harvesting crew that had a reputation for being tough defenders of the union. When I asked Lemus how things were going in the celery, he shrugged. When I told him I wanted to try my hand at contract work he spoke with a voice infused with skepticism. If you think you can hack it you could try my crew. The crew was short a few people; the union hadn't sent anyone out to fill the spots: "Si l'haces, puedes agarrar un dispatcho en la oficina." If I made it the job would be mine. This was a good arrangement for me, because even though I thought I was in pretty good shape I didn't know if I could handle celery work and I didn't want to be on the payroll if I wasn't going to make it. That would be like taking money out of the other workers' pockets. With good reason, the union was reluctant to dispatch people if they were not sure they could handle the job. If I made it, the crew would give me a cut for the day. If I didn't, the time would be on me.

The following Monday I showed up at the field as Lemus had directed. When I arrived without a celery knife he just shook his head, and I felt foolish. But the foreman handed me a knife. The celery knife is actually like several knives in one. It's about half the length of a machete with cutting edges on two sides—on the long side, like a conventional knife, and at the head of the knife, where a second blade flares out forming a cutting edge three or four inches wide. This is the edge the *apiero* (celery harvester) uses to cut the bunch from its root. The cutter pushes that edge at the end of the knife under the plant. If the cut isn't a clean one, the long edge of the knife is used to make a second, clean cut of the root side of the plant leaving the butt of the plant smooth. Then the cutter flips the bunch over and cuts the top of the bunch to leave a straight cut across the top. This is the way the celery was packed in the boxes to be sent to market.

Lemus told me to work near his burro, a table with wheels where he and other packers placed the celery in boxes according to size. There were 24s, 36s, and 48s, each corresponding to the number of bunches per box. The 24s were the larger-sized bunches, hence fewer per box. The burro rolls over the cut rows, and the packers pick up the cut celery, sort them by size, close the boxes, and lay them on the ground behind the burro.

By the time I got my knife, sharpened it on its various sides, and prepared to settle into my row, the burro was already several yards ahead. The foreman was cutting my row ahead of the burro. I cut my row up to the empty spot and then went back and forth picking up the cut celery and placing them on the burro. Finally, after I got all the celery up from the ground, I went to where the foreman was cutting, ahead of the burro, which was on a row just off to the side, and began to cut, as fast as I could. At first I thought I was doing well. I was even able to cut some of the stalks to the right depth with one stroke, maybe one out of every five or six times. I cut, trimmed, and dropped; cut, trimmed, trimmed, dropped; cut, trimmed, trimmed, trimmed, dropped; cut, trimmed, trimmed, dropped; cut, trimmed, dropped, my body bent forward 45 to 90 degrees the whole time. I was moving fast, as fast as I thought humanly possible, but awkwardly. My heart was racing. I stripped to my T-shirt, and the sweat from my forehead dripped onto my arms. I pushed harder, and the burros, the packers, and the other cutters moved steadily ahead of me. Before long, they were yards ahead. When I looked around it seemed as though the other cutters were moving at a more leisurely pace than I. I tried to copy their movements, but my cuts were getting wilder, either too deep, hitting the ground, or too high, dismembering the plant, and I kept falling further behind. The foreman came over to help, but I knew I was lost. I was like a frantic tortoise in the race with the hare, but a hare that wasn't going to stop for sleep. I gave up the race, but stayed on to help the foreman catch up the row. When the two of us caught up with the burro, I handed him the knife. "Siento como un perro con tres patas" (I feel like a dog with three legs), wondering if such an expression really made any sense in this circumstance. I felt lame. It was my first and last day in the celery.

La Posada

In November of 1971, barely a year after the "accidental" Pic 'n Pac strike forced the company to agree to a union contract, Pic 'n Pac declared it was going out of business. The 137 families that worked for the company and lived in the company's La Posada trailer camp were told to leave. Local growers and the press depicted Pic 'n Pac's "demise" as proof that the union would drive growers into bankruptcy and ruin the local farm economy. The story of the eviction of the Pic 'n Pac workers from their trailer camp was one of the first covered by *El Obrero*. In the course of it, the paper had a long interview with one of the members of a committee of residents fighting to save their homes. Her story, edited slightly, went like this:

> My name is Concepcion Lucio. I am 26 years old. My family and I have lived in La Posada since 1965. In my family there are my mother, father and 13 brothers and sisters. My oldest brother and sister are married and have small families and often live with us too.
>
> My parents are from Mexico, and came to live in Texas when I was born in 1944. We settled in the Rio Grande Valley which has a lot of citrus. My father worked as an irrigator, sometimes 24 hours a day, weeks at a time, and was paid $15 a week. Around the summer of 1958 we began to migrate throughout Texas picking cotton, trying to find work for all of us. In 1962 my family went to Washington to work and then over the next few years traveled to Oregon, Montana, Idaho, and Indiana. We always returned to Texas in the fall so that we could go back to school. After school we would work a few hours every day picking tomatoes.
>
> Life in Texas was always very hard. Although we always worked very hard as much as possible, we never had enough for food and clothes.
>
> Then in 1965 we began hearing radio announcements advertising for strawberry pickers in California. The company was Salinas Strawberries, which later became Pic 'n Pac. They had a representative in

the Rio Grande Valley and we went to visit him. He said that with the size of our family we could make $1,000 a week, and the company would pay our travel expenses to get there.

We were all very excited. We left right away with $175 from the company. When we arrived we moved right into La Posada. Most of the families here today came about the same time we did and under the same arrangements. We started working right away by the hour until we were experienced, and then we worked piece rate. We never made $1,000 a week. With eight of us working, we managed about $700. Working conditions were not good. Men never got any rest periods and there was only one toilet for both men and women. We used to pay $49 a week for our trailer. Still, we were making better money than in Texas. Every winter we still went back to Texas. We began to think that going back to Texas cost too much, maybe we could stay in Salinas all year. All my younger brothers and sisters were in school in Salinas and all our friends were here too. So for the last three seasons our family has lived in La Posada year round.

The money was better here but the people were angry because the company was always pushing us around. When we worked by the hour, the company always pushed us to work faster and faster. At the end of the season when there weren't too many berries, we would ask for a wage guarantee or a little more for each box, but the company always refused. We could never do anything about these problems because we never organized ourselves as a group to fight for things. We were too scared.

In late August of 1970 we were faced with the same problem of the berries getting real scarce. Then the strike came to the valley and we went out too.

After walking out of the fields everybody came back to La Posada and met with César Chávez. TV cameras were there, too. We got organized. We had a picket line at the entrance to La Posada mostly older people and the kids. The rest went to the ranches to picket. We were a real strong group and sometimes we would picket other ranches too. When the anti-strike injunction was handed down many of us were arrested rather than stop picketing. But we won the contract and for the first time we felt secure and really free. The day of the contract we threw a party. We weren't scared any more because we had a union to back us up. Some families joined the lettuce boycott and really made sacrifices for the union. My brothers went to Boston to picket SS Pierce.

After the contract it was like being born again. For the first time you could speak out and not be afraid.

We knew that Pic 'n Pac was having troubles. They bought a half million dollars' worth of strawberry machines that didn't work. They had too many supervisors and many didn't know what they were doing. So when Pi c'n Pac announced that they were going out of business we were not surprised. But we were really shocked when they announced that they had sold the trailers.

They had just planted new berries, so we knew that there had to be work. But why couldn't they come to us and try to arrange for keeping the camp? On Oct. 10, 1971, everybody got an eviction notice saying that we had seven days to leave La Posada. We didn't have any idea where to go or what to do.

We went to the local county agencies, but no one really wanted to help. We asked for Camp McCallum and that was turned down. We asked for a loan to buy La Posada, that was turned down. We asked for a housing project to be built, but no one listened.

The government officials only listened when we put pressure on them. . . . We cannot expect them to give us anything unless we fight for it.

Pic 'n Pac is in court to get an immediate eviction for the 60 families that are left. But we will not leave here until we have some place to go. We think that by fighting for our homes we are helping many people of Salinas who face the same problem, because there isn't enough housing. We hope to see a lot of low-income housing built that could benefit many people as a result of our struggle. We know that the growers are scared because we are fighting to stay and become a permanent part of this community. And then we will have some power to make some changes for all the people.

The La Posada families fought the eviction for some time, but they lost and in May 1972 forty remaining families were evicted by squads of police.[27] The people were now camped with their families on the side of the road with no place to go. Some of the youths from La Posada put a sign on one of the tents calling their encampment My Lai, the Viet-namese village where U.S. soldiers massacred 500 people, mainly women, children, and old men in 1968.

Strikebreakers' Rebellion

In October of 1972, just two years after the general strike, Freshpict, sub-sidiary of the Purex Corporation, announced it was ending lettuce and celery production. After Pic 'n Pac went out of business, its owner, Dave

Walsh, continued harvesting strawberries without a union contract and the workers went after him. The strike was long and contentious, and the workers found themselves up against court injunctions meant to break the back of the strike. Arrests were frequent, as strikers challenged the judge's orders.

Not long after Pic 'n Pac, D'Arrigo Brothers also refused to renegotiate with the union when that contract came due in the winter of 1972. The company complained publicly, "Every time we try to exercise our management rights . . . we have been met with wildcat strikes and slow-downs."[28] They refused to negotiate and a strike began at their operation in Eloy, Arizona, in December. By March the strike had spread north as the harvest season approached in Salinas.

With workers in short supply the companies turned to the labor contractors who were more than anxious to break the strikes. The UFW hiring hall had undercut contractors, and their existence was threatened. They formed an association to fight back and joined hands with the Teamsters and growers to conduct war against the union movement.

One day a Stockton contractor arrived at the Stewart Hill camp in Salinas with a bus full of strikebreakers. A crowd of strikers greeted them. A fight erupted and some camp windows were broken. The strikebreakers were mainly black. They knew nothing of the dispute. When they realized a strike was on, and there were workers determined to enforce it, they refused to leave the camp for work. The enraged contractor evicted the strikebreakers from the camp and flatly refused to bring them back to Stockton. Their situation was precarious. They had little money and they needed a place to stay for the night.

That afternoon, I'd just gotten off work when I got a call from Jerry Kay, who was coordinating the Pic 'n Pac and D'Arrigo strikes. "Hey," said Jerry, "we've got about twenty strikebreakers from Stockton who walked out of the camp over at D'Arrigo and they need a place to stay. S'pose they could stay at your place?" I looked around our living room with its worn easy chairs and a floor lamp with a missing shade we'd found waiting innocently out on an Alisal street corner. There was plenty of floor space. "Sure, bring 'em over." We put beans and rice on the stove and bought tortillas and chile. With that kind of food you could feed an army cheaply.

That night we stayed up late with the Stockton visitors, men in their late twenties to mid-forties. Some were addicted to the bottle, not unusual among people who relied on part-time fieldwork for survival. They talked about the false promises that lured them to Salinas. And a few talked about the paths that led them to the fields.

Henry, a soft-spoken man with thick hands and shoulders, had come a few years before from Seattle, where he'd had a good job as an assembler at the Boeing aircraft plant. Competition was heavy among the aircraft companies that had grown fat during the Second World War. In the late 1960s Boeing bet heavily on a new airliner, the 747. By 1971 few had sold and Henry found himself downstream with 60,000 other Boeing workers, washed out of a company tottering on the edge of ruin.

Henry drifted down from Seattle, where homelessness spelled death in the winter, to the Central Valley towns where work was plentiful if poorly compensated and where the weather outside, in Henry's words, "could chill you, but not kill you." He left behind the wreckage of a family torn apart in the economic turmoil and the psychological fallout that came soon after. Henry was fairly new to the farm labor scene, but others who knew well the heat of tomato picking in the Central Valley jumped at the chance to work in the coolness of Salinas.

It was a night filled with stories of the streets, day labor, and "slave" (labor) contractors. In the morning we brought the "strikebreakers" to the bus station. The union strike committee passed the hat and raised funds to send them back home.

Billboards and a Worker Named Jack

Jack Deaton, a Pic 'n Pac worker and striker, came from a state in the South. After serving a stint in the marines, he ended up traveling in Mexico. Wandering one day through the streets of Cuautla, Morelos, near the town of Ayala where the Zapatista rebellion began a half-century before, he exchanged friendly words with a woman in the street and decided he wanted to get to know her. As he and Lenore would later tell the story, Jack followed her home and insisted, to her mother's chagrin, that he wanted to see her. Lenore's mother told him to leave. He did. But he came back. His persistence paid off and Jack and Lenore began a friendship that quickly developed.

It was Lenore who brought Jack north, not the other way around. She had been working in the strawberries in Salinas, and she introduced him to the fruit from a position low to the ground. Jack got the knack after a painful apprenticeship, and he and Lenore worked together in the berries, adept enough to make a hard-earned but decent living at it. When the union struggle hit the valley, they were part of an active group of workers who immediately jumped into the battle.

When Pic 'n Pac went out of business and owner Dave Walsh tried to duck the union while still harvesting berries, Jack and a core of workers pursued a strike that lasted for months. Jack landed in jail more than once for court injunction violations.

In the summer of 1972, the growers put an initiative on the California ballot called Proposition 22. It was born of the growers' sudden interest in giving the workers a chance to choose their union through elections. It was actually a brazen attempt to legally kill the farmworker union movement in its tracks. It provided for union elections to be held when there were an equal number of permanent and seasonal workers on the job. Since most growers had many more seasonal than year-round workers, most farmworkers would be automatically disenfranchised. The initiative would have banned boycotts and imposed fines for advocating them. It would have allowed for a farm strike to be halted for a sixty-day cooling-off period, enough time generally for the growers to bring in their crops. The initiative was advertised as a fair measure to give farmworkers the right to decide their destiny. It received a lot of favorable publicity, and the union and pro-union forces mobilized against it.

The backers of Proposition 22 had a big advertising budget. They purchased billboard ads across the state for their "Yes on 22" campaign. Some of these billboards ran along Highway 101 through Salinas and down the valley. One day at the union hall in the weeks leading up to the election, Jack and I and several other workers and union staffers were talking about the election with Richard Chávez, the head of the field office. "You know," said Richard, "there's a Proposition 2 on the same ballot with 22." He looked around at us to see if we were paying attention. "That proposition 2 has something to do with medical care or doctors or something, I heard that it's a positive thing, it would be good if it passed." We were all paying attention, but it wasn't totally clear what he meant, so he continued. "If I had the wherewithal, I'd support that proposition. It's expensive to put out ads, you know, like the ones out on the highway." There were some nods and "cómo nos" (Ya, of course).

Several days later Jack and I were at the hall and we saw Richard. We were both pretty tired, having been up most of the night riding around with Roberto Garcia and his compadre who served as lookouts while Jack and I practiced our climbing techniques. "You wouldn't believe what we saw out on the highway today," said Jack. "You know that doctor's proposition 2, I think it's gonna win. They got all these 'Yes on Proposition 2' signs all up and down the highway!" Richard nodded happily. I don't know if Richard noticed the paint on Jack's hands, but I did.

I helped as best I could to oppose Proposition 22, but in general I was not enthusiastic about elections. This was the same year the antiwar candidate, George McGovern, was running for president and there was a big debate among activists over whether to build support for him or not. The first election I had taken an interest in was 1964 when I was in high school. Lyndon Johnson was the "anti-war candidate" running against the hawkish Barry Goldwater. It was an election that will live in infamy for many sixties people. Johnson won in a landslide on a promise not to send "American boys" to Vietnam. Not long after his election, using the phony Gulf of Tonkin incident, Johnson escalated the war, eventually provoking such rage that he was forced to withdraw from the electoral race in 1968.

Decisions about war and most crucial life-and-death issues in capitalist democracy are not based on the "will of the people" but on the will of people who control the levers of wealth and power. Their decisions are based on the needs of the system they serve and control. By buying into their electoral shell game, the people actually forfeit their will, which can only be expressed through active, and usually massive, resistance.

I saw in McGovern's candidacy a move to divert energy from that powerful movement that for a precious moment was giving the people a sense of their power and ability to change things. It was really the old order, seeking to reassert its political control by convincing the rebels that there were well-placed government allies on the side of the people. I believe that most of the people around *El Obrero* agreed with that position, but it was nevertheless quite controversial among many in the radical and antiwar movement, who argued that by not supporting McGovern one was actually betraying the Vietnamese people because McGovern would have shortened the war if elected. And as it turned out, it was Nixon, the pro-war hawk, who withdrew U.S. soldiers from Vietnam in 1972.

One Chávez's Pain, Another's Anger

One day, perhaps six months after *El Obrero* first came out, I was at the union hall when I spotted Richard Chávez's somewhat portly figure. Even from a distance you could see how his walk responded to an ache in his lower back. He gestured to me and I followed him to his modest office a few steps from the dispatch windows. His usual casual friendliness was more a neutral formality. I chalked this off to the back pain that seemed more serious than usual. He was also carrying a can of beer in his hand. I had never seen him drinking at the hall before.

He sat down uneasily on the old easy chair in his office and talked without looking at me. He spoke hesitantly and emotionally. "Last weekend we had a meeting at the union headquarters." He paused to move in his seat, trying to find a spot to elude the pain. "César was pretty upset. He jumped all over me. It was about you guys' paper." There was the sound of distance in the way he said "you guys." "César heard about how the paper was being sold out of the union office to the crews and he blew up. He came down hard on me, yelled at me pretty bad, in front of every-one. He came down really hard." It was apparent that the pain was not just in Richard's back. "Can't let you guys sell that paper here anymore." "How do you feel about that?" I asked Richard. He answered with annoyance in his voice. "I have to do what the union wants." "But what do you *think* about it?" I repeated. "César has the bigger picture. I've gotta do what the union decides. Man, he was really angry," Richard repeated, as if to give a release to the pain that was evident in his voice. "He jumped in my shit big-time. I can't let you guys sell that paper out of here anymore."

4. THE BATTLE LINES SHARPEN, SPRING 1973

Coachella: La División del Norte

IT WAS EARLY EVENING. The union hall on Wood Street was getting crowded. Chairs placed in rows only a few feet from the pinewood dispatch windows at the front end of the hall extended back to where the white and black banner announced, "Viva la Causa!" An aisle left room for people to make their way to the benches along the walls or find a spot to squat in the front. Still more tried to squeeze in, and a crowd packed around the door and out onto the sidewalk, craning and straining. Had the meeting begun?

I stood at the back of the hall and watched Marshall Ganz at the front of the room, looking professorial, his shoulders slightly rounded, a belly spilling lazily over belted slacks, sipping coffee from a paper cup and pushing up eyeglasses that had slipped down his nose from perspiration in a room heated by closely packed bodies. Marshall was known as César Chávez's right-hand man and the union strike coordinator. He smiled and looked from side to side at the gathering crowd. Certainly he must have been satisfied with the large turnout to this emergency meeting.

The murmur of voices in the room was punctuated now and then with the squeal of a child hanging on a mother's neck, or yanking restlessly on a father's arm. Here and there a shout came from someone in the crowd beginning to feel restless, even as they were settling into their places. "Viva la huelga!" "Viva César Chávez!" More vivas. "Compañeros y compañeras," Marshall began, setting his coffee cup on a table by the dispatch window. He scanned the crowd, gauging the mood. A mass of mostly dark-eyed humanity stared back at him. There were teenage girls with tender eyes and hair hanging to their mid backs; middle-aged women with hair to their shoulders, some wearing hats or scarves; men of various ages, with thick, dark curly hair bursting out from under baseball caps or graying strands peeking out from under wide-brim straw hats. There were some tall, strong men, with wide mustaches and dark beards, shoulders hardened by the years of heaving lettuce cartons, middle-aged men and women thickened with age and physical work, mostly a Mexican crowd with a scattering of black, white, and Asian faces. It was a generally good-humored crowd, buoyed by the energy and excitement of a historic moment, and at the same time nervously anticipating the outcome of this new bend in the road.

"Viva Marshall!" someone shouted to a roll of laughter. "Que viva los campesinos!" answered the strike coordinator, laughing with the crowd, which echoed back, "Que viva!"

"Who is here?" he asked, finally. "What companies?" Workers from different companies registered their presence to shouts and applause from around the room. Interharvest made up the largest group, but there were some from D'Arrigo, Pacific, Harden, Hansen, Cal Coastal, Oshita, Dave Walsh, Mann Packing, Finerman, Admiral, Trevino, and others. Even a few workers from Bruce Church called out to hardy applause.

"Then it's time for some singing," the strike leader proclaimed, "De Colores" and "Solidaridad Para Siempre," the Spanish version of the old Wobbly song "Solidarity Forever" minus its radical imagery. No new worlds arise from the ashes in this version, just people loyal to their union. "Que viva nuestra unión," the song concluded.

Finally, Marshall Ganz introduced the main business at hand. He spoke quickly in a Spanish that flowed fluently but with a decidedly non-native accent. "It's not an exaggeration to say that our union, our struggle is at a crossroads," he began. The buzz of the crowd was gone, in its place a silence of stern faces and concern. "Grape contracts signed in 1970 with Coachella Valley growers are about to expire. The growers have refused for some time to seriously renegotiate their contracts. We are certain they are going to sign with the Teamsters Union. This is the biggest challenge we have faced. The growers think farmworkers can be forced back into the days when we were at their mercy and had no recourse, no organization. Are they right?" A chorus of "No!" followed by "Huelga! Huelga!" Then, "Abajo los rancheros!" "Abajo los Teamsters!" "Viva la union de campesinos!" and "Viva la unión de Chávez." If there was any question that the news from Coachella would be intimidating to this crowd, it was quickly dispelled.

What followed were details about the tactics the growers and Teamsters were using and the union's plan to deal with it. Ganz spelled out the union's plans in light of the challenge: volunteers were needed from among the Salinas workers to help initiate the strike in Coachella. Salinas volunteers would be called "La División del Norte," recalling the army of landless peasants under Pancho Villa that swept down from the states of Durango and Chihuahua to the Mexican capital to drive out the tyrants and back up their burning demands for land and freedom. Now this new "army" would swoop down from Salinas to Coachella to spearhead a struggle to beat back this effort to break the union. The proposal was met with cheers and shouts of determination and defiance. Who was ready to volunteer? Hands shot up, more cheers, more excitement, more anger.

I stood next to Mary Ann Sullivan, a woman in her early twenties. Her light, freckled face stood out in this crowd of generally darker complexions, much as her Boston accent stood out the first moment I heard her speak several weeks before at the union hall. She'd come with her thinning crew for a meeting over a grievance. Even though she'd only been in town a short time, she was already gamely trying to use her Spanish. When I kidded her about her "Bostonian" Spanish, she said, without missing a beat, "If you want to hear something really funny you should listen to you Californians speak Spanish."

As the meeting broke up, office staff with clipboards worked a crowd to sign up volunteers for Coachella. The union might be beaten back, but it would not go quietly. I looked at Mary Ann with a question, but I had no real doubt from her emotional response to the union's exhortations that she was going to Coachella.

UFW contracts with Coachella grape growers were set to expire April 16. Early morning on April 15 people gathered around the buses that sat on the lot beside the union hall. I saw many familiar faces from the thinning and broccoli crews, union meetings, and conversations.

I sat with Mary Ann for the ten-hour ride south. We worked on a crossword puzzle. Mary Ann put me to shame with her quick answers. We chatted with the people around us about what might be ahead. And we talked about the twisted paths that led us to Salinas.

Mary Ann was born and raised in suburban Boston. Like so many other restless youths in those years she'd left home not long after high school, looking for a way to assist in bringing in the new world, or at least discovering the old. Her travels eventually took her to an Alaskan fish cannery, lured by hopes of adventure and promises of good pay and spectacular surroundings. The pay turned out to be somewhat less than promised, the adventure soon wore off, and the beauty of the Alaskan summer was trumped by a dark, frigid Alaskan winter. Her migration south eventually brought her to Salinas, to see for herself what all the fuss was about in the lettuce fields.

Now, only weeks after arriving in Salinas, Mary Ann Sullivan was about to jump into the thick of struggle in the fields.

Talk on the bus turned to speculation about Coachella. A judge in Indio had issued an injunction limiting picketing even before the contracts had expired. This was not going to be some quiet protest. But then, who wanted quiet protests? Change only comes by confronting injustice. The workers around us shared their stories about the 1970 strike and about struggles of various kinds in Mexico, from issues over land and water to strikes and internal union battles against sellout leaders, to an uprising in one municipality by local residents infuriated over corruption and a stolen election. The güeros in the group talked about the struggles we'd seen, against the war in Vietnam, and about the civil rights movement. In this bus we were no strangers to conflict. There was feeling among us that there was a connection among all these conflicts, and we all tried to express in various ways that commonality.

Songs also kept the spirits up. There were the Spanish songs popular in the union, and I tried to recall the stanzas in English to the Joe Hill song, "The Preacher and the Slave": "You will eat, by and by, in that glorious land beyond the sky. / Work all day, live on hay, you'll get pie in the sky when you die." We had fun going back and forth between English and Spanish, but some of it got lost in translation.

From time to time someone would sermonize on the significance of our adventure, referring to the history of struggle that had been the lot of farmworkers and "la raza" ever since the expansionist-minded gringos ("No offense to all our güero friends") had taken the land by force. Once again there was a feeling of a connection with something bigger. We felt eager and apprehensive at the same time. There was no doubt that all of us "Division del Norte" people ardently wanted to strike a blow at the growers and their henchmen, the Teamsters. People were up for a fight.

It was late afternoon by the time our caravan coasted past the Salton Sea and hit the Coachella Valley. It was a warm mid-April day, but snow from an unusually wet winter and cool spring still clung to the San Bernardino Mountains, which could be easily seen to the east. On the way to the town of Coachella we drove through a wide, flat valley, a patchwork of irrigated vineyards, fields, and date farms. Less than a century before, this land was a vast expanse of low-lying desert, a deadly stretch of land for many would-be gold seekers who tried to cross it.

In ancient times, this area was the bottom of a huge lake that stretched from Indio to the Mexican border and covered more than 2,000 square miles. The lake was created by one of the diversions of the mighty

Colorado River. The silty waters of the river deposited thick layers of sediment on the lake floor. Then, around five centuries ago, the meandering Colorado shifted course once again, leaving the lake without a source, and it dried up until only a hot but fertile desert remained.

This desert was home to the Cahuila Indians, whose history in the area stretched back to the days of the great lake. They remained on the land even as the lake dried up and disappeared, adapting to the new environment. They survived this cataclysmic change, but nearly succumbed to various invasions that came after 1492. The last and most devastating began with the Gold Rush of 1849 and the fevered rush for land that followed it.[1]

In the late 1800s the Southern Pacific Railroad took control of the land and its water rights. With the discovery of water in artesian wells fed by the runoff from the nearby mountains and an aquifer left over from the lake, agriculture became possible. By the 1940s Coachella was part of the gigantic water project that tapped the Colorado for the burgeoning coastal metropolis of Los Angeles. With water came the metamorphosis. The land had potential for riches. First came date trees, imported from Iraq and Algeria in the early 1900s. Then came grapes, citrus, avocados, and other crops.

Coachella played a prominent role in the Delano grape strike of 1965–70, when Filipino grape workers, in the words of Philip Vera Cruz, a farmworker leader, "delivered the initial spark" by going on strike to demand higher wages.

Filipino grape workers made up an important part of the labor force in Coachella grapes. Since the 1920s Filipino farmworkers in California's valleys faced racist oppression, segregation, and violence, but they also had a history of struggle and resistance. They had an astute knowledge of the industry and some shrewd and experienced leaders. By 1965 their ranks were aging and their numbers were dwindling, but they were still a force in the table grapes.

On the eve of the grape harvest season that begins in Coachella in April, trouble was brewing. The Bracero Program, which ended in 1964, had been used by the growers for decades to keep down wages and undermine working conditions. Now with bracero labor unavailable, the growers wanted to flood the fields with green-card holders and the undocumented. To attract enough workers to the 1965 harvest they were offering $1.40 an hour (up from $1 an hour in 1963) to workers recruited from Mexico, but were refusing to pay more than $1.25 an hour to locals, including Filipino workers.[2]

Unlike other grape-growing areas, the Coachella Valley did not have a large permanent population of workers who depended on the grapes after a winter with little work. Growers relied heavily on Filipino workers from Delano for the harvest. Coachella grapes are the first in a long summer of table grape harvests that begins in the southern semi-desert valleys and move north. These Coachella grapes ripen as early as late May and can bring high first-of-the-crop market prices. The Filipino workers calculated that Coachella growers would have a difficult time finding enough replacement workers quickly enough to get their pricey early grapes to market and would not risk a long strike. As the harvest approached in early June, Filipino workers, under the leadership of Ben Gines, a Filipino from the Agriculture Workers Organizing Committee (AWOC), forged unity with Mexican women crew leaders and demanded $1.40 an hour and 25 cents per box of grapes.[2] The growers at first refused but after ten days of striking around the Coachella Valley town of Thermal, the growers gave in and settled for the higher wage.[3]

But when the grape harvest reached the Arvin-Lamont area, the next big harvest on its march north to Delano, the growers dug in, refusing to budge. They even lowered the wages they offered to $1.20 an hour.[4]

The Filipino workers decided they would not to be pushed down without a fight. They were not naïve about the forces they were going to come up against nor the odds against them, and this provoked tension and debate over whether to continue the strike. But in the end they resolved to continue, voting to strike on September 7 at the Filipino Hall in Delano. The next day they went on strike under the leadership of AWOC organizer Larry Itliong.[5]

The Filipino workers stayed in their labor camps in Delano and refused to leave them. They appealed to Chávez's National Farmworkers Association to join their struggle. On September 16, 1965, in Our Lady of Guadalupe church in Delano, hundreds of Mexican farmworkers shouted their determination to join the Filipinos in what would become broadly known as the Delano grape strike.

No one could have foreseen that it would last for five years. Field rebellions are a part of California history. And many such efforts made significant, if temporary, gains in wages and conditions. But the growers were largely successful in isolating them from outside support, using the local media to label them as the work of hooligans, thugs, criminals, vagrants, malcontents, outside agitators, subversives, and, of course, communists (reserving for themselves the right to define what communist meant) to drive a wedge between the strikers and the broader public. Meanwhile, growers used influence over local courts and police to impose injunctions and arrest leaders and break up organizations. They hired vigilantes to intimidate or beat up workers and burn labor camps. They took advantage of the poverty of the workers and the seasonal and migratory nature of the work, which made the sacrifice of a prolonged struggle very difficult for even the most passionate of workers and facilitated recruitment of strikebreakers. They succeeded in defeating any permanent organization of the workers, and they believed that their efforts this time to crush the strike would succeed.

But some things had changed. By the 1960s nearly 90 percent of Californians were living in cities, removed from the grower mentality that dominated rural farming areas and the rural media. The proportionate influence of the growers was thus diminished along with the dominance of agriculture in the state's economy.

Changes within the composition of the population also shook up the balance of forces in the state. This included a growing population of Chicanos and Mexicanos with ethnic and family ties to people in the fields—growth that took place despite persistent efforts to contain and reverse it.[6]

Changes both internationally and within the United States were also bringing about a shift in the mood of the people. In the 1950s the Cold War spurred the vast McCarthyite campaign of political repression, especially of those sympathetic to socialism. Anti-communist purges in schools, in the arts, in unions, and other institutions, along with a virulent propaganda campaign, aroused fear and ravaged progressive influence in nearly every field.[7] But as the 1960s unfolded, McCarthyism began to give way to a sense of defiance. Perhaps nowhere was a changing mood more evident than on college campuses. A new postwar generation was coming of age that saw the world in different terms than those promoted by the Cold War propagandists who dominated the media and shaped curriculum in public schools.

Most central to this awakening was a powerful and radicalizing element that had never expressed itself with such intensity, determination, and moral force—the awakening of black people. Shifts in the world situation and changes in southern agriculture, especially the mechanization of the cotton crop, pried open cracks in Jim Crow segregation through which a movement emerged, bursting like a raging flood through the levees of repression that sought to contain it. From the civil rights movement to the Black Liberation struggle, black people brought a wave of energy, passion, and enlightening reality that reshaped the landscape of American politics.

The generation coming of age in the sixties saw the history and social studies books it was weaned on mocked by the reality they saw around them. The freedom riders, sit-ins at segregated restaurant counters, marches in defiance of dogs, bullets, and clubs, and eloquent denunciations of centuries of unspeakable brutality wrenched open the door to the blazing light of long-hidden realities. Civil rights struggles and rebellions awakened society to a crass, lynch mob reality in the South and to a more subtle, but certainly racist setup in the North. The war in Vietnam, which also began in the early 1960s, directed light to an arrogant and brutal foreign policy that spit on the sovereign rights of other countries. On the campuses, where a new wave of activism was met with repression, freedom of speech looked like the freedom to mouth official lies, and otherwise keep your mouth shut. For many people, especially the youth of the postwar generation, the epic saga "America the Beautiful, Land of the Free," was losing its power to enthrall, and began looking like some cheap B-movie.

Politicized youths and others began to look at social issues with a more discerning eye. And what came into their view as well were farm-workers, alternately pictured as either beaten-down wretches, incapable of anything but a paternalistic handout, or happy pastorals, blithely har-vesting crops with the joy and glee of a "Juan Valdez." A new view of rural workers would soon emerge, and there was a newly awakened audience ready to embrace it.

In 1965, from a strike barely sustainable under conditions in the grapes, a farmworker movement emerged, with an international grape boycott drawing strength from a powerful social upheaval across the country and around the world. It forced the mighty California grape growers and wine makers to recognize a union of farmworkers. On July 29, 1970, twenty-six Delano area growers representing 42 percent of the table grapes in California sat down and signed contracts with UFWOC (the organization formed by the merger of the NFWA and AWOC) at the union's Forty Acres complex in Delano.

It was early evening when our bus pulled up to Coachella's Veterans Park, a large square of grass, trees, park tables, and benches a few hun-dred yards from city offices in the center of the town. We were greeted happily by a crowd of local workers and union officials who must have been uplifted by our arrival, since we greatly expanded their ranks. At a rally that followed, Marshall Ganz and local Coachella officials like Frank Ortiz, made no qualms about the importance of volunteers from Sali-nas. The following day Coachella growers would claim publicly that, with the termination of their contracts with the UFW, acceding to the wishes of their workers, they had decided to sign with the Teamsters union. Any further problems would be attributed to infighting among the unions, to which grape growers would claim neither say nor responsibility. This was a clever but not original strategy to undermine the strike and the boycott. Only actions in the fields, powerful enough to cast doubt on the claim of popular support for the Teamsters, could trump such a scenario. Though it was never openly stated as such, it was evident that as things stood the union was far from confident it had the support among the grape workers to pull off the kind of action that would be needed to make a strong challenge.

After eating dinner in the park, we were assigned places to sleep. I went with several others from Salinas to the home of a Coachella resident, a tractor driver and his family. He was a veteran worker, probably in his late fifties, a longtime union supporter who worked on a small ranch that was not going to be part of the strike. We were up before dawn and out to the park where cars, pickups, and vans waited to take us to the fields.

By daybreak we stood on the margins of a grape field, part of the huge holdings of Tenneco Inc., which ran into the millions of acres. From the edge of the road looking into the vineyard we could see rows of vines converging in the distance. A crew was working well into the vineyard, kneeling before the vines and barely visible from the road. This was grape-thinning season and the young light-green Perlettes, the first variety to ripen, needed to be thinned so that the remaining grapes could grow large enough to be marketable. Without thinning, the crop would be lost.

We were the initiating force of the strike to come. Officially we were at the field to picket and encourage the workers to leave. But we all knew that we were going in. If the workers in the vineyards lacked the initiative or confidence to walk out, it would be up to our invading force to give them that confidence.

We stood. We paced and waited. Several Sheriff's Department cars were parked just down from our picket line. One worker in a wide-brimmed straw hat marched up and down the line, speaking to the several hundred of us who stood stretched out along the field's edge. "Compañeros, compañeras, camaradas, the people in this field are not our enemies, they are part of us. They are our brothers and sisters. Our enemies are the growers and the big bankers and the corporations and the Rockefellers who have forever exploited our country and enriched themselves off us. Remember that these are our people, we must explain to them why we are here, and why we must strike, to defend what we have won in our struggles."

We had arrived in Coachella with a new word on our lips, *zánganos* (drones), a word the union was now using to express contempt for the Teamsters; in sentiment, closer to "parasitic, good for nothing, SOBs." "Estamos peleando los rancheros y los zánganos" (We are fighting ranchers and drones), the worker said to us.[8]

Suddenly our line began to move and we entered the field. I ran into the vineyard not far from where Mary Ann was running. Shouts of "Huelga!" could be heard up and down the line. We ran, our hearts pounding, our feet sinking slightly into the soft soil. Like mini-subs we dove below the green canopy with the little tight green bunches, dove under the wires laced with green vines. We settled next to a small knot of thinners as they knelt in the shade of the vines. Words began to flood out of us, excitedly. Mary Ann and I took turns. "Huelga," she said in her Boston accent, "Júntense con la huelga." They want to break the union, the organization of the workers, we've got to stop them. The thinners were quiet. The words *zángano* and *huelga* and *lucha* spread out among the vines.

A hand grabbed my arm. Boots passed by stomping heavily in the path between the vines. I pulled my arm away and scooted under another row, dodging and weaving. My shirt got stuck on a wire; I pulled it away and it ripped. Words flowed faster. "Huelga, vámonos. Look at the sheriffs. Look who's protecting the growers—who's on their side, who works for the growers. What justice is this? They want to break the spirit of the workers and destroy any organization. Vámonos ya. Walk out with us." Then two hands on my neck pulling me back, and I see people leaving the vineyard. A striker falls forward on to the ground, pushed from behind by a khaki uniform. The grape thinners watch and listen. There's a lot of shouting now, "Huelga!" "Everybody out of the field. Struggle for your rights!" "Viva los campesinos!" "Viva la huelga!" If the thinners were moved by our words or actions, would they join us now with the eyes of supervisors and foremen on them, with the sheriffs in the field?

I walked from the field, a sheriff's deputy just behind me, his hand on the back of my neck, but no handcuffs. I felt like pulling away and running, but there was really no place to go. "No violencia!" picket captains were calling out. Tell that to the sheriffs, I thought, recalling the striker shoved to the dirt. We walked to the sheriff's tan bus. We were frisked quickly. A union legal observer stood to the side with a clipboard. She shouted to us as we were entering the bus, "Tu nombre? Cual es?" (What's your name?).

A metal screen separated us from the driver and the deputy, sitting shotgun. As the bus started up, a Swiss army knife appeared. Screws began to turn—the metal kind. Someone handed the screwdriver to me. I undid the pieces that held a window shut and passed it on. Windows began to open, shouts shot out and fists shot in the cool morning air. Shouts of encouragement from the edges of the road were met with ardent calls from inside the bus as it lurched forward—"Abajo con los sherifes!" "Viva la union!" "Abajo los rancheros y los zánganos!" Bus furniture was coming undone as the little Phillips did its job. The bus roared with the collective voices of protest, laughter, and shouting, joy and anger, but mostly anger. Strikers on the margins of the fields bellowed their huelgas and vivas, arms waving, fists and V-signs, as our bus pulled away from the field.

If anything, the shouting grew louder as we were herded through the jailhouse doors into a large holding cell. Everyone who could do so grabbed the cell bars as they closed on us and we shook them for all we had. It was all about noise, all about converting anger into decibels, into the only form of resistance available to us at that moment. Sheer, outraged noise. The sheriff's deputies shouted back at us. Scores of us now shouting, shaking, raging at the injustice of being jailed for defending the union, for demanding rights, for rebelling against what should never have existed in the first place, however each one might have interpreted that.

The deputies were also in a rage. "Shut the fuck up!" "Shut the fuck up!" But that was the wrong tactic for them. It only stoked the strikers' outrage more sharply at them for their role as chumps of the growers, for their clumsy attempts to silence us, and for the sheer stupidity of their response. New sounds merged with the "huelgas," the "abajos," the "vivas." It was derisive laughter, sarcasm so hardened and honed that it should have been declared a lethal weapon. But how could they confiscate it? And it came in its most withering, deadly, fashion from the mouths of the women strikers. If words could kill. The sheriffs pounded the bars with their clubs trying to smash a finger not fast enough to get out of the way. The shaking of the bars, the smacking of clubs on metal, the shouting—jailhouse rock!

The men were separated from the women and placed together in a large cell. Still, the shouting and singing continued. As the hours crept by, the men began to tire. And then the shouting and cursing, like a flame burning down to ashes, weakened. Only smoldering embers. That was in the men's area. Not so the women. Their shouts and chanting and singing could be heard throughout the jail, well into the night.

The men and women were taken one at a time to the booking section. Here we were fingerprinted, and the deputies took down our personal information on a booking sheet. But there was resistance at every step. A campesina held her hand clenched in a fist refusing to be fingerprinted. Bodies went limp as they were being taken to the booking area. As I was waiting my turn to be booked, I heard a deputy ask an older farmworker his name. "Guadalajara Jalisco," came the reply. If the deputies knew anything about Mexican geography, they didn't let on. "How do you spell that? Your last name is Jalisco? Is that with an H?"

Near the booking area was a solitary cell enclosed by a heavy metal door. The cell was bare except for a metal bench mounted on the wall and a hole in the center of the floor from which dirty water periodically backed into the room. While I went through the booking process, I heard more shouts of "Viva la huelga!" and "Abajo los sherifes!" from behind the metal door. This was Spanish with a decidedly Bostonian accent: Mary Ann! A deputy, clearly annoyed by the chanting, pounded his fist heavily on the metal door. But the shouting only increased. He opened the door and took a menacing step toward Mary Ann, who was sitting on the bench, her feet tucked away from the rising water. The deputy yelled at her and she just kept it up. "Huelga!" The deputy slammed the door. "Well then rot in there! Fuck you!" We were getting on their nerves.

Later the men were taken from the large collective cell, which was the eating room, and placed in small individual cells. As I was being taken to a new cell, a deputy grabbed the glasses off my face and I instinctively grabbed back. We ended up on the ground and another deputy grabbed my neck in a chokehold and I nearly passed out. They dragged me to a cell and threw me in without my glasses, and I hit the side of the cell opening as I was pulled in, bruising my shoulder, but fortunately not my head.

We were finally fed late that evening. The dinner included unusual amounts of lettuce, a practice that would be noted by strikers in other jails that summer. We refused to eat the lettuce in solidarity with the lettuce boycott. The male strikers sat and talked, but the sounds of shouting from the women's wing could still be heard.

By the following evening the word was out that we would soon be released. The mass arrest had broken into the national news, and pressure was on the Sheriff's Department to let us go. We were released pending trial on the charges against us. Holding hundreds of strikers in jail was not working to the growers' advantage.

Later in court, Jerry Cohen, the UFW attorney, would argue that the union had not been notified of the injunction that we had allegedly violated and we could therefore not be held liable. And so within several weeks the charges against us were dropped. Once again, bringing farmworkers in large numbers to trial was not the kind of publicity the growers were seeking.

Our release from jail was cause for a rally, and we were greeted by a noisy demonstration as, one by one, we left the prison. Emerging from the jail we saw a picket line, crowds of people, and a flatbed truck with amplified sound. Each arrested "striker" was invited up to the truck to say a few words to the crowd gathered around. I was released around the same time as Mary Ann and Pam, a friend and a collaborator with *El Obrero*. We all went up on the flatbed together. When I was handed a mike, I said, "Viva la huelga, abajo con los rancheros y sus títeres los sherifes." And, "Nosotros ganaremos!" (Up with the strike, down with the ranchers and their puppets the sheriffs. We will win!) But my mind was somewhat in a fog, and I couldn't find any more words. Marshall Ganz, who was emceeing the event, turned to me and asked, "Is that all?" "That's it," I said. But it wasn't long after climbing down off the truck that I regretted not having said more. There was one thing in particular I regret not having said, and that was acknowledging the women. Their tenacity, their spirit and militancy in the jail, to say nothing of their sharp tongues, stood out to me then, as they do to this day.

The mass arrest was the first of what would become a long summer of struggle, arrests, and brutal reaction.

Teamster "Organizers"

Before we arrived at Coachella, we knew we'd be facing Teamster goons. This was not new. In Salinas, Teamsters' so-called organizers appeared to help the growers whenever there was a dispute involving pro-UFW workers on ranches with Teamster contracts. The Teamsters were thoroughly hated by the majority of farmworkers, and they made no pretense of appealing to the workers' desire for justice. Their appeal was to power and the threat of physical violence.

Rumor had it that a Teamster local in Los Angeles had recruited the Teamster "officials" who were all over the Coachella area when we arrived there, standing guard at vineyards where work was going on. Officials or not, if these guys had been paid by the pound they'd have left the valley rich. Hardly one could have weighed less than 250 pounds, and they all looked as if they were wearing tire chains under their shirts, or maybe ate them for breakfast. They were mercenaries making $67 a day, a small fortune at a time when farmworker wages hovered around $2 an hour. Their leader, a tall, lanky local Teamster official by the name of Ralph Cotner was purportedly the nephew of a local grower. He wore a black hat (no kidding) and drove a yellow El Camino, always at high speeds. His habit of wearing black golf gloves led to rumors that he wore brass knuckles. It was also rumored that he was "packing."

The Teamsters officials were there to intimidate. As the strike progressed they became more violent. Over the course of the summer there were many reported instances of Teamsters beating striking workers.

Every afternoon there was a rally at the park in Coachella. These were the central political focus of the strike. At a rally the first day out of jail it looked like the numbers of strikers had swollen considerably. The actions of the first days of the strike had raised spirits of the workers in the valley. Several growers who had been waiting to see what would materialize that first day signed with the UFW. This included one of the larger growers, Lionel Steinberg, and another by the name of RK Larsen. They represented 15 percent of the table grapes. They agreed to a joint union/

grower-run hiring hall. The Teamsters contracts with the remaining 85 percent of Coachella growers allowed the use of labor contractors, long notorious for their abuses of farmworkers. The Teamsters also signed a contract with the Farm Labor Contractors' Association.

As the word got out about the actions in Coachella, farmworker union supporters from Los Angeles and around the region began to show up. In the evening rallies, workers who'd walked out that day were introduced to the crowd. Whether all of these workers had, in fact, chosen to walk out spontaneously, or had been previously organized to do so in order to create momentum for the strike, I don't know. But the effect was powerful, as workers were brought up to the microphone to "testify" about why they chose to strike.

Strike activity in Coachella began very early in the morning. Before first light even gave a hint of another day, both sides were out scouting the valley. The union sent out cars to do reconnaissance, to find out where scab crews were working, usually by following the company or Teamster vehicles or through tips from union sympathizers in struck companies. Once it was determined where work was going on, cars and vans of strikers would pull out from the central park area.

Both sides played cat-and-mouse games. The companies would send empty buses, windows covered by plywood, out to a field, drawing union cars in pursuit. It was not unusual for union pickets to go off in one direction as a diversion to draw the Teamsters away as the main "strike force" headed for another field. Several times I found myself in a car caravan hastily sent off with no particular destination with the yellow El Camino and other Teamsters cars and a couple of sheriff's cruisers in hot pursuit. It was amusing to drive around trying to elude pursuers, all the while making sure they stayed within eyesight behind us. A friend, who'd come with a group of Chicano students to a Coachella picket line, saw the Teamster goons running to their cars to give chase to a departing caravan of strikers, evoking shouts from pickets, "Hey, you're being paid to be gorillas, not rabbits!" These comic elements existed in an environment that was otherwise deadly serious. And the threat of violence was ever-present.

The strikers set up sound cars to talk to the workers in the vineyards. The Teamsters sent their beefy squads to guard the entrances to the ranches as the first line of defense against efforts to invade the fields, and they sometimes set up their own loudspeakers with music to drown out the strikers' agitation. Their favorite melody was "Bye, Bye, Blackbird." Sheriffs were usually present. While the media portrayed the sheriffs and police as *intermediaries* between the conflicting interests, striking farmworkers looked at them as little more than grower goons in uniform, paid for by taxpayers.

In some areas the union set up small picket lines. In others, a large force of strikers was concentrated to influence those working and to look for openings to invade the fields and chase them out. The Teamsters set up their lines to "protect" the strikebreakers. The two sides were constantly maneuvering.

In the afternoon we'd follow the work crews as they were leaving the fields for home. At night, when possible, strikers went to the houses and camps to talk to the strikebreakers. This became more difficult as time went on because the growers were putting guards at the camps. Sometimes these tactics paid off and workers would agree to either not work or to walk out the next day, something that required more courage but which had a very positive effect on the morale of the strike.

A confrontation occurred toward the end of the first week when a crew of pickers was put into a field directly off the road while club-wielding Teamsters and sheriff's deputies stood guard. The Teamster goons made obscene provocations to the several hundred strikers who were in an angry mood. Deputies were out in force decked out in riot gear. Sheriff's Department buses and vans stood by. It looked like a setup. But the strikers were not taking the bait and no arrests resulted from it.

With passing days the beefy field guards were getting more threatening on the picket lines, and I witnessed confrontations between groups of pickets and the Teamsters, who openly carried clubs, undisturbed by the sheriff's deputies while we were repeatedly harassed for carrying flimsy picket signs.

Lightning assaults at fields to get workers out and mass picketing in defiance of injunctions led to arrests, which mounted to the hundreds and continued throughout the summer as the strikes headed north with the crop.

Enrique and Virgilio

After the first night in Coachella, we were moved to longer-term housing, in small cabins in a labor camp near Mecca. My roommates were Enrique Guzman and his son Virgilio, whom I knew from an Interharvest broccoli crew. They hailed from a small village in Oaxaca and traveled every year to work the spring and summer in Salinas. Enrique was among the millions of corn and bean farmers in Mexico who lived (and still live) on the margins of existence, at the mercy of price and market fluctuations and agrarian policies that favor big landowners. It only took a couple of bad years and the pathetic looks of hungry kids to convince him that salvation lay in seeking a living outside Oaxaca, to the north. When Virgilio was old enough, he began bringing him along. Now they spent the major part of the year in Salinas, returning to Oaxaca only several months of the year, from around Christmastime to the beginning of the lettuce thinning in February.

Enrique was a good cook and prepared some simple but tasty meals in our little camp cabin. He confessed to his craving for his wife's mole sauce, known as one of the best moles in the village, he said proudly. Mole, a complex mix of chiles, nuts, spices, and chocolate, can be found in many varieties. It requires skill and patience to prepare. Enrique's wife had her own recipe, which she was reluctant to reveal. But Enrique knew her secret. One evening, with a twinkle in his eye, he said he was willing to reveal it to me. I waited, expecting some exotic ingredient I would probably know nothing about anyway. "It's the cocoa tree in our yard," he said, dispelling the mystery. "The fruit of that cocoa tree is the secret to that great mole."

Enrique, Virgilio, and I spent our days, sometimes into late evening, out in strike activities. At night we had time to talk, and Enrique would reminisce about his life in rural Oaxaca. He had stories of the local folklore of a culture than spans many centuries. But the story I recall best was about a frightening incident he had as a youth.

Enrique was walking from his home to a town some distance away when a sudden thunderstorm sent him running for cover. The lightning and rain were ferocious, as if the sky itself was on fire, and the wind and thunder made him feel the anger of the forest around him—the anger of the spirits that Enrique believed inhabited the forest. It was getting dark when he came upon a building near the path he'd been following, and he was able to pry open a window and get in.

It was a strange building, unlike anything he had ever encountered. As the dark thickened and the thunder diminished, he felt more and more uneasy. He sat on the floor in one corner, trying to stay warm, hoping to wait out the night to continue his journey in the morning. Everything around him was now pitch dark, with only the sound of the wind and rain thrashing at the windows. Suddenly, a loud clattering sound erupted from within the room along with a strange flickering of lights. His mind, already tense from the thought of the spirits that roamed the nighttime forests, spun into panic. He wanted to get out and run away, but outside the rain and wind were pounding the building with such force he dared not. Once again the clattering erupted, continuing for a longer time. He was sure it was an angry spirit cursing his trespass. He hid in his serape and awaited the worst. After tense hours he fell asleep. In the morning he awoke to find himself in a room filled with machines he'd never seen before. Daylight brought relief from his

THE BATTLE LINES SHARPEN, SPRING 1973 / 149

paralyzing fear, and he was able to continue his trip. Only later did he discover that the strange room was a railroad telegraph office and the clattering a telegraph machine. A simple enough story, but for Enrique it had implications for how he understood the world. He now had a word to describe the origin of his childhood fears, and fears that affected others in his community—superstition.

The Coachella grape strike evoked a significant outpouring of support from a broad section of society. Clergy, students, representatives of various ethnic groups, labor unions, fighters for different causes from ecology to Native American rights, workers from different industries, artists, and others. Many came to Coachella to express solidarity and walk the picket lines. The strikers warmly welcomed these supporters, introduced at evening rallies. The rallies helped to bolster morale. They also set the political tone of the strike.

The union was carefully promoting certain allies while shunting others. By far the greatest emphasis was put on the leadership of organized labor, especially the AFL-CIO and big unions like the United Auto Workers and liberal politicians. Nearly every visiting politician was accorded a hero's welcome. Of course, these were by and large Democrats. Ties between the union leadership and Democrats had been developing at least since 1968 when Bobby Kennedy visited César Chávez during one of his early fasts. Watching these affairs I found it difficult to stomach the adulation for representatives of a political party responsible for the nuclear bombing of Japan, years of hellish war in Vietnam, and the invasion of the Dominican Republic, to name just a few atrocities under Democratic regimes. Yet here they were, being hailed for their support of farmworkers!

Many union officials spoke to the daily rallies, expressing solidarity. There were unionists who extended a genuine hand of solidarity. Some extolled the glories of the labor struggle, employing an overblown (if not outright phony) rhetoric that I suspect they'd stored away years before, thinking they'd never use it again. For me one of the most disturbing aspects of these rallies was the adulation accorded George Meany, head of the AFL-CIO. Meany was praised as a great ally and friend of the farmworkers—the same George Meany who'd bragged before an assembly of business executives that he'd never walked a picket line; the same Meany who put the power and prestige of the most powerful federation of U.S. unions at the service of a murderous U.S. policy in Latin America and other places. When the CIA overthrew Guatemalan president Arbenz Guzman in 1954 and replaced him with the butcher Castillo Armas, they did so with the assistance of George Meany and labor groups directly linked to the AFL-CIO. Arbenz, it should be said, incurred the wrath of the CIA by threatening to take land from the mighty United Fruit Company in order to distribute it to poor and landless peasants. Castillo, who replaced him, outlawed all trade unions in Guatemala and began a prolonged period of slaughtering progressive unionists among many others, with nary a peep from Meany. This was only one of many such actions backed by Meany and the American Institute for Free Labor Development (AIFLD) group he supported.[9]

One afternoon as the rally emcee was falling over himself in praise of Meany, I said to the woman next to me, a nurse who worked at the union headquarters in La Paz, "Do you suppose they're talking about the same George Meany I know?" The nurse confessed her own revulsion with Meany, which she said was shared by other union volunteers. "I've been told César feels the same way," she said. "But the union is in a difficult spot and needs Meany's backing." Yes, the union was in a difficult spot. But what was the price for this "support"?

I shared with Enrique and Virgilio my concerns about George Meany and how what he represented was antithetical to the whole struggle for justice. Neither of them had any background nor knowledge of U.S. labor history, which was hardly surprising. Enrique had confidence that Chávez knew what he was doing, and he was not happy with me even speculating that something was not right. It strained the atmosphere in our little cabin, and Enrique lost interest in talking to me. Virgilio, on the other hand, was not enamored with César Chávez and his politics, which he considered reformist and not that visionary. But then, he said, "this is America" and "maybe that's all one could reasonably hope for." Neither one of them could really imagine a revolution in a place as apparently affluent as the United States. Even when I related my experiences and stories about the rebellions of black people and the massive resistance of soldiers, the disenchantment of students and youth and their turn to revolutionary ideas, the country beyond the fields still looked to Enrique and Virgilio like a massive impenetrable fortress.

Virgilio and I shared a common respect for the rebellious souls of the world. And we had a common disdain for Republicans and Democrats, which we regarded as parties of imperialism with slightly different styles and rhetoric. But our views diverged on other matters. Across the world this was a time of great debate, especially intense among politicized youth and students, over what future course humanity could pursue in light of such intense injustice, staggering inequality, and horrific brutality. That debate reflected the sharp division in what was regarded as the international revolutionary or Communist movement, between the Soviet Union and China.[10] This debate found its echo in the fields as well, most often, but not always, among youths influenced by the student movements in their countries. Virgilio and I spent many hours, on the picket lines and off, discussing the relative merits of the Cuban and Chinese revolutions and the theories of people's war, promoted by Mao, and the focoism associated with Che Guevara.

Between Pincers

AFL-CIO officials came to Coachella to assist the strike, but they brought with them AFL-CIO politics. One expression of this was the political buttons they distributed to strikers and supporters. It had a U.S. flag and the slogan, "Buy American." What the slogan meant in practical terms was foggy, but the real point was the button's ideological content, loyalty to America (corporate America, to be more precise) and its flag. It was wrenching for me to see people engaged in a movement for justice wearing a political symbol associated with massacres, invasions, and unjust wars in pursuit of exploitive aims, from the wars against the native peoples of America through Vietnam.

At the start of the strike any striker who wished was free to pick up a bullhorn or mobile loudspeaker and appeal to the workers in the fields. This agitation was interesting and often moving because the strikers poured out their feelings and understandings in very passionate and creative ways. They spoke about the ranchers and the years of exploitation under the Bracero Program, racism, and abuse suffered as farmworkers. There were references to the United States' theft of land from the Indians and from Mexico, and to the enslavement of blacks. Mentioned too was the historic aggression against Mexico—the invasions, the pitiless murder of Mexicans by the invaders, the plunder of Mexico's resources, *prestanombres* (U.S. companies using Mexican names) used by American interests to hide their control of Mexican land, production, and resources. Politically minded workers connected the growers' exploitation of farmworkers with a worldwide system that was guilty of crimes in Vietnam and other parts of the world. They appealed to the rebellious sentiments of the workers in the fields to join the struggle *para la justicia!*

But the freedom to express such views over the loudspeakers did not last long. As picket captains chosen from among farmworkers and AFL-CIO officials took charge of the loudspeakers, the political message came under tighter control, and agitation was reduced in scope, often to a repetition of a few slogans like "Abajo los Teamsters," "Que viva la union de Chávez!" or "Chávez si, Teamsters no."

The overall atmosphere within the strike began to take on a more controlled and even repressive tone. Only on the surface did it appear as though workers were free to air their opinions and therefore fight for their views at the meetings. In practice, a lot of orchestration and manipulation worked against such possibilities. In Coachella it began to feel as if the open democratic atmosphere one generally felt in Salinas in those days was being sucked away, like air from a closed chamber.

Sometimes comments from professional unionists were quite overt: "The UFW has got to start acting like a real union not a social movement," which echoed the criticism in the grower press. I felt this was really aimed at the more socially conscious and radical sentiments of the farmworkers. A "real union" acceded to the interests of the system as a whole, to which it demonstrated its loyalty while limiting its demands and protests to a "fair" share of the spoils of empire. But farmworkers, largely refugees from a country plundered by that empire, oppressed as a nationality and as immigrants, and held down as a lower caste, were not readily incorporated into such a scheme.

After the first week in Coachella, a union official called some of the Salinas volunteers together to ask us to stay around. I told him I had to return to Salinas. We had planned a demonstration there to celebrate International Workers' Day and I needed to be there to help organize it. The official looked at me narrowly and said sarcastically, "I'd rather make revolution than celebrate it."

I left Coachella with a feeling that the effort to crush the farmworker movement was not only coming from the growers and the Teamsters. Some of their allies—liberal politicians and some major union leaders —were just as determined to suppress unruly and potentially radicalizing influences of the movement in the fields. The difference is they were willing to see a union, shorn of any rebellious edge, continue to exist. They were willing to see the body of a farmworkers' union survive so long as any radical heart and spirit had been wrenched from it.

The farmworkers were being attacked on two fronts. But they also had many allies and the potential to bring to the fore a lot of support. The world was still in turmoil over the war in Vietnam, and the influences of the civil rights movement, the struggle of women for equality and liberation, and the anti-colonial struggles were still reverberating. And the farmworkers themselves were far from ready to roll over.

In early May the union announced that George Meany had pledged $1.5 million to assist the grape strike.

May Day

Several hundred people from the fields, canneries, local factories, and schools came to a May Day rally in Salinas that spring of 1973. Though the majority were farmworkers, the rally reflected that the movement, especially in the fields, was alive in other areas as well. The spirit of struggle unleashed by the 1960s and the farmworker rebellion continued to influence the political environment.

In Texas, workers from a huge garment company, Farah Pants, had gone on strike and, motivated by the example of the farmworkers, began a nationwide boycott of Farah Pants. Organizers from that strike were traveling the country, and several spoke to the May Day gathering at Sherwood Park.

From the back of a rented flatbed truck, in the shadow of the Salinas rodeo grounds, farmworkers spoke about Coachella, local strikes, and their determination to fight for justice in the fields; cannery workers spoke about struggles against speed-ups and harassment on the job; students and antiwar activists denounced the criminal war in Vietnam continuing behind the camouflage of "Vietnamization"; women active in the feminist movement spoke of the victory earlier that year in the historic struggle for the right to abortion.

There was a section of the world that had torn itself away from the imperialist system and was seeking to forge a different kind of social system, one that augured a different future. How that would happen was vague and full of contradictory views, and tended to get overshadowed by the immediate struggles at hand, but it was an element spoken to on that May Day

The local farmworker union officials who worked in cooperation with the Revolutionary Union and the *El Obrero* staff to organize the Salinas May Day event would soon find themselves under a barrage of criticism. Different trends in the movement and the union were becoming increasingly at odds.

Breaking into the Lettuce

By May the Salinas harvest was in full swing. For a time the previous winter I drove tractor, disking and plowing fields, alone but for the birds that came to feed on the worms and seeds left in the wake of plowing. With spring approaching, I worked on an Interharvest broccoli crew, and when the work slowed I cut lettuce by the hour for Sam Andrews, an outfit that produced chopped lettuce for McDonald's and Burger King.

Now, back from Coachella, I had my mind set on a lettuce ground crew. There was a mystique of sorts that surrounded the lettuce workers—*lechugueros*—on what was called the ground crews. They had a reputation as a tough group, and after 1970, militant fighters. Arguably they were a key component of the 1970 strike. The slowdowns and marches of angry *lechugueros* in defense of their new union contracts shook up the valley. They had a certain strength they brought to the struggle, which was thought of as "toughness" but was really a result of being organized and a highly skilled group that was hard to replace. And this, in turn, was related to the nature of the lettuce industry.

Lettuce was and is big business. In the early 1970s it was worth $273 million a year, $175 million in California alone. Between May and November the Salinas Valley produced on the order of six million heads of lettuce *a day*, supplying 70 percent of the total lettuce consumed in the country. A large percentage of the total acreage devoted to vegetables was planted in lettuce. As one description of the business put it in the early 1970s, "Lettuce is to the vegetable industry what Chevrolet is to GM—the volume product, the financial backbone, the meat and potatoes, the cash crop, the action."[11]

Lettuce is not grown to feed people; it's grown to make a profit. Any grower who forgets that will soon be looking elsewhere for a livelihood. However, profit depends on market price, and market prices fluctuate.[12]

When vacuum cooling was invented in the 1950s, cutting and packing lettuce for market became the task of a crew in the field, the ground crew. The growers had a need for trained, efficient, and mobile crews that could be brought into action quickly at any time in the yearly harvest cycle, in accord with the dictates of the crop and the market. Prices in the lettuce market were volatile. For a grower the difference between turning a profit and losing money could be a matter of days. So getting lettuce harvested at the precise time in its growing cycle, especially when market prices were up, was of crucial interest to them. [13]

The lettuce crop migrates with the seasons, moving south in winter and north in spring and summer. Thus ground crews tended to remain together and travel as a unit from Salinas to Firebaugh-Mendota, Huron, Blythe, or Poston/Parker Arizona, Brawley, Calexico, Yuma, and so on, year-round, in rhythm with the growing seasons. Working by piece rate, lechugueros could make more than other types of field workers so they tended to stick with it for years. This is a key factor why Salinas became the fortress of the union struggle in those days. Lettuce workers were a more consistent, organizable, year-round workforce than workers in grapes, or other fruit or vegetable crops. If you were looking for workers that fit the stereotype of the meek and helpless farmworkers, scattered, disconnected, incapable of defending themselves or fighting effectively, submissive and resigned, you would *not* find them among the lechugueros.

I looked forward to breaking in as a lechuguero, to the physical challenge of working on a ground crew, and the better pay it offered. Easier said than done!

Work on a piece-rate ground crew required experience and physical endurance. It's virtually impossible to keep up with the experienced workers without considerable practice. On such a crew it's not the foreman or supervisor who'd stop you if you were not up to doing the work—the crew would. That's because piece-rate work was *en bola*, in a group, not individual. Boxes packed by a crew on a given day are divided among them. Anyone not doing his share drags the crew down. And because cutters and packers advance through territory, anyone too slow is left behind, forcing a crew member to do extra work to help, an impossible burden to handle for long.

I learned ground-crew lettuce work like many other workers, by splitting a job with another inexperienced worker. After working this way for several weeks for a contractor, I decided to go it alone. At Sun Street near the corralón there were a number of camps where labor contractors picked up workers to fill out their crews—a kind of informal labor shape-up.

With my lettuce knife and small file in their cardboard *funda* resting in my back pocket, I approached Willie Morales, a stocky and surly labor contractor with a loud, commanding voice and a head of thick curly hair boiling out from under his *cachucha* (baseball cap). Willie was working for Pacific Lettuce and he was short cutters and packers that day. "You're a cutter and packer, eh?" he said, looking down at the yellow water container in the back of his El Camino. "Ya, I am," I said. "Sabes cortar y empacar?" he said, asking the same question in a slightly different way. "Como no" (sure), I said, "tengo mucha experiencia." Actually, at that point, I couldn't pack to save my life, but I felt I could hold my own cutting. Sometimes, depending on the group you're with, it's enough.

"All right." That's all Willie said to me. I had to ask around to find out that his foreman had space in his van for a ride to the field.

It was a typically damp Salinas morning, and the lettuce was wet, slippery, and cold. Workers often wore gloves at such times to keep their hands from getting numb. I had no gloves. But I was too nervous to let a little cold and numbness distract me. I had only one thought on my mind—*moving fast*. After finding two partners, and learning, to my relief, that one preferred packing, we set off on our rows.

The lettuce was not ideal. A lot of it was soft, without well-formed heads and unevenly mature, which required measuring to find which heads were ready to cut. But there must have been a good price and strong demand to cut in this marginal field.

I stepped into the irrigation row between the beds of damp, green lettuce, bent over, and cut, moving my body back and forth, cutting, trimming, placing the trimmed heads on the center row for the packer. Moving . . . you've got to keep the knife moving . . . stabbing under the plant with a sharp quick stroke, hoping for a smooth cut, then flipping the head over to strip off excess leaves and, if needed, another cut to get a smooth stem. When the rhythm is right and your instincts are working well, you can cut lettuce with one stroke and lay it down in the row without further trimming; this is when you feel like you're really in your groove, so to speak.

I went forward for several hours, as quickly as I could, groping for the good heads, without pausing to look around me. Only when the foreman called for a break did I dare stand up. When I did, I found, to my great relief and joy, that I was in the middle of the pack of cutters! I was over the hump in my debut as a lechuguero.

If all there was to harvesting lettuce was cutting and putting it in boxes, a machine for that purpose would have been put in the fields by now. The lettuce on that day was not well formed, but the market allowed for it anyway. Still, you couldn't cut every head, because some of them were clearly too open and unformed to be marketable. So, selection was necessary. A head that is passable one day may be left in the fields the next. This was a matter of judgment and experience. Where human lettuce cutters have the ability to select lettuce and make judgments based on the vagaries of the market, communicated to the worker through the foreman or supervisor, machines, at least up till now, do not, at least not economically.

Ground-Crew Joys and Sorrows

The basic units of the ground crew were the trios: two cutters and a packer. Add to that several box closers and loaders, sometimes a water-boy to wet down the lettuce, and you had a crew. There was also a stitcher on a truck to make boxes, essential for the operation, but stitchers were a different category of workers, most often Anglos or occasionally chicanos, and usually under the same contract that covered Teamster drivers. The metaphor here was hard to miss. The stitcher-driver made boxes for the whole crew, making an amount on each box. This added up to a sum higher than any of the crew on the ground could make. And he stood on the bed of the truck, above the crew on the ground. This was a racial/ ethnic, economic, and physical divide, but this is the way the system was organized.

On a good day a crew would cut and pack "*un carro por trio*," a truckload for each trio: 640 boxes of twenty-four heads, 15,360 heads of lettuce per trio, 153,600 heads per crew of thirty-five. If you do the math, that's fourteen to sixteen heads per minute per cutter for an eight-hour day. And sometimes you could do that production in six or seven hours, moving through the field like some crazy plodding machine in a posture our hominid ancestors had the good sense to abandon many millennia ago.

Moving in that unnatural position that long, at that speed, day after day, wreaks havoc, and it was a rare individual who could handle the stress past his forties. I knew only one older worker on a ground crew. He was perhaps sixty. They called him El Toro because he was built like a bull. The younger workers held him in high regard. He held his own. He was the exception that proved the rule. Add to the stress of such work, the rigors of migratory life, including being away from one's family most of the time, and no easy access to health care, and you had a life with a great deal of physical and psychological stress.[14]

Still, on a good day on a ground crew, it could almost feel like play. Well, that's a bit of an exaggeration, but if you felt in sync things just clicked. The lettuce itself mainly defined a good day—small, firm, and nearly round without a lot of extra foliage, but enough to provide a cushion and allow the heads to be packed firmly and with a stem that was easy to cut smoothly, all ripe to cut. We're assuming a mild Salinas temperature, with the cooling winds blowing off Monterey Bay. Of course, a good day also depended on your physical and mental state of mind. When all the stars of weather, lettuce, and body aligned, you could tear up the field, as it were, do a *carro por trio* by one o'clock and put $80 to $100 in your pocket, good money in those days. And the afternoon to burn!

But also possible was a field of lettuce that, for whatever reason—variety, left in the field too long given the temperature, too large, or worse, misshapen and hard so that cushioning foliage had to be stripped just to get it to fit in the box, or lettuce with discolored leaves that had to be stripped off or with little sections turning to slime that had to be cut out—work became hell. In fact, put a crew in such a field, add heat to the mixture, and you'd have a day that would make hell seem like a vacation spot.

There were days when you felt you were struggling for survival and losing. As a cutter you felt awkward and off balance with lettuce too large to hold in your hand. It would slip off before you could properly smooth the stem, and because of its awkward shape, it was hard to hit at the right angle or put in orderly fashion on the *"hilo."* As a packer you were jamming the heads to make them fit, catching a nail painfully on the side of the carton. Such events were frequent enough to keep a packer's nails sore and discolored. For as long as I packed lettuce all my nails were constantly black with bruises.

There were days when the finished pack was far from the ideal of four neat rows of heads, perfectly aligned with a slight slope toward the middle of the box, and you had to adjust the heads to give them the semblance of order the company demanded. Only the most skilled packers, and I was not among them, could pull off such a trick. And to top off your good fortune, on days like this the company men, bugged by their sales department, might just pay a visit to the crew to hassle you for your pack. What does a grocery store buyer know about the misery that comes with such a box? And if they knew, would it make a difference?

Even on good lettuce days, enough heat could destroy you. I remember days during hot spells, or when cutting deep in the valley past Soledad, where once cool bay winds arrived mean with heat, and by late morning you were already cooked. At a certain point, from the lack of salt and other minerals, you couldn't sate your thirst, and your body began aching with a deep, wracking pain that made you think that maybe death was a welcome alternative. With the crew pushing each other, and with *un pedido* (an order) that had to be filled, you could do nothing but shout out to whatever beings may or may not hear your suffering: "Chinge su madre, que pinche dolor!" (Mother fuck, what pain!).

Such conditions of work were not only uncomfortable, but dangerous and potentially fatal. It's called heat stress.[15] On such days, returning to the bus was our salvation, liquor stores our oasis, beer our medication. Cold cans of beer, a bag of potato chips or chicharones, a bottle of hot sauce, and you began to feel restored. Beer, the salve and savior, was both a blessing and curse. It numbed the body and restored the liquid balance. But it could also be addicting and often was. Sometimes the beer would continue. On a Friday, with a fat paycheck, the temptation to have just one more beer before going home sometimes proved fatal. I knew workers who'd leave the field with a big check on Friday and be in the field on Monday morning borrowing from a crew member or asking the foreman for an advance, flat broke, the rent and food money in the cantina's till.

This is not to say that working in lettuce was all suffering, not at all. We were working, outside, with the sun and wind and a beautiful valley spread out around us. At times there was more playing, goofing, and kidding going on than you could find in a lot of jobs.

Battle in the Grapes: Summer of 1973

Summer approached and unfolded, and a grape strike became increasingly volatile. By the end of April, strike activity in Coachella was cooling down, but about to heat up in the much bigger grape growing areas to the north, first in the area of Arvin Lamont, then Delano.

As May began, seventeen grape growers in Arvin Lamont dumped their UFW contracts covering 10,000 workers and signed with the Teamsters.

On May 10, George Meany announced a contribution of $1.6 million to the UFW strike fund. That same day a Kern County judge issued an injunction limiting picketing to four people at any entrance or exit to a vineyard.

The Coachella grape harvest began weeks late because of a cool spring. One grower complained that grape-thinning costs were two to three times normal because pickets and the bullhorns disrupted work. Later, the UFW claimed that nearly 50 percent of the grapes in Coachella were lost. But the growers didn't budge.

On June 1, in an Indio restaurant, Mike Falco, a Teamster heavy, sauntered over to where John Banks, a Catholic priest and UFW press liaison, was eating with a reporter from the *Wall Street Journal*. The Teamster sat down across from the priest, mocked him, and with a swing, smashed his nose.

By mid-June Coachella growers were complaining about low-quality grapes due to "inexperienced Teamster workers." Cool weather delayed the grape harvest in many areas.

On June 23, 180 Teamster "counter-pickets" attacked 400 UFW pickets at an asparagus field southeast of Thermal.

A few days later Teamster guards at a ranch near Arvin charged into a UFW picket line with clubs, beating UFW strikers.

On July 5, following the fights on the picket line and bad publicity, the Teamsters pulled their guards out of the grape vineyards.

Labor contractors under Teamster agreements complained that Teamsters were not signing contracts with growers fast enough, leaving them stuck with paying the promised Teamster benefits.

By mid-July, Gallo and Franzia, two of California's largest wineries, formerly under UFW contracts, signed contracts with the Teamsters.

In Firebaugh 350 melon workers refused to sign with the Teamsters and were locked out of their camp.

On July 18, hundreds of UFW strikers were arrested in the Arvin area for violating a court injunction limiting picketers at struck ranches to one picketer every 100 feet.

On July 19, 1,000 picketers massed at Fresno County farms, and 350 were arrested for violating a court injunction. Arrested picketers were taken to the Fresno County Industrial Farm, then to county jail. The *Fresno Bee* reported: "Deputies said they tried to *avoid* arresting any women or children, although many were among the pickets at the ranch. It eased the arresting process and one deputy added, 'Let's face it. Those women are vicious. The men are no problem.'"

That same day, the *Fresno Bee*, on its front page, wrote: "50 pickets ran through a cantaloupe farm and chased out scabs near Five Points"; 827 arrests were recorded in two days. New injunctions limited bullhorn use to one hour a day.

On July 20, the *Fresno Bee* noted on page one that 435 pickets were arrested in Fresno County, and thirty-two more in Tulare.

The owner of the Jack Harris ranch in Five Points began disking under his melon crop because he said he was "tired of strikes."

Also on July 20, farmworkers arrested on the picket lines refused to sign citations.

In Kern County authorities *refused* to arrest 500 strikers for trespassing because of lack of jail space.

On July 21, 128 strikers were arrested even while 600 strikers remained in Fresno jails. Both the industrial farm and the jail were jammed with arrested strikers. The city began looking for more jail space.

A Kern County judge ordered 439 jailed strikers, arrested for picketing in Arvin Lamont and Shafter Wasco, released. Strikers refused to leave unless all jailed strikers were released.

Three busloads of longshoremen and other labor supporters came to Delano from San Francisco and Los Angeles to support the grape workers on strike.

On July 22, a *Fresno Bee* reporter stated: "In almost hit and run fashion, the UFW has been picketing and striking throughout the valley, creating some labor shortages and taxing law enforcement agencies and the judicial system." "More than 1,600 arrested this week."

In late July, 300 to 400 melon workers walked off the job, and growers had problems getting replacements.

Telles Brothers, owners of Tri-Produce, Inc., and John Guimarra of the Delano growers said growers wouldn't sign with the UFW unless the hiring hall was dumped.

On July 23, the UFW charged that nine prisoners in a Fresno jail were forced to run a gauntlet between twenty sheriff's guards who beat them. Strikers were forced to sleep on concrete floors without blankets, and on bunks without mattresses. One prisoner reported on conditions: "Lying in stagnant filthy pools of water created by overflowing toilets. Rats run free through the cellblocks. Only 25 percent of those arrested were allowed phone calls."

On July 24, a county clerk from Reedley, Gladys Bowden, told the press: "There's such a mess at that jail you wouldn't believe it. We can't get through, there's no communication."

On July 25, 435 more strikers were arrested at Long Ranch. The front page of the *Fresno Bee* pictured a long line of farmworkers waiting to get on sheriff's buses.

The same day, sixty farmers arrived at the Song Ranch with clubs and sticks. Farmers remained in the orchard where forty workers picked nectarines.

Then, on July 26, 2,000 workers at a UFW meeting voted to strike Delano growers.

The press reported that Fresno police spent "far more than $102,000" in overtime pay due to strikes. In Kern County overtime pay cost $25,000.

The press reported on July 26 that more than 2,000 arrests took place the previous week. A San Joaquin court ordered limits on picketing and bullhorn use.

Harris Farms Inc. of Five Points put its melon crop up for sale for 1 cent per pound because it couldn't get anyone to harvest them.

On July 27, Kern, Fresno, and Tulare counties reported 2,200 total arrests. Some strikers were arrested two or three times. Of 439 arrested the previous day, 267 were green carders.

City official complained of $122,000 in police overtime expenses in Fresno. That didn't include jail costs.

On July 29, the Central California Farmers Association representing 800 farmers met to plan ways to assure a supply of labor.

Coachella growers claimed it was a "terrible" marketing year because of the weather and boycott, not the strike. Some said only the weather caused the problem.

On July 30, UFW talks with Delano grape growers collapsed.

On July 31, 300 strikers were arrested in Southern Fresno County, including priests and nuns.

On Wednesday, August 1, the *Fresno Bee* reported, "The UFW marshaled more than 3,000 pickets. In Fresno County Tuesday 313 were arrested including 40 priests and nuns."

On Thursday, August 2, the press reported that Chávez offered the growers arbitration, by someone appointed by George Meany, of any contract dispute between UFW and the growers.

The same day 150 strikers were arrested at the Song Ranch near Reedley. Those arrested included Dorothy Day, head of the lay Catholic Worker movement; 2,000 to 2,500 UFW supporters were picketing in the morning.

Friday, August 3, Teamsters and the AFL-CIO held talks. It was reported that one element of the talks would be UFW acceptance of the National Labor Relations Board (farm laborers are not covered by the National Labor Relations Act). The papers reported 3,000 strikers arrested in the two previous weeks.

On August 7, a Fresno paper reported on renewed efforts to pass a farm bill to allow for union elections.

On August 8, 430 UFW supporters were still being held in jail, as Daniel Ellsberg and other personalities were reported on the picket lines.

On August 9, the Teamsters, the UFW, and the AFL-CIO held talks in Burlingame. Four hundred strikers still held in jail were told they would be released under the condition that they would not picket again. A sit-in by seventy-five UFW supporters thwarted an attempt to evict seventy-one striking farmworker families, including 400 children, from Gallo housing.

On August 10, two UFW pickets were shot while entering a field to overturn grape boxes. Neither was badly injured.

Reverend Eugene Boyle, jailed in a Fresno County jail, called the jail "a medieval tomb-like sarcophagus." Criminal charges against 249 UFW supporters were dropped because of lack of facilities to try them.

On August 14, Nagi Daifullah, a twenty-four-year-old farmworker supporter of the UFW from Yemen, was killed in Lamont when he was hit from behind by a sheriff wielding a heavy flashlight.

On August 16, Juan de la Cruz, a sixty-year-old farmworker and one of the original strikers from 1965, was shot and killed on a picket line near the Guimarra Vineyards outside Arvin. A twenty-year-old Filipino worker was later arrested and charged in the shooting.

On August 17 more than 5,000 people, including a contingent of Yemenese farmworkers, marched in Nagi Daifullah's funeral.

On August 18, the UFW executive board met for ninety minutes, reportedly with sharply differing views about whether the strike should be continued.

On August 20, charges against 167 strikers for unlawful assembly were dropped and told nothing would happen to them if they didn't get arrested for six months.

On August 21, 5,000 people participated in a mass and funeral for Juan de la Cruz. They marched six miles from Arvin City Park to Arvin District Cemetery. Among the supporters of the union were Joan Baez and Taj Mahal.

On August 22, 250 UFW strikers stormed a vineyard at Franzia Brothers to drive out "14 non-union employees." Some of the fourteen were armed with clubs.

On August 23, UFW pickets rushed melon fields to drive out scabs.

The wave of struggles in the fields was without precedent in its extent and duration. From April until August courts in five counties handed down sixty-three injunctions to limit the strikes.

Salinas Wildcats

Rumblings in the fields also rolled through Salinas. In early June, lettuce prices were peaking, at a robust $10 a box. A ground crew from the Bruce Church Company stood gazing at a lettuce field that had been cut over twice before. Meanwhile the foreman was unloading a contraption from a company pickup that had been introduced into the fields the year before by Bud Antle, a little handcart that held a lettuce box while it was being packed. The workers referred to the device as the "*el burrito*," the little burro, or or "la burra." The burrito was supposed to improve the look of the packed lettuce, but it slowed the work substantially and was therefore unpopular with the workers. Looking over the field, one lechuguero commented, "No ganaremos ni pa' comer aquí. Ya vamanos" (We won't make enough here for food. Let's get out of here). They refused to enter the field and after a time were returned to the company camp.

On arriving at the camp crew members were given slips of paper informing them they were fired for refusing to work. The crew headed down to the Teamster headquarters on Market Street to demand that the union fight for their jobs. At the office of Local 890 they were told everything would be taken care of. The next day the crew was informed by the company that they were permanently fired. Anger spread out like a shock wave. All the ground crews refused to work and headed to the fields to set up picket lines with Teamster flags. When a Teamster official informed them they could not strike with that flag, they headed to the UFW office. The Teamsters, who could not allow a strike without jeopardizing their relations with the growers, called for a general meeting of Bruce Church workers.

A Bruce Church Striker

Richard, a longtime Bruce Church lettuce worker, whom I knew from my first Interharvest thinning crew, sat at his dining-room table with a six-pack of tall beers in a paper bag on the chair next to him, relating the blow by blow. He grinned as he described the Teamster meeting: "This guy Louie was leading this meeting, at the Teamster hall. This may be the first meeting ever of farmworkers at the Teamster hall. It was the first time I stepped into that place. Then Louie sees some UFW people, from the office, in the group and he says, 'We're not having this meeting as long as the UFW people are here.' 'Then we're not meeting'—that was Francisco, from my crew. So everybody just walks out of the meeting. Now it's not just the lettuce crews but everyone who decides. No way, man. I'm outta there."

Richard takes a long drink from a tall can and berates me for drinking so slowly. "You'll be all night drinking that," he says with his mischievous grin. "And I got to be up early in the morning . . . to go to the picket line. You know I'm a *huelguista*" (a striker), he says with special emphasis and with a hint of irony. "Then Mike Payne comes to the camp the next morning." Richard finishes the tall one, crumples the sides with his large hand and places it in the paper bag and pulls out another. "We went there to go out to the picket line, but Mike Payne wants to talk. You know Mike Payne?" Before I can answer Richard says, "He's the general manager of Bruce Church. Payyyne," he says drawing out the vowel sound. "You know, like *dolor*. That's what I told the guys at work," Richard says with an intensity that grows with the alcohol he keeps pouring into himself, "Mike Dolor." "Miguel," I remind Richard and he laughs, "Ya, Miguel Dolor." I laugh at the thought of the conversation and the seriousness he's giving to it in his account.

"So Mike Payne—you know who he is, right?" He repeats, a habit of repetition that tends to accompany his beer drinking. "He tells the guys at the camp, 'you can come back to work, we'll give the crew, the fired crew, another chance.' But it's too late now because everybody's all riled up! 'We're not braceros anymore,' they're saying and they tell Mike, I mean, Mr. Payyyne, 'We'll let you know'—about going back to work. But no one wants to go back." Richard looks slyly at me. "They've been held down too long, been oppressed too long, they remember what mister Payyyyne said to them . . ." says Richard. "About the strike?" I ask. "No! About the houses," Richard says emphatically. "The houses?" I repeat. I've haven't the slightest idea what Richard is talking about, but I'm used to these unexpected tangents in his conversation. Talking to Richard when he's drinking is like riding with a wild driver who might turn unexpectedly on a whim. "What did he say about the houses?" I'm trying not to get annoyed. Richard leans forward, his neck stretching in my direction, "About how he doesn't want any of the lettuce guys buying houses in town." "Why is that?" "He says because they're not intelligent enough. Mike Payyyyyne doesn't want these guys to settle in Salinas, he only wants intelligent people settling in his town." "He said that?" I say, shocked that anyone would be so openly crude and condescending. Richard is still leaning toward me, his big outstretched hand holding a tall can, "Ya. 'You guys should keep traveling,' he said to the guys. 'Don't settle down here, we don't need you here.' That's what the Payyyyne said to the guys."

The best I could do was shake my head at this. "That's why the guys don't want to listen to Mike Payyyyyne," Richard says with a kind of melodramatic intensity. "That's why the guys want to rebel, they want to rise up," and again Richard laughs, but his normal sarcasm is laced with a noticeable strain of indignation, unusual for him.

"Better be careful, Richard," I said. "You're gonna start sounding like one of us." Richard ignores my remark, but he says in a loud whisper, "I got to be careful so La Loca doesn't hear me." At that moment Maria, a white woman in her late fifties with graying hair and a fleshy face, enters from the kitchen and sits at the table with us. "I heard what you said you old boozer. I walked a picket line with my dad before you were old enough to suck your mama's nipples," she says. She has a beer in her hand, and she takes a small sip and looks at Richard.

"You shouldn't talk that way with guests here," says Richard, scolding. Maria answers back quickly, "I suppose Bruce has heard worse in his life. Isn't that right?" I nod, lamely. "I know what a strike is," Maria continues in her somewhat raspy voice, taking more sips of beer as she talks, "I'm from the Dust Bowl crowd, don't think we didn't see our share of troubles and fights." "But this is different," says Richard, with a sidelong look and mischievous smile. "This is revolution," he says now giving a little laugh. "Well," Maria says sharply, "you'll probably be drunk when it happens and miss the whole goddamn thing!"

"Still, it's more serious now," says Richard. Maria nods. "Maybe so, Richard, I don't have a crystal ball. You're a grown man, you can do what you think you gotta do." "You didn't want me to strike in '70," says Richard, annoyed. Maria looks at me, "Would you go out without strike bene-fits and nothing in the bank? That strike was a long shot. And anyway, I didn't think those guys were that united to win a strike. And guess what?" Then she stops, maybe thinking better of what she had intended to say. "So what finally happened with Mike Payne?" I asked, filling in the dead space in the conversation. Besides, I was interested in that. "Mike Payyyne," says Richard, "thought he could talk everybody back to work. But the guys remember what he said to them. And then guys start talk-ing about how we pay dues to the Teamster but we get nothing for it. So people started yelling and he just left." Richard laughed at the memory of it all. "A few of the Chávez guys said they all should strike. And here we are. Now I'm a *huelguista*." He savored the sound.

The strike spread to the rest of Bruce Church's fields. The workers set up picket lines. Teamsters sent several carloads of goons to confront people on one of the picket lines, and allegedly brandished guns and threatened the strikers. Word about that aroused disgust throughout the valley, and workers from many companies organized by the UFW ranch committees began showing up at the picket lines and at rallies.

Lettuce ground crews at Salinas Lettuce Farmers Coop camp on Airport Boulevard met at their mess hall one evening and decided to strike, too. The next day company buses escorted by Teamster organizers showed up at the camp. Company officials were moving in to try to force workers onto the buses. Lechugueros from Interharvest and other ranches were tipped off and showed up to support the wildcatters. They blocked the entrance to the camp, preventing some of the Teamster organizers from entering. Soon the Teamsters were surrounded by a growing mass of workers, and the temperature started to rise. One of the Interharvest workers, who stood maybe five-foot-five, took a fighting stance and angrily challenged some much larger Teamster "organizers." Despite his small stature, he wasn't getting any comers, perhaps because he wasn't alone and because he had a reputation. This wasn't just bravado; he had a black belt and his own school for karate in Mexicali.

Then a contingent of police, sirens blaring, screeched to a stop in front of the camp. They formed a skirmish line separating the two sides, allowing the Teamsters to leave the scene unscathed.

Several hundred wildcatters and workers from various companies now showed up at a Bruce Church field. Teamster officials showed up but were outnumbered by strikers and fled. This time they were followed by carloads of farmworkers. When the officials reached their office at Market and Sanborne, they locked the doors and began firing out the windows at their pursuers.

Incidences such as these continued to roil the valley throughout the summer. Monterey County's sheriff and Salinas's police department complained publicly that the cost of policing the wildcat strikes throughout that summer of 1973 was double that spent during the general strike summer of 1970.

Inspired by the anger and the desire of the workers to resist, César Chávez held a meeting with the Church workers and promised there would be another Salinas general strike, and this time, he swore, neither the courts nor anyone else would break the strike. There is no reason to doubt Chávez's sincerity. But it was not to be. The wildcat strikes eventually lost steam and a general strike never materialized. Forces were in motion that would push things in another direction.

A Strike Called Off

In Delano, the situation was tense, perhaps explosive, as the grape harvest approached. Fully one-half of California's table grape crop was on the line.

In early August George Meany made a television appearance on the heels of a much-publicized meeting with Teamster head Frank Fitzimmons. The meeting was billed as Meany's attempt to resolve the dispute between the Teamsters and the UFW. As events would prove, the Teamsters had no intention of resolving the conflict in favor of the UFW and such meetings and the headlines they produced only created greater confusion among the public.

In the aftermath of the killing of Nagi Daifullah and Juan De La Cruz, the UFW Executive Board voted to call off the strike. The anticipated battle in Delano never happened. Strikers were asked to go to the boycott.

When the decision to abandon the strike and return to the boycott was announced to the striking workers, some of them offered to turn in their strike benefits and continue the strike without them. Neither the mainstream press nor the union's own paper reported those sentiments.

It was not going to be easy to revitalize the boycott and turn it into the kind of massive social movement it had been in the late 1960s. Things were changing socially. The powerful activism of the earlier period was diminishing. And there were other problems. The public was confused. And pressure was mounting to rein in the movement in the fields. New funding was not forthcoming from the AFL-CIO. George Meany was down at the mouth. He indicated that despite the AFL-CIO's desperate attempts to save the UFW from defeat the strike had done poorly.[16]

"Illegals" Take the Fall

Labor contractors were recruiting people to break the grape strike. The UFW denounced this loudly. But it took the issue further: it denounced the recruitment of "illegals" to break the strike.

The first time I heard "*los ilegales*" being singled out as strikebreakers in Coachella, I was stunned. It had to be a mistake, an unthinking slip of the tongue of a union supporter caught up in the passion of the moment. When I asked about this among the picket captains, I found both confusion and hostility. Soon it became clear that this was not an errant comment, but official union policy. Not only were "illegals" being denounced as strikebreakers, the union began making a public issue of demanding that the Immigration Service come and deport them!

This was hard to fathom. There were undocumented workers among the strikebreakers, but they were not the only ones. Undocumented immigrants were part of the strikes and part of the union. But even more, "illegals" were the most abused and mistreated section of the people. To single them out—could that be anything but divisive? And to think that the INS—whose operation was geared to serving the interests of growers and the government, both in terms of "opening the gates" when farm labor was needed and deporting workers at the end of the harvest, and carrying out deportations when political expediency dictated—would act in any way that would benefit the long-term interests of farmworkers or be a positive force for the union movement by deporting "illegal" strike breakers seemed a bit, well, delusional.

There was great controversy among farmworkers and many union activists about the union's position. I and others around *The Worker* found ourselves sharply at odds with some of the activists we'd been friends with and respected.

The arguments sometimes got intense and bitter. Those who supported the union's position argued that gains in the fields couldn't be consolidated so long as the growers had a steady supply of workers from Mexico to undermine strikes. This had to be stopped by any means necessary. If that meant appealing to and putting pressure on the immigration authorities, so be it. They argued that the union had to do what it was doing to survive, that the union leadership didn't prefer that kind of a stand but they had the responsibility of running the union. Those who opposed this policy of appealing to the INS were accused of being second-guessers, of criticizing without having to bear real responsibility.

To be provocative I asked, "What if labor contractors brought in black workers to break the strikes? Would you support an appeal to the KKK if that organization could get rid of strikebreakers?" People would deny the analogy held up. But what I think it came down to was the migra was a "legitimate force," part of the state, therefore their actions (terror) were more justified than the actions (terror) of vigilantes like the KKK.

To believe that anything good could come from pressuring the INS to aid the union struggle is to believe a myth about U.S. Democracy, to believe it is a government standing *between* contending classes and interests in society. In this view of democracy, different classes, farmworkers and growers for example, vie for influence. The growers generally have the advantage because of their money, but sometimes the poorer classes can muster enough strength to offset this and get the INS, for instance, to sometimes act in the interests of the oppressed.

The state, far from being neutral, rigorously upholds the interests of capital. The very existence of capital—private ownership and control of the means to produce things—depends on the exploitation of labor. This is sacrosanct and always will be under bourgeois democracy. No matter how much "pressure" is brought to bear through argument or protest, you cannot change that basic nature.

Promoting the view of the capitalist state as a neutral arbiter fits quite well with a dominant myth, that the Republicans represent the interests of big business and the Democrats the interests of the workers, oppressed groups, the poor, the lower middle class. Rhetoric aside, so far no microscope yet invented has been able to detect the subtle and minute differences in actual immigration policy as practiced under Democratic and Republican administrations.[17]

The farmworker movement, powered to a great degree by a deep hatred for all the ways Mexicanos and immigrants are mistreated, exploited, and marginalized, was a powerful force that energized the union movement and served as an anti-chauvinist pole in society. But what happens when such a movement is diverted into opposing the undocumented? Once you unite with the system's enforcers against another section of people, you are now promoting the corrosive logic of supporting the oppression as long as *I get my cut*. It is the soil from which reactionary, anti-immigrant, and discriminatory movements are engendered. It was argued that farmworkers understood that the "anti-illegals" campaign was just a tactical maneuver to aid the union in its immediate battles. But that fails to take into account the ideological effect of such a campaign, which can only sap the progressive energy from a movement. It was an indication of the direction in which the union was headed.

As the strikes proceeded north, the call for the migra to stop the flow of illegal strikebreakers grew in intensity. It became the union's principal preoccupation.

A Paper Burned, Another Banned

When Guadalupe Varela didn't show up for work for several days on the lettuce crew, I began to wonder. We were trio partners and we had become friends. When he married earlier in the summer, I was his best man. After the wedding there was a large reception in a rented hall in the middle of a Central Valley barrio, filled with people from the neighborhood.

In front of a group, lined up appreciatively in front of a large beer keg, Lupe hung his thick arm around me and announced jovially, "Ya somos campadres! Cómo la ves?" *Compadre*, as I would gradually come to understand, was more than a friendship; I was now like family.

Perhaps that explains my concern for Lupe's absence. And since Lupe rarely missed work, his absence for a good part of the week was notable. At the union hall that week, I saw him sitting in his van. He looked exhausted. "Where've you been?" I asked. "Hey, compadre," he said, his distinctive large eyes nearly rolling back into his head, as though he'd just taken a healthy shot of tequila. "I just got back from La Paz. Man, compadre, I am fucking tired." "I thought you went to La Paz on the weekend. What were you doing back there again?" I asked. "Delivering papers." "Delivering papers? Isn't that where you picked them up?" "Well, ya," Lupe said gripping the steering wheel, "I picked them up, but then I had to bring them back."

"You're just messing with me now," I said pretending to be annoyed. "No. I delivered the papers, but then I had to bring them back to La Paz so they could be burned." "Burned?" "Quemado, prendido fuego. Let me put it this way, compadre," Lupe said, straightening up now behind the wheel, "César's not happy with your friend Ruth. I think she's packing her bags right now to leave La Paz." "They kicked her off the *Malcriado*?" I asked, really curious now. "And out of La Paz. Maybe California. Like I said, César's pissed."

"She put some stuff in *Malcriado* that César didn't like. You know those wildcat strikers in Detroit, something like that. She put some stuff in the paper that was critical of the United Auto Workers. César hit the roof. I heard he didn't like the article about Chile that much either. So after delivering all the papers from La Paz to Sacramento and coming back here, I had to go back to Sacramento and pick up all the damn papers I'd delivered around the valley and take them back to La Paz. I just got back. I don't think I got any sleep in three days."

La Paz was the union headquarters, and Lupe was one of the main distributors of the union paper, *El Malcriado*, a job he did on his own time on weekends. Every issue he'd load up his van and drive down the San Joaquin distributing thousands of union papers to stores, restaurants, social agencies, clinics, and so on, especially to those places frequented by farmworkers. "Move over, Lupe, I'll drive you home, man," I said to him. "No, but thanks, compadre. I'm gonna sleep here in the van for a while, then I'm going home and sleep till next week!"

When I left Lupe, I thought of Ruth and all she'd been through. I had known her years before when she was studying and teaching in Santa Cruz. She showed up in Salinas earlier in the summer soon after her return from Chile where she'd been working in the barrios of Santiago with groups who were part of Salvador Allende's Unidad Popular. Allende was elected president of Chile in 1970, and there were great hopes that his regime would lead to positive changes for working people. When I saw Ruth in June or July, we talked about her experience, what she'd seen and learned. She was hopeful that the great activism among the poor and disenfranchised people, along with students and progressive groups, would lead to a new, more just and more independent kind of society, free from domination by the United States, Anaconda Copper, and other big business interests. We even debated some about the idea of a peaceful transition to socialism, which was a concept some people in Chile believed was possible. There were others who believed this was dangerously illusory. I found myself in the latter camp.

Ruth was passionate and hardworking. After returning from Chile, she got a job working in the fields and as a volunteer with the union office. It was not long before she was sent to La Paz, where her writing, editing, and language skills were welcomed and she was made editor of the union paper, *El Malcriado*.

I saw Ruth again in Salinas in September, shortly after the Pinochet coup that overthrew the Allende government. She was in torment, emotionally torn apart with worry and heartache. She had been unable to communicate with her friends in Santiago. The word was coming out of widespread military roundups and murders of members and supporters of the Unidad Popular; of the horrific situation in a Santiago's National Stadium where people were beaten, tortured, and shot by the Chilean military. In that stadium Chilean soldiers, in an act of sadistic savagery, cut off the fingers of Victor Jara, the Chilean folksinger, before executing him.

It was no secret to people who followed events in Latin America that the CIA was behind the coup. You didn't have to wait for the *New York Times* to reveal insider information from "unnamed sources" or for a Senate hearing to reveal the truth to "shocked" politicians. If the average person on the streets in Chile, if politically aware people in the United States, knew that the CIA was working to get rid of Allende long before it happened, then certainly the U.S. media and politicians in Washington also knew. Blood was on the hands of the U.S. government as much as it was on the Chilean military's.

So after the September 11 coup, it was not hard to understand why Ruth would seek a way to denounce it, expose the brutality, and point out how the United States was implicated in it.

But it wasn't the article on Chile as much as the Detroit wildcat article that prompted the paper burning. The story out of Detroit was also compelling. Detroit in the summer of 1973 was a place of tense conflict, centered on the auto factories, as increased competition was putting pressure on the auto companies for greater productivity (exploitation),which resulted in intense speed-ups on the production lines. In 1946 three million vehicles rolled off Detroit's assembly lines. By 1970 that number had risen to eight million. In that same period the number of auto workers increased by less that 50 percent. Increased production was achieved by mechanization and by pushing production workers faster and longer under unsafe and unhealthy conditions. The companies called this automation. Black workers in the plants, placed in the hardest and most dangerous jobs, were disproportionately hurt and even killed by these speed-ups. They called it "niggermation."[18] A rash of protests against dangerous conditions hit the auto plants. A mood of defiance, especially among those influenced by the radical political climate of the times, was spreading into the shops.[19]

An important form of protest was the wildcat strike, that is, not authorized by the union. The first big wildcat of that summer of 1973 took place at Chrysler's Jefferson Avenue assembly plant, where 90 percent of the workers in the metal shop were black. Poor conditions in this shop were aggravated by the racist attitude of a white supervisor. Seventy percent of the shop workers signed a petition to remove the supervisor, but both the management and the union disregarded it.

In late July, two workers from that shop, Isaac Shorter, twenty-six, and Larry Carter, twenty-three, climbed into the electric power control cage and locked themselves in. By pushing a button, they halted the assembly line at the start of the first shift. They said they were prepared to continue the occupation until the supervisor was removed and they were granted amnesty. Shorter and Carter held out for thirteen hours, protected and fed by other workers of various nationalities, including workers from other shops who huddled around the cage with chains in case anyone tried to remove them by force. In the end the company agreed to their demands.

A photo taken of Isaac Shorter and Larry Carter being carried from the plant on the shoulders of their jubilant fellow workers after the successful Jefferson Avenue strike became symbolic of the whole wildcat insurgency in the summer of 1973. The photo made it into the local Detroit paper and into hundreds of alternative and labor-oriented newspapers around the country—and onto the front page of El Malcriado.[20]

Because the wildcats took place in defiance of the United Automobile Workers (UAW), they were an embarrassment to the UAW leadership. That these wildcats made it on to the front page of El Malcriado was mortifying for the UFW leadership, which had received financial and political support from the UAW. So while Lupe was racing down the valley collecting issues of El Malcriado from surprised shopkeepers, boycotters in cities around the country were gathering copies wherever they'd been distributed. According to one story, UFW's boycott staff in Detroit combed through the halls and offices of the UAW headquarters frantically gathering all the copies of the paper. They succeeded in gathering up all of them, except one, a copy that had already found its way onto the desk of Walter Reuther, UAW president.

The *Salinas Worker* also carried a front-page article about the wildcats. About a week after the *El Malcriado* affair, I walked into the union hall and was pulled aside by Roberto Garcia, who was working in the Salinas field office. He wanted to talk to me, but he didn't want anyone to overhear. I had known Roberto since my first weeks in Salinas. In the wildcat days in the seasons following the 1970 strike, he'd gotten a reputation as a union militant. We had been on friendly terms, but as political conditions were changing our relations were becoming more strained.

Before the 1970 strike Roberto was a foreman for a labor contractor. When the strike broke out in August, he was busy recruiting and transporting scab crews into struck ranches. One day, while trying to bring a busload of strikebreakers through a picket line, a man stepped in front of his bus, forcing Roberto to stop. The man was his father. According to the story Roberto liked to tell, he got off the bus, joined the picket line, and never went back to work for the growers. He became part of the strike and then a union organizer and field office rep.

Roberto spoke English and Spanish fluently and emanated self-confidence, traits that served him in his foreman days and now in his new role. He was formidable in appearance—not tall, but wide, thick, and stocky with a bulldog face and large thick neck and hands. He looked like a brawler, and he could play the role. Roberto could be both disarmingly good-natured and charming, and he could be intimidating. He used these qualities to his advantage.

Roberto was an early promoter of *El Obrero* around the union hall and once confided that workers liked the "stuff you guys put out" better than the union's stuff because of its more militant edge. But things were changing. And as I was standing facing him in the small office behind the dispatch windows, he was coldly serious. "I got the word about the *Worker* paper. It can't be sold around the union hall any longer—that's it. You can't distribute it around here now. OK? You heard me, right? Don't talk to me about it. No, I'm not interested in talking about it. You got problems with that, call La Paz." He was proving to be a good organization man.

Gallo by Submarine

I was confronting a major invasion of ants in the kitchen of a duplex on King Street in the Alisal district where I was living when Juan Aguirre came by. He was a ranch committee member from Almaden Vineyards at San Ardo. We first met on a picket line at Brown and Hill Tomatoes in King City and then a number of times at union meetings. He'd passed the word about May Day in the King City area and came with his family to the event at Sherwood Park. But I hadn't seen him since then.

"What brings you all the way up here? You didn't come to help me with the ants, did you?" "Problems with ants, heh?" he said. "I'll switch with you. I'll take your ants, you can have our *ratoncitos*." "Which ones, the ones in your house or in the government?" He laughed and we sat down at the kitchen table to talk over some instant coffee.

Juan was young and enthusiastic about the union and changes taking place in the fields. He'd come to the United States when he was very young and so spoke Spanish and English fluently. He took an interest in the Chicano movement and struggles in the black community, in international affairs and the war in Vietnam, to which he was strongly opposed. He saw U.S. involvement there and other places around the world as part of an imperialist agenda of domination. He took an interest in events in China, Cuba. and elsewhere in the so-called socialist world. And we would often talk about these things when I saw him. But this visit was for reasons closer to home.

"How's the grape-picking business?" I asked him as I handed him the jar of Nescafé. "I'm glad you asked," said Juan, "because that's what I'm here for, to talk to you about *piscando uva* (harvesting grapes). You know Gallo signed with the Teamsters, right?" "Ya, along with just about everyone else."

Gallo, Franzia, and a few other wine producers, like Almaden and Paul Masson in San Ardo, signed contracts with UFWOC early in the five-year strike and boycott that began in Delano in 1965. Easily identified product labels made wineries more vulnerable to a boycott. Ernesto Gallo, especially fanatical about grabbing "market share," feared a boycott might thwart his goal of making Gallo the biggest wine dealer in the world. By 1973 one-third of all the wine consumed in the United States was produced by Gallo. And Gallo used 25 percent of all the wine grapes grown in California in his operation, though the company only grew a small percentage of that on its 3,500 acres of vineyards. So Gallo signed with the UFW in 1967 and again in 1970, which was clearly an important victory for the union.

But when the tide turned in 1973, Gallo swam with it. In late June, after months of "fruitless negotiations" with the UFW, Gallo signed with the Teamsters, claiming, as all the growers did, that this reflected the will of his workers. Gallo publicly objected to the union hiring hall that was part of the UFW contracts. Gallo said this was a hardship for his longtime and loyal workers, mainly Portuguese immigrants from the Azores. Such was the common complaint of the growers. But curiously, while they objected to the potential unfairness of the union hiring hall, they had no problem turning the fate of their workers over to labor contractors, the human equivalent of hungry vultures. Gallo fired many of his "longtime, loyal workers" and hired others to replace them and, at the same time, moved to evict striking workers and their families from the company labor camp in Livingston.

"So, you're here to recruit pickers for Gallo now, and you knew I'd be a good choice for that?" "That's right," said Juan, "I'm surprised you guessed so quickly." "Must be our mutual love for the growers," I said, "we just think alike." Juan laughed at that. "OK, so you're ready to work?" "When do we start?" "Monday," said Juan. "You, Antonio, and I are going to Livingston to work for Gallo. The union has a plan for us." "Ah, the union. So we're going to be spies for the union!" "Submarinos!" said Juan. "How long?" "Just a few days. I can't stay away from work that long, nor can Antonio. How about you?" "I'm working in the lettuce right now but work is slow. I can get away for a few days."

We arranged to meet on Sunday for our trip to Livingston. On the ride there we discussed the union's plan. We were to work with scab grape pickers for several days, and then, at an arranged time, strikers on the picket line would invade the field and we, inside, would do whatever we could to "discourage" the strikebreakers from continuing to work for Gallo. What that meant exactly, none of us knew.

We arrived in Livingston on Sunday in the early afternoon. Our bodies, used to mild summer temperatures on the coast, felt sapped by the dry Central Valley heat. We went by the Livingston union hall hoping to see Aggie and get more information, but the hall was nearly empty, though I did run in to Pam Whalen, who had recently moved to Livingston to help Aggie as a volunteer. Pam had just gotten a job at Foster Farms processing chickens on an assembly line. It was an unpleasant job and the pay was lousy, but Pam was happy and enthusiastic. "Working in such a factory may have its downside, but it does provide punning opportunities, not found in every chickenshit job," she joked. Pam was interested in union organizing and saw promise in that factory.

Unable to make contact with UFW officials, we went looking for the place to sign up as strikebreakers. We had no problem finding the right place. We drove into a Gallo ranch and found the office to sign up. There were a couple of security guards outside, and we assured them we were there for work. As we stood outside the office, we overheard the guards talking. I heard one, an African American, say to the other, a young white fellow, "You know what's the word, right?" "What's the word?"

"Thunderbird!" The guard laughed. "I heard that," said the white guard. The young black security guard continued, "That's Gallo's thing, Thunderbird, Ripple, the ghetto drinks, for the winos, man, it's cheap rotgut. I seen people rot away on that shit. But Gallo makes out like a bandit selling that shit."

I knew that Thunderbird was a Gallo brand. The union pointed this out in their boycott literature. I knew that Thunderbird was a drink often favored by street alcoholics because it's cheap. What I didn't know was that Thunderbird was jacked up to 21 percent alcohol to give drinkers a quick jolt. Nor did I know just how consciously this drink was developed to target the black community.

In the late 1950s, when Ernest Gallo was consumed with a passion for expanding Gallo Wines' market share, he had his marketing crew go out into the cities and neighborhoods to sniff out new opportunities. Perusing liquor stores in the Fillmore neighborhood of San Francisco, one of the marketing people noticed that these stores routinely kept lemon juice and lemon-flavored Kool Aid near the racks with white port wine. By asking around, he discovered that customers liked to mix the lemon juice to cut the sweetness of the port, giving it a more balanced flavor. From this discovery, Gallo came up with the idea of mixing white port and lemon juice in a drink and marketing it to the black community. This was the origin of Thunderbird, which became Gallo's number-one-selling product and put the ecstatic Ernest Gallo over the top of competitors, beating out Italian Swiss Colony in the race for best-selling wine companies.

To ensure that Thunderbird reached its target market, Gallo engaged in an aggressive promotion campaign, going so far as to litter skid row gutters with empty bottles of Thunderbird to increase "product awareness."[21]

It was obvious to us that the black security guard was not just talking for the benefit of his fellow guard, but for all the dozen or so potential strikebreakers, standing around the area. He was laughing about Thunderbird in a light, joking way, but there was sarcasm in the mix and a hint of bitterness as well, maybe like the lemon in that sweet port. He felt free to put down Gallo to an audience of strikebreakers and peons of Gallo who couldn't care less about the company. His manner also spoke to his "in your face" brashness.

We signed up at the Gallo office to pick grapes. We each filled out a short application and were escorted to the strikebreakers' camp. It was a cluster of little huts of wood with a roof overhang and screens but no glass on the windows. It was one room with two bunk beds and sink at one end with a small counter next to it. In front of the sink was a small table and chairs. There was a single light bulb dangling from the ceiling. At the Gallo office we were given a propane-powered green camp stove to do our cooking, and each of us also got a blanket. The bunk beds had dirty mattresses with no covers. The single blanket meant no hardship since the nights were so warm any blanket at all would seem oppressive.

It was late afternoon by the time we had moved in to our new quarters, and we went out for a bite to eat. We went to a Mexican restaurant, hoping to overhear something or learn something about the strike, but nothing. We talked about our "assignment" and concluded that we would try to talk to as many strikebreakers as we could to let them know just how fabulously rich Gallo had become from the labor of his workers, and point out to them how he treats them now. Since we were bilingual, we thought we could reach a number of people. That was about as far as we knew how to plan.

Early in the morning we made our way to the Gallo office to catch a bus to the vineyard. The bus drove us through a noisy picket line with sheriffs standing guard, along with others who were probably Teamster goons. There was a shed and an open space in the middle of a large vineyard, and here a group of us, the new scabs, were given a brief orientation about the picking, shown how our tractors worked, handed shiny metal tubs to hold the grapes and a small curved grape knife for cutting the bunches.

Work was done in teams of three to five people. Each team had a tractor and a gondola. As the tractor was moved between the rows of vines, each member of the group would cut the grape bunches into the tubs and then dump the contents into the gondolas. When the gondola was full, one of the team would drive it to the weigh station, where the gondola would be weighed and its contents dumped into a large container, from where it would be taken to the washer and then to the crusher. After weighing, a company weigher would mark the team's card with the weight and grape varietal, which would determine its value since each varietal paid a different rate per ton.

Once the gondola was emptied, it would be driven back to where the group was working to begin the process again. The faster and harder we worked, the more we would share at the end of the day. We were going for weight.

A Gallo foreman assigned George, a white guy in his fifties, to work with us. George was short, with a reddish complexion and short light hair that was turning gray. He had the flushed look of someone who drank too much. George was from the South, slightly noticeable from his accent, and had been on the road for years. When he talked about himself and his background, I thought of Roger Miller's song, "King of the Road," though George's road in life did not seem as romantic as the song.

It was early and still pleasantly cool when we began to cut grapes. We sat kneeling under the vines, our knees in the dirt, our tubs just in front of us, reaching up to grab the bunches of small red grapes, which may have been pinot noir, a grape named for its dark pine cone-shaped bunch. I was tempted, as no doubt all new pickers are, to push a few of these little round sweet things into my mouth. And they were delicious, sweet, juicy, and delightful—at first. As time went on the delightfulness tended to dissipate, and the sweet juiciness lost some of its appeal.

After our first gondola was filled to the top, Antonio jumped on the tractor and headed for the weigh station. When he returned a while later, he said to Juan and me, "We got a problem." Dropping his tub under the vines and sinking to his knees he explained, "I tried to talk to the guys out there lined up with their tractors, but most of them don't speak Spanish *or* English. They're Portuguese!" So much for plan A.

As we worked, we could hear the noise of the picket line in the distance. Morning coolness gave way quickly to heat, and then more heat. By late morning it was sweltering, and then really sweltering. The dirt we sat in began migrating up our bodies and onto our faces where it mixed with the sweat that oozed out of us forming little streaks, made sticky by the addition of the grape juice that gradually became part of the mix.

It was late morning when George turned, startled at the sound of a thump and then another thump as Juan and I emptied our tubs into the gondola. "What the hell you guys throwing in there?" "A little of this, a little of that." "You guys throwing rocks in there?" "Rocks, dirt." "What the hell, man!" George looked wide-eyed and upset. "You can't just throw shit like that in there!" "Take it easy, George. This is a strike. We're strikebreakers. Look around. Gallo's got a few people, not nearly what he needs to harvest all his grapes. He needs us, so he ain't easily gonna fire us. Besides, he doesn't want to see some disgruntled scabs walking out to join the picket line, right?" "Ya, George," said Juan. "And Gallo's a fucking millionaire and his money comes from peons like us. Do you think he appreciates that? Look, he dumped his own people when they just tried to get a little break, a little security, a little something better for themselves."

George wasn't that happy about our dumping habits, either out of fear of being fired or some sense of moral obligation to his employer, a morality, I would venture to guess, his employer didn't share. Poor George found himself picking grapes with a group of nihilistic psychopaths, but what could he do? I worked next to George and spent some time talking to him about Gallo, but I didn't let on, yet, why we were really there.

It was shortly after noon when I started feeling light-headed. I realized I hadn't eaten since the night before, except grapes, and I didn't think I'd fare too well without food. One of Gallo's foremen was making the rounds, a young blond-haired guy, and I called him over. "When's lunch?" I asked. "You can eat any time you want," he said cheerily. "No.

I mean, when do you serve lunch?" "We don't serve lunch, you have to bring your own food." "No one told us that!" I said. "Hell, we'll never make out here all day without food." I called to the others, "Hey guys. They don't serve food to the workers here. Whatya say we go out and get some food?" At that the foreman became more accommodating. "Listen, hang on, I'll see what I can do." And within a half hour or so we all got sack lunches: a sandwich, chips and a soda. It was a Happy Meal, before McDonald's ever thought of it. It was skimpy, considering the calories we were burning up in that heat, but I couldn't resist the temptation. "Listen, guys, if they're gonna feed us great shit like this, whatya say we just say fuck the strike and stay here and work?" Juan and Antonio just nodded, "Ya right." George looked at me with a puzzled expression.

We got our last card for the day marked and rode back to our camp. We were filthy and exhausted and hot. Back at the camp we headed for the toilet and shower room. The facilities were poor. Some of the toilets were stopped up, thin wooden grates on the floor the only barrier between us and fetid water. The shower water had a bad smell to it, and the water was only as warm as the heat it had absorbed from the pipes it ran through. Still, the relief of getting the sticky mud off our hands, arms, and faces was tremendous. After the shower we sat for a while outside our hut and enjoyed the still warm, but cooling day, relieved that the stinging heat was now fading with the setting sun.

The next day was to be the moment of truth. At noon we were to walk out and raise hell as the strikers streamed into the vineyard to drive the strikebreakers out. We talked over several possible scenarios, including pulling the wires out of the tractors or knocking over a gondola in the chaos we assumed would be going on. But there was not a lot more we could think of doing.

The next morning I again worked next to George. We could hear the shouts from the picket line. "George," I said, "you hear that? That's the people on strike. They're pissed off because we're taking their jobs." "Ah, don't mind them. They're all crazy. Just causing trouble." "Ya, but we're taking their jobs. And they're out because Gallo wouldn't bargain with them, wouldn't respect them even though they worked for him for years. We're taking the bread out of their mouths and their families. It's not right, what we're doing." George said, "You think like that and you'll be crazy, man! Don't mind that shit, it don't have anything to do with us." A while later I said, "George, we're really not here to work for Gallo, we're with the union, the strikers. We're here to help the strike. At noon we're walking out and the strikers are coming in. Do you want to stay here, or go with us?" George was a bit shaken by the news, but recovered quickly. "Well, I can't stay here by myself." "Can you get a job somewhere else?" I asked. "I suppose so." "So come out with us. You can join the strike for a while." He said he had to think it over. After more discussion he said, "I don't know about joining the picketing, but I'll leave when you leave." We all shook hands with George.

At noon we threw our tubs in the gondola and jumped on the tractor and rode out to the weigh station screaming, "Strike, huelga! This place sucks! Gallo sucks! Stop working! Leave! Gallo's a bloodsucker! Gallo sells bad wine! Join the strike! Viva la huelga! Gallo es una mierda, un chupasangre!" and other such things. But the other pickers, if they heard us at all, looked at us as if we'd just taken lunatic pills. No one from the picket line came in, so whatever noise there was came from us. And it wasn't very impressive. Even the Gallo foremen looked more confused and perplexed than angry. We walked out. But we walked alone.

We were greeted warmly on a picket line with several hundred people. I said hello to Aggie and Pam, and they introduced us to some of the strikers. George was with us, but perplexed. Roberto Garcia was on the line, and I asked him why no one had gone in the vineyard as planned. "There was a change of plan," he said. But he didn't wish to discuss that subject further, at least not with me.

It was later that afternoon when one of the strike coordinators called the Salinas submarine crew together. "Before you go back to the valley we've got something you could help us with." Why not? We jumped in a car, one of the union's fleet of dusty old Valiants, and headed off. A few minutes' drive from the picket line we parked on a side road and walked up a dirt path to a clearing hidden by some trees and bushes to a makeshift parking lot filled with vehicles familiar to people around the farm labor scene—large American-made sedans and station wagons, an occasional pickup or van, probably not one of them less than ten years old. Farmworker cars. Our squad leader held out a large paper bag. As we pulled cans from the bag, she said, "We've got about fifteen minutes, let's see what we can do." Later, as we left the lot, walking briskly toward our car, I looked back at the parked cars, "SCAB" and "ESQUIROL" in bright reds, oranges, and yellows scrawled on their sides and windows. It wasn't something I felt any joy or sense of accomplishment doing. But I accepted it as something that needed to be done as part of the struggle.

A Pamphlet and Controversy

Throughout the summer of 1973, committees had been active in a number of cities in support of a boycott of Farah Pants. These committees had organizational ties to the Revolutionary Union. As the grape strike spread the length of California, these committees began to turn their attention to the grape strike as well, with the goal of organizing support for them in the cities, especially in California. This included sending caravans of workers and students to the strike areas, such as Modesto where Gallo was being struck. As part of this effort a pamphlet was published about the field strikes, placing them in a historic context of struggles in other eras in California's fields. The pamphlet noted important battles going on among different sections of workers in the United States. It stressed the commonality with the ongoing strike and boycott at the Farah plant in El Paso, where, in May 1972, 4,000 garment workers had struck for the right to be represented by a union. The strikers were virtually all Hispanic and 85 percent were women. And the pamphlet touched on the wildcat actions in Detroit. In this context it criticized the UAW leadership for suppressing the wildcats.

The pamphlet was overwhelmingly supportive of the UFW, and it vigorously condemned the Teamsters Union and its alliance with the growers. It had a composite picture on the front of farmworkers with a small UFW eagle on it, and it was distributed in the name of the "Salinas Citizen's Committee in Defense of Farmworkers." It was being circulated in the communities and workplaces in the Bay Area.

The committee had sent a representative, a former UFW staff member, to talk to Chávez to inform him of the solidarity work it was doing. But when the pamphlet appeared with its criticism of the UAW leadership's repression of the Detroit wildcat movement, it immediately came under attack by the union leadership. The UFW's paper, *El Malcriado*, carried a criticism of the pamphlet, and Chávez threatened to condemn it personally and publicly. He even threatened a lawsuit over the use of the union symbol on its cover. The goal of these committees was to rally mass support for farmworkers on the basis of their fight against the growers and thus to spread the sparks of this struggle to other sections of the working class. We were taken aback by the union's hostile reaction. Though there were certainly important differences between the committee and its views and that of the union leadership, there seemed to be no reason why there could not be unity on common points. We viewed an open dispute with the union to be damaging, something negative for the movement and something that would make it difficult for the committees to function. So we concluded that the situation had to be cooled out. Some clergy, who'd worked with the union in the past and were close to the committee's work, wrote the UFW leadership defending the pamphlet. A meeting was requested on behalf of the committee, and Chávez agreed to one. I was part of the group that drove to the union's headquarters in La Paz to meet with César Chávez.

When the union relocated its headquarters from the "Forty Acres" compound in Delano to La Paz near Keene in the Tehachapi Mountains southeast of Bakersfield in 1971, it was in a moment of heady optimism. With the powerful 1970 Salinas strike coming on the heels of the victory in the grapes, tens of thousands of workers were now under union contract.

For César Chávez the previous twenty years had been an eventful ride. In 1952 he was a young man living in the San Jose barrio who caught the eye of Fred Ross, an organizer for the California Services Organization. The CSO, associated with the community organizer Saul Alinsky, was developing a reform campaign aimed at empowering the growing Chicano population of California. Ross recognized the spark in Chávez, and soon he was working under Ross's guidance as a community organizer.[22]

Chávez's odyssey to farmworker leader began in 1958 when, at the behest of the CSO he went to work in the Spanish-speaking community in Oxnard, a fertile farming area on the California coast north of Los Angeles. The CSO's organizing strategy rested on voter registration, elections, and work around immediate community issues. As Chávez began to preside at house meetings, a mainstay of CSO's organizing method, he heard local residents voice anger and frustration at the lack of jobs on the nearby farms.

These were immigrants who had settled in Oxnard to make their living in the fields. After Operation Wetback in the mid-1950s—an infamous campaign of ethnic cleansing aimed at the Latino community—the federal government pushed farmers to expand their use of braceros. Braceros were popular with the powers that be because they had no legal right to protest, could be used to lower wages and working conditions, and as long as they remained braceros could not settle down in the country. They fulfilled the white establishment's ideal for a non-white workforce that provided "production not their reproduction."[23]

The law stated that growers could employ braceros *if* there were no locals available and willing to work. But like most facets of the Bracero Program, this provision was violated, and aggressively so.[24] Growers and government agencies worked hand in hand to keep locals from getting field jobs. When a "local" managed to find work in celery, tomato, or carrots, growers simply claimed they were not up to the job and fired them.

Under Chávez's guidance these abuses were documented and used to pressure federal agencies to enforce the law. Small breakthroughs in securing a few jobs encouraged people from the community, and a struggle began to take shape. There were marches to back up the demands for jobs, including one that grew to many thousands.

The Oxnard experience ignited Chávez's interest in organizing farm-workers. But this was not the path the CSO wanted to take, and Chávez was asked to give up the project. Not long after he left Oxnard, the organization he built fell apart and, according to a disappointed Chávez, was consumed by infighting and divisions. Oxnard foreshadowed the farm-worker organizing work that would come. It also foreshadowed Chávez's inclination to favor local residents over braceros and later the undocumented, in a way that tended to divide them rather than unite them against their common oppressor.

The Oxnard experience left Chávez with an intense interest in organizing farmworkers, and confidence in his ability to connect with them, to lead them. Within several years of leaving Oxnard, Chávez gathered his family in an old station wagon and headed to the heart of California's table grape country in Kern County. He had decided to take on the ambitious goal of building a farmworker organization.

Chávez had proven an energetic organizer with the talent for creative tactics. As he had done with the CSO, Chávez and the organizers who formed the core of what became the National Farmworkers Association held house meetings where they learned of the issues that weighed most on the workers. Here, one can be fairly sure, the stories of exploitation and abuse moved them. Yet the conservatism of the period and an awareness of the history of defeated farm organizing efforts made them wary of direct confrontation with the growers. The outlook was more long-term and gradual.

But events rapidly changed the terrain. First came the end of the Bracero Program, then the Filipino-led walkout in the grapes in Coachella and the looming battle in Arvin Lamont and Delano grape vineyards, which brought the Filipinos' call for Mexican workers to join them in a strike. Chávez hesitated to join the strike but then reluctantly agreed when it was clear that not to do so would have set back the organization.

Some 800 to 1,500 people gathered at Our Lady of the Virgin of Guadalupe church in Delano on September 16, the day of Mexican independence, to decide whether or not to join the strike. The gathering was filled with references to Mexican struggles for independence and revolution and the mood was "upbeat and energetic." One local farmworker activist called on the workers there to become true "sons of Zapata."[25] This was a potent moment for a people with a long history of being targets of racist oppression and exploitation, invasion, humiliation, and plunder of their homeland—all the more so in the context of a country shaken by the civil rights movement, and a beginning antiwar movement, with movements of liberation and revolution stirring across the globe.

The grape strike that began when about a hundred strikers showed up on the morning of September 20 at the NFWA's Delano office would face all the difficult problems that agricultural strikes had encountered many times in the past. But the context was dramatically different, and context would prove decisive.

But what is clear in hindsight can be far less so in the heat of the moment, with all its noise and contradictions, with all its weighty immediacies. And here I believe it is to their credit and of historic significance that once the strike was thrust on them, Chávez and the NFWA leaders' sense of outrage and the desire to advance beyond the confines that history had consigned to farmworker struggles led them to seek ways to sustain the Delano grape strike, even as the strike, at the end of the harvest season of 1965, was running into difficulties endemic to all such efforts. Sensing from the contact with students and others who came to support the grape strike that there was a public sympathetic to the reality of struggle in the fields, Chávez and the NFWA leaders put that reality on the march, from one town to another, and into the big cities.

A breakthrough came in the spring of 1966 at a moment when the strike was at low ebb. What began as a small march out of Delano built momentum as it moved north and became a major event by the time it reached the state capital in Sacramento. The grueling 250-mile walk aroused farmworkers and their allies in the small farming towns, but it also connected with a larger national audience and revealed the new mood that had begun to emerge. The strike broke through the encirclement and annihilation campaign the growers counted on to crush it. The grape boycott that followed put the growers on the defensive.

UC Berkeley students and civil rights veterans began to appear in Delano and became an important part of the union's mostly volunteer staff. Newly politicized students, and the more reformist-oriented Chávez, who came from a conservative Catholic background, did not make a perfect fit. But there was a great sense of unity and common purpose. While the farmworker struggle surged forward, there was much to hold people together: the empowerment of people long denied and the improvement of starkly oppressive conditions in a land that loved to boast of its high standard of living. Nor could it be said that Chávez and the NFWA (and later the UFWOC) leadership were immune from the influences of the powerful waves of struggle battering the U.S. empire.

Efforts to rein in the farmworker struggle, which developed and intensified over time, came from powerful systemic forces. I had seen up close how the more radical voices of farmworkers had been suppressed in Coachella. I was not alone in noticing a sharp contrast between the more open and democratic atmosphere in Salinas and the more closed and "controlling" climate one sensed the closer one approached the union's command center.

There were powerful pressures that would come down on any leader in Chávez's position. There was the socially conservative outlook of Chávez himself, limitations imposed by historical social divisions, and so on. How all these factors combined is an equation difficult to untangle, but as the conservatism grew it clashed with other views and passions within the movement. Vietnam is a case in point. After President Johnson's massive escalation of the war in 1965, opposition to it quickly emerged on college campuses. Dr. King publicly denounced the war in a famous speech at The Riverside Church in New York in April 1967, a year before he was assassinated in Memphis. Chávez, despite criticism from others in and around the union, refused to take a public stand against the war until 1969. By that time it was politically safe to do so, since prominent Democrats were staking claims as antiwar candidates.

It was early afternoon when we pulled up to a guard shack at the UFW's complex at La Paz. This former tuberculosis hospital had been purchased for the union by a friendly movie producer.[26] I never quite understood why Chávez had chosen such a place, so far from the fields, for the union's headquarters. In that period some thought of it as the seat of the empire. Representatives from ranches all over California and Arizona made their way to La Paz for meetings. Farmworkers were bused in for education sessions. Union volunteers and staff lived and worked there in buildings that once housed a hospital, but they were isolated from the farmworkers they served. Could this isolation have been, as some have suggested, part of the point of why Chávez moved the union's headquarters there?

I saw little of La Paz; we had no time to look around. We were immediately escorted to the building where Chávez had his office. After a few minutes he showed up. In this second meeting I attended with him, his greeting was less than cordial. There wasn't much sense of the friendly, modest man I had shaken hands with in Salinas several years before. Facing the four of us who represented the support committee was a businessman, a hard-nosed negotiator. He treated us like one of the growers might have at times treated him, as someone in an inferior bargaining position. The meeting had barely begun when Chávez punched up a number on his telephone and asked to speak to his lawyer, Jerry Cohen. "Jerry, is that lawsuit against that farmworker support committee being prepared? OK. Hold off on it right now, I'll let you know right away." No niceties, no small talk, no philosophical discussions, no light stories, no effort to examine common or divergent views; in fact, no effort to personally connect in any way, just hard ball. When I tried to explain the purpose of the pamphlet, Chávez cut me off. In the end we agreed to republish the pamphlet with the remarks about the UAW leadership deleted. In return Chávez agreed to publish an article in *El Malcriado* vindicating the pamphlet. No such article to my knowledge ever appeared.

The Color of Privilege

On some weekends, I accompanied a friend who drove a big rig for his family's business. This could be a grueling affair since the business was headquartered in Los Angeles. We'd drive out of Salinas to L.A. by car in the afternoon, pick up the 18-wheeler around midnight and head up to places like Half Moon Bay, San Mateo, Millbrae, and even San Francisco to pick up flowers. Then we'd return to L.A. with our load. The two full round-trips covered 1,300 or 1,400 miles over two days. My job was to keep the driver awake, which I had plenty of incentive to do. On a few occasions my friend Chad put me behind the wheel of the rig, but I was no match for it, especially on hills! The gearing system, along with all the other issues involved in moving and stopping a vehicle of such size and tonnage, was not something to be handled on the fly, at least not by me. And Chad really had no patience to teach me. So I looked for a place to learn to drive such a rig.

One day, after coming off work early from a broccoli crew, I stopped by a lettuce sorting shed on Abbott Street that I knew used big rigs, and I asked for a job. My proposition was, teach me to drive a big rig, and I'll work part-time for free in your shed until I can drive on my own. I wasn't so hot on driving a rig for a living, but I wanted to learn how to handle one.

The owner of the shop was in his office when I came in. He was in his fifties, stocky, with a large bald head. I stood behind one of those four-hinge doors where the top and bottom open separately. I had the look of someone just out of the fields, and when he came to the door he noticed my rain boots. I had just begun explaining my request when someone came up to the door and asked something in Spanish, which no one in the office understood. So I translated. "Where do you work?" the boss asked. "I'm working on a broccoli crew," I said. The owner's eyes widened. "Listen, son," he said as he opened the lower half door of his office and came out, "I wanna talk to you." He put his arm around my shoulder and directed my attention to the parking lot. "You see that car there?" He was pointing out a late model Chrysler Imperial, a car I loathed as one of those overwrought American monstrosities with too much chrome. "That car could be yours," he said. Was he going to give me the keys? "Actually I know how to drive a car, it's a truck I'm interested in learning to drive." He gave a sort of abbreviated laugh, but pulled me around. "Let me show you something, son." I was ready to chuck the whole thing right there, but he had a vise grip on my shoulder and directed me to a cooler room where several dozen people, a majority of them women, were coring and chopping lettuce coming down off a belt, depositing the chopped lettuce in a bin from where it was wheeled to another area and bagged. This was lettuce destined for McDonald's, Wendy's, or some such place.

"You speak Spanish. You work in the fields. So you know these people; I betcha know how to handle them." He could have been talking about a piece of fish. Handle them? "I really just want to learn to drive a truck . . ." "Listen," he said again, this time like he was talking to a recalcitrant son, and here I'd just met the man less than ten minutes before, "I need a foreman in this cooler. You'll start out with a modest wage, but if you stick around it will build up fast, trust me." I'm sure he meant what he said, which is why I wanted to get out of there as soon as possible. To hell with driving a truck. "OK," I said. "A foreman job in the cooler. When do I begin?" "You can start now, if you want, this afternoon." "Well, I really have to get home, I haven't eaten. But tomorrow, I'll start tomorrow. What time do you start?" "Eight o'clock. But come in at 7:30." "Sure," I said, happy to be out from under his friendly embrace.

If I'd been out of work, starving, and had a sick mother who depended on me getting this job to save her life, I might have considered it. But none of these were factors. Still I was impressed. Without even knowing me, this insightful businessman had discerned my suitability for the foreman job: I was white.

5. FIRES STILL BURNING

WHEN THE DUST CLEARED after the 1973 harvest season, the union held few contracts. Among them were the Coachella table grape growers Steinberg and KK Larsen, who signed just after the Coachella strike erupted; the wineries Almaden, Paul Masson, Vie Del, Novitiate, and Napa Valley vineyards; Interharvest and the strawberry grower Pik'd Rite in the Salinas and Watsonville area; a lemon grower, S & F in Ventura; and citrus workers at Coca-Cola ranches in Florida. The farmworker movement was facing a full court press. The year 1973 saw it stripped of nearly all table grape contracts, Franzia and Gallo wine company contracts, its contract with vegetable grower D'Arrigo Brothers, who had signed with the Teamsters in May, and Finerman, a vegetable grower located mainly in the Imperial Valley and Arizona areas, which broke off negotiations with the UFW in June.

In April, Freshpict, the Purex Corporation subsidiary, one of the first companies to sign following the 1970 strike, and which, at its height, controlled 42,000 acres of vegetable growing land in California, Arizona, and Colorado, announced it was selling off much of its Salinas and Imperial Valley vegetable growing operations. By July 1974, Freshpict announced it was going out of the business altogether. In April, a Federal Trade Commission judge ruled that United Brands (formerly United Fruit) should be forced to give up its farm operation in Arizona and California and barred from the fresh produce business for ten years. If carried out, the ruling would dismantle Interharvest, which accounted for 11 percent of all U.S. lettuce shipments and destroy the mainstay of the UFW in the Salinas and Imperial valleys.

By late summer of 1974, the *New York Times Magazine* published a long article by Winthrop Griffith titled "Is Chávez Beaten?" It was the journalistic equivalent of a funeral dirge.

In response, César Chávez, drawing on Mark Twain, was telling crowds at rallies, "Rumors of our death are highly exaggerated." Nor did being around the fields in Salinas feel like impending doom. The union movement still retained a lot of its energy, fed by a mood of defiance among farmworkers in the face of the adversity.

Brush Fires

In the winter, spring, and summer of 1974 things were still smoldering in the fields and brush fires were erupting. There were large strikes in Stockton in the tomato and cucumber fields, in San Luis, Arizona, in the lemon orchards, in the central San Joaquin Valley in the melons. In February the UFW successfully shut down the Imperial Valley for several days in an action called to demonstrate defiance of the Teamsters–growers alliance. The stoppage covered all crops—lettuce, asparagus, melons, sugar beets, onions, and so on. On the evening of the stoppage, asparagus workers came to the Calexico union office and stated their intention to continue the strike for increased wages and UFW recognition, a determination that did not waver despite the union's insistence it had no funds to support the strike.

These struggles were both a continuation of the agitated environment of the previous year and the organized efforts of the union to fan brush fires into larger conflagrations as in the melon strikes that César's *primo hermano*, Manuel Chávez, organized around the Firebaugh area.[1]

Speaking before the UFW's second convention in Fresno in the summer of 1975, Chávez stated: "In 1974 . . . we engaged the growers in more strikes covering more geographic areas and [involving] more workers than at any time in our thirteen-year history"—an observation that was, at the same time, meant as a warning.

I spent much of the harvest season of 1974 cutting and packing for several lettuce outfits. After work I occasionally walked boycott picket lines at local grocery stores along with other, mainly farmworker, volunteers. In front of a Safeway in Salinas an elderly woman snatched and crumpled the leaflet I handed her and yelled at me, "Go back to where you came from if you don't like it here!" "You mean Long Beach?" I said. "You know what I mean," she said crankily as she hurried by.

"Economism"

Putting out the *Salinas Worker* continued to take up a major part of the time of a number of us—writing, translating, laying out, distributing. A number of stores in the Alisal district were regular outlets for the paper, and we were able to get hundreds out through them. The paper was getting better known in the camps, and farmworkers were supportive of it, so it was possible to distribute larger numbers in a shorter period of time.

But there were also ongoing concerns about our efforts. What had motivated most of us was the desire to be part of a revolutionary movement that could realize the promise of a different, more just society. This was a gigantic undertaking into unknown territory and there was lots of pressures to settle for something less, maybe a little reform here or there to *aflojar las cadenzas* (loosen the chains a bit), as the saying went. In the movement in those days there was not much understanding of the distinction between the economic struggle in the workplace and the struggle for a different kind of society. There was a strong tendency to believe that the one would lead to the other. This worked to narrow the range of political work. One of the ways this was reflected was in the tendency to limit the paper's coverage to the struggles around immediate conditions such as low wages, poor working conditions, disregard for the safety and well-being of the workers, controversies with the unions, and so on. But to do so would be to abandon the principles that had motivated us in the first place and ultimately capitulate to the very machine we were fighting. All this was magnified by the fact that the revolutionary movement was beginning a long period of ebb, and like the tide moving out, it exerted a strong pull to find some political accommodation to the system. Discussions around such issues were part of the political life of the time.

Nixon

The year 1974 brought Richard Nixon's political demise. A march in Salinas echoed the demand across the country that Nixon be driven from office. Not everyone in this effort was in agreement on its motives or its aims. The democrats and many liberals saw in this anti-Nixon movement the restoration of democratic values after a period of reckless, autocratic behavior. For many radicals and revolutionaries Nixon was not a blemish on Democracy, but its true face, and his falling out of favor in the eyes of powerful interests had more to do with felt need to restore people's confidence in the system rather than any intent to restore democratic principles. U.S. prestige had suffered a beating in the Vietnam War period, and there was need to patch the tattered mask of America as the "defender of freedom and human rights."

Much of the establishment condemned Nixon for spying and carrying out dirty tricks on political enemies and erasing sections of a tape that contained evidence of the tricks, and offered this as reasons for his removal.[2] But to many of us, these were hardly more than the normal workings and infighting in a corrupt political system. Not mentioned in the mainstream media were the savage bombings of Vietnam and Cambodia, the invasion of Cambodia, the bloody coup in Chile that Nixon and Secretary of State Henry Kissinger helped arrange, and the murder of students at Kent State and Jackson State that took place under his watch. These were real, serious crimes for which Nixon, among others, should have been indicted. But these were not even considered offenses, let alone punishable ones, in the U.S. political system.

Pearl Street

In the late summer of 1974 I moved into a small courtyard on Pearl Street in the Hebbron Heights area of the Alisal. A collection of tiny shacks, arranged in a horseshoe shape around a dirt parking lot, and a few playground swings made up this modest courtyard. Each shack consisted of a bedroom, a tiny kitchen, and a bathroom so small that to sit on the toilet required propping your knees against the opposing wall.

The move to Pearl Street came under pressure from the landlord of the more ample duplex on King Street. The landlord lived in the adjoining duplex and grew cranky over the constant stream of newcomers to our part of the duplex, in apparent violation of the lease. When Betsy, a young woman who'd come to Salinas the previous year to test life in rural California, left the area, returning to Milwaukee to continue college, I was in no mood to wage a fight over the place, which in any case would have been too expensive to keep on my own. So I too moved. With few possessions, not much more than fit in my rusting van, my move proved fairly easy.

The little court on Pearl Street was packed with farmworkers and their families. While my tiny apartment was cramped, I did not have to share it with a family of children or relatives as others in the complex did. So any inconvenience to me was relative. I didn't mind. Living simply was preferable, and at that time I had no aspirations to live any other way.

Buak

Early in July 1974, Teamsters Local 1973—so named for the year the Teamsters succeeded in stripping away UFW contracts in the grapes— announced it had signed contracts with fifteen Watsonville apple growers. The first apple contracts of many to come, they said. "The best-paid farmworkers around," claimed the Teamsters of their new members in the apple orchards. It was a kind of arrogant show the Teamsters were putting on to convince the world that field-workers were now in their hip pocket.

The timing of the announcement seemed less than coincidental. It came just one day before a much publicized appearance by UFW leader Chávez before a large gathering of farmworkers at Alisal High School, where Father Higgins, a longtime church activist for worker causes and active around farmworker issues in the early years of the Delano grape strike, reaffirmed the support of Catholic bishops for the UFW and their conviction that the conflict in the fields was not a jurisdictional dispute but an effort to destroy real unionization. David Castro, Teamster Local 1973 spokesman, publicly challenged Chávez to a TV debate as he pro-claimed their new conquest of apple growers.

There were rumors at the UFW hall that Teamster apple contracts might get challenged in the orchards. As late summer lettuce work was slow, I headed to Watsonville to find out what might be stirring in the orchards. Others on *The Worker* staff encouraged this, thinking that a story from inside the orchards would make for an interesting article.

There was a strike among Watsonville strawberry workers, and the strikers were keeping an eye on the situation in the foothills where the apples were ripening. Through some friends among the strikers I was directed to a non-struck strawberry company where I worked a few days while I waited for apple harvest season.

Strawberry picking seems placid from a distance, but it is tremendously hard work. It requires long periods bent over the low-growing fruit. It requires nimble and gentle fingers to pull the berries off quickly and smoothly without crushing them and without removing the green caps, without which the berries are unmarketable. Making a living in the berries is no easy trick.

I watched the experienced pickers move down the rows. Their bodies pivoted from side to side and their hands disappeared under the plants and quickly emerged with fists full of fruit. They deposited the berries in flat wooden crates that sat in small moveable frames, like miniature single-wheeled wheelbarrows that the workers pushed in front of them as they moved forward. Once filled, the crates were carried to the end of the rows and recorded by a checker, who stood by a stack of empty crates. This was a harvest dance that had a quality of magic for a stumbling beginner like myself, struggling just to make enough to pay for gas and food for lunches.

Working in the strawberries also made me nervous because of a white powdery substance around the plants, something I was not used to seeing in the vegetable fields. Assurances that there was nothing harmful in this herbicide residue were somehow not reassuring.

A week into strawberries I heard that Buak, the largest apple grower in Watsonville, and one of the first to sign on with the Teamsters, was hiring pickers. It took no great persuasion to leave the strawberries and head for the hills that rimmed the Pajaro Valley, where fall held the fragrance of ripening apples.

I borrowed an apple-picking sack from Mickey, who'd once worked a couple of seasons in the apples, and headed up to the Buak orchard. Green Valley Road is a beautiful ride in late summer, with dry wild grasses displaying their shades of yellow against the dark greens of the shrubs and trees that lay in the hills' gullies and folds. The road up the foothills of the Pajaro passes small farm houses, rural homes, well-tended gardens, raspberry and blackberry vineyards, and open spaces of lush vegetation, at points overlooking Monterey Bay, the blue waters glittering in September brilliance.

The pleasures of the view distracted my attention. When I reached a high spot on the hill and a sign that said Hecker Pass, I knew I'd gone too far and doubled back. It was getting to be late afternoon, and I was beginning to think I wouldn't find the place before closing time. On the return down the road toward Watsonville, I saw a large sign on a big gray wood and tin building, "Buak Apples." How'd I miss that? I turned into the parking lot surrounded by huge stacks of large wooden bins of weathered wood.

In the warehouse I was directed to an office where I made my interest in apple picking known to the people who sat behind a counter. In a short time a tall man in a crewcut came out of the office. Without much question or scrutiny I was asked to fill out a short application form. I wrote my name and made up the other information I was requested to write. I rode a foreman's pickup to the area I would begin the following day.

In a grove not far from the Buak headquarters I stood with the foreman under what was to be my first tree. Tall wooden ladders were visible all around. Some apples had already fallen from the tree, which stood maybe thirty feet high; its branches, spread thirty or more feet across, were laden with red fruit, the lower branches bending toward the ground from the weight. The orchard had a pleasant, healthy smell.

I received instructions on the rules of picking. "First and foremost," the foreman said with great conviction, "never toss an apple from the ground into a bin. Fill the bin up to here." He placed his hand at the level top. "You'll get $5.50 for each of these you fill. Your task is to efficiently strip a tree of its fruit. So you've got to know how to attack it"—a military analogy that seemed to lend weight to his words. "That means you have to think about where you are going to place the ladder, and be systematic," he said, looking at me intently, maybe wondering how long I'd endure at a job where hard work can get old quick. "This is Indian Summer so I suggest you get here early, you'll do better in the cool of the morning. The heat can sap you."

I took his advice. I showed up early the next day. It seemed early. It was barely light. But workers were already busy in the trees near the ones I'd been assigned.

I couldn't recall if the field boss had said to pick from top to bottom or bottom to top. But it was from the bottom I began, lured by easy pickings at the outset. Picking from the ground, I was able to fill my apple sack and bin quickly. My energy and hopes were up. But soon I was out of apples within reach from the ground, and I began to climb the tall three-legged wooden ladder. Picking got slower and harder. The bin must have grown in size. My first estimate of a full bin in an hour turned out to be grossly optimistic. Hours went by. The bin and my ambition remained unfulfilled.

As I continued to pick, it was necessary to climb higher and higher into the tree. I began hanging on precariously while reaching out for a couple of shiny red ones. My leg slipped as I extended my reach and I grabbed a branch in time to keep from falling. It dawned on me that I was risking my neck for this shit!

As I picked, a few apples fell on the ground. I'd been warned not to put any apples from the ground in the bin, but as the day wore on and my arms grew painful and heavy, the temptation became too great. I picked up a few that seemed to have survived their fall unblemished. After a brief check I threw them in the bin.

It took me until the afternoon to finish my first tree and fill my first bin. I'd fallen short of my optimistic estimate by a factor of four or five. The foreman came around after I'd moved the ladder to the next tree and called me over. He pointed to the top of my first tree where a few clusters of apples hung in defiance. I kept my thoughts to myself as I lugged the ladder, now considerably heavier than in the morning, back to my first tree and crawled up through the branches, and hung from a high branch that swayed and strained under my weight while the foreman stood underneath watching to make sure I got them all.

When I wasn't hanging from the trees, I was sniffing around to see what was going on. During an afternoon break I went and visited a couple of guys working the trees near mine. These guys were experienced workers and each of them had already picked three times as much as I had. I found out that they considered the price of the bin to be too low. It was lower than the previous year, and they weren't happy about it. Buak would later claim that he had wanted to raise the rate for the bin, but, by general agreement, Watsonville apple growers had settled on the lower rate and he was obliged to abide by that. Whether that was true or not, it was apparent that the clever Teamster braggarts had managed, in winning their union contracts, to actually negotiate a *lower* rate than had previously existed!

These workers didn't have a high regard for Buak, or for apple growers in general. They had no idea that Buak had a Teamster contract, nor did they know anything about the Teamsters. No one had told them that union dues would be deducted from their paychecks. They had never seen a Teamster organizer, read a Teamster leaflet, or signed any authorization cards. They had a generally favorable impression of "la union de Chávez" but hadn't had much personal experience with it.

There was a supervisor at Buak named Frank, a Chicano with dark hair streaked with gray and combed straight back, who came around on occasion in his white pickup. He was pretty talkative, liked to joke around, and always referred to his boss as "old man Buak." Through him I was able to get an idea of where Buak's orchards were and approximately how many workers he had. It was pretty obvious that most of the workers were undocumented, but I only found out later that Frank had a little hustle going, charging each undocumented worker $10 *a week* for a phony Social Security number.

On the second day of work I sought out other workers more aggressively and began to talk more openly with them about the price of the bin. When I repeated what the workers had said the previous day, I found that the lower price of the bin was a source of considerable irritation. There were other grievances, notably that the foreman was only coming around with drinking water very occasionally, even though it was getting into the 90s during the day. I told them I thought that a real union was necessary, not the Teamsters who were only there to keep out a real union. I also told them that I thought that "la union de Chávez" was the best one, but that its policy on workers without papers stunk and that it needed to be changed, and that there were people in the union who wanted to change it. Though my earlier enthusiasm for the union and its leadership had diminished, I still believed it to be a positive force and very much needed, otherwise I would not have promoted it. However, I did not want to deceive these workers, to get them to risk something without knowing what it was they were getting into. I also told them I was a supporter of the union and that I had come into the orchard to help the union scope out the situation. It was my understanding that there was a plan to begin a strike there fairly soon.

Most of the workers I talked to were pretty young, in their late teens or early twenties. A few had participated in union actions in other areas of the state, but most, from what I could tell, hadn't been directly involved in any union struggles. For the most part they listened without comment to my suggestions about the need for a union, but I felt from their mood that if a strike were brought to them, they'd join it.

During the lunch break that second day, I asked the foreman if he'd mind bringing water around more often to those of us who were "doing the work." He didn't appear to be too happy with me making such a request or the fact that I was talking to the other workers, or that I *could* talk to them. I could tell he wasn't crazy about me in general, but we got our water.

The next morning when I arrived at the little cluster of trees that had been assigned to me, the foreman was standing over one of my bins. Apples were piled up on one corner, and he had dug down into the bin and said he found a couple apples with little brown spots where they'd been bruised. "You been pickin' these off the ground, haven't ya! You fucking ain't worth a shit, ya know that." I knew right then that any chance of a promotion was out. "Go pick up your check, asshole." The last time I had been kicked off a workplace was in 1969 when I was called in to the Coast Guard base commander's office and told to leave Government Island military base and never come back. I was happier on that occasion than this one. But I wasn't heartbroken this time either, just taken aback by the abruptness and vehemence of it. The field boss was pretty upset that some of his apples might have gotten ruined. But he had no idea just how many of Mr. Buak's apples were going to go to waste that season.

After I picked up my check, I rode over to a picket line at a strawberry field in Watsonville. Roberto Garcia, head of the Salinas office, was out there on the line and I told him what had happened at Buak. I told him I thought that the situation was favorable for a strike. There was a group of strawberry strikers around listening. They were going to be part of the strike force to hit the apple fields to get the strike in the apples going. As I related what I'd found out in the orchard, I said that the whole thing should be thought over carefully. "Most of the workers, from what I could tell, were illegals. Are you sure we want to initiate a strike among a bunch of potential scabs?" Roberto, with whom I'd argued about the union's position on undocumented workers, did not appreciate the joke, much less being challenged in front of the strawberry strikers. Nor was it easy for me to do. In addition to his rather intimidating presence and his union authority, he wasn't above using that fact that he spoke Spanish fifty times better than I did, to his advantage. He shot back something about me being all caught up in illegals (a bleeding heart?) in a manner that was clearly mocking.

On the way over to Buak's orchard I rode in the car with Roberto, and he told me, in his way, "You can hold any opinion you want about things as long as you remember that the union calls the shots." I thought, Wow, you actually allow people to have their own opinions? But I kept it to myself.

We entered the same orchard that I had been fired from that morning. We entered with a dozen or so cars, with union flags flying, horns blaring, shouts of "Huelga!" over the bullhorn. As we got out of our cars, the pickers were climbing down off their ladders. They dumped the apples out of their sacks and came hesitantly toward us. As they gathered around, Roberto told them that the union was calling for a strike to challenge the worthless Teamsters contract and to win real benefits. Did they even know there was a contract? Buak had lowered the price paid per bin from the previous season. That was unfair, but they would need organization to challenge that. The choice was theirs. If they wanted to strike, there was no guarantee they'd win, but the union would back them. The union could pay some strike benefits but they were minimal. Did they have any questions? Silence. Then a hand went up. "How much were the union strike benefits?" "Twenty-five a week," said Roberto. Did they agree to walk? "Vámonos." It was on.

With apple strikers in our cars we hit other areas where workers were picking. Everywhere we went, the workers came down off their ladders to listen. *Everyone* walked out.

The first days in a strike are the easiest. Spirits and anticipation are high. It's like a party. It's the long haul that wears down the spirits and the resources—and, of course, the employers are well aware of this.

Those first few days of the apple strike the picket lines were large. There was as yet no injunction. A lot of strawberry workers joined the apple workers and walked the lines. Some of those strawberry strikers would remain during the whole strike as a backbone of it.

All of Buak's pickers had come out, and most were on the lines those first days. We asked them about the conditions in Buak as ammunition to popularize the strike. We got plenty to talk about. On the first day of the strike, with no guards in the orchards, nor sheriffs mobilized, it was possible to go into the orchards. Some of the apple workers I'd met on the job wanted to show me around. Many were living in makeshift shacks under the apple trees. They'd built these crude shelters out of discarded cardboard cartons attached to a wood frame and covered with sheets of plastic. Inside these "casas de carton" were army-style bunk beds where four to six workers slept. For the privilege of bedding down in these huts the workers paid $14 a week each—$224 to $336 a month. In those days you could rent a nice big house in the city for that much. Their meals consisted mostly of cold sandwiches and unheated canned food, since there were no kitchen facilities, and, needless to say, no bathroom, shower, sink, and so on.

A few of the luckier workers lived in barracks facilities with indoor plumbing, but they were in the minority and the place was also overcrowded. Housing would turn out to be the issue that most put Buak on the defensive.

Besides rent and $10 a week for a phony Social Security number, the workers paid $11 for an apple sack, $4 for transportation to the orchard for those who didn't live under the trees, and $8 a month for Teamster dues. Ninety percent of the workers were without papers.

The first day of the strike began with soaring spirits. Strung out along the road that bordered Buak's orchard, workers shouted and sang and joked and watched the idle trees as they swayed in the breeze, their branches heavy with ripe fruit.

But the happy moment was broken abruptly around eight in the morning when a green bus, several green vans, and a car drove up Green Valley Road past the suddenly quiet picket line. La migra! Nearly every apple striker on the line, and some other workers as well, clutched their union-provided sack lunches and looked to the trees, plotting their escape. There was deadly silence as the caravan of green vehicles pulled up across the street. Someone began to shout "Huelga!" and the line exploded in shouts. The migra agents climbed out of the vans and buses and stood by them as we shouted, some of us with fists in the air, in their direction. "You touch any of us, we're all going to jail!" Meanwhile the lead agent, Mr. Sills, a tall man in a green uniform, with thinning gray hair, crossed the road to talk with several UFW officials. "Old Man Buak," who'd come that morning to see the show, looked on.

"You guys in charge here?" Roberto, his arms tucked in his pancho, and Santos, a young official from the Watsonville union office, nodded. "The Santa Cruz sheriff called us," said Mr. Sills, his arms folded in front of him, staring off into the trees, maybe calculating how many "wetbacks" his agents could realistically catch if the line bolted into the orchard. Leaving such an open escape route was a gross violation of the rules of immigration warfare. Wouldn't look good. "Said there was eighty wets in hand here. Don't look that way to me." He looked down at the ground, his shoe making a little semicircle in the dirt. "I don't think there's anything for us to do here," he said slowly, looking now over his shoulder at the agents standing ready. Now it was the turn of Old Man Buak to shove the dirt with his foot, but this was more a kick of frustration. Mr. Sills walked back to his car, motioning to the agents as he did. They retreated to their vehicles as a cheer went up from the line. "Huelga, cabrones!" "Que viva la huelga!" "Abajo la migra!" It was the first victory of the strike.

That celebration too was cut short. Twenty Teamsters from Salinas showed up, stopping right around the same spot as the migra had, exiting their cars with icy stares. This set off several hours of sharp-witted barbs, chants, slogans, and denunciation, until a lot of us were getting hoarse from shouting. Elias, a large and good-natured worker, who had a small farm in the area where he raised zucchini and pigs and who could be counted on to add a joke to almost any situation, now stood in the middle of the road, a few yards from the Teamsters. "Donde están los miembros manzaneros de los timstos?" he asked sarcastically, his arms extended. "Donde están sus miembros leales, cabrones! Pinches fraudes!" (Where are your loyal apple worker members? You fucking frauds!). There was laughter from the picket line. People were having a great time.

In the 1970s apples were still the biggest cash crop in the Pajaro Valley. More acreage was devoted to apples than to any other crop. Strawberries were beginning to come into favor, and their gross income per acre far exceeded what was possible in apples. But apples were still a mainstay and an important part of Watsonville's identity, and so the fact that there was a strike in the orchard was big news in Watsonville and the local paper, the *Pajaronian*, carried a story on its front page every day of the strike.

The walkout was sharply embarrassing for the Teamsters, and it was to become more so as the strike went on. After the first day or two of the strike, Buak declared to the press that he was thankful for his Teamster contracts because he was sure to get help with his crop. The Teamster officials crowed that Buak would soon have more than enough workers, because lettuce was winding down and Teamster lechugueros would soon be on their way to the apple orchards. All any of us around the strike could say to that was, "Ya, right!"

With the apple strike hitting the papers in the area, the union (UFW) officials were very pleased. This was clearly publicity they were looking for.

Yet, after the first few days of the strike, after getting the strikers to sign union pledge cards that entitled them to a small strike benefit and put the union in a position to claim to be representatives of Buak's apple workers, after several days of rumors that Manuel Chávez was going to come to help lead a general strike in the apples, the union's attention to the strike dropped off sharply.

A few days into the dispute, Roberto Garcia asked to see me at the Watsonville union office. His previous irritation was gone, and he was all cordiality and good humor. The success of the apple strike had buoyed his spirits, and perhaps his standing in the union as well. He was forming a committee to head up the strike, he said, and I, along with some of the strawberry strikers, was chosen for it. I was pretty put off by this. Wasn't this an apple workers' strike? Hadn't we called them out with the promise to fight for better conditions in the apples? Shouldn't apple workers be on this committee? Shouldn't the strikers have a chance to choose their committee? But Roberto would have none of this. Once again I was reminded about who was "calling the shots." I said I wouldn't be on any committee without apple workers. That ended the meeting. And we barely talked to each other for the rest of the strike.

On the third full day of the picket line lots of full bins were coming in from the field. Carlos, who worked at the Watsonville union office, and Pedro, a striking strawberry worker, snuck into the orchard to check out who was working. As they were lurking among the trees to get a look, they were spotted by Teamster goons. As they tried to leave the orchard, a Teamster with a club came at them. They turned to head another way, but as they did several more Teamster guards came at them and knocked them to the ground. The first Teamster began beating them with a stick. Pedro tried to defend himself, and the stick came thudding down on his upraised arm, breaking it.

When word came of the beating, the Teamsters claimed that Carlos and Pedro had been caught trying to shake a picker down off the tree. We wanted to put out a leaflet denouncing the Teamster thuggery, but the local UFW officials didn't want this, arguing it would anger people too much and might cause things to "get out of control."

The following day spirits were down. There was a need to talk about things. On the picket line a number of strikers and supporters got together—apple strikers, strawberry strikers, including Pedro with his broken arm; my old pal FJ, who was working in the celery in Watsonville and had joined the strike the first day; Carla whom I knew from the coffeehouse days and had come down from the Bay area beginning what would be many years in the fields; and Mickey, who took off time from the lettuce to join the line. There were others there as well, people from the Watsonville community who would come to the picket line at times throughout the strike to support it.

Clearly the situation with many of the apple strikers was precarious. Their small strike benefits, $25 a week, would not carry them long and finding housing and providing food was a big problem. Some understandably had moved on or were considering doing so. But if the strike could be carried forward, if strikebreakers could be kept out of the orchard, not only would the Teamster alliance with the growers be weakened, but Buak might be forced into concessions and others might follow.

We needed to find out where the strikebreakers were coming from. We needed to broaden the publicity of the strike and broaden support from the community. We needed to step up agitation on the picket line. We agreed we would fight to win as much as possible in the strike without resorting to blaming anyone among the people. We would keep our opposition aimed where it belonged, against the growers and the system that lives on the exploitation of the farmworker for the private gain of a few.

The next day on the line we got a big break. One of the strikebreakers turned out to be a spy for the UFW's side. He reported that Buak was "losing his ass." Buak had some scabs, he said, but they were inexperienced, working mostly by the hour. A labor contractor from Salinas, Jaime Amezcua (whose strike-busting career began back in 1970), was bringing them in. Production was way down. The first week of the strike they harvested 200 bins. "A bunch of those have apples that'll probably never make it to market," said the spy with a bit of a wink in his eye. Buak needed at least 3,000 bins a week to bring in his crop.

In fact, the strike was hurting Buak bad. Watsonville's apple industry had been on the decline for more than a decade. The market in fresh apples, by far the most lucrative, was being taken over by Washington State apples. They were gaining a better reputation, justified or not. But the fact that Watsonville apples ripened sooner than those of Washington, as much as ten days sooner, gave Watsonville growers a potential edge at the beginning of the season when prices tended to be higher. Whoever could get their crop harvested earliest stood to gain in the lucrative fresh fruit market. Therefore, the first few days of the harvest were potentially crucial to the bottom line. Apples that could not be sold as fresh could be sold as juice apples or to processors of dried fruit but at considerably lower prices. Clearly, with the strike, these were Buak's only hope.

We began following Amezcua's bus as it left the orchard. Meanwhile in Salinas, there were allies of the strike and partisans of the union who were also keeping an eye out. Early one morning, Amezcua parked his bus near the corralón, just off Market Street. As word got out about a bus that was waiting to pick up strikebreakers, hundreds of workers, in the area waiting for their own rides to the fields, massed around Amezcua's bus. No one could get near the bus, let alone get on.

After several mornings of that, Amezcua changed tactics. A group of us strikers from Watsonville had been scouting around in the early morning and spotted Amezcua's bus on Alisal Street across from the county jail and the sheriff's office. As we approached the bus, Amezcua leaned on his horn, stuck his head out of the driver's window, and began screaming for help. Soon, a line of sheriffs, their faces protected by Plexiglas shields, filed out of a building across the street. Batons in hand, they lined up to guard his bus while fifteen to twenty strikebreakers meekly came on the bus. It was rumored that some of these were prisoners in the county lockup given early release for agreeing to do "community service," but we were not able to substantiate that. After spending some time near the bus, pleading with the strikebreakers to leave, to no avail, we strikers threw up our hands. All the strikers looked thoroughly dejected. "Vámonos, ya nos ganaron ahora!" (They won out today, let's get out of here).

As we were driving away, in the direction of Watsonville, the driver of the car I was in made a U-turn and headed back toward the labor contractor bus. I was about to ask him where he was going as we pulled just about even with the bus, which just then starting forward. Suddenly there were a series of whooshing sounds, and the bus sank low to the pavement with four flat tires! Our driver let out a yell, shook a closed fist at an astonished labor contractor, and pushed his hand onto the horn as we sped past the bus.

By now Buak was raging. Since the beginning of the strike, his son, who was in charge of the cooler operation, had insisted that everything was normal and apples were arriving in sufficient numbers. But this was also part of the psychological war that is part of every strike. Despite these defiant words, in the second week of the strike, the Watsonville *Pajaronian* ran a front-page headline, "Teamsters letting me down, Buak says." The large force of laid-off lettuce workers the Teamsters promised to deliver turned out to be a myth, as was predictable. The chance of experienced lettuce workers coming to work in the apples was unlikely enough. That they would come to break a strike on behalf of the Teamsters was about as likely as the apples picking themselves. Buak complained openly that the burden of finding strikebreakers had fallen to him, and, without saying as much, it was apparent that his efforts were, excuse the expression, not bearing much fruit.

But Buak and Amezcua weren't giving up. The second week of the strike a small number of the original strikers went back when Buak offered them $7 a bin. From what we could tell, they worked a few days and moved on, the money helping to pay their expenses to their next destination. This was not an uncommon pattern in the field strikes. Workers would walk out, strike for as long as they could or felt motivated to hold out, and then move on, usually to non-struck ranches or areas.

The strike turned into a kind of guerilla war. There were incidents of strikers hitting the enemy virtually under their very noses. A worker from

Calexico spent a week walking the Buak picket lines. He had spent the previous months traveling around the state from strike to strike engaging in the battles from asparagus in the Imperial Valley to the lemon orchards of Yuma, to the tomato and cucumber fields of Stockton. He had become a kind of roving, professional striker. He had a ton of stories to tell.

Not long after the flat tire incident, Jaime Amezcua managed to bring several busloads of scabs into a Buak orchard. They were working an area pretty far from the public road, outside bullhorn range. We tried to come up with some plan to either drive them out of the orchard or disable the buses, but we couldn't get close to the scene because of the guards and sheriffs. We were standing around feeling frustrated when the campañero from Calexico came up to us with a sly grin on his face. "No preocupes," he said: Don't worry. "Amezcua's going to have some problems leaving the ranch today." And at that he lifted his jacket revealing a handful of wires of various colors he'd "found" under the dashboard of one of Amezcua's buses!

The virtual absence of the union's leadership on the picket line allowed for certain radical sentiments to be expressed more openly and freely. This was largely done through the agitation to the strikebreakers.

The bullhorn by the orchard was a public forum for any strikers or supporters to express their indignation, outrage, sarcasm, or irony. This was a psychological war, where the point was to wear down the morale of the other side. Some of the farmworkers on the strike line had plenty to say about an array of issues concerning the robbery by the growers, discrimination against Mexicans and immigrants, and the injustices of society. Sometimes it was strictly appeals to class loyalty, at other times broad denunciations of society, exposure of the growers, the police, or migra, or calls for a radical response to injustice. Sometimes a bullhorn was used to advise those at work in the orchard on the proper workstyle of a strikebreaker. With inexperienced pickers as strikebreakers we found Buak was paying by the hour. Strikers gave them sincere advice. "Slow down, take it easy, take a break! Buak needs you like a worm needs an apple, he can't fire you!" Sometimes, if we were close enough, we'd even see them laughing at these taunts.

One day while we were on the picket line with our bullhorn aimed at rustling branches at trees off in the distance, we saw an unusual sight. A half-dozen strikebreakers were heading our way. They emerged from the trees greeting us and several of them were shouting "huelga" and "apple strike." The leaders of this small group turned out to be two young "chucos" (street youth) from the Salinas community who had, from all appearances, gotten on a scab crew with the explicit purpose of getting other strikebreakers to walk out. In this they succeeded quite well.

Francisca, a strawberry worker from Michoacan, was a powerful agitator on the picket line. Short, with a somewhat raspy voice, she let her outrage ring out with the indignity of a people forced by the heartless exploitation of a homeland to emigrate, only to be exploited and mistreated again in this new land. On the picket line she explained her feelings about this by way of stories. One of them involved a visit to her family in Michoacan. She'd gone home on a trip bringing some fruit she'd brought from the United States. After greeting her mother, Francisca presented her with a gift of a large beautiful melon. "Que bonito!" said her mother as she inspected the fruit with a U.S. company label on it. "If only we could grow fruit like this in Mexico!" "Mama," said Francisca, handing her mother the large round fruit, "this melon is from Mexico!" Once again, the best of Mexico's agricultural products, along with its prime-age working population, were coming north.

The picket line rang with denunciations of U.S. immigration policy and appeals to the undocumented immigrants that made it clear that we opposed the whole notion of "illegal workers," and that anyone working in the United States should have the same rights, that the policy was aimed at intensifying exploitation, and that in any case, the border itself had been imposed illegally through an unjustified war and broken treaties thereafter. And speaking of the border, hadn't the United States violated the sanctity of other countries' borders by scores of invasions of places like Mexico, Nicaragua, Panama, Vietnam, Korea, etc.?

Just how much effect this propaganda had is difficult to judge. In one situation it just may have saved my hide. One day a group of strikers, taking advantage of one of the few moments when the sheriffs were not around, ran into the orchard to chase the scabs out. We were carrying sticks but didn't intend to do more than scare people, and it worked. Some scabs left and never came back.

The next morning we were setting up our picket line outside the same orchard when a sheriff's car pulled up to me. "Amescua's filed charges of assault on you," the young deputy said, holding the paper in front of me. He asked me to step into his squad car. FJ was on the picket line that day and got into his car and followed us into the grove where the labor contractor bus was parked. I was sitting in the squad car as FJ got out of his car. Amezcua came running excitedly toward FJ shouting, "That's the guy. That's the one that was clubbing my people." FJ hadn't been on the picket line that previous day, and he was not the person Amezcua had first indicated to the sheriffs. "Well, the guy you told us about is in the squad car." The deputy pointed to me. "Oh, ya," Amezcua corrected himself, "that's the guy."

The deputies then brought a young Mexicano, probably nineteen or twenty, over to identify me. I'd seen him in the orchard the day before, and for certain he saw me because we'd been just a few feet from each other. He came over to the squad car and stood for a time looking at me through the open door. He smiled slightly before he spoke, "No, no reconozco a este tipo" (No, I don't recognize this guy). Jaime Amezcua had a fit, but they had to let me go. The sheriff's deputies assured me that a false accusation report would be filed on the incident. How fortunate that would be I could not have imagined.

I wish I'd had the chance to meet this fellow later to find out why he lied for me that day. Why did he take that risk of pissing off his boss? Was it fear of the strikers? Or did something in that strike give him a sense that what was happening on the picket line was really in his interest? Anyone's guess.

As nearly always happens in such strikes, an injunction was handed down limiting picketing to a ridiculous degree, one picket every 25 yards. We ignored it when we could, playing cat-and-mouse with the sheriffs.

Since Buak employed a number of African American guards, we addressed ourselves to the commonality among the striking workers and field-workers and black people who had suffered greatly from the same capitalist hands. Mexicans dispossessed of their land and livelihood, forced to migrate to survive, blacks robbed of their freedom, enslaved for centuries and brutally discriminated against. Weren't blacks and Latinos sent in disproportionate numbers to fight in Vietnam? This appeal to solidarity against a system of exploitation also had its effects. There were occasions when these guards showed their sympathy to the strike, or tried to remain neutral when they could.

The strike got considerable support in Watsonville. We tried to intensify that support by leafleting, mobilizing car caravans around town, and even by a solidarity march with people who came to support the strike from the Bay area. There was support from the community, and people from the town came out to the picket lines, sometimes bringing food or something to drink, like coffee and sweet rolls (*pan dulces*) in the mornings. During the second week of the strike there was a rally at the plaza in Watsonville's downtown area. César Chávez was due to come with Teatro Campesino, but they couldn't make it. Still the rally, with speakers from local union officials and strikers, along with music from a local mariachi group, drew a crowd of several hundred.

As the Buak strike continued, its leadership pretty much fell (by default) to a group of *Worker* newspaper staffers, strawberry strikers, and a dwindling number of apple workers. Though only a few apple strikers stayed around to the end, not one of the original Buak strikers went back to Buak for more than a few days.

The Teamsters frequently showed up at Buak's ranches to act as guards. The mere sight of them aroused considerable anger in the workers. The Teamsters would stick around to the end of the picket line and escort Amezcua's buses to discourage us from following them to find out where the strikebreakers were being dropped off. One day, as a bus left the field, three or four carloads of Teamsters fell in behind it. We followed them onto Highway 1. The Teamster cars blocked both lanes of the highway and slowed down to allow the bus to get ahead. One of the more daring strikers gunned his engine and swerved onto the right shoulder, fishtailing in the dirt but managing to hold on and pull in front of the Teamster cars.

Highway 1 between Watsonville and Salinas is an undivided four-lane road with lots of fast-moving traffic. Even under normal circumstances, it's dangerous to drive. As we sped down the highway, the pace quickened and the maneuvering became more and more dicey with striker and Teamster cars trying to outrun each other, swerving, and several times almost colliding.

When we got to Salinas, some of us hunters suddenly became the hunted as the Teamsters, using CB radios, tried to trap us. Several Teamster cars were following the car I was driving. I made a turn to get away from them up a side street, but a third Teamster car was coming down the opposite way directly toward us. It turned quickly to block the street. It looked as though we were going to be trapped in a vise. There were other strikers in the car with me. Pedro sat next to me on the front seat, his broken arm still in a cast. We just looked at each other and grabbed for anything that might serve as a weapon. As we approached the Teamster car in front of us, I was able to swerve onto the sidewalk and find enough clearance to get around the car.

Mickey was not so lucky. He and Carla were in his car being tailed by a Teamster. As he tried to ditch the car behind him, the guard arms of a railroad crossing came down, blocking his way forward on Market Street. One of the Teamster goons, a particularly obnoxious one who was killed by his girlfriend a few years later, came up to Mickey's car carrying a large wrench. Mickey had his window up, but he lowered it so the approaching goon could see the gun he had in his hand, the barrel aimed straight at his chest. The goon stepped back, grunted, and walked away.

The Buak strike cost "Old Man Buak" dearly. It was estimated that well over half his crop never got picked. Undoubtedly, he suffered other losses from poor work—like bruised apples being thrown in the bins by the strikebreakers who knew they could get away with it. On top of that were expenses for security guards, the labor contractor, and so on. Well into the strike the union sent a telegram asking Buak for negotiations but he never responded. It is certainly possible that his losses were cushioned by help from other growers who had a lot to gain by keeping the union out of their orchards.

We tried to make the most of the strike politically. We put out a special issue of *The Worker* during the strike in which we hit particularly hard at the issue of "illegals," exposing the cruel conditions the growers imposed and upholding the tenacious struggle that the strikers put up. But because in those days we overestimated the importance of the workers "learning from their own experiences," we didn't do the kind of political work to expose the system that might have been possible.

Although at first it was difficult to understand why the union had pulled away from the strike, it was FJ who pointed out that it was perfectly consistent with evolving strategy. There was growing interest within the political establishment to see an end to strife and struggle in the fields. The union was interested in seeing as much struggle break out as possible in order to prove that without its intervention, without grower recognition of it and guarantee of its existence, there would be no peace. The UFW was saying, we hold the key, if you want peace, get the dogs to back off. The Teamsters can't ensure peace, but we can. These "publicity strikes" were part of a union strategy.

Arson

Fall was approaching when the Buak strike ended. I returned to Salinas to the one-room shack on Pearl Street that I had seen only rarely during the strike.

I hadn't worked in weeks, nor was I receiving strike benefits, so I was pretty broke. But I was able to find a job almost immediately at Paul Masson in San Lucas, just south of King City, working on a crew with the Margarito family. The Margaritos were strong union supporters. I'd known Tony, the father of the clan, for several years, through picket lines, marches, and meetings. We got along fairly well, even though our views on the union and its policies were diverging. Tony, like many people then, was reluctant to criticize the union, even when there were things he disagreed with. He thought this could only weaken it while it was under attack. I argued with him that the union's strength was the workers and to the extent that anyone divided them, even the union leadership, they were weakening the union and the larger struggle.

Tony lived with his family in Salinas and, like many farmworkers, worked different crops at different times of the year. The fall wine grape harvest was one of those crops. Some of his family—the ones who were not in school at that time—worked together in the grapes. This was fairly common in the grape crops, which are well suited to this kind of arrangement. We worked as a crew, six of us—Tony, his wife, their three older children, and myself, with our tractor and gondola—each with our grape pan and small curved grape knife. We'd leapfrog down the vineyard until we'd filled the gondola. Then one of us would drive off to the scales while the other crew members filled their pans with whatever variety was being picked that day. Usually we'd work one variety for two or three days: Pinot Noir, Emerald Riesling, Gamay, Gewürztraminer, Pinot Chardonnay, and so on. Each variety paid a different price per ton, depending on the weight of the berry. It was hard and dirty work, but it was pleasant too, working with that family. The weather was warm as is usual in grape-growing areas, but without the oppressive heat there had been at Gallo. The Margaritos were experienced, kind, good-humored, and they taught me well. The team worked together well.

With the vineyards in San Lucas, a good fifty miles south of Salinas, I had to leave early and usually got home late in the afternoon. One day I came home from work and found my room turned upside down. Clothes were strewn everywhere. My bed, a mattress on a piece of plywood resting on milk crates, had been turned over, and all the boxes of books and papers underneath tipped over. My dresser drawers had been emptied on to the floor. Even the cupboards in my tiny kitchen were flung open and the few pans and dishes pulled out on to the stove and into the sink. On the dresser I found a search warrant issued by a judge from the Salinas Superior Court and signed by someone named Captain Miracle. I laughed at the name, and for a second I thought this might be a joke, but the official-looking paper and the serious disorder in the room spoke otherwise.

What were they looking for? I was tired, hot, and dirty and in bad need of a shower. So I began to undress. In my bedroom/living room I had a wooden barrel that stood next to the front door. Usually, the first thing I'd do after work is throw my work clothes in that barrel so I wouldn't sit down on anything with them on. I began to peel off my clothes and had my shirt off and my pants undone when there was a knock at the door. The front door was mainly glass but it was covered by a shade. I peeked out from the shade and saw a guy in a tan, corduroy jacket. In my exhausted and somewhat dizzy state of mind, it didn't occur to me to be concerned about this, until I opened the door, one hand clutching my pants. "Drop it! Drop the fucking gun!" a voice screamed. The voice came from behind a barrel that looked like a howitzer, no more than six inches from my nose. "What gun? I don't have a gun." All I could do at that point was react by instinct. I held my hands in the air, and very quickly.

A second plainclothes grabbed them and forced them behind me. Meanwhile the corduroy jacket had holstered his gun and was pulling the dirty clothes out of the barrel.

How many times have cops thought they've seen a gun and shot first before finding out for sure? Here they were out to arrest "a dangerous radical" living in a "forlorn shack" in the heart of the barrio. It's not hard to imagine that had I been black or Mexican, I'd have had my face blown off by a nervous cop who would know that killing such a person would always be excused with the argument, "I thought I was in danger." These thoughts were actually going through my mind at the very moment I was being cuffed and, still half-dressed, led out the door. My plea to be allowed to shower was emphatically denied, and now I stood in the open air in front of a small crowd of children who'd stopped their playing to see the spectacle in their courtyard.

"Would you mind telling me what this is about?" I asked. Sure, the corduroy jacket said, "You're under arrest, for arson. Last night some buses were firebombed, I suppose you don't know anything about that?" My car was parked in a little carport attached to my house, and the police demanded my car keys so they could search it. "Do you have a search warrant for the car?" I asked them. They were kind enough to explain to me my options. "Either give us your keys, or we'll have your car towed in and torn apart." I was fairly sure that was legally a crock of shit, but I didn't protest. Maybe this could be brought up later. They checked the car, inside and out, looking, they said, for flammable material for firebombs but also reading letters I had on the front seat. They then put me in their squad car and we headed for the county jail.

On the way to jail the cop riding shotgun turned to me, "You know this guy Amezcua?" "Ya." "He swears you told him you were gonna blow up his buses. That true?" "No," I said. "Well, that's why you're here."

I was booked and held on $15,000 bail. I began to think about motives, alibis, witnesses, and the like, and I was beginning to think that there was a chance, maybe even a good chance, of being convicted of the fire. It dawned on me how relatively easy it is for someone to be brought up and convicted for something they had nothing to do with. In this case there was a labor contractor anxious to testify that I had threatened him (witness), I was heavily involved in a strike that he was trying to break (motive), and I was asleep after a day in the grapes when the crime occurred (no alibi). What if by chance I happened to have some flammable material in the garage (evidence)? I thought of the incident at the Buak orchard when Amezcua accused me and then couldn't identify me. I thought of the young strikebreaker who looked straight into my eyes and shook his head and said, "I don't recognize him." The sheriff's deputies said at that time that a false accusation report would be in their files. At that moment it seemed like that just might be my salvation.

I used my right to a phone call to call the union. I was told that the union would help, but that publicly they were going to disassociate themselves from me so as to avoid bad PR. Why bad PR, I thought. I hadn't done a goddamn thing.

I spent the night in a tiny county jail cell trying to read a cowboy novel I found on my bunk, by the light shining in the corridor and shining through the bars of my cell. The next day I read the cowboy novel and watched TV through the bars.

In the late afternoon a guard called my name, and I was led to a room with a table and several chairs. They sat me down and told me to wait. I thought a lawyer had been sent to see me, but the blond-haired fraternity type, in his late twenties or early thirties, who walked in a few minutes later was no lawyer. He sat down and smiled, shook my hand, and introduced himself. Then he pulled out his badge. He was Agent X from the FBI.

The whole point of the FBI is to find out information, and they are trained to do that. Sometimes their tactics are subtle, sometimes more direct. But it is always a mistake to talk to them about anything. In this case, the agent didn't begin with any questions. He started going on about how he'd been in Puerto Rico and had grown to respect the independence movement there. I knew nothing about the movement in Puerto Rico, and very little at all about Puerto Rico. So I couldn't comment on anything even if I wanted to, which I did not. I should have excused myself politely at that moment, but I decided to hear him out. It was obvious he was trying to gain my trust and sympathy. After a while, he began to get impatient and started asking me directly about things. Was I being treated all right? "No complaints," I said. Did I want to talk about what happened? "No." Was I happy with the outcome of the strike? At that I told him I was feeling homesick for my cell and would like to return. That ended the interview.

I don't think Agent X had the slightest interest in the strike. If the conversation had continued, he would have likely expressed sympathy for it and tried to appear as a friend of the farmworkers. Nor was he there because of the arson charge. He was fishing for information useful to weakening or destroying any oppositional political movements.

During periods of popular upheaval the FBI sometimes tries to come off as sympathetic to progressive causes such as civil rights. This is a hoax. The FBI is implicated in the murder of Malcolm X, Martin Luther King Jr., Fred Hampton, and other important leaders. They carried out and continue to carry out operations designed to discredit, divide, and destroy progressive movements that represent obstacles or dangers to the functioning of the empire in its repressive, brutal doings. To believe the FBI is anything but the implacable enemy of all genuine progressive movements and of the struggle of the oppressed is to engage in self-deception. To think you can outwit them, or psych them out, which to some degree I believed at the time, is to be blinded by one's own foolishness.

Early in the afternoon of the following day I was told I was released, charges dropped, for lack of evidence.

I went to FJ's place that night to let him and others in Watsonville know what had happened. I got a call shortly after arriving there from Ken Dursa, my former roommate, asking how I was. "Fine," I said. "Why do you ask?" "I was concerned about you being in jail." "How did you know I was in jail?" "From the TV," he said. "It was on the news!" "It was?" "Ya, a Captain Miracle, talked about you tonight. He said they'd arrested you and believe you're the person responsible for a string of arsons at various facilities around the city." So now I was the mad arsonist! It seems that Captain Miracle's comments were broadcast on the evening news just about the same time I was being released for lack of evidence. "Wow," said Kenny, as the timing became clear. "Sounds like there's a lawsuit there somewhere."

Lawsuit

The union's legal staff refused to live at the UFW headquarters in La Paz. The union's chief counsel, Jerry Cohen, was important enough to the union that Chávez didn't push the point. That's why I was able to find Jerry in his office in downtown Salinas. Cohen had a reputation as an in-your-face attorney, able to match wits with the growers' lawyers, conservative judges, and the like and usually come out on top.

He knew of my case, and of me, apparently, because soon after walking in to the office I was challenged by him, though indirectly. "You heard of that group, that nationalist group that defends Juan Corona, haven't you?" he said, almost as soon as I'd introduced myself. I'd heard something about it. And I knew about Juan Corona, a Yuba City labor contractor accused of murdering dozens of farmworkers who'd worked for him. It was said that he buried the workers in the peach orchard of a nearby farmer who discovered the freshly dug ground on his property and called the local authorities. It had come out in the press that Corona had exploited alcoholics and other down-and-out folks for some time, keeping them in a state of semi-slavery by paying only small amounts of their wages, usually just enough to feed their alcohol or drug habits and making it difficult for them to leave.

These itinerant workers were owed large sums of money, and Corona figured he could avoid paying what he owed them by just getting rid of them. He counted on their isolation, estrangement from their families, and the indifference of society to their plight, to get away with this ghastly crime. That's what it appeared from the press accounts.

"You know why they defend Corona?" Cohen went on, referring to a Chicano group protesting his prosecution. "They defend him because he's *Mexican*. And because he's Mexican he's just being persecuted," he said with more than a bit of sarcasm. "And anyway, weren't a lot of the farmworkers he killed white?" I didn't know enough about the strength or nature of the evidence against Corona, the nature of the group's objections, or even what the group was, to say much. "Listen," said Jerry, "this is such an off-the-wall, narrow, divorced-from-reality way of looking at the world—an irresponsible, knee-jerk nationalism. If you don't have any real responsibility for what goes on, for the fate of people, what the hell, it doesn't matter, you can take any kind of position. But if you're fighting for something real and have to be accountable for what you do, if real people's lives are affected by what you do, things look different."

I knew by now what he was getting at, but he was using what one might call a straw man to do it. Raise an obviously weak argument and defeat it to make a point. Defending someone like Juan Corona only because he was Latino—if, in fact that was the motivation—was certainly not defensible. But Cohen's real point was that criticizing the union's stand on undocumented "illegal" strikebreakers was tantamount to defending Juan Corona. Undocumented immigrants used as scabs were scabs, period. A scab is a scab, is what Cohen and others close to the union leadership liked to say. Any other circumstances were irrelevant. They were being used consciously or against their will, but they were being used to defeat the union movement, to defeat the struggle to organize farmworkers, the struggle to give workers the collective strength with which to liberate themselves from growers' oppression. Scabs were tools of the enemy and needed to be fought against by any means necessary. Because of their vulnerability, the growers and labor contractors more easily manipulated the "illegals," and it was difficult to organize them. They often feared association with the union, not because they were bad, but because in their conditions they are intimidated. Furthermore, since it was in the interest of all farmworkers that the union succeeded, deporting the undocumented strikebreakers was in the broader interests of the undocumented as well. This was the argument. Jerry didn't have to lay it all out. I'd heard it before.

Cohen was a strong defender of that policy. And he was enmeshed in controversy around it. Every summer lawyers and law students associated with the National Lawyers Guild, a progressive organization of lawyers and law students, volunteered with the union. They had done valuable work as legal observers and legal investigators. However, a great many of them refused to have anything to do with the anti-illegals campaign, and because of the union's insistence that all union staff, including volunteer staff, adhere to all union policies, it was becoming impossible for these lawyers and law students to work with the union. This had become a very contentious issue because the anti-illegal campaign was now the union's *main* priority in California, taking precedence over boycotts and strikes.

The legal staff was deeply involved in the "illegals" campaign, with the union's legal staffers spending long hours gathering statements from strikers, residents in rural areas, and neighbors of suspected undocumented workers. They were gathering evidence of collusion between the INS and growers, documenting the INS failure to enforce immigration law and failing to act even when there was clear evidence as to the whereabouts of the undocumented, as when, for example, the union informed them of the location of such workers.

Declarations gathered by union staffers included inflammatory testimony attesting to the bad, even malicious, character of the undocumented. These declarations were used to pressure politicians to get the migra out "doing their job." They were used to appeal directly to the immigration agents. Chávez wrote personal letters of thanks to those who joined the anti-illegals whistleblowing campaign, praising them as friends of the movement. It was a glaring example of how negative stereotyping of a group can begin to take hold when it is encouraged by influential sources.[3]

Opposition among lawyers and law students to this policy resulted in an internal battle in the National Lawyers Guild. The Guild took a stand against the UFW's policy and advised its members not to participate in any union activities aimed at cooperating with the immigration agents against immigrants. This position enraged some top UFW leaders, and Jerry Cohen wrote a terse letter severing the relationship between the union and the Guild. Union attorneys were asked to do likewise and were severely criticized if they failed to vigorously defend the union's position.

We on *The Worker* strongly opposed the union's policy on a number of grounds, including philosophical ones. It was shortsighted to develop a policy to achieve a limited and immediate goal without regard to the long-term damage it could cause.

I tried to interject that point into the conversation, but it was not to be. Jerry was not interested in debating the point. "My time is limited," he said, "and you're here about that false arrest case, right? I think we ought to get to that; this office has a lot to deal with."

He then proceeded to quickly summarize the union's strategy in my case with the police. "The cops shit all over themselves on this case," said Jerry. "We've got 'em by the balls. We're going to send the Salinas Police Department a few hundred interrogatories. The cost of answering them will be greater than settling this thing out of court. They'll settle." He handed me a thick file of papers with the questions to look at. The questions aimed at uncovering the department's procedures for investigating crimes, and how it had proceeded in this case, eliciting information that would have been very time-consuming to produce, even if the police were so inclined to provide it. Cohen made it clear that the union was not going to pursue a more aggressive case against the police; it was not that important to them. And I accepted that.

Of "Illegals" and Ideologies

At that moment I was more interested in pursuing the controversy Cohen had raised. For people like myself with a revolutionary point of view, the most significant aspect of the farmworker movement was its challenge to the exploitation and national oppression of Mexicanos and other oppressed peoples. Among the most blatant expressions of that oppression was the way in which immigrants were stripped of their legal rights by being labeled undocumented. This is a system that lives off the plunder of other countries like Mexico and then uses and abuses the people forced by that plunder to emigrate to survive.

The immigration police are the enforcers of that system. Calling on the INS to "do their job" meant endorsing that role, blunting the reality they represented while inducing people into collaboration with the system. It was a policy that trained people to think of the migra and the government as allies or at least as a neutral authority that could, with enough pressure from below, act in the interest of the people.

And here, I suppose, was the practical side of the policy for the UFW leadership. Whether it was consciously conceived this way or not, it put the union in closer alliance with the political system by increasing people's faith in that system. It therefore yielded positive results, not by pushing the INS to help against strikebreakers, which seldom happened in any event, but in strengthening an alliance with the Democrats and other liberal representatives of the system.

A dynamic was in motion. The illegals policy alienated the radical and progressive forces—not only outside but also inside the union—at the same time as it brought the union closer to a policy favorable to a U.S. ruling class still struggling against the radicalism and revolutionary sentiments unleashed by the upheavals of the 1960s.

Bowing to Israel

This dynamic was not as clear at the time as it is in retrospect. It helps explain another incident at that time. At the end of 1973 César Chávez circulated a letter to the union staff that was later made public, in support of Israel. It came just months after the 1973 Yom Kippur War and Israel's triumph against the armies of Egypt and Syria. Chávez's statement said in part: "As individuals committed to the cause of freedom, concerned with the fate of victims of racial, ethnic and religious prejudice and discrimination, we feel a particular sense of solidarity with Israel's struggle to survive as a democracy in peace. As persons of Mexican-American backgrounds, we share Israel's aspirations to integrate people from vastly different backgrounds and to provide them all, including Arab and Jew alike, with the benefits of an advanced social system. . . . We appeal to our government to provide Israel with material aid to those in need and moral influence to bring both sides to the bargaining table in the hope of achieving peace."

This statement caused an uproar among some progressives, who wondered how the union could support a state that oppressed and discriminated against an entire people, the Palestinians. Support of Israel has been such a key element of the U.S. strategy in the oil-rich Middle East, and anyone seriously interested in allying with either political party, Republicans or Democrats, must adhere to it. How much this declaration of support for Israel was taken up on the initiative of the union or due to pressure from AFL-CIO president George Meany or other allies of the union is not clear. But the implication was obvious. This was an open and clear ideological accommodation to empire.

Disgrace in San Luis?

A few months after my conversation with Jerry Cohen, I received a check for $500 from the Salinas police. I received the money by forswearing any further legal action on this case.

Around the time I received this settlement, I was walking down Alisal Street near the union hall when I heard someone call my name. On the corner across the street stood a stocky man in his early thirties with short, wiry brown hair. It was his voice, not his figure, that I first recognized.

I knew Ruben Martinez from union and other political activities. Most recently we'd spent time together on the picket lines at Buak where his volatile personality and occasional outbursts of anger made people uncomfortable with him on the line.

Ruben's brother and sister-in-law were longtime community activists in Watsonville who threw their support behind the farmworkers' union during the 1970 general strike. But their relationship with the union soured over what they said was its growing coziness with the political establishment. The union in turn denounced the Martinez family as crazy and irresponsible militants.

Despite his family's criticism, Ruben worked with the union. The union found his bravado style and his bent toward physical action useful, and they found a place for him within a special section headed by Manuel Chávez.

After greetings, Ruben asked about how things had gone with the Buak strike, and I gave him some of the highlights. When I told him about the police and the arson arrest and the settlement, he got very upset. "Oh, my brother, the union screwed you, man! You should have gotten your own attorney and burned the cops' asses for what they did to you, not some shitty little settlement like that!" I told Ruben I wasn't really interested in spending a lot of time on the issue, but he was not placated. He thought I could have won a big suit against the city, and I was foolish not to pursue this. Maybe he was right, I don't know.

Wishing to change the subject, I asked, "What about you, Ruben, you still working for the night crew?" This special union crew did things not publicly acknowledged, and I knew Ruben and a few others involved with it. "Ya, I've been working with them," said Ruben. He did not sound happy about it. "We just got back from San Luis."

I'd heard about the big strike in the lemon orchards near the border in Arizona opposite the town of San Luis Rio Colorado. There the union's campaign against illegal strikebreakers was raised to a whole different level. The word was that the union set up tents along the border to stop workers coming across the border, to prevent them from breaking the strike. There were rumors about union actions on the border, not very pretty ones.

"What went on down there?" I asked. Ruben looked away and slapped a light pole hard several times with his open hand. He shook his head. He looked at the ground and then at me; his face was contorted as if he were in pain. "I'm not proud of what I did there, brother, OK? I'm not proud. Fuck no. I'm not proud of it, not at all, not at all." That's all he would say about it. But his emotional state made me think the rumors were true.[4]

6. NEW LAW, 1975

A DECADE HAD ELAPSED since the movement in California's fields began, a decade that encompassed upheaval on a global scale: growing economic instability, financial arrangements in place since the end of the Second World War discarded; the Middle East oil embargo; and perhaps most crucial of all, the U.S. defeat in Vietnam. The image of panicked officials packing helicopters on the rooftop of the U.S. embassy in Saigon marked the humiliating end to the greatest military defeat in U.S. history.

The Cold War between the United States and the Soviet Union was about to enter a new, more dangerous stage, and so those with power saw a need for order on the home front. The government had moved to put down the struggle of black people, combining political repression and assassination with economic concessions and civil rights legislation. A high point of anti-colonial struggle and political rebellion had passed, and what the 1960s had wrought in terms of pulling the mask off U.S. democracy and inflaming the passions of liberation and revolution was now coming under ferocious counterassault.[1]

The rebellion in the fields that emerged with, and in some ways merged with, the broader social movement, could not but be influenced by these changes. The union rode the upsurge in the fields, encouraged it, and gave it political direction, but was now coming under great pressure to put it down.

The repression unleashed during the summer of 1973 failed to crush the union movement in the fields and had, in reality, unleashed even greater, more widespread agitation. Union allies, such as big unions and Democratic politicians, sought another way to still the waters and restore "peace" in the fields. When Democrat Jerry Brown won election as governor in California in November 1974, a way was open to a political compromise the UFW leadership felt it could live with.

The union encouraged the strike wave in 1974 with an eye on a quid pro quo, that is, to win a favor in return for one it was prepared to grant. The message was clear: there would be no peace in the fields, no end to strikes and boycotts, unless the union was granted the concessions that would ensure its survival. The stage was set for the Agriculture Labor Relations Act, the ALRA.

The campaign to pressure the INS to deport "illegal" strikebreakers and the statement in support of the state of Israel were unmistakable signals: the UFW, however much its development was intertwined with the rebellions of the 1960s, was moving ideologically into the camp of the imperialists. It was willing, indeed it had to, break with progressive forces to do this. As there is punishment for those who remain steadfast and refuse to make peace with the system, there are rewards for those who move into its protective shadow. The union demonstrated its ideological will to do just that. It would now seek its political reward.

The Race Is Won

It was the first week of June 1975. It was early morning. Despite the approaching summer solstice, it was still dark as I stood on a corner on Market Street in the Alisal. Farm labor buses passed by, whining and rumbling as their driver foremen revved their engines and jerked their sticks into gear. A group of broccoli workers in their yellow rain pants and dark rubber boots walked toward a bus that pulled to a stop on a side street adjacent to where I stood, their rubberized gear rustling with each step as they mounted the bus. Other workers stood on the opposite street corners. Still more approached silently from the side streets of the barrio, or emerged from the small wood houses that sat along Market Street between fruit stands, used clothing stores, and bars.

It was a relatively warm morning. The air was still and dry and most workers came without jackets, some even in short-sleeve shirts. Their rubber gloves hung out of back pockets; lettuce knives and sheathes stuck out of others. Colored plastic mesh bags bulged with thermoses, and there were hats of many descriptions to ward off the intense summer sunlight a few hours away.

Eyes strained to identify the colors and letterings of the buses and vans as they approached, a task made more difficult as the orange-yellow glow of the street lights distorted their normal colors. I kept an eye out for a bus from the Finerman Company.

In the darkness, several figures made their way up the street. They passed out leaflets as they walked, and the workers nodded their heads to their remarks as they moved along. I recognized them as union office staffers and farmworkers active in the union. "Buenos dias. Mira, ya ganamos, compa. La victoria es nuestra," I heard them say as they approached. I grabbed a leaflet and strained to read it by the dim glow of the street light across the street. At the top there was a graphic of a runner crossing the finish line, his head thrown back victorious as his chest broke a tape. The headline read "Ya Se Ganó La Carrera!" The race is won! On June 5, 1975, the California legislature had approved the Agriculture Labor Relations Act, known forthwith as the ALRA, setting up a process of union recognition elections in the fields.

A rating of union leaflets put out over the years would put this one, announcing the passage of the ALRA, high on the list of the best known and most widely distributed. It signaled a major change, a major turning point in the history of the farmworkers' movement and the beginning of a new era in the fields.

The ALRA

The growers and the union had demanded an election process at different times over the previous ten years, usually when they thought the outcome would go their way or when the call for elections served a public relations need. During the Delano strike and boycott and in Salinas in 1970, growers called for elections. At times, these election calls came with conditions ensuring a favorable outcome for the party promoting them. In 1973, the year grape growers turned their contracts over to the Teamsters, the UFW called for elections to counter growers' claims that they were "obeying the will of their workers."

In 1935, in the midst of a deep economic depression, waves of strikes, factory occupations, and other labor rebellions rocked the country. A union election process under the National Labor Relations Act was one outcome. Agriculture was excluded from NLRA labor protections. As the situation in the fields heated up in the late 1960s and into the 1970s, there were calls from different quarters to include agriculture in its provisions. The UFW opposed this because the NLRA's provisions were ill-suited to union organizing among seasonal agriculture workers. Delays allowed under the NLRA between submitting a request for elections and conducting one would not work in the fields, where a harvest would likely be over by the time the election was held. The NLRA also prohibited secondary boycotts, like boycotting of supermarkets carrying grapes, a crippling restriction for conducting a boycott of a product that comes without any clear labeling.

The Agricultural Labor Relations Act represented a compromise more favorable to a farmworkers' union. It allowed union organizers access to the workers in the fields. It set up a process for elections to be held soon after the required number of authorization cards was submitted. In the political terrain of 1975, with the Democrat Jerry Brown as governor of California, the union had some leverage over who would sit on the Agricultural Relations Board. In fact, the board selected to oversee the work of the ALRA was weighted in favor of the union, with Bishop Roger Mahoney and Leroy Chatfield, both supporters of the UFW, among the four pro-UFW members of the five-person board. But the ALRA was part of the government apparatus and, in the final analysis, turf favorable to the growers and the powers that be.[2]

Confessions

The UFW used religious symbols, especially "La Virgin de Guadalupe," as a unifying element among the people from Mexico. The origin of "La Virgin" dates from 1531 when, the story goes, a young peasant, Juan Diego, was visited by an apparition similar to the Virgin Mary, but with facial features indigenous to Mexico. This was just ten years after the small, but aggressive invading army of Spaniards led by Hernan Cortez, cleverly and brutally playing off difference among the peoples of central Mexico, defeated the Aztecs in their magnificent city of Tenochtitlan. Diseases, horses, religious superstitions, and conflict among rival peoples in central Mexico aided the conquest.

When the blood dried, the Spanish held political control over much of Mexico. Capturing political power was a first decisive step, but it remained to firmly establish their hold on the many peoples in the area. Their arms had proven superior, but would people submit to their rule? The Spanish Catholic authorities hailed the "miraculous" appearance of an Indian Virgin as proof of the superiority of their religion, and it gave them a potent local symbol to combat the influence of the Aztec gods and the gods of other indigenous societies in Mexico the Spanish sought to supplant.[3]

Two hundred and eighty years later, the Virgin of Guadalupe was carried into battle by the forces of Mexico's independence rebellion led by the priest Father Miguel Hidalgo. The symbol the Spanish colonizers created and promoted to solidify their rule was now claimed as a symbol in the fight to defeat them.

For many farmworkers, La Virgin was as much a symbol of national unity as a religious one. Though religious devotion among the farmworkers was and is certainly a potent influence, religious piety is not universal and there was plenty of opposition to the Church as an institution, if not the idea of God.

People sometimes asked about my religion. I told them I was born into a moderately religious family but now, I'd confess, I was an atheist. For many fellow workers, the idea that I was an atheist was shocking, and it sometimes aroused interest and even concern. Profess belief in socialism or revolution and it aroused interest. But since many in Mexico and Latin America considered themselves these things, and there were plenty of farmworkers who used such labels to describe their own sympathies, the labels had a limited shock value. But atheist? That was another matter, and it often sparked comments like "How could you *not* believe in God?" There were times when you could sense a fear, as if disbelief in God was inviting a terrible calamity. Even people who were not particularly devout or didn't put much stock in religious observances or institutions had this fear, which came from an early and intense indoctrination. For most, God was a given.

When the opportunity presented itself, I would try to explain the origin of my belief because I did believe in many things, just not a "god." Serious disbelief in God began when I was thirteen. It corresponded with an intense interest in evolution. The obvious incongruities between the science of evolutionary theory and religious teachings forced me to question my religious teachers and, ultimately, religion itself.

Religion, it seemed to me, had very few answers to the interesting mysteries of life. The Bible had its colorful stories, its songs, and poetry, but science had a vast and growing storehouse of information about the world, the solar system, the universe, and life. It had a method for exploring the world, increasing knowledge and uncovering the amazing ways things worked and changed. Religious method consisted of accepting things on faith. When it came to understanding the world, religion was, by contrast, pale and simplistic, inconsistent, impoverished, and sometimes horribly mean-spirited. Not that science has never been distorted and misused. But religion was stuck on hold, retelling stories from thousands of years ago from one small corner of the world as if little of import had occurred outside its narrow "biblical" time and purview.

Of course, there were many deep philosophical questions on people's minds that influenced their belief in god. "Why are we here?" "How did we get here?" "What happens when we die?" Many people believe that there are no answers to these questions outside religion. Science offers answers, or a method for seeking them. It doesn't offer soothing promises.

On the other hand, to the *hell* that exists here on earth for many people, science does offer a methodology for getting at a truthful explanation for its existence and for seeking ways to change things. It's a methodology that helps clear away the notion that all is ordained by a god and therefore outside the purview of humans to change it. This can empower people to seek solutions, a big help to real, living human beings.

While belief in God was, in my experience, nearly universal in the fields, reverence for the Church was another matter. John Dury, who came to Salinas to work on an antiwar project around 1972 and ended up staying and working in the fields, found this out on an Interharvest thinning crew and related his experience to me.

Interharvest had a policy of allowing workers to take off work early on Good Friday. It was not a paid holiday, just a pass to leave work to go to church. When Good Friday came around, John expected his crew to take the opportunity to honor their religion. He was surprised when nearly everyone worked through the day. Not only that, there was pity, even ridicule, for those who left early. "They'll lose money, people said, and for what? To sit for half the day in church, bored?" This caught John by surprise and aroused his curiosity.

"Why aren't you observing this holiday?" he asked. "We're bad Catholics," they said without remorse. And as John related, they went on to explain:

Many of us come from the ranchos in the same area in Michoacan. We were poor farmers. Life was always pretty hard for us there. In our area there was a large *terretaniente*, a landowner, who was rich and politically powerful. He abused us with his power and that created great resentment.

Every now and then an animal, like a goat for example, would stray from this rich man's farm onto the land of one of us poorer neighbors. Under the right conditions this could be cause for celebrating our rare good luck—a goat to make an excellent meal for us all! Of course, we understood this was a sinful act—enjoying this goat that didn't belong to us!

The priest of our church always told us that sins would get us into trouble with God, but that if we confessed our sins we would be forgiven. Under other circumstances we might have confessed to the priest on the chance that this would save us from later grief. However, we made an exception in this case. We understood that confessing this "sin" would certainly lead to *immediate* grief. For it was certain that the landlord would hear of this confession—perhaps even before the Lord himself. And it would be the landlord, not God, who would deliver the punishment. We did not trust the priest nor religious authorities in general. The Church was a close friend of the landlords. *That* relationship we were very clear about.

Lettuce and Communism

We vegetable workers were a very productive workforce. A modest lettuce crew of thirty-five could harvest and pack 150,000 heads a day, enough to feed a small city. At the height of the lettuce season this sliver of land called the Salinas Valley produced around six million heads of lettuce a day (as well as many other farm products), 70 percent of the lettuce consumed in the country, with a lettuce harvesting workforce that numbered a few thousand. Working out this math made me think of the disconnect between what we produce and could produce with the rational application of science and how the things we make are distributed. And I thought of how the many do the work, while the few who control this work and make it miserable for us get the lion's share of the fruits of our efforts. What if we did things differently? Shared everything. It made me think of communism.

I looked around at the crew and thought about the fabulous amounts of production passing through our calloused and beaten hands. And as Karl Marx noted, the enormous production unleashed by modern industry created the basis for a world in which all of humankind could participate in many aspects of life and culture, not just production. Yet, in this world we hardly had the energy to crawl into bed at night, let alone participate in any meaningful way in science or the arts. We had no say in the organization of production, let alone the administration of society. Nor were we encouraged to do so. Farmworkers are cast into the pit called "beasts of burden"—end of story. Obviously something would have to change before a communist world could come into existence based on this enormous productive system.

Sometimes a discussion would kick off at lunchtime—backs propped up against lettuce boxes, the odor of food mingled with the smell of the soil and fresh-cut lettuce, and I'd look across the ground littered with sweaty shirts and weathered faces and imagine a world where what we were doing went on voluntarily—in the sense that we were working for the common benefit of the larger community—and there would be no stigma connected to "manual labor." A world in which what we were doing was a conscious contribution to securing the needs of society and not some alienating effort done under a coercive hand for an "alien" force that used that wealth to advance private interests. And tomorrow or next week, we might be discussing developments in astronomy or learning to perform a new musical arrangement or debating production issues or governing policies.

The idea of such a cooperative society is not unappealing to people whose lives are restricted to being implements of production. But it was often discounted on grounds of human nature. "We can't even agree on minor things related to work, how do you suppose you'll ever get people to agree on how to run society?" Or, "We're not smart enough. And the smart people will always take over." Or, "People are too self-ish. Somebody'll always find a way to get over on the next guy." My own understanding strained under these objections, and questions and arguments trailed off as we rose and returned stiffly to our rows.

In those years of the 1970s I felt that our growing capacity to produce would somehow, someday, assert itself and yield a new social order, bursting through the old shell that could no longer contain it. Humans were on a march to this better future, and, though much could delay it, nothing could ultimately stop it. And in that I was skirting close to a different form of religious thinking—only this god of mine was historical necessity!

I no longer hold this view. For better or for worse we humans have no such god to ensure our destiny. Only mighty struggles, guided by our best efforts to understand the world as it is, can make such potential a reality. There is no guarantee.

But the potential is there. I watched as it pulled out onto the highway on its way to feed the nation.

Lettuce Morality

Years after leaving the fields, I ran into a former lechuguero I'd worked with at Cal Coastal. He'd become a supervisor for a lettuce contractor. "It took me thirty years," Tony said with great conviction, as we sat in his company pickup, "to realize that what we were doing in the fields was producing food. I always have to insist to the workers about that." At first, I didn't understand what he was getting at. But as we talked it became clear. As a supervisor he was now critical of the careless attitude of workers, especially those working piece rate, who were more interested in the quantity than the quality of their production. Tony concluded that workers lacked a moral commitment to their work, failed to appreciate the value for human sustenance of what they produced. I realized that this morality, however worthy, will never be more than a secondary issue in a society where everything, including essentials to the well-being of people, is judged by its capacity to yield a profit. Growers may be sentimental about their lettuce, but in the end, if it doesn't yield a profit it has no value.

"Ya, the workers sometimes show a lack of concern for the product they're harvesting," I said, recalling my own attitude as a lechuguero, "but don't the growers show the same lack of concern when they disk a field of good lettuce because the market price is low?" Even if they feel bad about disking (as the worker *may* feel bad about packing a box of crushed, unmarketable lettuce), they would not hesitate—can't hesitate really—faced with the dictates of the bottom line. The grower that allows morality to stand in the way of cold economic calculation will soon be looking for other employment. Only when we live in an economic system where things are consciously produced to benefit society as a whole will the divide between human needs and human production be breached and we can talk of a world where moral responsibility for things produced for the benefit of people and the earth will be more than advertising rhetoric.

We argued for a while on this issue. Finally Tony said he'd learned through his years as a supervisor to appreciate the growers' point of view, an assertion I had little doubt was true.

Planets and Orbits

When humans get treated as mere instruments to produce, and their existence flattened down to fit the needs of production, they can begin to internalize negative views of themselves and one another. Some of this comes out in the terms people use. For example, farmworkers frequently greet each other with, "Hey, que pasa güey!" (which translates to something like, what's up, dumb ox?). The frequent use of "güey"—ox—reflected some of this negativity even as it was used in a joking, playful way. And every once in a while you needed to remind yourself that you and the people around you were human beings, as capable of soaring creativity as anyone, with that potential restricted by a restricting social order. It might make you consider what people could be like in a society that valued them as people and provided the opportunity to give expression to that fuller humanity.

One day John was reminded of this on his thinning crew. He had a partner on that crew named Antonio, and they spent a lot of time talking about different things related to work and their lives, and their ideas of the world. One day Antonio pointed to the sky and remarked about the movement of the sun around the earth. This stopped John in his tracks, until he realized that from an empirical point of view, this is exactly what the sun's movement looks like. Antonio had had little formal education. But he had a curious and creative mind, and he wanted to know what John knew about the subject. So, for a time, during breaks and lunch John related to Antonio what he knew about such matters, even drawing a diagram in the dirt with the handle of his hoe of the solar system, the planets orbiting the sun, and the rotation of the earth. It was a riveting experience for Antonio, who had never been introduced to this science before, and for John, to see the effect this information had on his friend, and how it opened up a new perspective on the world for him.

Finerman

Among the farms and agribusinesses in Salinas, Mel Finerman may have been the most purely capitalist. Like a stripped-down car, shorn of all but its essentials, the company was built for maximum performance, which meant making money for its investors. Not for Finerman was the show other growers made of their civic mindedness. The Churches and D'Arrigos, Hansens, Hardens, Antles, Oshitas, Crosettis, and Merrills—family-owned or at least family-initiated businesses—relished praise as stalwarts of the community. Their positions of prominence in the Salinas Valley were displayed in permanent offices, equipment yards, in some cases their own coolers and sheds. Their buses and pickups usually bore their names and logos. Even Interharvest, the United Brands behemoth, which had come into the valley as an outsider, had its own camps and recognizable trucks and buses, and thus had an image of stability and standing, if not popularity, in the community of growers.

Finerman had neither such presence nor, perhaps, pretensions. Even the Finerman office, in a rented building in the middle of old-town Salinas, had an impermanent feel to it. It had once been a branch of the Bank of America.

In the movie *The Sting*, which opened in 1973, Paul Newman and Robert Redford are con artists who find a way to bilk a hoodlum of his money. They convert an empty warehouse into a realistic-looking, bustling betting operation. After losing a fortune in the betting house, the hoodlum, played by Robert Shaw, returns to the establishment, only to find it returned to its empty warehouse state. Going into Finerman's office, you felt like this too could be a front, and that the next time you came to pick up a check, it might just be an empty building, strewn with discarded boxes and abandoned filing drawers left in haste in a move to greener pastures.

Mel Finerman signed with the union after the 1970 strike, then in 1973 followed other growers and dropped the UFW, seeking the shelter of a Teamster contract. And he did so for the same basic reason the others had taken that route, to maintain control over production, and the instruments of production, the two-legged kind.

I got hired at Finerman in the late spring of 1975, and it was now midsummer. One day we were in a field near the Firestone Tire factory, just outside of Salinas, when several cars pulled up to the field. Out came people who looked like company officials, in slacks and long-sleeve shirts. They were accompanied by a Finerman supervisor. They came walking up the rows, somewhat gingerly, toward us. Elias, one of my trio partners cutting in front of me, turned and smiled. "Aquel señor allá" (that guy over there), he said pointing to a man in a gray sports coat, "el es dueño de la parcela aqui" (he owns this land here). The foreman had told him that. Then he laughed. "I guess he brought the wrong shoes." The landowner had on light suede shoes. The field was still damp from the heavy morning mist, and he was having trouble keeping his shoes from getting muddy as he carefully stepped his way forward toward us. Just seeing someone out in the fields with such shoes seemed funny.

Elias didn't know anything about the other men who'd come with him, but we guessed they were investors in the company. They made their way out to where we were working to view the operation, looking curious, as one would expect of people watching a worksite like this for the first time.

It felt odd with them in the field. Every day we worked semi-conscious or oblivious to the relationship between our work and the wealth that the companies were accumulating. But here, with someone clearly unconnected to the fields, the work, or the workers except by way of a kind of abstract ownership of the land, cast it all in a slightly different light. I was not judging the landowner; he might have been a good person, kind, generous, socially conscious, a contributor to righteous social causes. Or he might have been a narrow-minded bigot. He may have inherited the land from a relative, or he may have purchased it as an investment. He may have worked the land at some point and been pushed out by more muscular capital. It made no difference. Otherwise invisible threads connected his well-being and ours. Whether he made money on this land, or went into debt paying taxes on it, depended on us. Some of our efforts, our sweat, our pain, a part of our waking day, and our energy went to produce wealth that would go into his pocket, to use as he wished, be it contributing to Vietnamese war orphans, buying the latest-model Jaguar, or funding the Daughters of the American Revolution.

I felt a strong sense of alienation and distance from these men walking toward us. It was more than the slacks and dress shirts. If we had chanced to eat at the same restaurant, we would not likely have noticed any great divide, but here they felt like alien beings.

I was aware of how oddly *I* might be perceived by the visitors. The rest of the crew, Mexicans, would be taken for granted as belonging in the fields. This was a given. If the whole crew were PhDs from prestigious Latin American universities, they would have seemed, with their brown skin and baseball caps, in their proper place in the universe. On the other hand, they may have looked at me with pity or contempt. This was the underside of being from a privileged group.

To the owners and investors we were, regardless of our backgrounds and ethnicities, really just instruments of production. Maybe they would feel grateful for us; maybe they would consider us troublemakers or overpaid. Maybe they would not think about us at all.

After the visitors left and we broke for lunch, Elias and I and our other trio partner began talking about the visitors, about the land, and about what it all meant.

I learned early in life, as do most schoolchildren in the United States, the story of the purchase of Manhattan. The Indians who occupied that island, in their childlike innocence—so the story goes—sold the island, destined to become the great center of world capital (as in money) to Dutch traders for a few shiny beads. It was only later, and outside of school, that I learned that the native occupants of Manhattan did not sell the island since the idea of selling land and exclusively owning land was not part of their social outlook. To the native people, the trading of gifts signified an agreement to share the land. It was the Dutch who interpreted this as a sale, a permanent change of control, and acted accordingly, driving the native people from their land, confiscating it for their use, and with slave labor building a big wall (the origin of Wall Street) to keep the Indians from returning to retrieve what they had lost.

The fact that Indians could not sell land because that concept did not exist in their culture was an insight that changed forever my view of the world and especially what is referred to as human nature. Apparently, human nature regarding ownership of land is not some fixed and frozen category but varies with the development of society. I related this story to my trio partners, and then Elias said he had a story to tell me, also about land and about feelings toward it.

Elias's Story and the White Rose

Elias had an uncle who lived in a *rancho* (village or town) in the state of Morelos. The uncle was a small landowner and a teacher. He was someone held in high regard in the community. One day the uncle received a visit from an official of the ruling PRI party from a nearby town (Partido Revolucionario Institucional, or PRI, was then the ruling governing party of Mexico). The official was cordial and friendly, remarking on the uncle's good reputation and the confidence that others had in him. The uncle found the praise and high regard suspicious, and was hardly flattered by it. He was not a political man, but he knew enough about the PRI not to trust it. He was, after all, in the state that produced Emiliano Zapata, and it was politicians of the PRI type who murdered Zapata, even though they later built statues to him and endlessly praised his name in public ceremonies.

The PRI official left without stating any particular purpose other than to meet the uncle, but he returned several weeks later for another visit. This time he brought a representative of a corporation that had an interest in a development in the area of the village. They were not specific about the project, but they said it was something that would be greatly beneficial to the community, would bring jobs and revenue, and help the community with school facilities and other institutions. As a teacher, the uncle would certainly be interested in something that would bring resources to the school. So they said.

The PRI official wanted Elias's uncle to meet the people behind the project. These were outsiders, the PRI official confided, and could not be expected to understand the community and its needs. The uncle could play a role to ensure that the project was carried out with the interests of the people in mind. The uncle listened patiently but uneasily to these two friendly men, trying to figure out their real motives. When he asked what the project was, he was told he'd be given all the details later.

He soon found out. A week after the second visit, the man, who represented a company with both Mexican and U.S. investors, returned. This time the man revealed a project that would bring tourists to the area. Once again the man praised the project as a great boon to the community and insisted that the uncle, as a broad-minded, educated person, would understand and embrace it. Furthermore, in view of the uncle's prestige in town, the representative was certain his assistance would be of great value. The biggest hurdle was getting the right land for the development. If the uncle were to sell his land for the project, he would be paid a very good price. His help in influencing others in a positive way would be appreciated and generously compensated.

The uncle heard him out, thanked him for his confidence, but no, he could not sell his land. The land was part of the people and the culture. A revolution had been fought to secure the land. It was paid for in blood. Asking him to give up his land would be like asking him to sell his arms and hands. The land was the base and livelihood of the community. Without their land the community would cease to exist.

The company man was insistent. He offered the uncle not only a generous amount for his land but a bonus if he agreed to sell. If he helped him with the others, he would be in line for a bonus for each of them as well. Once again the uncle refused. The offer of bribery angered him, and he began to express his feelings. If the man wanted to talk to other small owners, he was free to do so, but the uncle would not sell his land or try to convince others to do so.

The company man was discouraged but did not give up. He offered a greater reward and then, also, some warnings. There were people who were set on the project and had invested time and money in it. It had to go forward. They would not be happy with the obstacles that stood in their way.

The uncle countered that the promised benefits to the community might not appear if people sold the land. People in Mexico had seen a lot of this "progress," and it always ended up benefiting someone else. Progress always seemed to be to the detriment of the peasants. Progress had driven thousands off the land into the big cities. What good was revenue if their community was destroyed?

The company man expressed surprise that the uncle was such an unreasonable man. He warned Elias's uncle that he should wake up to economic realities. The world is changing, he said. There were economic powers that could not be resisted for long. The peasants with their quaint ways were an anachronism. They could barely produce enough to feed themselves and their families. Here was an opportunity for progress.

Fuck your progress, the uncle later confided to his family. To the agent he said, Progress for you is no progress for us. Do you know how many people around here have had to leave for DF (Mexico City) or el Norte?

You're arguing against yourself, the man said. This project will bring money here to this community.

But the uncle wasn't going for it. As far as he was concerned, whatever money came to the community by this investment would go to the owners. The people might get a few low-paying jobs, probably serving tourists. But he didn't want any part of it.

Thus the lines hardened. And the enmity grew.

I said to Elias, "So he didn't sell the land to the company?"

No."

"Y entonces, que pasó con tu tio?" (What happened to your uncle?)

"Desapareció más tarde. Encontraron su cuerpo en una zanga fuera del pueblo, con veinte balazos." (He disappeared and was found in a ditch with twenty gunshot wounds.)

"Le mató porque no quiso vender su tierra. Que mierda!" (Killed because he wouldn't sell his land. What a bunch of shit!) "And the project, what happened to it?" "It was a big scandal and the local people protested. The local PRI people at one point had to flee for their lives. There was no way the project could go forward, so it was abandoned. But the PRI found a way to take vengeance on the community. The whole thing was a big mess."

And what about the investors, people who may have just innocently invested some money in a development in Mexico. I wondered if they had any inkling of the trauma they caused by investing in such a land deal.

I said, "That's something like the White Rose story." The *White Rose* was a novel by B. Traven, a German immigrant who wrote stories set among the indigenous people of Mexico. I first learned of Traven and his books on a trip to Mexico in the winter of 1973. There I began reading, slowly and with difficulty, a series of books called the *Jungle Novels* about the enslavement and rebellion of the indigenous people of Chiapas. Later I found *La Rosa Blanca*, the story of an indigenous peasant community whose ill fortune resided in being located on land coveted by a U.S. oil company. Like Elias's uncle, the patriarch of the White Rose community refused to sell the land, with tragic results.

The similarity between the White Rose story interested Elias but didn't surprise him. "Stealing land from indigenous communities and peasants has been a way of life for a long time in my country. You know, there was a revolution fought over that!"

I tried to convey my fascination, not only with the stories of this German writer but by the writer himself. Traven steadfastly refused to reveal his true identity. Only after his death were some of the details of his life confirmed by his widow, and the world discovered that Traven, who had claimed to be from the United States, perhaps to protect himself, had German roots.

Traven was part of a revolutionary movement that swept Germany after its defeat in the First World War. Rebels in Munich took power in the city and declared a socialist republic. The republic was short-lived. The counterrevolution mobilized ex-soldiers called Stahleim, for the steel helmets they wore, to crush the revolt. By a stroke of good fortune, Traven was able to escape the country, eventually making his way to Mexico where he spent time among the peasants in the indigenous states of Oaxaca and Chiapas. Here his rebellious soul flourished in the rich soil of a people whose own inclinations toward rebellion were nearly five hundred years in the making.

Why my interest in this German writer, Elias wanted to know. Maybe in part because my father, who grew up in Munich, related events of those days to me as he recalled them. He was a young boy when the Munich Soviet Republic (Münchner Räterepublik) was crushed. And a few years after this, he saw an obscure right-wing political organizer walking his dog on the street in front of an apartment just up the street from his own home. Later, when Hitler was on the rise politically, my father saw him and his Nazi partners driving Munich streets. My father was there in the early 1920s when Hitler's party tried to seize power, only to be defeated and Hitler sent to jail. And he was there when Hitler came to power in 1933 as the German chancellor. By the late 1930s my father's sister, near a nervous breakdown from the intense pressure put on Jews, implored my father to make preparations to leave. They found a way out with help from a cousin in Chicago, but their parents could never get a visa necessary to leave Germany.

But the story didn't end there. Here I address the reader since these facts were not known to me at that time in the fields. During the Nazi era a group of young Germans formed an underground opposition to the regime in Munich. And they called themselves the White Rose. They were probably the most successful anti-Nazi resistance group in Germany and, it seems, they were inspired by the stories of the indigenous people of Mexico.[4]

Union Convention

In mid-August 1975 the United Farmworkers held its second biannual convention in the same arena in Fresno where it had held its first convention in 1973. The situation was quite different and the mood more optimistic. In 1973 people were under siege, having just lost nearly all the grape contracts. Now, with the ALRA, there was anticipation that things would improve.

A number of people associated with *The Worker* went as delegates to the convention. I was not among them, but we all had worked on a resolution concerning the issue of undocumented workers and intended to present it at the convention.

We believed in the principle that anyone living and working in the country should be accorded basic human rights and allowed to live and work without the fear of persecution. The resolution called on the union to use its power and prestige to raise the demand for an end to deportations. A movement to end deportation would impact the community. Every time the migra came to deport people, every time a migra van was seen cruising a neighborhood and lying in wait outside a church, people would take heart knowing that there was a movement to end that kind of harassment. It would help build a sense of resistance and strengthen the union movement as a defender of human rights. And though the chances of winning such a demand were not good, certainly not without a massive campaign to end deportations, it would be a positive way to educate the people about how immigrants were being victimized. It would have the effect of uniting people and serve as a platform for educating them about the underlying cause for immigration in the first place: the inequalities between exploiting countries like the United States and exploited countries like Mexico. Besides, deportations were a weapon used against the union; they undermined the willingness of workers to get involved. People to whom we showed the resolution, including workers on our crews, viewed this approach favorably.

But it was not to be. The resolution never made it to the floor. It was presented properly according to procedures, but it was sidelined and suppressed, even though it found support on the floor among delegates. When one of the delegates who supported the resolution got up to speak about it, the mike was turned off and a music group started up to drown out his voice.

The Union Executive Board offered its own resolution. It proposed to fight for the undocumented. It said in part:

> WHEREAS, illegal workers often suffer more at the hands of the growers than legal residents, and
> WHEREAS, the United Farmworkers of America is dedicated to liberating all farmworkers who suffer regardless of color, creed, ethnic origin, religion or residence status,
> NOW THEREFORE BE IT RESOLVED by the membership of the United Farmworkers of America, AFL-CIO, sitting in convention in Fresno, California, that this organization urges the enactment of legislation granting amnesty to all illegal workers, and
> BE IT FURTHER RESOLVED that if growers can bring illegal workers to this country for the purpose of exploiting them, then we can organize illegal workers to liberate them.

With union elections about to begin the UFW continued with its pragmatism, this time tilting in the direction of undocumented workers who would be an important constituency in many ranches. But the resolution, by using the amnesty language ceded to the contention that "illegals" had to be forgiven for some offense, and it skirted the issue of deportations that was really the heart of the question.

Fired from Finerman

It was a warm day in fall and we were cutting in a field in North Salinas. It was a second cut field, meaning that it had already been harvested once. Not only were the remaining heads of lettuce in this field more dispersed, they were oddly shaped and difficult to handle. To make matters worse, late-season lettuce was flooding the market, bringing prices down. Growers were barely making their break-even price. Company men were swarming the field, inspecting the lettuce in the boxes, complaining about quality. It was a nervous market.

It was one of those days when the work is difficult and the money lean. Every normal pain is amplified and multiplied, and you're impatient to get it all over with. I was packing and cursing, my fingers sore from hitting up on the edge of the boxes. Elias came with a tall stack of boxes from the stitcher—he prided himself on the number he could carry at one time—and after dropping the last box in front of me, he nudged me in a way that was uncharacteristically serious. He pointed to a trio several rows over. There were boxes of lettuce overturned, their contents spilled on the ground. A supervisor was going up their row and dumping the lettuce. Half a dozen boxes at least had been dumped this way. I stopped my packing and went over to that line. Packers were standing around watching. The supervisor was cursing in English: "You gotta do better than that." He then jumped to the next line and started doing the same dumping routine in that row. Apparently, Finerman lettuce was not doing well on the market that day.

Watching this display of anger, of boxes being shoved over, of hard work spilling on the ground and the disrespectful anger of the supervisor, I got angry. The problem with the packing had much more to do with the lettuce we were harvesting than any failure of the cutters or packers. "Es por eso que necesitamos una unión!" (This is why we need a union!) I said this loudly so others would hear me. "Como nos insultan, nos chingan por su maldita lechuga, sus chingadas ganancias. Que nos importa, sus pinches ganancias. En qué nos beneficia? Fíjense, como la compania nos trata como mierda." (Look at the way they insult us—how they fuck us over for their shitty lettuce and their fucking profits. What do we care about their fucking profits. How do we benefit? Look at the way the company treats us like shit!) The reader might find the language a little salty, but believe me, that was just normal speech in the fields. The supervisor turned to me and came over to where I was, along with the foreman. "You go to the bus. We don't need you here anymore!"

"OK," I said. I began walking to the bus.

Then, I heard someone's voice. "Vámanos muchachos. Vamos todos!" And without much more comment, everyone began walking to the bus. The foreman came over and there was a discussion. The company offered to call it quits for the day if the crew finished up the load—a few more boxes from each trio. They agreed.

When we got back to Salinas, a number of us drove to the union hall. There we were directed to the new office of the ALRB on Laurel Drive. About a dozen of us drove over to the storefront office of the bureaucracy set up to oversee union elections and handle related issues. The place had just opened up, and we were apparently among its first customers. One of the office people in a suit and tie stood a little dazed as we traipsed in— dirty clothes, sweaty faces, dusty boots. An office worker, a young Latino, asked us what happened and we gave him a short report. I was asked to fill out a form. And then, a young woman in her mid-twenties, short and slender with medium-length blond hair, came up to me. She put out her hand. "I'm Susan," she said; "I need to ask you some questions."

We went into a little cubicle, and I told her what happened as she took notes. This was her first day on the job, her first job since graduating Berkeley's Boalt Law School. She was a socially conscious law student full of vigor with the prospect of using her legal knowledge and lawyer status to do some good for people who are more often victims of the law, or who could never afford a lawyer if they needed one. After talking to her a little while, it became obvious that she was sympathetic to the union movement. Once I finished with my account of what had happened on the crew, she assured me that in this case the company was clearly in violation of the new law. Companies were specifically prohibited from firing workers for their union views, she said. I was a lead-pipe cinch. And what would it mean to win, I asked. "You'll get back pay for all the days you miss until the case is settled. And you'd have your job back. Do you want your job back?" She laughed. "Ya, I suppose I do," I said.

I wasn't so sure about her optimistic assessment, but I appreciated her enthusiasm and her confidence. "If we win this case, can I buy you a dinner?" I asked. "Of course," she said.

Susan

I received a letter informing me that I was to be compensated with back pay from Finerman along with the restoration of my job, and I called Susan at the ALRA office. "I told you," she said, when I thanked her for her help. "Well, I promised a meal; dinner?" Several evenings later we went to a restaurant housed in an old church on Pajaro Street with the very Salinas name, East of Eden.

My relationship with Susan began on a harmonious note, but it turned stormy before long. It should not have been difficult to predict this. We had a lot in common on one level. Both of us were from middle-class Jewish families from Southern California. We both abhorred the injustice we saw in the world. We both had opposed the war in Vietnam and believed in the civil rights movement, the women's liberation movement, and so on. But our outlooks and goals in life were very different. I was no less middle class than she was in upbringing, but I had no desire at that point to live a middle-class life, whereas she did. Despite her abhorrence of injustice, she felt that there was little chance of really ending them, so she settled for acts to alleviate them to the extent she could by her own actions. I had a burning in my gut against all the injustices I perceived, and nothing could calm it. I wanted to get together with whomever I could to pursue some way of ending injustice and what I understood to be its source.

We could be friends, but these different views implied a different lifestyle and the attempts to reconcile the differences satisfied neither of us and led to periodic bursts of anger and frustration, and eventually separation.

We argued over differences of opinion. The arguments began not long after we started going together. The first argument I recall was about homosexuality. Up to that point much of what was the Marxist movement had developed a position on homosexuality that was both superficial and mechanical. Basing itself on a "reductionist" view of evolution, some Marxists concluded that homosexuality was unnatural, was in opposition to the basic need for species to procreate, and therefore must be a result of relationships distorted by class society. In the capitalist era, Marxists concluded, homosexuality was a product of capitalism in its decadent declining phase. This was the view I adopted and argued for, and it collided with Susan's. She did not see homosexuality as something negative at all, just part of human sexuality, more broadly defined. We disagreed and argued. As I was concluding that Susan had a more liberal attitude toward the system, I decided that she must be wrong on this too. This was my mistake and wrong way of thinking.

It would be years before I would conclude (and others I knew who considered themselves revolutionaries as well) that these views on homosexuality were *demonstrably wrong*. It was a sobering lesson, a lesson in the need to be willing to question one's own views and to consider other arguments seriously. Everyone is susceptible to religious views, not necessarily a belief in God, but views that hold themselves above serious scrutiny, views that become a part of a faith or dogma, guarded consciously or otherwise from evidence that might show them to be in conflict with reality.

Union Elections

The Agriculture Labor Relations Act was set to go into effect on August 27. In July, in anticipation of the elections, the Teamsters renegotiated contracts with 135 growers, mostly in lettuce. The new contracts increased wage and fringe benefits 25 percent. The minimum wage rose from $2.50 to $2.92 an hour. Piece rates went up 4 to 6 percent. The growers and Teamsters were taking out a little UFW insurance.

The ALRA office opened on August 28. That same day the Salinas police carried out raids in seven labor camps claiming they were looking for stolen goods. Thirty-two immigrants were arrested and turned over to the INS—the largest mass arrest of undocumented immigrants ever made by Salinas police. In Watsonville, forty more immigrants were taken in. The UFW loudly protested the roundups and denounced it as a ploy to intimidate immigrants in anticipation of the coming elections. Three UFW officials were arrested at the INS office in Salinas, an action that had a very PR feel to it.

By September, union elections were being held almost daily in California, with the UFW winning the majority, but not the large majority, of them.

The UFW won eighty-six elections the first month of voting, with a total of 13,410 votes, 52 percent of those cast. The Teamsters won seventy-three elections with 8,037 votes, 31 percent of all votes. The No Union option received the majority nineteen times, with 4,175 votes, or 17 percent of votes cast. After the second month of voting, the UFW had won 114 of the elections to the Teamsters' eighty-six. The most lopsided vote was at Interharvest, where the UFW won by 1,167 votes to twenty-eight for No Union. At about the same time, the Teamsters won a big victory at Bud Antle. Statewide, by the first week of October 30,000 farmworkers had voted in union elections at 267 farms. Thirty-six of the UFW victories were on ranches covered by Teamster contracts. This included nine of ten union elections among Watsonville apple growers.[5] The other elections either went No Union or were indecisive—disputed ballots being greater in number than the margin of victory for either union. In the Salinas-Watsonville area the election wins were about even.[6]

Such statistics alone did not tell the story. Elections at some ranches were held among workers who had been strikebreakers. And though strikers were technically eligible to vote at formerly struck ranches, finding them and getting them to the voting place was a challenging job.

The Teamsters had the advantage of incumbency. Before the elections the UFW had fewer than twenty contracts covering 10,000 of California's 220,000 peak season agriculture workers. The Teamsters claimed over 400 contracts covering around 50,000. The growers could often be counted on to aid the Teamsters side.

Nevertheless, the election broke the stranglehold the Teamsters held on many contracts. The UFW won elections in some of the key companies, like D'Arrigo and Bruce Church, which had been fighting the UFW for years.

But these were election *results*. It remained to be seen how many of these would be certified after the delays and challenges that the growers would soon become extremely adept at using.

La Corrida

The union elections campaign was heading south with the crop, and Susan, as an ALRA lawyer, was moving with them to the Imperial Valley. Mickey and I decided to follow "la corrida" south with the crop. Susan and I arranged to meet in Calexico.

La corrida is the circuit the lettuce takes as it follows the sun through its seasons. As the fall harvest season ended in Salinas, it shifted to other areas, such as the Mendota-Firebaugh and Huron, both a few hundred miles south of Salinas. The Finerman crews were being run by the contractor Willie Morales in Huron, a small farming town off Highway 5 near Coalinga and the Harris Ranch.

The Huron harvest season is short. Crews arrive as the crop matures and usually take a couple of weeks to complete the work. I arrived there a day before the harvest was to start. Morales/Finerman had rented a camp in town, a typical wooden barracks structure, with no insulation, just a cement slab, plain wood walls, and roof. It had a large heater suspended from the ceiling that stayed on too long and overheated the barracks.

In one corner of the room, old mattresses were stacked in a pile next to a stack of rough, thin blankets and coarse materials to use as sheets. We all grabbed from the piles and made up our army cots in the big, long, open barracks room.

Rain came early that fall. It rained the day I arrived at camp, and it continued to rain for days after. The barracks sat in a dirt yard that turned marshy with the downpour, so that we had to slosh through mud to go from barracks to bathroom to mess hall. It was impossible to keep the floors in any of these places clean, and so we got used to shuffling in the mud, inside and out.

The harvests that follow the Salinas fall "deal" (a name the growers use for harvest) and predate the Imperial Valley season are much smaller than those at either end of the harvest season, and the market can get hungry. Scarcity feeds the price and with the rain hammering central California, the alchemy of the market turned lettuce lead into lettuce gold—the price shot into the stratosphere.

It's nearly unheard of for lettuce crews to work in the rain. But that's exactly what that hot market led us to do. We sloshed in the mud, cutters struggling to stay on their feet as they bent over to slice the heads; packers sliding as they grabbed the heads three at a time and lowered them into boxes. Normally the cardboard lettuce boxes would turn soft with such water, but the company got cartons that had a thicker coat of wax or some such protection. It was a messy affair, and a dangerous one, especially for the loaders who had to toss the fifty- and sixty-pound boxes onto the trucks while struggling for footing in the bog. All this suffering, and dangerous conditions too, and we were making next to nothing.

We had a huge crew, twelve or fourteen trios, so it looked like some production was going out, but work was slow and ugly. And the ugliness spread like some waterborne disease into our moods. In a couple of days it was an epidemic.

It started with grumbling. "Ain't this the shits, man?" Then some suffering soul started shouting and soon, without plan or forethought, packers sat down on their boxes and foremen and supervisors huddled and debated. Soon they agreed to raise the price of the box a dime or so. It was enough to salve our souls, wrinkled by the moisture soaking our skin and bones.

The rains stopped after the first week, and the work turned more or less normal. Huron had but one street with any commerce, a few restaurants, and small grocery stores, so there was little to do after work and dinner but lie in our cots and stare at the bare beams or play a game of Conquian.

After Huron, we moved to the Parker-Poston, Arizona, area for several weeks of harvesting near the Colorado River. Parker is part of an Indian reservation, and it was the sight of the largest Second World War concentration camp. Japanese from the Salinas–Watsonville area were bused there in the winter of 1942, many coming directly from the horse stables at the Salinas rodeo grounds clutching the sole suitcase or bundle each was limited to bring along. The sand-swept desert with its broiling summers became their home until the end of the war. I didn't know this about Poston at the time. Looking back, I sometimes wonder if our weathered barracks were left over from that internment camp.

Winter in Poston was sunny and cool. Irrigation water from the nearby Colorado had transformed that desert area into a lush and fertile strip of farm land.

There was a small town near the camp, a welcome escape from the drabness of the barracks. I spent some nights at one of the bars drinking beer and chatting with the locals from the tribe who hung out there, people from the Navajo, Hopi, and Mojave tribes who lived on the reservation. I remember especially the women—their long hair and chunky physiques, their friendliness, their storytelling and fun-loving personalities. I remember them as genuine, warm, and accepting, and I felt comfortable in that place drinking beer with them.

After Poston, I met Mickey in El Centro. He had taken a different route south with the Bruce Church company on his first corrida. We got a motel together at a weekly rate and waited for the start of the season in Calexico. The Imperial Valley harvest was a few weeks away, and our money started getting short. To conserve, we ate just one meal a day, at a smorgasbord restaurant near our motel. We ate until we were stuffed, and then we stuffed ourselves more, our jackets and pants pockets bulging with rolls and bread to carry us through to the next meal.

Shorty

The harvest was approaching, and we began to think of our next move. There was a cutter on the Finerman crew who went by the nickname "Shorty." With good reason: he stood about five-three. When Shorty heard that Mickey and I were looking for a place in Mexicali to take advantage of cheaper food and rent, he asked if he could come in on an apartment with us. We agreed, and Shorty found us a small place on Madederos Sur in a district near downtown called La Colonia Industrial. The colonia was off one of the main thoroughfares and a short drive to the *garrita*, as the border crossing was called.

Shorty was somewhere in his early forties. He had a small mustache and thinning curly hair, with gray beginning to march up his temples. He had a strong, wiry frame and an aura that spoke of an energy wound tightly inside him.

All my dealings with Shorty had been positive, but I'd also heard rumors that he had an emotionally explosive side. As I got to know him better, it became clear that his reputation as someone not to be messed with was as much a mechanism of survival as the product of a malevolent outlook. At least that's how Shorty told the story.

Shorty insisted on more than one occasion that life as a very short male required more than just a pleasant outlook. He could not survive, let alone find respect, he assured us, without nurturing a reputation that would give potential tormentors pause. As this was a reality outside my realm of experience, I felt in no position to pass judgment. And so I listened quietly in our tiny apartment kitchen to Shorty's tales of danger and combat.

One weekend Shorty disappeared and didn't show up again until work the following week. When he did, he asked the foreman for an advance because he'd lost his week's pay in a dispute in Mexicali bar. I learned the long version later in our kitchen. Shorty swore that he'd just had a few drinks and was only trying to be friendly with a woman in the bar when her boyfriend, who Shorty claimed was a lawyer, got irate and physical with him. In the ensuing altercation the Mexicali police showed up. There was never any question, said Shorty, whose side the police were going to take, and so Shorty, the farmworker, was hauled to jail. Between the police and other inmates Shorty's pockets were vacuumed clean. Only aggressive action, he said, kept shoes and shirt in his possession.

Richard, who'd followed la corrida to Mexicali that year, also had an encounter with a Mexicali cop. He came out of a Mexicali bar one weekend night, fairly late, and "*la chota*" stopped him on the street, probably looking for a tip as well. Richard was in no mood to accommodate him, and the alcohol had made him brasher than his sober self, so when the cop started harassing him for being drunk Richard said, "Con mi chile engordes!" A literal translation in English, "Get fat on my chile," has a figurative meaning in Spanish. Perhaps unimpressed by the clever insult, the cop shoved Richard to the ground and then arrested him. He spent the rest of a long weekend in the Mexicali jail where he paid an exorbitant tab for room and board before he was allowed to leave.

Shorty liked our radical politics. He had no love for the system on either side of the border. Shorty also despised the condescension that supposedly "ignorant peasants" like himself felt from various quarters. The fact that we emphatically denounced this class and racial chauvinism, and defended the people who were subject to ignorant, racist crap, greatly moved Shorty. That and the fact that we shared the travails of lettuce work, is why we got along well. He was not an activist. Politics for Shorty was at most a spectator sport. Yet on days when Mickey and I would get up extra early to cross the border to sell *El Obrero* in Calexico at the various spots where buses stopped to pick up workers, Shorty sometimes came along. He was not interested in distributing the paper. He had a hard time reading it, and if there was an article that really interested him we'd read it to him. He didn't feel comfortable talking about politics. But when he said he'd be there if anyone messed with us, I believed him.

Mickey and I, and occasionally friends from Mickey's crew, would wander the dark morning streets of Calexico to where knots of workers waited for buses or lined up at the "fayuca" trucks to buy their coffee or morning sweet rolls.[7] The largest of these spots was El Hoyo, an irregularly shaped parking lot rimmed with a chain-link fence on the edge of an arroyo through which wound the New River. This was the line between two countries. Across the arroyo was a colorful fence that marked the border on the Mexican side.

In all these spots we'd jump from bus to bus or group to group, distributing as many papers as we could before we had to hook up with our own crews for work.

"Acts of God"

Madrugarse is a verb meaning to get up early in the morning. "Early morning" is "*la madrugada.*" For farmworkers in Mexicali who cross the border to work on the U.S. side, *madrugarse* has its own special meaning.

Work in the fields generally began as soon as there was enough light, but long before that, the lines of cars and bodies spread behind the border waiting to enter the U.S. side to work. Add to that the growers' requirement that workers get to the buses early and the frequent long rides to the fields in places like Yuma and Blythe, both about a hundred miles from Calexico, and *madrugarse* could easily mean 2 a.m. Add to this the fact that a cold night could leave the lettuce slightly frozen and uncuttable—cut a frozen head of lettuce and it will turn black—and then have to wait in the fields several hours until the thaw, and workdays stretched into interminable hours.

Leaving Mexicali in the dark of early morning and returning in the dark of night was the norm on those December, January, and February days. And that was when the weather was good. Sometimes, after a long ride to the fields, rain would either delay work or force it to be cancelled altogether, in which case your whole day was for nothing.

This painful reality led workers to demand compensation for lost time. Though the company would claim, "We're not responsible—act of God!" And this was even specified in some contracts. But it wasn't God, people would say, who drove us in the goddamn bus, was it?

Sometimes the rancor from the crew was such that the company would concede a few hours of pay. And union contracts later included clauses that obligated the company to pay if they brought the crew to a field prematurely. The company figured out how to get around that obstacle, adjusting their actions so that crews waited on the buses in Mexicali rather than at the edges of some field.

Long hours were not the only discomforts suffered on the long Yuma or Blythe rides. On the roads to these towns, farmworkers encountered other misfortunes.

Road Hazards

On a January morning in 1974, Pablo Arellanos, a driver for labor contractor Jesus Ayala, began a two-hour, 130-mile trip from the Imperial Valley to Blythe near the Arizona border. It was 3:30 a.m. Pablo had been up since 2 a.m. picking up workers for the High and Mighty company. Pablo was tired from the 260-mile round-trip to Blythe the day before. It was still dark when the old farm labor bus reached the outskirts of town. The bus was in poor repair; its brakes did not function well and the headlights needed adjustment. As it rounded a curve next to an irrigation canal, the bus's wheels left the pavement, hit the dirt to one side of the road, and skidded down an embankment into cool murky canal waters. Inside the bus, the impact with the ditch broke seats loose and they flew forward, trapping and crushing the driver and pinning passengers under debris, so that they could not escape the rising water. Among the nineteen who died there were men, women, and teenagers, including a father and his three teenage kids.

Several thousand people attended a funeral the following week at the Calexico armory for those killed in the bus crash. It would be pointed out by the UFW many times that High and Mighty farms, for which Pablo Arellanos worked, had a contract with the Teamsters.

Other dangers lurked on these roads. Mickey, who worked several winter seasons with the Bruce Church company, made the long commute to their fields in Yuma. In an interview he related the following experience from the winter of 1977.

Every morning during that winter harvest season, we would board the company bus in Calexico in the dark, me with a 7-Eleven cup of coffee and an *L.A. Times*. Everyone else had his or her own rituals. We all sat in the same seats day after day, more or less. I sat with the young guys in back. Couples sat in the middle, and single women, both mothers and daughters, in front close to the driver.

Most of the lettuce machine crew crossed the border from Mexicali every morning. A few, with questionable documents and no family on the Mexicali side, stayed in one of the motels that dotted Calexico near the border. Sometimes six or eight crammed into one room.

It was an hour and a half to Yuma where the company had most of its winter fields. In the shortened daylight hours of February, we moved in the dark each way. I'd sit with the young guys in back and work on my Spanish, trying hard to understand the slangy jokes, the barbed innuendoes, and regional accents. From time to time, I would circulate our newspaper, *El Obrero*, and engage the *vatos* (guys) in political discussions about imperialism, capitalism, Chávez's union, Mexican politics, and general current affairs. With these guys, if you couldn't prove yourself in the daily work of cutting lettuce, they really wouldn't listen to you about anything else. So, I felt pretty good that I had their respect on both fronts and that we were friends and *compadres*.

We might have shared a lot of the weal and woe of those harvest months, but in one respect my situation was not at all the same. Most of the crew had official green cards. Some just birth certificates, and others got on with fake green cards. Those who didn't have some kind of card, or one they had confidence in, usually didn't ride the bus. They made the drive in a car. It was safer than riding the bus. Without papers a person was never safe. Even with them you never knew when the Border Patrol would stop and harass you.

It was a February day, like most others. After cutting in Yuma, the bus worked its way back to Calexico. But first we stopped on the outskirts of Yuma for a soda or beer. For the young guys in the back of the bus it was quarts of beer and pints of spicy Clamato juice. At the time, there was nothing like a good ration of beer to ease the throbbing in the lower middle of your back from a rugged day of stooping and rising ten to twenty times a minute to cut that lettuce and put it on the shelf for the women to wrap in cellophane. It could be real cold in the winter dusk of the desert, and even the beer could not save us from the cold and stiffness that would set in eventually. In those school bus–type seats, it was impossible to find a comfortable position.

This day, however, we had a second stop. There's an agriculture inspection stop near the Arizona-California state line. As a general rule we'd be waved through. But this time when we arrived at the checkpoint, the driver was told to pull off to the side, and we were boarded by a couple of Border Patrol agents (migra), checking for papers.

These guys were the original cowboys: hats, boots, very bad Spanish, guns, and badges. They worked their way down the aisle, asking each person to show them their green cards. I saw a couple of guys looking very uncomfortable. Maybe they forgot their cards or lost them, who knows. The migra noticed them too, and went up to them and was going to take them off the bus. When I saw this I said, "Hey man, why don't you get yourself an honest job." This tall migra heard me and came real close, "What did you say?" he screamed at me. I repeated what I had said, and he grabbed my jacket and pulled me out of my seat and off the bus. He took me behind a shed at the edge of the inspection station, and I thought, oh shit. He started yelling about respect and slammed me up against the shed a couple of times. My head broke the glass window behind me and my glasses got twisted. Then he took me back to the bus and patted me down. After a few more shouts and screams, he told me to "get the fuck out of here."

The people on the bus said, "You gotta do something about this!" And I said, "Do I have any witnesses here?" The people shouted, "Yes!" Later I went with a few of the crew to the migra office to file a complaint. Of course, nothing ever came of it.

Mele

That winter I worked the ground crew with Finerman; Mickey, the lettuce machines with Bruce Church. But one day we coincidentally worked adjacent fields near Yuma. At morning break we met at a dirt access road at the edge of the field. As we were talking, we heard a commotion and saw the green immigration vans heading from various points in our direction. As we stood there, a fellow came up to us. At first sight he looked a bit strange. He wore thin-soled street shoes and clothes more appropriate to someone out shopping on Calexico's commercial strip than stomping around a slightly muddy lettuce field. He was short, about our height, with a dark complexion and thick wavy brown hair. As he approached, he extended his hand, and we each grabbed a thick, strong, calloused hand.

"Talk in Engliss, mi frind," he said in barely intelligible English. "What?" "Talk in Engliss." He turned his head slightly behind him to call our notice to a green migra van driving slowly up the rutted access road that skirted the field where we stood.

Mickey turned to the figure before us and grabbed his shoulder and said loudly, "Hey, that was one of the funniest jokes I ever heard, man." "Ya," I said, "I told that joke to some friends I know; man, they almost split a gut over that one." "When are you coming over?" said Mickey, and we went on with small talk as the van passed us. The van's passenger side was facing in our direction with its window down, an agent peering out at the field. We nodded to him and he nodded back as we kept up our conversation. For his part, the immigration agent, a young guy with a crewcut, had a vacant look, as though his mind may not have been in exactly the same venue as his peering eyes would indicate.

For the unsuspecting observer we could have seemed like a gathering of hearing-impaired engaged in disjointed conversation. But as the van passed and then turned and left the field, our conversation partner showered us with "thank you's" and "mi frinds." This was our introduction to Mele.

We began talking to him in Spanish. "Mi nombre es Mele, no sabia que ustedes hablan Español, pero me salvó!" (You saved me!) He grinned happily. We gave Mele a brief description of our own distaste for the migra and introduced ourselves. Little could I have imagined that this was the beginning of a friendship that would last across decades.

Mele was not really a farmworker, as one could have guessed from his clothes, but he'd come across the border with a permit borrowed from his cousin. This was his first job in the fields, and he was working as a waterboy for a ground crew, the only hourly job on such a crew. He expressed no real interest in getting further into the art of lettuce harvesting. He was only out temporarily to make a little money to supplement the income from his neighborhood mechanic shop in one of the new colonias in Mexicali.

His cousin's permit allowed him to cross into the United States, but only within fifteen miles of the border. It didn't grant permission to work. Mele was concerned about the migra, not so much because he feared deportation, since he was going to return to Mexico that evening anyway, but rather that if they found the permit they would rescind it. There was also the inconvenience of possibly losing his job.

Having exchanged our introductions and established the fact that we also lived in Mexicali, Mele insisted that we visit him at his home. He tried to explain how to get to his colonia. Once there, he said, we could easily find someone to direct us to his place. But Mexicali was still for us an indecipherable maze. "I'll meet you where you live," Mele suggested, "Sunday morning." It was agreed.

The Imperial Valley

Salinas is often called the "Salad Bowl" of the country. The Imperial Valley is Salad Bowl South, or the Winter Salad Bowl.

The Imperial Valley was once part of an immense lake known as Cahuila that covered the area from the present-day Salton Sea to the Gulf of California, six thousand square miles. For many millennia the Colorado River, carrying ten times the volume of silt as the Nile, brought materials washed down from the eroding slopes of the Rockies and scoured from the walls of the mighty Grand Canyon, part of the huge drainage area that covers 8 percent of the entire land area of the continental United States, and deposited them into the lake. When the lake dried up it left exposed the legacy of the mighty river, a fertile potential that Indian groups and later, on a far greater scale, Anglo settlers would exploit.

In the 1850s surveying parties were sent by the U.S. Congress to find suitable passageways for an intercontinental railroad. One of those parties explored the southern reaches of California and arrived in the region of the Imperial Valley. There a geologist by the name of William Blake saw the potential of that dry lake bed. Blake observed that wherever water was applied to the desert, soils, trees, and grasses grew lushly. The region bordered one of the major rivers in North America, the Colorado. The implications were obvious.

News of the potential of the border area spread. But it wasn't until around the turn of the century that conditions for turning potential into reality, and cash, were feasible.

This was the era of the consolidation of monopolies, of capital seeking new sources of investment, of big engineering projects like the Panama Canal, which sliced a continent to stimulate trade. To this southern desert in California came entrepreneurs full of reckless confidence, seeking their fortune. Like the gold seekers who ravaged the rivers and countryside of Northern California in the frenzy for mineral wealth some decades before, the entrepreneurs who came to the Imperial also sought fortunes. Everything else was secondary.

These were not farmers, but speculators. They started the California Development Company and set about to divert waters from the Colorado River through a canal to the Imperial Valley, where they calculated that with the coming of farmers they could make a fortune in land and water rights. They hired a Canadian engineer name Chaffey who studied the matter and found a way to channel Colorado River water through a fifty-mile canal on the Mexican side of the border (on land then owned by U.S. interests) to Calexico. Here gravity would bring it north to the dry Imperial Valley.

Water began to flow in the spring of 1901. By the fall of 1903, a hundred thousand acres of fields were being irrigated. A settler population reached 2,000, and continued to grow afterward. But the river had surprises in store. Silt filled Chaffey's channel inlet, reducing the flow to a trickle. Efforts to dredge and divert the water coincided with a season of heavy precipitation in the large Colorado watershed and a corresponding large runoff in 1905. The Colorado overwhelmed efforts to control it.

For several years, and two seasons of unusually high water, through a half-mile breach torn in Chaffey's gate, a huge torrent of water churned its way north through the Imperial Valley toward the great depression south of what is today Palm Springs. The Imperial Valley lay under a sheet of water eight to ten miles wide. Where the waters converged, they formed new rivers or scoured out paths of old ones, carrying huge quantities of earth, calculated to have surpassed by four times the amount excavated for the Panama Canal.

The waters ripped away most of the town of Mexicali and nearly swallowed Calexico. They obliterated two important lakes and the small settlements near them.

The water flowed eighty miles north of the border and accumulated at the low point, forming a huge new lake. As it flowed, the water picked up the salt that lay on the land in the soil. The result was a 450-square-mile lake with salt concentration second only to the Sea of Galilee, dubbed the Salton Sea. It took several years to finally close the breach and bring under control, at least temporarily, one of the largest and most powerful rivers in the world.

The valley recovered. By the 1920s large-scale lettuce production began in the Imperial Valley. It would soon become one of the most productive agricultural areas in the world and the leading source of winter vegetables for the United States. But this potential could only be realized with another resource—workers. Driven by lack of land and low wages, people from the interior of Mexico began migrating north to the border city of Mexicali. The Imperial thus acquired the cheap water and cheap labor it needed to make a dry land bloom.

New Law, Controversy, and Elections in the Imperial

The harvest season of 1975–76 saw the continuation of the union elections that had begun in late August in Salinas. Shortly after the start of the harvest season in the Imperial, the union called for a meeting a few blocks from the border to discuss the union elections. The meeting was held in a school auditorium, and it drew a good crowd. Marshall Ganz ran the meeting, pacing across the auditorium stage, microphone in hand, discussing the ALRA and the election process, the advances the union had made, the pitfalls that lay ahead. I arrived late and was just settling into a seat when I heard Ganz say, "Compañeros, we have a special visitor to our meeting tonight." I heard my name called. "Bruce was fired from the Finerman Company in violation of the new law. A complaint was filed and he won his case. We have an example of the power of this law. He won back pay and his job. Que viva la ley!!" The crowd responded with "Viva!" The remarks caught me flat-footed. I thought I should say something about this, but it took too long to find the words, and the agenda, as they say, moved on.

Ganz's remarks were really a polemic, though the great majority of people gathered there could not have known this. Shortly after the passage of the ALRA, *The Worker* published a controversial article, widely distributed in the camps and community, in which it recognized the law as an important achievement for consolidating farmworker union organization, but warned against reliance on it. *The Worker* article argued that the law, the legislature that set it up, the court system that would enforce or arbitrate it, were the turf of the system, of the capitalists, apparatuses set up to enforce their rule, at the heart of which is exploitation of labor. It was not wrong to make use of these laws when possible, but to preach reliance on them would put people in a passive position and sap the strength of the movement. These institutions were not neutral and could be easily manipulated to serve the interests of the growers, which they most certainly would be.

There were strong pressures at work to set the union up as the guarantor of peace in the fields in exchange for a place at the master's table. If that were to happen, the union would no longer challenge the exploitation of the workers and the endless abuses, but find ways to reconcile these in the name of preserving its position and power.

Whatever union officials may have felt privately about the law, this was not the public position of the union, so Ganz was polemicizing against this argument. [8]

In the union election process the Teamsters had some of the advantages of incumbency, to say nothing of the support of the growers. But the UFW still had some of the creative spirit of the upstart. The UFW sought to expose the Teamster contracts from every angle, and the election campaign advanced amid a furious blizzard of UFW leaflets.

Leaflets criticized what the UFW called "*impuestos durmientos*" (sleep tax)—the practice of forcing workers to come early and wait for hours before leaving for the fields. This was a hardship imposed on the workers to give the growers and contractors more flexibility in dispatching crews long distances.

There were leaflets that recalled the horrific bus accident in Blythe in 1974, pinning the blame on the Teamsters for failing to enforce safety standards on farm labor buses in a company under their contract.

Leaflets criticized new work methods introduced by the growers, like the introduction of the burra, the lettuce cart that slowed down work in the contract lettuce and made it more physically difficult.

Leaflets upheld the union hiring hall as a protection against discriminatory practices and favoritism from the companies and contractors, while acknowledging there were also abuses of favoritism at times in the way the hiring hall was managed.

The leaflets pointed out that the Teamsters rarely if ever held meetings and that Teamster crews had no union representation. Still others denounced the Teamster retirement dues deducted from paychecks, claiming they were being used to finance mobster activity. The UFW played on the perception of the Teamsters' mobster connections (much as the Teamsters retaliated with charges of UFW "communist" leanings).

Leaflets referred to the lack of any grievance procedure in Teamster companies, and therefore any method to combat speedup or poor working conditions.

UFW leaflets pointed to the lack of compensation to workers for time spent in transportation to work.

Some leaflets were reprints of checks for holiday pay negotiated in union contracts but usually nonexistent on the non-union ranches.

Other leaflets showed the payoffs some workers had received from the UFW's medical plan for health services, and pointed to the health clinics set up by the union in some areas.

Many of the leaflets were artistically stark, sharply sarcastic, relentlessly exposing the hypocrisy that was the Teamster-grower charade.

When elections were held in December and January in the Imperial Valley near the Mexican border, the UFW won eleven of twelve contests. The UFW attributed the victories to the "enforcement of the ALRA," which reduced the intimidation workers felt from the growers.

Not long after, an election for Finerman was held, and the UFW came out the victor. The elections overall were a significant victory for the UFW. They demonstrated that on many Teamster ranches the majority clearly preferred the UFW. It demonstrated that among vegetable workers the UFW was building a stronghold, even if this was decidedly not the case in the UFW's birthplace, the grape vineyards.

But election victories were no guarantee of contracts. A backlog of stalled negotiations and worker grievances began piling up on the ALRB's agenda.

Mexicali and Flores Magón

Geologically the Mexicali Valley is a mirror of the Imperial Valley to the north. They are really one dry, flat, fertile expanse of land that once lay at the bottom of a huge lake. Now a border, decided by a war, politically divides them. History and geopolitics, not geology, have given the Mexicali Valley a sharply different reality from its twin to the north.

Porfirio Diaz, who ruled Mexico almost continuously from 1876 until revolution drove him from power in 1911, had a quest to bring modern capitalist relations to Mexico's countryside. Mexico's peasants paid a bitter price for Diaz's brand of "progress." Peasants were driven from their land; indigenous communities were dispossessed of their traditional lands. In large landed estates called latifundias, peasants labored in slave-like conditions. Mexico's resources were sold to foreign interests, and Mexico's economic structure came under the increasing domination of U.S. capital.

In Mexico's sparsely populated and undeveloped northern border area, Diaz ceded hundreds of thousands of acres to General Guillermo Andrade. After failed efforts to develop the Colorado delta area in partnership with U.S. entrepreneurs, Andrade, Mexico's consul in Los Angeles, sold out to Harrison Otis, the publisher of the *Los Angeles Times* and to Otis's son-in-law, Harry Chandler. They and their business partners became the *"dueños absolutos,"* the virtual owners, of the Mexicali Valley. Their Colorado River Land Company controlled 862,000 acres (340,000 hectares) and for thirty years they operated one of the largest cotton-growing operations in the world, making use of free water, cheap labor, and a strong U.S. market for their product.[9]

The growing discontent with Porfirio Diaz was channeled into an election set for 1910. Diaz's main rival was Francisco Madero, a wealthy landowner himself though unhappy with the regime's policies and monopolization of power. Madero was defeated in what was widely considered a fraudulent election. When Madero refused to accept the official results he was arrested, and discontent sparked into open rebellion that spread across the country.

In February of 1911, as revolution was rising in other areas of Mexico, a group of rebels, brought together by the Partido Liberal Mexicano of Ricardo Flores Magón, influenced by both Marxist and anarchist ideas, staged a rebellion in the Mexicali Valley. They took over the small settlement of Mexicali and fought off an attempt by Diaz forces from Ensenada to drive them out. Magón and his associates planned to take Mexicali as a step toward building a northern base from which to spread revolution, led by his party, to the whole country. Unlike Madero who proposed a program of reform, the core of the Magonista movement advocated the overthrow of capitalism, the seizure of property of big landlords and capitalists, and the establishment of a government based on communal ownership of farms and factories.

In 1911, the Mexicali Valley was a region with a small population far from the centers of Mexican society. To have a national impact, the

"Magonistas" had to break out of the area. The Partido Liberal Mexicano had a newspaper called *La Regeneración* with a fairly wide distribution. But it was no match for the mass media in creating broad public opinion. In that all-important arena the Magonistas ran into problems. They were a multinational group; a sizable part of the Magonista rebel army were Anglos with anarchist and socialist leanings, some associated with the Industrial Workers of the World. Reactionary newspapers in the United States and Mexico cited the participation of Anglos as proof that the Mexicali rebellion was actually a move by pro-U.S. "filibusters" to create conditions for the U.S. annexation of northern Mexico. This characterization as well as errors the rebels committed by failing to clearly publicize their aims undermined the broad initial support the rebellion enjoyed from progressive forces on both sides of the border. Unable to broaden its base, and weakened with internal divisions, the Magonistas failed to break out of the Mexicali area and were defeated there.

The Magonista rebellion fell far short of contending for power. Its political and organizational program would not have allowed accomplishing the radical changes its adherents hoped for. Yet it had significance as the first rebellion of the twentieth century to raise the banner of revolution against capitalism. And the name of Flores Magón would continue to reverberate positively among Mexicanos for decades to come.

Porfirio Diaz was driven from power in 1911. The revolution continued through twists and turns for many years. The party that finally emerged with power in its hands was no less capitalist than Diaz. Nor was it any more independent economically or politically from its imperialist master to the north. But it incorporated the word *revolution* into its name—Partido Revolucionario Institucional—and its leaders mastered the art of invoking "the Revolution" for every action to expand its power and enrich its ranks. It covered the country with streets and plazas named for the revolutionaries Zapata, Villa, Flores Magón, and others, whom the new ruling elite had fought against and even assassinated in the course of consolidating their power.

In the end, the revolution barely touched the Mexicali Valley. Land was still in the hands of wealthy men from across the border. Nothing had come from the revolution's promise of land to the landless.

In the 1920s a movement to seize the properties of U.S.-owned and -operated land company gained some momentum. There were brief land seizures by landless proletarians led by a former rebel colonel from Pancho Villa's army, but these efforts failed to achieve their aim.

Land ownership in the Mexicali Valley remained nearly the exclusive purview of wealthy U.S. interests until the Great Depression of the 1930s. As the Depression deepened, tens of thousands of Mexican workers lost their jobs or were driven across the border by the U.S. immigration. Many took residence in Mexicali.

Lázaro Cárdenas was the Mexican president in Depression-era Mexico. His government wanted to stimulate growth in the country-side and relieve mounting pressures from below, as the people asked: Where is the land to the landless the revolution had promised? Cárdenas launched programs of land distribution in various parts of the country, and he promised to break the hold on Mexicali land by pressuring Chandler's Colorado River Land Company to divide their holdings and sell tracts of land.

Yet very little changed until campesinos and landless workers, their patience at an end, took matters into their own hands by invading the private holdings and seizing land. The Cárdenas government met with representatives of the invading campesinos and ordered the formation of sixty-seven *ejidos*—collective farms—on a quarter-million acres, enough to provide livelihoods for 16,000 formerly landless peasants. Another 150,000 acres were distributed as private holdings to independent farmers and settlers, and Chandler's lands were ordered subdivided and sold under the terms of a 1936 agreement. The Cárdenas government nationalized land held by the Colorado River Land Company in 1937.[10] These reforms set off a wave of migration by land-hungry peasants. New villages sprang up in the Mexicali Valley, with names like Michoacán de Campo, Toluca, Querétaro, and Veracruz, reflecting the origins of the people who came gambling on a new life in Mexico's northwest. By 1930 Mexicali's population passed 50,000. Forty years later it was approaching half a million.[11]

The Colorado River is the lifeline of the entire region. By treaty the United States is obliged to deliver 1.5 million acre-feet of water to Mexico, about 10 percent of the river's normal flow. Unfortunately, by the time the Colorado enters Mexico, it has already picked up salt from fields on the U.S. side. Nor is there enough water to wash the salt out of the lands of the Mexicali Valley. Mexicali farmers must do with half as much water on average as their counterparts on the U.S. side. This results in crops that are inferior to those grown in the United States.

Mexicali and Mariachis

Mele, as he had promised, arrived at our apartment in Mexicali on Sunday. From there we drove to the colonia where he lived. Like many other colonias or barrios in Mexicali (and elsewhere), Mele's colonia felt like a makeshift affair. These were not the planned communities common in the postwar United States. They were and are communities of opportunity, once barren land now occupied by people with few resources and great needs. Mele's home, an eclectic affair of cinder blocks, tin sheets, plywood, and brick, occupied a lot a few "blocks" from his brother and sister, who had preceded him from their native state of Nayarit. Each lot was carved out by its dwellers, and then rigged to provide for cooking, bathing, and so on. As in many similar communities occupation by squatters or *paracaídistas* (literally "parachutists") preceded regulation, established property lines, and the like. There was, as yet, no indoor plumbing. Instead there was a wooden outhouse a few steps from the house, and a small free standing brick structure, the size of a closet, with an open door, that served as a shower. On cool days, water from the spigot outside the shower could be used to fill the large metal pan that was heated on a propane kitchen stove. On warm days, especially in the scalding summer, the water out of the tap would do. Mele's electric service, like many others, was tapped illegally from a nearby power line to light a few electric bulbs, or, in more affluent homes, a TV and stereo.

The streets of Colonia Aurora were unpaved and would remain so for decades, calling forth a stream of criticism of government inefficiency and corruption. Aurora then was not far from the outskirts of the city. The coming years would see it outflanked by an expanding ring of residential districts in a city that was slowly but steadily inflating, like an expanding balloon.

On our first visit to the colonia, Mele invited us to a wedding party. Dismissing our qualms about being unknown and uninvited he led us to a house surrounded by a fence. There was mariachi music and other sounds of celebration, and the smell of carne asada, birria, and frijoles— a gathering of the barrio. What struck me was the informality, the easy interplay among the generations and the matter-of-fact way two total strangers from another world were welcomed into a wedding party.

Norton and a Wildcat

In early February the UFW won an election victory by a wide margin at the Norton company. This was the second UFW victory at Norton, but the company challenged the results with the ALRB. The week following the election, after several days of rain, Norton lettuce loaders, fearing injury in the slippery mud, demanded a change in the method of handling the boxes. Every lettuce crew has its small sub-crew of loaders who lift the 50- to 60-pound boxes onto a truck as it moves through the field. On any given day the group of three or four loaders might handle more than 2,100 of these boxes. This is skilled and risky work, as I discovered when on a few occasions I joked with the loaders about their easy money and tried tossing some boxes on the truck. I could barely get the boxes on the level of the truck bed, let alone loft them high onto the stacks, basketball-style, as experienced loaders could do!

The loaders' protest was a serious one. Back injuries were common and could cut down a person's working life in a split second. I knew a number of workers whose lives were painfully constricted by their crippling back injuries suffered on the job and endless efforts to minimize the agony they caused. The company, however, was in no mood to cater to the loaders' defiance. They refused the loaders' demands, and fired them for illegally halting work.

As the cutters and packers were finishing up their work that day, the company asked them to load the boxes in the field, promising to pay extra for the work. When it became clear that the loaders had refused to load the boxes and had been fired, the cutters and packers also refused and walked out of the field.

The workers approached the UFW but were told to return to work and wait for the situation to be resolved in negotiations. Unsatisfied, the five Norton crews refused to work until the loaders were rehired. After several days of protest and lettuce about to go to ruin in the fields, the company relented. It refused to change the method of loading, but the protesting loaders were rehired.

On February 16, following maneuvers by pro-grower legislators in Sacramento, the Agricultural Labor Relations Board ran out of money and closed its doors. The Norton election and many others were left in limbo.

Returning North

With the end of work in the Imperial, Mickey and I prepared to head back to Salinas to await the spring harvest season. We were packing up to leave when Mele showed up with an old suitcase held shut by a thick rope. "Voy al norte," he said in his thick voice, "a ver que encuentro"—I'm heading north, I'll see what happens there. No problem. Mele had a visa to cross the border, so we would just meet him on the U.S. side and be off.

It wasn't until we were all in the car that we thought about the immigration check an hour or so north of the border. Every car is stopped and checked. What would happen with Mele? We pulled over to discuss our options. There was the trunk. It was small and cramped in my little Datsun. And we'd have to put all the luggage in the front of the car. Would that arouse suspicion? And if they caught us with this cargo, it wouldn't go down well for Mele, or for us.

I'll ride in the front, said Mele, proposing a scenario similar to our encounter in Yuma. I would drive and Mickey would engage in a one-sided conversation with Mele as we approached the checkpoint. With conversation in English going on, the migra might just wave us on. If he did check, Mele would look through his wallet and exclaim to his dismay that his green card was gone—must have left it home! At the worst, he'd be put in a migra bus and sent back to Mexicali and we'd have to start from scratch.

Then, someone said, isn't it the job of the migra to check people who they suspect might not have papers? Why wouldn't they check Mele? "Naw, they wouldn't check him 'cause they'd never suspect a couple of good ol' 'Mericans like us 'd be cavortin' with one 'a *them*.'" But then again, they might. And the consequences could be severe. We debated this for a while. In the end we made a decision based on that most scientific of methods, the coin toss.

We spent nervous moments anticipating the immigration stop. When it finally appeared in view, several green-clad agents standing next to each lane, my blood pressure rose. My temples throbbed, and I rolled down the window for air, feeling suddenly warmer. A tall young agent with close-cropped hair stood examining the approaching cars, an unlit flashlight in his hand. As I moved slowly up toward him, I saw in the mirror a line of cars slowing behind me. Now I sat even with the agent as his green eyes peered into mine. "Good evening," he said, "everything OK?" "Fine," I said. Mickey, to my right, was turning down the music from a country-western station. The agent looked over at Mickey, flashed his light into the backseat, with its luggage covered by a bright Indian blanket I'd bought at a stand in Mexicali. He looked toward the rear of the car, at the line of cars stacking up behind us. "Drive safely," he said, moving his flashlight forward with a slight movement of his hand.

Later in Salinas, buoyant with his successful journey and in a facetious mood, Mele said with a sheepish grin, "Me olvidé algo en Mexicali, tengo que regresar" (I forgot something in Mexicali, I have to go back). Mickey said, "I'm sure the migra would be happy to give you a ride back." "Ah, quizás no lo necesito tanto" (I can probably do without it).

The author in a lettuce field in the Imperial Valley.

Bud Antle lettuce machine, early 1970s.

Cominos Hotel: a former luxury hotel that by the 1970s was run down. It was an affordable place for farm workers and others but unpopular with city officials. In 1989 it was torn down.

A contractor's labor camp in the Salinas Valley, circa 1972.

Encampment of families evicted from La Posada trailer camp, 1972. One family posted a sign: "LaPosada—My Lai [Vietnamese village massacred by U.S. soldiers in 1968]. Same enemy—U.S. bosses and guns."

A ground crew harvesting in the Salinas Valley, 1970s.

Some lettuce workers on strike.

Longshoremen from San Francisco visiting the farmworkers'
union hall in Salinas, early 1970s..

Lettuce workers from the Norton company on a work stoppage in the Imperial Valley in support of loaders fired by the company, 1975.

Other lettuce workers from Norton on a work stoppage in the Imperial Valley.

Sheriffs and hired grower guards guarding a vineyard
during a strike, circa 1973.

Salinas lettuce workers marching in the Bay area in solidarity
with Farah and Oneita garment workers on strike.

7. 1976

THE UFW CONTINUED to win more elections. And though the UFW showed strength in the vegetable fields from Salinas/Watsonville to the Imperial Valley but little support in the major Central Valley grape-growing areas, momentum was on the UFW side in the contest with the Teamsters.

A new UFW slogan began to make the rounds: "Una Sola Union," one big union, and projections of an organization of tens of thousands across the country. For the Teamsters-growers alliance the handwriting was on the wall. By March of 1977 the Teamsters formally bowed out of the fields, keeping only the contract it had signed with the vegetable giant Bud Antle in the early 1960s.

But in Sacramento politicians allied with grower interests had succeeded in cutting off funding for the ALRA in February 1976. They tried to use funding leverage to implement changes to the composition of the executive board that oversaw the Act's implementation. The ALRB did not begin functioning again until July. A pattern was beginning to emerge. Growers were learning how to use political maneuvering and the ALRA law itself to channel unfavorable election results into a legal labyrinth.

For the United States, 1976 was a bicentennial year. The previous decade had not been a happy one for those believers and defenders of the American empire. The Vietnam debacle had much to do with this, but it was only part of the bad news. A whole period of social upheaval, now ebbing, left the image of democratic America deeply scarred. "Bourgeois democracy" itself was brought into question. A lot of myths lay shattered or at least badly damaged. The contention that the United States was built on the Jeffersonian ideal of "All men are created equal" was now a mockery for many who'd been weaned on this pablum in school. The Soviet Union, taking advantage of intense discontent and hatred of the United States, was contending for influence in parts of Asia, Africa, and Latin America. It could well be argued that the Soviet empire was gaining ground. A popular news magazine surmised that the "Soviet drive for supremacy could leave the U.S. isolated in a hostile world."[1] In this new, more contentious phase of the Cold War, "domestic tranquility" and support for U.S. institutions were seen by the political and economic elite as crucial for the maintenance of U.S. imperial power. The U.S. empire, though shaken, was far from defeated. It still had resources and reserves to restore its standing, and the Bicentennial provided the occasion to work on restoration.

The Bicentennial events were planned to celebrate the glories of America, but for those who saw U.S. imperialism as an oppressive force in the world, the Bicentennial offered an opening to engage these questions and ask different ones: Is this the best we can do? Is there another way?

For example, the Revolutionary Communist Party, formed in 1975 as successor to the Revolutionary Union, initiated a project to counter the Bicentennial message with the slogan "We've Carried the Rich for 200 Years, Let's Get Them Off Our Backs." In Salinas some of us took up the call and went (modestly) into battle. With a slide projector and an old bed sheet, we struck out for the labor camps and living rooms to compare our understanding of history with what the ruling institutions and media were promoting.

One could argue that we were almost preaching to the choir. Belief in American ideals was not particularly strong in the labor camps. "U.S.A. First" national chauvinism was on the defensive, but it was still rife in the land. Not here in the camps. Here history spoke a different narrative of the United States—more arrogant invader than beacon of freedom, more oppressor and aggressor than champion of human rights.

U.S. armies seized Mexican land in 1848 and invaded and occupied its capital, Mexico City. The United States bullied its way to war and then rubbed the noses of the conquered in the dust of stolen lands. Marines could sing triumphantly of the "halls of Montezuma," but Mexico sang of heroic youths who, in the lore of resistance, chose death rather than surrender to the Yankee occupiers at Chapultepec.

In 1914, interfering in an internal dispute with the Mexican government, the Marines landed in Veracruz with a massive naval fleet menacingly off the coast. To Mexicans it looked like the bully strutting his stuff.

In 1916, the U.S. Army once again invaded Mexico, under the command of General Pershing, to pursue the "bandit," Pancho Villa. But to

Mexicans, Villa was a hero who outfoxed his pursuers, who had to give up the chase and leave.[2]

What the United States did in Mexico was repeated dozens of times in Central America, South America, and the Caribbean to enforce unequal treaties, impose compliant rulers or dictate favorable terms for U.S. banks and corporations. Smedley Butler, U.S. general and twice recipient of the Medal of Honor, denounced his role as a "racketeer" for capitalism and defender of Wall Street interests in his 1935 classic, *War Is a Racket*:

> I spent 33 years and four months in active military service and during that period I spent most of my time as a high-class muscle man for Big Business, for Wall Street and the bankers. In short, I was a racketeer, a gangster for capitalism. I helped make Mexico and especially Tampico safe for American oil interests in 1914. I helped make Haiti and Cuba a decent place for the National City bank boys to collect revenues in. I helped in the raping of half a dozen Central American republics for the benefit of Wall Street.... Looking back on it, I might have given Al Capone a few hints. The best he could do was to operate his racket in three districts. I operated on three continents.

The U.S. media could rave about immigrants not respecting the country's "sovereign borders," but to many eyes from down south, this was nothing but grotesque hypocrisy. Many farmworkers would be more inclined to identify with Malcolm X's remark about black people: "We are not Americans, we are victims of America."

In the slide show and discussions there were many other issues related to the United States, from the original invasion of the Americas by Columbus to the annihilation of the native peoples and the mass importation of kidnapped Africans. There were commentaries on the barely known histories of slavery, Reconstruction, and Jim Crow segregation that continued until the 1960s. This history was not the consequence of some immutable racism in white people but of an economic and social system that grew on a foundation of exploitation and oppression, especially of nonwhite groups.

The slide show also touched on the historical evolution of the United States and other industrial powers as imperialists; the division of the world among them; and the stupendously violent wars over that division. Our presentation was history from the point of view of the conquered, the dominated.

The shows took place in barracks corners, projected on a sheet tacked to two-by-fours. The audiences sat on cots pulled into a semicircle around the slide projector—men from their late teens to veterans in their fifties and sixties, decades of labor deposited in their rough hands and thick shoulders. They were interested and leery. The younger ones, more outwardly cheerful, the older workers tending to the dubiousness that comes to people after long years have etched resignation into their outlook, who knew of promises broken and revolutions betrayed. Though they did not always have a clear understanding of how all that had happened in Mexico, they certainly knew that revolutions are not things to be toyed with.

It's a challenge to sense under the bedrock of the present the tectonic pressures building. Sometimes, what seems impossible can, under other circumstances, appear inevitable. But that is nearly always in hindsight. Hadn't the 1960s upsurge come out of "nowhere"? And hadn't the impenetrably sturdy edifice of society suddenly begun to appear remarkably shaky? Hadn't an invincible army nearly disintegrated in Vietnam? Hadn't a long-standing Jim Crow social order suddenly begun to crack? Hadn't the "silent" hands suddenly marched out of the fields into society's conscience? Could new pressures be building, quietly, nearly sight unseen?

The slide show discussions leaped beyond the narrow bounds of contracts, wage raises, and paid holidays. For brief moments it allowed us all, though limited by the difficult, restraining necessities of life and by our often narrow understanding of the range of reality, to glimpse beyond the *inevitable* to consider the *possible*.

Lupe's Housing Tour

It was a Saturday morning in that summer of 1976, and Lupe, my compadre, came to visit. After we greeted each other, he said, "I have something to show you, you need to see this, get your camera."

Lupe had left lettuce work the year before. He had at one time worked lettuce year-round, following the crop south. But now he was married, with a child, and had no interest in being away from his family for four or five months in the fall and winter pursuing the lonely life of the migrant lechuguero. So Lupe left the fields in search of year-round work close to home. He parlayed his fluent English and local savvy into a job with a company that did garbage collection.

His route took him to Prunedale and Aromas, small, semi-rural towns northeast of Salinas, in the direction of Watsonville. This is an area of rolling hills that attracted westward-moving farmers displaced by the dust bowl of the 1930s. It was appealing to country people because here you could get a large lot for a modest garden, chickens, maybe a goat, or even a horse. Prunedale was so named from an early settler who planted plum trees in an unrealized effort to make a go of fruit farming. Aromas, said to have gotten its name from the sulfur smell of hot springs in the area, is a land of rolling hills and strawberry fields.

It was through this area that Lupe navigated his garbage truck by the first light of day, hitting narrow lanes of dirt and gravel, and through field access roads the casual visitor would likely never see.

We turned off Highway 129 that leads from Highway 101 to Watsonville, and up Rogge Lane toward the little hamlet of Aromas. After a series of turns up gravel roads, we came to a clearing between fields surrounded by lean-tos and several small trailers with roofs split, sides peeling, and windows covered with plastic and tape. The trailers look uninhabitable, like the forlorn relics one might see in a rural wrecking yard. There were no people out in the clearing. The only sign that the trailers were occupied was a clothesline that stretched from the rear of one trailers to the branch of a tree that stood just off the cleared area. On the line was an assortment of work pants and shirts in plain blues and grays. Not far from the trailers was a water spigot, and under it was a large galvanized metal pan. "Take a look, compadre, how my people live," said Lupe. "And the pity of it is, they work for other Mexicans." We snapped a few shots and left.

From this clearing we went to another area along a narrow road that bordered a strawberry field. Once again we turned off into a clearing that bordered a field. Scattered about was farm equipment near what looked like a wooden tool shed.

Just to one side of the clearing, next to the field, stood a small cluster of trees. Near them were several large holes carved into the ground. In the hole, which was partly dug laterally under the ground to form a small cave, sat a crude fire pit. A circle of rocks surrounded the ashes of a recent fire. A few metal pots were stacked on the rocks. Filthy blankets lay around the fire pit and beyond them several wooden crates with clothes and other items.

We saw several more similar sights, snapping pictures and, luckily, encountering no one who objected to our presence, most likely because everyone concerned was off in the fields working. The sites were what I'd imagined hobo encampments to be. These were the homes of workers in the strawberries, working not for a contractor or traditional grower, but for *medieros,* or sharecroppers.

Medieros were, more often than not, Mexican farmworkers and their families, lured by the promise of escape from the life of wage workers to rent land to become a kind of small farmer. They were legally considered independent contractors, yet they were contractually tied to a farmer or landowner. Sharecropper relationships varied, but the mediero was responsible for harvesting the berries, and, in return, got a percentage of the price received from sale.

Sharecropping was practiced more frequently in strawberries than other crops. The sharecropping tradition in berries went back to the pre–Second World War period. Landowners found it advantageous to rent land to Japanese farmers who, due to the Alien Land Laws, could not own land. The Japanese were resourceful, ambitious, and knowledgeable farmers bringing skills to the cultivation of fruit that many landowners lacked, so the sharecropping arrangement was profitable. Japanese share-croppers were given a lot of latitude in the preparation and harvesting of the crop. But the outbreak of war with Japan and the roundup of the Japanese community brought this practice to an abrupt end.

Braceros replaced Japanese farmers, and hired labor replaced the share-cropping system. The end of the Bracero Program in the mid-1960s and the movement in the fields to organize farmworkers encouraged landown-ers and large farmers to turn once again to sharecropping. Some growers found sharecropping a useful way to avoid the pressures of the union move-ment and its demands for economic improvements by offering workers a piece of the action, making them "partners" as opposed to "employees."

The grower or owner usually prepared and planted the land and applied fertilizers and insecticides and so on. This kept the control of the land and crop in their hands; they had the access to capital necessary for farming that relies on expensive inputs like fertilizers, pesticides, and access to coolers.

The medieros of the 1960s and 1970s maintained the crop, weeded, cut runners, and supplied labor to bring in the crop, often relying on rela-tives or acquaintances to do so. Medieros with large families could put their children, nephews, and cousins to work, thus raising the collective income, even when—which was not unheard of—pay on an hour-to-hour basis was below that paid to hourly workers, and below minimum wage. There was a roll of the dice in this, a gamble that the market price would repay the hours put in. It was a gamble that paid off often enough to keep medieros in the game. But a crop doesn't wait. When the crop was there and family labor not ready at hand, medieros hired outside help to fulfill their contractual obligation. And because margins for the medieros were usually thin, they sought labor on the lowest rung of the hierarchy of the exploited, the most vulnerable and lowest-paid labor. Thus sharecropping turned strawberry medieros into small-time labor contractors squeezing out a profit with hired hands frequently living in wretched conditions.

The medieros were not the only alternative to wage enslavement that farmworkers pursued. In the early 1970s I became acquainted with a cooperative called Rancho de la Fe, which drew in some active and militant farmworkers around the union. I was given a tour of the co-op by Jose Perez, an early organizer of the UFW in the Salinas area, and was impressed by his enthusiastic vision for a cooperative farm movement that would help lift workers out of the thrall of grower exploitation and give them a dignified self-reliance. Yet the great hopes around Rancho de la Fe did not last, and a few years into the effort, it fell into internal disorder and then collapsed.

As Lupe and I mulled things over, there was a pull to look for the culprits and heap the blame on them for such wretched conditions in these clandestine places. The medieros, the most immediate at hand, seemed too vulnerable themselves to bear the label of villain. The landowners, many of them Japanese, who leased the land to the medieros, might serve the need, but weren't they really just small fry themselves? How about the banks that loaned the funds for production and demanded their pound of flesh in interest? Or the retailers like Safeway that used their marketing muscle to buy cheap and sell dear? Or the investors and speculators in all these various concerns, always clamoring for the highest return on their investments?

Here, it seemed to me, spread out before us, among the broken trailers and caves scratched out into the ground, was the wreckage of illusions that seek an escape from a system of exploitation, without actually ending that system.

Not long after Lupe's tour, the media and then the California Rural Legal Assistance and other agencies got wind of the situation among these strawberry workers and there were exposés in the local papers, and then legal action and talk of reforms. But the situation did not really change, and, given the system in agriculture, it was unlikely that it ever would.

Wanted Poster

From *The Worker* newspaper, October 1976, a Watsonville strawberry worker tells this story (edited for this book):

On the 23rd of September, the Border Patrol came to the Silliman Ranch (near Watsonville) to check people's papers. The green vans, guided by the tactical plan, entered the fields from many directions with the aim of cutting off any route of escape of its intended targets. There were about fifty of us—sharecroppers and others. Fifteen people ran. Twelve ran toward the hills, and three young guys didn't make it out of the field.

The Border Patrol began rounding people up. One patrolman got two. The name of the head patrolman was B. G. Harkendahl. He didn't do anything to them, he just said, "OK, next time."

There was another patrolman, a dark-haired Texan or Mexican, I don't know his nationality or his name because he took his name tag off his shirt. He was chasing another young guy. The young guy was scared, you could see the terror on his face as he ran. Right before the agent caught the young worker, he swung and hit him from behind with brass knuckles. He hit him so hard he knocked him down. And after the guy was down, he hit him three or four more times in the head. We watched the blood come out of his wounds, and the pain that replaced the fear on his face. Afterward we found out the young guy had two wounds one took twelve stitches to close and the other took eight.

Well, seeing something like that does something to you . . . The minute we saw that we came running to help him, so the patrolman wouldn't hit him any more. We came running and yelling, our hearts were pounding, our anger exploding—"Stop! Who gives you the right to beat us!?"

The young guy was still down. We said to him, "Don't get up." Then the agent grabbed him because he was going to get up. He was taking him out of the field. So we made a circle around them and said, "Why did you hit him!?"

People were still coming up to see what had happened and the agent threatened us with the brass knuckles. And he loosened his gun in his holster. We said, "Don't be such a son of a bitch!" We were all yelling then, saying that what he had done was so bad you couldn't give a name to it!

So the other patrolmen came running. We moved fast, we wanted the young guy to get medical attention, so we closed the roads with our cars, blocking the migra so they couldn't take him away to their migra prison. But the patrolman who was holding the young guy got to his patrol car, before we could block him in. He managed to get out of the field. He had to make a big circle, but he made it. We called the police, but by the time the police got there they'd gone.

When we were making a circle around the patrolman, the other patrolmen ran to help him. So the 12 guys that they'd already grabbed and put in the van forced the door of the van and ran free! We were yelling, "Run like hell!!" The patrolmen were running too, they were pushing cars off the road so they could get out. Some of the workers got away! We were really happy that we'd beat them. But they said, "We don't care, we've got a lot of work here tomorrow."

But they didn't show their faces the next day. And I don't think the one who beat up the young guy is ever going to come around here again. The next time they come we're going to be ready for them. Our children are in the fields and the way they drive someday they're going to run over one of my little girls. They've got no right to drive like that, and they've got no right to treat us like that.

The incident at the Silliman Ranch sent a ripple through Watsonville. Strawberry workers and others from the community formed a committee to address the outrage. Some of us at *The Worker* had people on the committee, and we decided that the beating could not go down without a response. FJ, who was part of the committee, said that when criminals are on the loose, the authorities put out wanted posters to warn the community and elicit support in seeking to bring the "wrongdoer" to justice. The Border Patrol abused the people, treated them roughly. In their hands, immigrants were humiliated, beaten, even killed. Was this not criminal behavior? Why not put out a wanted poster on the immigration agent who beat the worker?

This was a very popular suggestion and a group was assigned to work on the project. We were able to discover the name of the agent who did the beating, Agent Hawkins. But we had no picture and little chance of getting one from the migra. We decided we'd have to get our own. So we got a van, put curtains on its windows, got a camera with a telescopic lens, and stationed the van outside the headquarters of the INS. We had to have one of the workers who witnessed the beating in the van to identify the agent. It took time and perseverance, but we got our picture.

The "wanted poster" appeared all over Watsonville and Salinas, even, Lupe happily informed me, on the door of the Immigration office in Salinas. Within several days the INS announced that for the sake of the safety of Agent Hawkins, he had been transferred to Arizona. The press did not mention the beating, or the outrage in the community, but only mentioned that Agent Hawkins had been "threatened."

Communism Comes to Salinas

The great revolutionary Mao Tse-tung died on September 23, 1976. In the wake of his death, tremendous struggles took place in China, as a new group of leaders tried to reverse course away from socialism and restore capitalism. Mao recognized that the revolution that brought socialism was only a small first step in a transitional period in which the old class society is radically transformed, and that throughout this period, there is struggle between the old society and those who gained from it, and the new communal society trying to be born. Nothing guraranteed that the old order wouldn't be restored; the inequalities, habits, traditional ideas, and cultural forms that have existed over thousands of years of class society won't melt away overnight. Constant struggle to eliminate the old and give birth to the new would be necessary, and this was the motivation for the Cultural Revolution and just about everything else Mao did in the last years of his life. Unfortunately, his views and the actions of his supporters did not prevail after his death, and a process of state-directed dismantling of collective farms, state enterprises, and social welfare measures began, a process that continues today and has converted China from one of the most egalitarian nations in the world to one of the least. Advances in creating a new, revolutionary culture were turned back, and a culture of commercialism, sexism, and glorification of private wealth flooded in to replace it. Workers and peasants, struggling to become the masters of society in the Mao years, were reduced to marketable assets to be sold off at bargain prices to multinational corporations in the post-Mao society.[3]

Across the world there was debate about the changes in China.[4] Like many others who had been influenced by Mao and the events in China, I was watching and trying to understand what was going on there. At the same time, my own naïve assumptions about socialism, its inevitability and irreversible development, were sorely challenged.

I remember attending a conference of the U.S.-China Friendship Association in San Francisco. In one of the workshops someone in that organization upheld the reforms of the post-Mao regime and argued vigorously for new policies in Chinese factories.

After the Chinese Revolution of 1949 changes took place that greatly improved people's lives. But many of the habits of the old class society persisted, such as the relations between people in positions of authority and the peasants and workers. In many factories there were administrators who dictated rules and controlled finances, and there were workers who carried out production with little or no say in factory affairs, let alone broader social and governmental matters. Mass struggles would have to take place if peasants and workers were to democratically and collectively control the work they did and in which directions the larger society moved. One result of the class warfare brought on by the Cultural Revolution was that new systems of factory management emerged, engaging workers and managers in different combinations of collective leadership. For example, reforms in factories set aside time for workers to engage in study and discussions over political matters, including policies in the governing bodies of the state. These were experiments with a strategic vision in mind.

The post-Mao leaders began to denounce such practices as crazy and wasteful. They were clever to do this without directly criticizing Mao, instead blaming everything on supposed perverters of Mao's ideas, such as the so-called "Gang of 4." China, it was argued, needed to advance its production potential. Deng Xiaoping, who by the early 1980s emerged as the new leader of China, basically defined socialism as the rapid advance of production. The new capitalist leadership argued that expanding production created the material base to build communism. Therefore, the more quickly production expanded, the faster society would get to communism. Workers needed to concentrate on what they were in the factory to do—produce. The emphasis that had been placed on workers becoming the masters of society, of striving to narrow the differences between mental and manual workers, of transforming social relations on a more cooperative model, bringing forward a culture on that basis—to build a prosperous society without exploitation domestically or internationally and so on—all that was brought to an end.

At the U.S.-China Friendship Society meeting a debate took place over the new factory policies. Those who favored them criticized what they called the erroneous and destructive policies of the Gang of Four and praised the reforms that eliminated "wasteful" meetings and study sessions that detracted from the tasks of production. They supported policies that encouraged factory managers and supervisors to spend time on the production line working side-by-side with workers, thus ensuring some kind of production site democracy.

Arguments in support of these post-Mao factory policies and against workers' participation in discussions of important matters of state policy, in the name of increased production, struck me as ironic. In the fields we worked on some of the most productive farms in the world. On occasion supervisors and foremen would come around for different reasons and help out with the work. But such gestures could hardly change the social relations that existed in the fields and in society at large. If the new leaders in China were right in insisting that high levels of production and managerial beneficence were key factors in advancing a revolutionary new social system, then, hell, we must have been on the same track in Salinas!

Occasionally I talked to fellow crew members about these issues and my effort to understand changes in China. I was interested in their take on this debate around workplace policies. One day, I was packing, and one of my trio partners nudged me on the way to get boxes from the stitcher. "Hey, Güero," he said, pointing to a pickup heading our way on an access road, "hay viene el super—nos va ayudar llegal al comunismo!" (Here comes the supervisor to help us get to communism!). "Simón, a lo mejor nos va empujar, para que llegemos mas pronto!" (Yep, and he just might push us harder so we can get there faster!).

"Me" and J. Carter

The late 1970s witnessed a new mood of self-cultivation, of looking out for number one, that had gained ground. This was not a completely spontaneous affair. It was being promoted through powerful cultural outlets. It spawned organizations to help people come down off their "addiction" to social concerns, their activism and rebellion and transition into "changing yourself," not the world. Social consciousness was said to have become passé. Now, it was all about "me." The writer Tom Wolfe even coined this new era the "Me Decade."

In 1976 Jimmy Carter was elected as the "human rights president," softening the ugly images that B-52 carpet-bombing and napalmed children had seared into the consciousness of tens of millions around the world. Carter may have been folksy and humanistic, but when it came to defending U.S. interests, he could rattle the sabers as well as anyone. Image aside, he was not fundamentally different from the presidents before him, nor could he be, what with the exigencies of empire. In the face of growing contention with the Soviet Union, Carter threatened military force, including the use of nuclear weapons, in defense of U.S. oil interests in the Persian Gulf, in what became known as the Carter Doctrine. Thus began a military buildup in the region, which would continue through many presidencies in the decades to come.

In 1976 there was still a battle to be waged to win a union in the fields. The rebellious spirit of the farmworker movement, imbued by the aspirations of a better world, was waning, but there was still "La Causa," which to some degree embodied that idea. That too would change.

Proposition 14

When the ALRB ran out of funds in February 1976, cases of worker firings and other abuses pending before the board, as well as elections not yet certified, were left suspended in air. Such circumstances in any industry would cause difficulties. In agriculture the problem was greatly compounded by the harvest cycle and the mobility of the workers. Demoralization became a growing problem in the fields. The union sought more political leverage to prevent the collapse of the election campaign on which it had staked so much. It became more enmeshed in the machinery of establishment politics.

César Chávez looked for a way to protect the ALRB from becoming an instrument the growers could use to stymie the advance of the union. So began the campaign for a ballot proposition that would guarantee funding for the ALRB and at the same time guarantee the union access to the workers in the fields any time there was an election process. This was Proposition 14. Much of the union's attention was directed into gathering the hundreds of thousands of signatures to qualify for the November 1976 election.

Proposition 14 was written to guarantee union organizers open access to ranches to talk with workers in the run-up to union elections. The growers fought the proposition, relying on a massive campaign of distortion, claiming that it would amount to a general assault on people's privacy rights. This was, to say the least, pure demagoguery. People were unfamiliar with the particularities of farmworker organizing and confused by the fact that there was an election law in place, one that the UFW itself had hailed as a final triumph. This confusion favored the growers. Despite a massive effort by the UFW to mobilize all its forces behind Proposition 14, it was defeated by a wide margin.

A change was said to have come about in César Chávez as a result of the defeat of Prop 14, a loss of confidence in the public to rally to the farmworkers, a loss of confidence in the electoral arena as an avenue of struggle. But a more basic change had already occurred. Prior to the ALRA, the union waged legal battles to serve the struggle in the fields. After the law went into effect, the movement in the fields was *subordinated* to struggle in the legal arena. This would have an effect on how things unfolded in the months and years to come.

Norton Camp in Blyth

J. R. Norton was a medium-size lettuce company. I ended up at Norton during the late-summer 1976 harvest in Salinas. As the harvest wound down, I once again prepared to hit the road.

The first stop after leaving Salinas was Blythe, a swath of farmland in the desert near the California–Arizona line, one of those patches of arid land turned green by the transformative waters of the Colorado River that skirts Blythe's eastern edge. The town got its name from Thomas Blythe, a gold speculator in that area who managed to gain water rights to the Colorado in 1877.

Norton planted several weeks' worth of lettuce in the Blythe fall harvest. We lived in a camp the company rented outside town. Among labor camps I spent time in during those years, the Blythe camp stood out for its wretchedness. It was run-down and filthy. The bathrooms had a long line of toilets, many clogged and overflowing, with no division of any kind between them. The floor was covered with a layer of filth so thick it reached above a wooden grate that had been set down to "protect" us from the muck. Visits to the bathroom required boots for protection.

One of the few creature comforts one experienced as a farmworker was the after-work shower. After a sweaty day in the fields a shower took on a meaning it could only approximate for people in less physical jobs. In the Norton camp the shower gave off an obnoxious smell of sulfur, so showering lost all its appeal. After a few days I gave up on it altogether.

There was a lot of grumbling about these conditions. But the short duration and the sure knowledge we'd soon be out of there kept grumbling from becoming more than just noise.

Blythe is located on Highway 10, which links Los Angeles with Phoenix, Arizona. Blythe, in addition to the vegetable fields that skirt their way along the edge of the Colorado River, is notable as a major transit point and stopover for truckers and other travelers. The decent bathroom facilities available at truck stops and motels catering to long haulers were an attraction for me. I began bringing my clothes from the camp and taking sponge baths in the truck stop bathrooms away from the insults of putrid toilets and foul sulfur showers.

A Contractor and His Pistol

After the Blythe harvest, I was once again between crops, waiting for the Imperial harvest to begin. While I waited for Norton's Imperial Valley fields to ripen, I got an apartment in the area and a job with a local labor contractor who lived and owned a small bar in El Centro.

We were being paid in cash. Payday was on the last day of the week, which was Friday or sometimes Saturday. It was normal to be paid at the end of that last workday. One Friday we found out that we weren't working Saturday, but that we wouldn't be paid until the next day. We were told to be at the contractor's bar to collect our pay the following morning. I wasn't alone in being unhappy with this arrangement. But what choice did we have? People needed the money to get through the weekend.

The crew showed up around 9 a.m. and stood around outside the contractor's bar waiting for our pay to arrive. By the time the contractor arrived hours later, we were restive from the wait. We filed inside and lined up for our pay. The contractor stood with his foreman behind the bar and dispensed the money. The process was taking longer than seemed necessary, and it became obvious that there was something odd about our labor contractor that morning. His eyelids looked weighted and would occasionally roll down, nearly shutting his eyes. Then he would jerk his head back and open his eyes wide again. Sometimes he would laugh awkwardly and raise his voice in slurred speech. The man was drunk or damn close.

From all the stories I'd heard about labor contractors and their abusive treatment of workers, I had little sympathy for them. They were known to use their control over work to extract all kinds of favors, including sexual ones. They were infamous for cheating workers of their pay. Years later, I was angered but not surprised to hear from workers who'd put in long years with labor contractors only to discover upon reaching retirement age that their Social Security paycheck deductions had been pocketed, leaving them without the Social Security benefits they'd paid for and were counting on. This was just one contractor scam among many. Having a free hand to rob from their workers was a fringe benefit that kept a lot of them in the business.

As I got closer to the bar, I saw that the tipsy contractor had a revolver on the counter. The gun was disassembled. The trigger and barrel assembly was next to the cylinder. The cylinder looked empty of bullets, but I couldn't tell for sure. As my turn came and I approached the bar, the contractor picked up the revolver and looked intently at me. Then he began waving the cylinderless pistol around, stammering about how he didn't know what was wrong with it, that it didn't work right or something.

I wasn't afraid of the pistol; it was clearly incapable of shooting anything. But I was annoyed with the long wait, the lost Saturday, and with this drunken man in front of me waving his pistol around. I said, "No me apuntes con el pistola, OK!" (Don't point the gun at me!). The contractor looked at me with bleary, bloodshot eyes which now also had a glow of anger. "The fucking gun is not loaded, motherfucker—can't you fucking see that!" I said, "No le hace" (It doesn't matter). "I don't want you pointing it at me, or anyone. Just pay me so I can get out of here."

The contractor took what I said as some kind of a challenge, and he was not going to be challenged in his bar in front of his foreman and his crew, at least not by me. "Pinche cabrón, no ves que la pistola no tiene balas!" "Fuck off," I said, "just give me my money." All he had to do was give me my money and be done with it. But instead he pulled up the hinged section of the bar that served as an entry between the customer area and the back of the bar and came out toward me. "Don't you talk to me like that, you shit!" he said, and lunged toward me. The man was about my height, but definitely had a large weight advantage. On the other hand, he was drunk and not very coordinated. He grabbed me roughly, and we went down on the floor. I was able to break loose from his grip and jump up fairly quickly while he was still on the ground. He was having a hard time getting up, but not from anything I did to him, just the effects of the alcohol. I took my pay from the bar and walked out.

He was cursing me, but I got what I wanted. He looked like a fool, and I felt good about that.

Pablo and Maria

That winter I ran into Pablo Ramos on a street in downtown Mexicali. He was on his way to a little restaurant near the border for some menudo (tripe soup), which was the popular antidote for a Saturday morning hangover. He was carrying a bag with the strap over his shoulder. "Whatchya up to?" I asked. "As soon as I get rid of this little *crudo* (hangover) I'm going to my office," he said with a grin. His little *crudo* was the prize he earned from his previous night's bout with a bottle of tequila. "Your office?" I said. My skeptical tone was just what he was waiting for. "You think I can't have an office? I have to be a big shot to have an office? It's not only an office, it's an office with a view!"

After the menudo, we headed across the border for El Hoyo, the large lot that was a main farmworker pickup area. When we got there he sat on a bench under an overhang between the farm labor office and the fence that rimmed the lot. He took a portable typewriter out of the bag he was carrying and set it down on the wooden table under the shelter. "So here you are, my very doubtful friend," he said laughing. "My office. All I'm missing is a secretary."

"OK, but where's this great view you were bragging about?"

He pointed in the direction of the border fence, a brown wooden swath that snaked across the vista decorated with red spheres and blue triangles.

"So you have a view of a long wooden fence."

"Not just any fence. Look there," he said, pointing down. Between the wooden fence with its red circles and blue and yellow triangles and the large open lot of El Hoyo was an arroyo, with bare brown soil and a narrow river at its bottom, running slowly and darkly, with a cap of foam. The foam was so thick in places, it wasn't apparent there was any water under it at all.

"A view of the river . . . El Rio Nuevo," he said, "an office with a river view."

"Looks like El Rio Feo (ugly) to me," I said. Pablo laughed, with his trademark sarcastic edge. "And it doesn't look anything like new," I added.

"It was new some years ago."

"So why don't they call it El Viejo Rio Nuevo?"

He paused to think. "It's not that old. Maybe sixty years or something like that."

"So how does a new river come about like that?"

"Well, after your gringo ancestors stole our land they decided to steal our water from the Rio Colorado that flowed into the Mexican side. But the river got out of control and almost washed them all away. But this river was the result of that. So you see what your ancestors did?"

Pablo, like many campesinos, often used the word *gringo*. And sometimes they would apologize to me. But, to be honest, I never felt offended by it. I asked Pablo what he meant when he used it, and he said usually it just referred to white people from the United States. At other times, when he was angry, it meant arrogant bastards who think they have a God-given right to fuck over the rest of the world. In the first case, it seemed innocent enough. In the second, I shared his sentiments for the arrogant, ignorant, brutal bullshit that Americans had become infamous for around the world. I asked people where the word *gringo* came from, and the two versions I remember were that the soldiers who invaded Mexico with Pershing in 1916 sang a song, "Green Grow the Lilacs . . ." as they marched south. Thus, "Who are they?" "Oh, they're the Green Grows." The other version was that these soldiers were wearing green uniforms. The people expressed their anger at the invaders by yelling, "Green, go!" as in, "Yankee, go home!" In either case, the name is associated with invaders who stole Mexican land, treated Mexicans as inferiors, and exploited and plundered their land, resources, and people. Given all that, gringo seemed like a pretty mild and benign expletive. If gringo is a pejorative, it's at least a pejorative with historical content. It is contempt shown for unjust actions and brutish behavior. That is far different from the filthy, racist terms Americans have pinned on just about every non-white, and some white, racial and ethnic groups. You know what names I mean.

"Not my ancestors," I told Pablo. "My ancestors were Germans and they would never do anything bad like that." It was my turn to laugh sarcastically. "So somebody started dumping their shit in that river."

"Ya, it's more shit than river now," said Pablo.

It was evident that the small river was the only thing of consequence that stood between the wooden fence on the Mexican side and El Hoyo on the U.S. side. Aside from the wooden fence on the Mexico side, there was no fence at all until El Hoyo, and that was a simple chain-link fence. "Too bad the river's so messed up," I said. "This would be an easy place to cross over."

Pablo's expression became more serious. "I've seen people cross with nothing but their underwear, with their clothes in plastic bags on their head, wading through the typhoid or whatever's in there. I've seen groups of women cross and then I once saw them turned back by the migra with their guns drawn. I'd hate to go within five yards of that stinking mess."

Then he could not help himself: "You see all the shit people have to go through to come here!" It was Pablo's favorite humor, laced with irony.[5]

People were milling around the Farm Labor office and the covered area where Pablo and I sat. Workers came to the office for services, and sometimes they'd have to fill out papers. Pablo made a few dollars assisting those who had trouble navigating the forms. One man came up to us and asked Pablo if he could help with some papers he had to fill out. He was maybe sixty; his hands were thick and his fingers gnarled. He wore a sombrero with a little tassel that hung down at the back. He pulled a paper from his shirt pocket and unfolded it carefully, placing it down by the typewriter. Pablo picked it up to examine it. "Let me ask you some questions," Pablo said to the man, who then sat down next to me. "Sit here," I said, and told Pablo I was leaving him to his office work, and he invited me for dinner with Maria. With the memory of her cooking still with me, I readily agreed. We arranged to meet later in the day.

I first met Pablo in Salinas when we worked together on a broccoli machine. He was in his early thirties: short, with a slight build, long dark hair, a long face, and a mischievous smile. He grew up as an orphan on the streets of Calexico. His father left his mother shortly after he was born, and Pablo never knew him. His mother died when he was around eight, and his only relatives were on the Mexicali side—an aunt and several uncles. But he was never very close to them, and he grew up mostly on the streets. His first language was Spanish, but he learned English as a child and so was fluent in both languages. He was clever enough to have learned to read and write fairly well in both English and Spanish, which proved useful. Sometimes he'd lend a hand with translation of an article for *El Obrero*, or with proofreading.

Pablo spent the spring and summer months working in a variety of jobs, both contract and hourly, in harvesting and occasionally irrigation, moving the big sprinkler pipes, which had become the common mode of irrigation since Bruce Church began using them some decades before. But he worked most often in the contract broccoli, where we spent many hours in conversation.

One day we worked late in the broccoli. It was toward the end of fall, and so it was nearly dark by the time we got back to town. We were both extremely hungry. I gave Pablo a ride home from the Safeway parking lot where the bus let us off, and he invited me to eat at his small cottage to the rear of a house on Sanborn Road. His apartment was in an upstairs unit behind a house and not visible from the street.

Pablo was living with a woman named Maria. She was stocky, of medium height, and had long dark hair. Pablo called her La India. They had been living together for a few years, but this was the first year Maria had come north with Pablo. She didn't work in the fields but did laundry and ironing for some working families, mostly out of her small cottage. I thought she must have been bored staying home most of the day in their little apartment.

After Pablo and I threw down a few shots of tequila, Maria came into the living room. There wasn't much furniture and we sat on the floor by a small coffee table. There was one chair, but there were some pillows on the floor and we sat there, drank tequila, and waited for food.

Perhaps it was the intensity of my hunger or the stimulus of the tequila, but it was a meal so delicious that the pleasure of it remained with me long after I scooped up the last bits of juice and beans in the last piece of tortilla. It was not a fancy meal—thin beefsteak, beans, nopales, rice and handmade tortillas, some jalapeños. But it was fantastic. I don't know how she managed to create such a delight with these simple ingredients, but it was the case.

As in nearly all the Mexican households I visited, the men would sit and be served by the wife or a daughter, a niece, or any other woman in the house. I felt uncomfortable with that arrangement, though I usually didn't make an issue of it. But being pretty well acquainted with Pablo, I knew I could say things to him without him taking offense. So I questioned this arrangement of wife as servant. The tequila made his face a bit flush, made his sarcastic laugh louder than normal, and he launched into a defense by saying that he worked all day, Maria was not working outside the house, so it was only fair that she did the work in the home, including the cooking and serving. "I know you believe in women's equality," said Pablo, "but there is reality." He took another sip of tequila. "We can call it a division of labor—does that make it OK? Ya, women get the short end of the stick. But we men don't have it so great either—us field-workers. I know," said Pablo, perhaps anticipating a reply that I had yet to formulate, "we can't ever be liberated unless everyone is liberated, but we have to live in the meantime."

He then poured me another tequila and insisted I drink a toast with him "to the liberation of all of us from this fucked-up world." Pablo could read between the lines of the establishment press. To a certain extent he had broken the code. Like most Mexicanos I knew, he was bitterly cynical about the government and about "*la política*," by which people meant the system in Mexico and elsewhere. There was a deep distrust for leadership in general and a belief that anyone who rose to a position of political leadership would sell out. One of the phrases people used to describe this was "*puro convenencia*," pure self-interest. People did not expect that anyone could really rise above this.

284 / LETTUCE WARS

Pablo had a sadness in him, a tendency to depression, and you might say in psychological terms that he "medicated" with occasional but devastating binges of alcohol. More than once when he disappeared from work, I'd see him on the street, pretty messed up. I scolded him and struggled with him about this, about how he had things to offer the world, but it was a tough battle to win. I learned that this greatly saddened Maria as well.

Pablo's Mexicali home was an adobe house located in the newly forming colonia on what was at that time the outskirts of the spreading border city. Dry shrubs surrounded the square brown structure. The place had thick walls that enclosed two rooms. One was a combination living room and kitchen; the other was a bedroom off the kitchen. Toilet facilities were in a wooden outhouse.

The floor was a cement slab, which in the living room was covered with several layers of rugs. There was a couch against the wall facing the kitchen area and a table underneath a window whose frame was not perfectly set in the wall, leaving a space off to one side of it. There were only a few lights for the rooms, and they came from a wire brought from outside through the space between the window frame and the adobe surrounding it. The wire was split in two, with each section leading to a different part of the room, where a hook in the ceiling held each with a small fixture and a light bulb, probably around 60 watts. The house was fairly dark, even in daylight. But I had a feeling that the adobe structure kept the inside cool in the blast-furnace days of summer.

Pablo and I talked over another delicious dinner. We drank beer. Pablo laughed about my barroom altercation with the labor contractor, but suggested that if someone like him had tried a trick like that, the outcome would have been different. We spoke about the union elections. He had caught some of the skepticism circulating about the union, and it fed his own inbred cynicism, as did our discussion about China, and what was really going on there. Pablo was sure the bad guys had come to power, but he based this as much on his dark view of the world as on any evidence coming out of China itself. Maria remained in the background, busying herself with recharging our supply of warm tortillas and cold beer and clearing the table after we were done eating.

Pablo drank without much pause, and by nine o'clock he was semiconscious on the couch. I had no idea where we were in Mexicali and no interest in exploring the area at night. Nor did it seem like Pablo would be in shape to guide me downtown to the Hotel San Antonio where I was now staying. With Maria's assent, I decided to stay for the night, and I prepared a spot on the floor near the couch.

Maria was putting things away in the little kitchen area, which was a sink, a wooden table, and a stove powered by propane from a metal tank that sat upright near the stove. I thanked her for the food and said if she persisted in feeding me, she might never get rid of me. I found out she was from Tabasco in southern Mexico. There she had three children, but came north because it was hard to find work to feed them. Her mother was taking care of the kids. From what I could tell, the father of the children had left her and them and now she was sending money home to help support them. Maybe someday she would bring them up north, but not now. Pablo gave her some money at times to send home, and she made money, helping people at a laundromat not far from the colonia.

When I told her how I felt uncomfortable with the men always eating and the women always serving them, she laughed. I didn't know if she would think I was crazy, but she understood quite well. She said that as men go, Pablo was pretty good. Except for his drinking. But he was never abusive to her, as others had been with women she knew. And even with the restricted life in Mexicali and Salinas, she was freer now than when she lived in the south in the village where women's lives were tightly proscribed. I said I didn't like the way men treated women, but I understood that men were taught that way, that society molded them that way.

I told her how I had had to confront my own instilled male attitudes. A group of feminist women had come to Seaside from Berkeley to visit the GI coffeehouse project. They were critical of the "division of labor" at the coffeehouse, where women were most often consigned to jobs like cooking and making coffee. One evening a group of women, coffeehouse staff, and visitors took over the place, filled with GIs who'd come in to hear music and talk. They caught everyone's attention and then played the Tammy Wynette song "Stand by Your Man." I was groping around trying to translate this song title: "Pararse junto a tu hombre," the literal translation, didn't do it. So I said, "Apoyar su hombre a pesar de su estupidez" (Support your man no matter how stupid). Maria laughed heartily at that. "Well," I said, "the women were really angry at the song and at us for assuming they would do the dirty work in the coffeehouse, clean the dishes, and all that. I too was angry. I thought, here we're trying to organize against the war and these women are focusing on our minor errors. They shouldn't blow up differences with the men in such a way as to threaten our important work. They're nitpicking, looking for things to criticize us about. They are raising their grievances above the larger and more important issues." Yet the event shook the men up and made us think. Later I realized that my attitude was largely bullshit. Just because we had become active in opposing certain injustices did not mean we were free from distorted social relationships and backward attitudes. Maria listened patiently to all this. Then she said that she hoped to be able to work and support herself so she could decide about things in her own life. She said she knew women who were very badly treated in their relationships, but they accepted this as their fate and obligation.

I asked Maria about her husband, the man who had walked out on her and left her with the children. Her face turned somber as her stocky body slumped. For a moment I thought she was going to fall and I would have to catch her. A sense of dread and regret swept over me. Why did I open my stupid mouth? She caught herself and turned to me. "Lo siento, Bruch," she said, her eyes welling up and in that instant I too felt tears cloud my eyes, and I didn't know why, but with the intensity of the sadness that rose to her face and in her voice I couldn't help myself. I felt foolish to be near tears when it was her torment, not mine.

I didn't push the conversation, and Maria did not take it any further. She wiped her face and went into the bedroom and brought out a large, warm blanket and put it down on the rug in the living room area. Pablo was still asleep on the couch and I rolled up in the blanket and tried to sleep. "Hasta mañana," Maria said. "Hasta mañana," I repeated from my cocoon.

Hotel San Antonio

Richard's old haunt in Mexicali was the San Antonio. This is where Mickey and I ended up during that and subsequent winter harvests. The hotel was only a few blocks from the border crossing, along a strip of hotels, clothing stores, bars, restaurants, and taco stands in Mexicali's downtown. Rooms were cheap, far less than what you'd pay on the Calexico side. We never paid more than $3 a night for a room.

I always had the same room on the third floor at the rear of the building. The rooms were small and plain and nearly identical, with cement floors, a beat-up chest of drawers, and an army-style cot with a thin mattress. The cot's springs complained loudly whenever you put your weight on them. The bathroom had neither door nor shower curtain, and when the shower was on, it tended to wet the entire floor, which was by design, since the drain was in the middle of it, not in close proximity to the shower itself.

It was said that the hotel had hot water. But these were only unconfirmed rumors. There was never hot water after 5 p.m., which meant that farmworkers rarely could look forward to a hot or even warm shower, since we rarely got back from work that early. There were times when, having arrived in Calexico in late afternoon, I made a hasty dash for the border and the hotel determined to confirm the hot water rumor, only to be disappointed every time.

Years of such experiences led Richard, a regular at the San Antonio, to devise a method of showering that Mickey and I attempted to imitate. Richard kept a bottle of tequila on the dresser near the bathroom entrance. A quick swig, a run to the shower—in theory the warmth of the descending tequila would balance the frigid cold of the heatless water—then another dash for a swig, until cleanliness was achieved. I tried this method a few times at Richard's insistence but found it unsatisfying. I still felt painfully cold, only cold and tipsy, especially since the showering took place on an empty stomach. So I preferred the public bath a block or so from the hotel, where a hot shower cost the equivalent of about 50 cents. I also skipped showers some weekdays, reasoning that I was only going to get dirty the next day anyway.

The Hotel San Antonio in winter was known for hosting two categories of occupants—farmworkers and prostitutes. There was a lot of joking that went on about that. There were, for example, the late Friday night concerts that reverberated down the hotel's spare hallways, symphonies on creaking bedsprings. This Friday night affair attests to the fact that prostitution, like most everything else in that border area, moved with the rhythm of agriculture. Friday night had two special qualities: it was pay night and often the night before an off-day in the fields.

Ficheras

One day after work, I was sitting and drinking a beer by myself in a bar up the street from the San Antonio when one of the women who worked in the bar as a *fichera* (a dancer for money), whom I'd seen around the hotel, came and sat down next to me. She scooted up close and draped an arm over mine. Just as suddenly a man appeared at the table. His eyes held a glaze that spoke of too many drinks. In an aggressive tone, amplified and stupefied by alcohol, he asked the woman at my side what she was doing. "I just came to sit by my boyfriend a while," she said quietly but firmly, giving my arm a squeeze. At that, the man gave a disgusted grunt, looked around, and then staggered off toward the bar. The woman's name was Gloria, and she thanked me and asked if I would buy her and myself a drink. "Sure," I said, and she called the bartender over who served us. She explained how her customer had been getting obnoxious with her, and she thanked me again for playing along so she could get rid of him.

The term *fichera* comes from the small coin-like token, a *ficha*, which customers use to pay the women for dances. At the end of the night the women turn the *fichas* over to the bar for pay. In the bars I was familiar with in Mexicali, the women also got a fee for every drink their customers bought. Encouraging customers to drink was both a means to a livelihood and playing with fire.

After we were served several drinks, mine shots of mescal that I chased with a little lemon and hers a drink that looked similar, I began to feel the effects of the alcohol. How was it that she could drink and seem so unaffected? Gloria handed me her glass and asked me to taste it. Cream soda! It was then that I realized that not only do the ficheras have to make their money dancing with strangers; they have to employ some pretty realistic acting qualities. Their clients expect them to drink alcohol, and this, in addition to their own desire to drink, is one of the motivations for buying drinks for their dance partners. To prove that the drinks are having the desired effects, the women pretend to become more friendly as the night goes on.

After that night I greeted Gloria when I saw her at the San Antonio. I was shocked to find out that she lived there with three small daughters. One night, when business was slow, Gloria came over to where I was sitting, and we talked for a while. This time she didn't ask me to buy any drinks. We'd become friends, and I was happy to talk to her. She gradually unfolded pieces of her life's story that led her to this job as a fichera. I learned that she'd been married to a man who believed her role was to serve him and have his babies. After each child he gave her no time to recover. Shortly after the third child, he came to her one night and she resisted. It was too soon, she told him; she needed time to rest and recover. The fact that she protested was too much, and he beat her. I saw the scar across her lower jaw that testified to the beating. To add insult to that injury, he took up with another woman, and she found herself on her own with three small children. Though her daughters were very young, she had no choice but to leave them alone in the room when she had to take care of things, and, of course, work at night. After I found out about the children, I began, from time to time, to pick up groceries on the way home from El Hoyo and drop them off at Gloria's room.

Beer, a Paycheck, and a Friday Night

Through Gloria and a few other women I got to know by living at the San Antonio, I got a glimpse of the world the ficheras inhabited. And I also got to know a bit about the side of those men who sought out their services as respite from the loneliness of the migrant life. The following is the not altogether uncommon tale told by a farmworker friend on a repentant Monday morning.

It had been a long day, a long week. The beer on the way back to town after a hard week softens the pain, tranquilizes, brings some liquid equilibrium, but it's Friday and it can do little for the loneliness that seeps into the space the physical pain once occupied. It doesn't dampen the urge for human contact, but it appears to make that quest more attainable.

It's Friday and a fat check for a week's sweaty labor, even after the check-cashing joint takes its cut, becomes a reassuring lump on your thigh as you enter the dark cantina, filled with smoke and music and laughter.

Soon there's someone by your side, smiling and teasing, her hands on your arm. You might be among the most *pisoteados* (oppressed people) on the planet, *bien jodido* (really fucked over), but still you are male and there are things in the culture that assure you there are *shes* in this world rightfully yours to pursue—biology and ideology. You look at her smile with those eyes of "later tonight" and feel the tightening in the groin.

The booze (*el pisto*) starts to flow. "Hey, cantinero, un tequila, por favor!" The music, *la música, un conjunto,* a music group "compa, una canción, por favor"—a song please, friend. You reach for the lump on your thigh, and anything is possible—the men and women lining the bar, the laughing crowds at tables, clapping to your selection of music. "El Rey, que suave compa!" "Con dinero y sin dinero, hago siempre lo que quiero!" (With or without money, I do what I want!) A round for the table, beer, then tequila. "Gracias mi amigo, y gracias por tu amistad," they nod toward you. The thanks are genuine.

The fields, the pain, the loneliness, are all a thousand miles away now. The music, the laughter, then the dancing, her warm body and the dampness just below the fabric of her dress, the hint of perfume in her hair, a powerful seductive warmth radiating from below her abdomen; the beer, the tequila, the music, the friendly calls, the laughter, the lump smaller now, but still there; her smile, her eyes, her mouth as she laughs—companionship, relief, forgetfulness and that ever-present urge. The smile is worth some pesos, the laugh and those eyes even more. More laughter, more dancing, a head on your shoulders, the lump becomes more generous, the room more hazy, the tightness more palpable. Another song, another round, another dance . . . "En la penca de un maguey tu nombre, unido al mio . . ." Your voice, gravelly and shaky, sounds robust to your own late-night ears, eyes cast about a room now in some kind of undulating motion . . . but you want this to go on.

"Hey amigo, ya vamos a cerrar," says the bartender looking down with dark eyes and a small, dark beard. "It's closing time."

Already? "Espera cantinero!" Wait, just one more song, just one more, you say, staggering to your feet. The lump has melted, but you have enough for a song, one last song, and some pesos for your laughing, smiling partner. Tonight, aqui te doy, for tonight, we'll be together tonight, I'll make it a good night for you, you say, or you think you say. The haze is thicker now, including the haze on your tongue.

You want to hold her right there, the tightness has become painful. "OK," she says, "but, wait, I have to use the ladies room you know." OK, outside, I'll see you outside. "Wait for me there"—a wait-for-me-smile as she moves away.

The room moves. Little lunges now to keep your balance, like you're on a ship at sea. Then the door to the street and the cool air of early morning, the rush of people, some staggering, slurred speech, cops cruising. Where is she? Ya está cerrado la puerta. The door's locked! Still she's not here. The lights go out inside. The lump is almost gone, a few thin bills are all that's left of the $500 you came with. But all you can think about is that warm, damp back and the relief that will come holding her, pressing her flesh to yours . . . A van, a door opens, a shape, a familiar shape pushes in. It's her, in the van—the van, beginning to move. You step into the street now as the van passes. You turn and run, and your fist smashes into the back door of the retreating van, once, twice, three times. Pinche puta, cabrona! Pinche cabrona engañosa! A car weaving down the street barely misses you as you stagger back to the sidewalk and then stumble back to the hotel.

The fucking pinche menso, que soy yo! (What an idiot I am!) competes with the painful tightness and the anger. You blew the fucking rent. Now you'll have to ask for an advance from the pinche mayordomo. Que pinche suerta tan gacho! What fucking bad luck!

8. DISCONTENT

IN THE SUMMER OF 1977 I was working at Interharvest on the number 7 crew, the low-seniority ground crew. Interharvest had a rotation system, meant to give each crew roughly the same amount of work; it was feast or famine for us all.

Toro camp, on Hitchcock Road a few miles from downtown Salinas, was the Interharvest ground crew camp. Many of the ground crew lechugueros lived there or, like me, came there in the early mornings to catch a bus for the fields.

From a distance Toro camp looked like a lone white ship floating on a vast brown or green sea (depending on the season). Up close, the ship became a cluster of long white wooden barracks arrayed in a square pattern surrounding several equally spartan structures that housed the kitchen and eating area, and the bathroom and shower facility. These were all plain white buildings with green-trimmed wooden windows.

The camp sat on a large asphalt lot that extended on three sides from the outer perimeter of the buildings to the surrounding fields and roads. The asphalt grounds were undisturbed by vegetation save the odd weed that managed to liberate itself through the aging blacktop.

To the west of the men's camp stood a family camp of wooden cabins laid out in a row facing the access road. Between the two camps was a grassy lot with rusting children's swings and playground apparatus and usually a modest collection of worn autos taking advantage of cheap long-term parking.

Toro camp (as of this writing, it still exists as a bracero camp) is surrounded by fields that extend for a good distance in every direction. To the west they abut the boundary of Fort Ord; to the north they extend to Highway 1, which skirts Monterey Bay; to the east of the fields are the rolling hills that lead to Boronda Heights; and to the south they face Spreckels and beyond.

In the mornings I made a short commute from Salinas to Toro camp when the light of day had yet to cast its hint on the horizon. Like the other semi-awake denizens of the camp, I made my way into the cocoon of a waiting bus for the dream-like trip to the field.

Sometimes I spent time at the camp after work talking to people and, occasionally, eating in the dining hall at the invitation of a crew member with the assurance, "We'll work it out with the cook." As camp food went, this was plain but tasty—generous portions of meat, often thin steak, salads, beans, rice, salsa, and tortillas. Its relatively high quality owed to the organization and vigilant pressure the workers put on the company.

At Interharvest I became good friends with Tony, a veteran lechu-guero from the bracero days. After the program ended he got his green card, which in those days was a fairly simple affair because the growers were desperate for experienced workers and the INS, skirting the messy issues of legality invented a special category—the "commuter green card"—and made them available to the workers they needed in the veg-etable and fruit crops. Tony, like many other lechugueros, was the "ideal" worker. Tony and his family lived in Juarez, so the social costs of families, education, health care, and so on, were born by Mexico. U.S. growers got skilled workers in the prime of their working lives on the cheap. By some accounts, green carders were a better deal than braceros because the growers had no contractual obligations for housing, wages and other labor costs.[1]

Tony had been with Interharvest since it was formed in 1968, and he was second or third in seniority on the highest-seniority crew. He was a socialist and made no secret of it. We became friends based on our mutual interest in radical politics. Tony's father was a peasant activist in Mexico, working among the small and landless farmers in one of the northern states. Tony didn't follow his father into activism but held on to his father's disdain for the tyranny of wealth.

Tony had a family in Juarez, which he saw only occasionally. There were seven kids, though not all of them were biologically his. A lot of his earnings went to support them, and he lived, like many others, frugally, doing the year-round corrida from Salinas to Mexicali where he worked in the winter.

One day, when our crews arrived at about the same time at the camp, Tony and I got into a conversation that followed us to the dining room. After eating, Tony said he wanted me to meet one of his buddies, so I walked with him to the barracks behind the mess hall to one of the long rooms with little more than walls, windows, and a cement floor. Many of the workers hung sheets or blankets from rafters around their bunks to form small compartments for privacy. In one of these, with a hanging blanket pulled open, we found Carlos, sitting back in his bunk reading and listening to the little console radio he had on the orange crate next to his bunk.

Carlos nodded as we came in, and reached over to turn down the radio. I had seen Carlos around, and may have spoken to him on some occasions, but I had never been formally introduced. He looked to be a little older than Tony, maybe his mid-forties, with a stubble of a beard flecked with some gray. His hair was short and curly, and he wore a blue work shirt opened to around navel level, revealing a V-neck T-shirt and a partially exposed chest with sparse strands of hair. As he looked up, I saw his eyes were dark and alert. "This is my friend Bruce," Tony said, but he pronounced it Bruch, one of the common mispronunciations of my name. (Bruce was an unusual name for most farmworkers. There was only one Bruce that most had any acquaintance with, the company Bruce Church. Due to the cumbersome sound of that name, most farmworkers referred to Bruce Church as "La Brocha," the brush.) Carlos stretched out a thick, calloused hand, with the black nails of the lettuce packer. "Mucho gusto, Bruch," he said, imitating Tony. "Siéntate," he said, raising himself up against the curved bar of the cot. "Enséñale tu biblioteca" (show him the library), Tony said to him. "Le interesa" (He's interested in that). At that, Carlos reached down under his bunk and dragged out a suitcase tied with a frayed rope. Carlos untied the suitcase, flopped the case onto the bed , and opened it. Inside was a collection of books in Spanish. Among them were titles I knew: Lenin's *Imperialismo, La Etapa Superior de Capitalismo*, Engels's *El Origen de La Familia, Propiedad Privada y el Estado*, Marx's and Engels's *El Manifesto del Partido Comunista*, among many others. Included was literature on Cuba, and some books by Mao, including *Sobre Las Contradicciones* and *Sobre La Práctica*. These, it was clear, by the interest he showed in them and the care with which he kept them, were Carlos's treasures.

After briefly talking about some of the books we'd read in common, Carlos began laying out some of his views on society and his vision for the future. Carlos was confident that socialism would triumph one day. It had to, he said; capitalism is causing us too many problems. The tendency for some to get richer and richer and many others poorer would one day lead to an explosive situation that could not be controlled. The fact that the capitalists, in their frantic search for more and more profit, were driving countries into ruin and people into rebellion meant that eventually that rebellion would sweep the world and the capitalist game would be over.

He said he sensed that people were getting more and more restless about this. In this better world he would, he insisted, still work in the fields, but not for a company. For him work was natural and healthy. Exploitation was not. The work in the fields would be for the benefit of the people, to feed them, to feed society. "People would know what they were working for," he said. "Not like now. Do you know what or who you're working for?" he asked. "Is it some people in New York? Or some stockholder in—" He paused trying, to come up with a name. "In Cheecago?" Tony and I shrugged. "We don't know," said Carlos. "In Mexico we know we work for the güero," he said, referring to the United States, and laughed. "If we don't even know who we work for, how can we claim to have any say over anything we do?" In Carlos's new world workers would have more say over how things were organized and how work was carried out. And "there would be more to life than just working. We'll study, we'll engage in sports and other activities, not just be animals working in the fields, but real human beings participating in life." As Carlos spoke, I had the vision of some kind of ideal labor camp, with schools and sports facilities and the like. I thought about the struggles in China and said that I thought workers would have to become much more involved in how society itself was run, not just about the operation of this or that factory or farm.

I think that Carlos viewed socialism as some kind of ultimate, finished product, which was a common view in those days. But a new socialist society is dynamic, full of struggle and contradictions.[2] But I also understood that an essential point for people like Tony, Carlos, and other politically aware workers was the aspiration to live in a world where people were not used and abused so others could accumulate wealth that was alienated from them and used for purposes counter to their interests.

It was far easier for people to conceive of revolutionary change in Mexico or other oppressed countries than to imagine such a thing in the United States, sentiments magnified by the isolation farmworkers felt from the rest of U.S. society, including other workers. I'd heard politically minded farmworkers argue *they* were the working class in the United States, and everyone else was middle class. In many respects farmworkers were not part of the larger industrial laboring class, but a separate caste, set apart by low wages, poor working conditions, and social isolation, discrimination, and an apparatus of harassment and deportation. And they were separated also by cultural differences that were expressed in the term *obrero campesinos*—workers from peasant backgrounds. This caste aspect was true even in those cases when farmworker incomes were equal or above workers' incomes in other areas of the economy. Geographic isolation and language also separated farmworkers from the one group who most closely shared their social conditions: African Americans.

Carlos knew something of the history of U.S. workers and believed there was a basis for unity across the boundaries of race and nationality. And he subscribed to the view that this class could and would become conscious of itself and the role it had to play to bring into being a better world.

Carlos also spoke of the United States in imagery popular at the time—as an octopus, its tentacles extending across the planet, sucking up resources and wealth. In this imagery national liberation and independence movements would sever the tentacles, bloodying and weakening the beast and creating the internal conditions for change. In this way the U.S. empire would be taken to task. Such were some of the views that had currency as radicals like Carlos looked beyond their immediate situations and struggled over how the world might change.

Other people in the barracks drifted in and out of the conversation. And then rather quickly talk shifted when a worker on one of the nearby bunks sat up and said, "Estan hablando de sueños compa" (You're talking of dreams, brother). "Y aquí vivimos con pesadillas" (And here we're living with nightmares). He began talking about problems in the company, on the crews, and of an irksome feeling that things were not going well. The union was not backing the workers in their problems with the company. The real money being taken home in wages was diminishing with rising prices. One worker, who had just come from the shower room, a damp towel draped over his shoulder, stopped to relate, in a tone of frustration, his effort to get compensated for family medical bills. Where's the money for the medical plan going, he said with some exasperation. "A los politiquillos de Sacramento, primo" (to the political hacks in Sacramento, cousin), said someone else nearby, echoing a growing sentiment that their concerns were being pushed to the side for other interests the union was pursuing, interests that had more to do with becoming part of the political establishment. What particularly angered the worker who raised the medical plan problem was the dismissive tone of staff at the union hall when he sought help. Nor was the ranch committee very helpful, he said, and he angrily cursed the head of Interharvest's union ranch committee, Armando Ruiz.

And so it went for a while. Others joined the chorus, and the conversation shifted into the immediate day-to-day concerns. A mood of discontent had been growing for some time. There was general disappointment and disillusion with the contract signed with Sun Harvest in 1976, which many felt was inadequate. But the tone of the anger and the intensity of the feelings expressed now were on a different level. I had not heard that kind of anger, so broadly and intensely expressed by the workers and directed at the UFW.

Chávez, a New Vision, and a Rally

It was billed as a major speech, and several thousand farmworkers came out to hear what César Chávez had to say in the gym at Hartnell College. People were still hungry for the inspiration that the movement had brought them and that Chávez represented. This was summer 1977.

The meeting began with a movie about the grape strikes that had shaken the state in 1973 and 1974. It showed the arrests, the repression—workers cringing in the face of brutal sheriffs, the mass arrests. There was some good footage, but I didn't like the film. I didn't like the farmworkers as victims, which was its message. Maybe it worked as boycott propaganda. But I felt embarrassed and bothered watching it. Do people only show solidarity to those who seem helpless? Had people rallied to support the Vietnamese because they couldn't defend themselves? I don't think so. My image of farmworkers after working and living with them for these years was not one of weakness or helplessness, not by a long shot.

César Chávez spoke, reminding people of the struggles they had been through, and what they had accomplished, the obstacles they had overcome. Now they had a law that protected their right to organize, to choose a union, a new day had begun. Now they and the union, together, were in a position to make big advances. "Una sola union"—one big union for farmworkers. This was the goal, and the goal was in sight. What could a big union like this do? It could lift the workers to new heights, heights of economic stability and well-being. Just as the craft unions, the plumbers, carpenters, electricians, and the like had achieved great material gains for their members, bringing them the American dream, so the farmworkers were on the cusp of realizing such an achievement. This was the vision, the goal that the union was approaching. People needed to stay focused on this goal: to realize what they had so long aspired to.

As we filed out of the gym, I thought about what had been proposed, and the more I thought about it, the more impossible and uninspiring the whole thing seemed. I was not a big fan of the American dream. Dreams are great as long as they're not built on other people's nightmares. And there were plenty of nightmares to go along with this dream, enough to give you sleepless nights. Like Jackson Browne said, "Doctor, my eyes, tell me what is wrong. Was I unwise, to keep them open for so long?"

There were other glaring problems with the speech. By 1977 a new phenomenon had begun to appear that affected the well-being of workers in the United States—runaway shops. After the Second World War, and because of U.S. economic supremacy, wages, especially those of white and skilled workers, had risen substantially, but now there was downward pressure on them due to increasing competition from newly emerging industrial powers like Japan and Germany. The status of these privileged sectors was in decline, and it seemed unlikely that farmworkers would be able to buck that trend. And then there was the matter of national oppression. The civil rights movement and Black Liberation struggle, the Chicano movement, ethnic studies battles on the campuses, and the farmworkers' struggles, all were to some degree rebellions against discrimination and oppression. Important changes had taken place, but the structures of oppression were still there and had a way of reasserting themselves in new and vicious forms. By 1977, affirmative action was already under attack. The overall position of farmworkers had changed little. The INS was still out there actively harassing and hounding people; an unofficial apartheid for immigrant workers that confined them to the lower-paid strata still existed. This trend of sustaining the economy on the backs of low-paid immigrant workers was increasing, not decreasing. Chávez's speech had not really touched on the kinds of oppression that had given rise to the movement in the first place, that had provided much of its powerful energy.[3]

Around the time that Chávez delivered the Hartnell speech, he wrote a letter for union staff on "union business and purpose." It was an extraordinary call for a restructuring of the union and a reassessment of its outlook and goals. As the letter stated, "A clear, simple and penetrating theory of the business rather than intuition, characterizes the truly successful entrepreneur (all of us on staff are entrepreneurs) who must build an organization to endure and grow long after he is gone. . . . What is our business, what it will be and what should it be is the central question. Unless the basic concepts on which a business has been built are visible, clearly understandable, and explicitly expressed, the business enterprise is at the mercy of events." This new theory and outlook to bind the union contained not a word about the struggle for justice, dignity, and equality that the union movement had come to represent for so many people. "For our own salvation," the letter argued, "we must raise the question of what is our business clearly and deliberately, and answer it thoughtfully and thoroughly. This question will cause counter-argument and disagreement."[4] In fact, the letter did generate arguments and disagreements from union staff and volunteers who objected to this business union vision. The letter anticipated a period of argument and disagreement. But there was no hint of the intolerant treatment to be accorded those who actually dared to disagree.

298 / LETTUCE WARS

Union Convention and a Filipino Guest

The UFW held another convention in Fresno in August 1977. I went to Fresno for the convention with a few other people from the paper, which was now called the *The Worker from the Salinas and Pajaro Valleys*. We wanted to keep up with what was going on in the union and distribute the paper, aware that this could be a dicey affair. From past experience at such events, I knew the union leadership had an active security staff that "discouraged" anyone not officially sanctioned by the leadership from exerting any influence, even if it was distributing a leaflet or a newspaper.

We'd heard that César Chávez had recently visited the Philippines as a guest of the president, Ferdinand Marcos, and that a representative from the Philippines was going to be at the convention. There was quite a bit of buzz about this. Marcos was a notorious figure. Under his regime, which began in 1969, the Philippines had become one of the staunchest allies of the United States in Asia, firmly backing the U.S. war in Vietnam and allowing unrestricted use of U.S. bases on the islands as staging areas for the war. Marcos was also infamously corrupt, using his position of power to enrich himself and his cronies.

In 1972, as his unpopularity and a nascent insurgency threatened his hold on power, Marcos carried out a coup, suspending elections scheduled for the following year. In the course of consolidating his hold on power and to crush growing opposition, his government jailed, tortured, murdered, and disappeared many people. Among the victims were revolutionaries, union activists, peasant leaders, and members of bourgeois opposition parties. This was the government that Chávez visited and even praised on his return home.

The rumor that the union had invited guests from the Philippines government to speak to the farmworker convention proved true. The first day of the convention the Philippines' Consul General was introduced to the assembled delegates. He was accompanied onto the convention floor by a group of Filipino farmworkers. There was a noisy show of enthusiasm from the convention to this guest. From where I sat in the gallery above, I noticed some people around me jump up and applaud at certain moments, as if on cue. It was apparent that some scripting had gone on and what seemed spontaneous was actually planned beforehand.[5] When the Consul General was announced, these same people clapped and cheered. Others around them joined in, creating the impression of broad enthusiasm, well out of proportion to what was happening on the floor. I saw Roberto Garcia among the convention delegates on the floor, his heavy frame bouncing under his poncho, whooping like a football cheerleader as the Consul General marched to the podium. The sight of such excitement for the representative of a regime that had banned union organizations and repressed dissent seemed beyond bizarre.

The security at this convention was extremely tight, and the guards, most of them from Delancy Street (a San Francisco based group that provided services for substance abusers and former prisoners) were pushy and aggressive. Not only was it nearly impossible to distribute any literature in the convention area, even talking to people was difficult because the guards were emboldened to stand right by me and others from the newspaper while we attempted to communicate with people. I made my discomfort over their gangster-like tactics known as broadly as I could under the circumstances.

At one point I ran into Phil Vera Cruz near the convention grounds and managed to talk to him for a short while. Vera Cruz was the union's second vice president and had been part of the struggle from the early days in Delano. He was one of the original grape strikers from AWOC that walked out in the Coachella Valley in 1965. He was well respected and regarded as someone with integrity. I didn't know it then, but he'd been the only union executive board member to oppose the union's policy on "illegals," a stand that took some courage. I asked Vera Cruz what he thought about the appearance of the representative from the Philippines, and I was not surprised to find him very unhappy. "I hope you'll say something publicly," I said to him. "This is such a betrayal of what the union represents for many people and a betrayal to the people." Vera Cruz made it clear there were things he strongly disagreed with in the union and with Chávez, but he was reticent about speaking publicly of them for the sake of maintaining unity in the movement. I wondered why unity should be maintained in a movement that was taking a reactionary stand.

There were union people I knew from Salinas who defended the invitation to the Philippines representative on the grounds that it could help the union win support from Filipino farmworkers. With the union setting its sights on becoming the union for all farmworkers, it was important to find ways to overcome the antagonism Filipino farmworkers felt for the union. If developing ties with the Philippines government could help, why not? So went their argument. But why were Filipino workers alienated from the union in the first place? I never heard any good explanation for that.

The second day of the convention, another Filipino guest, Blas Ople, was introduced to the gathering. He was the Secretary of Labor in Marcos's government. Having the Secretary of Labor of a regime that essentially outlawed unions at the farmworkers' convention was a pill that made many people gag. The outward display of unity began to crack following the secretary's speech. One of the union's Filipino organizers stood up, went to the microphone, and, after thanking the secretary for his remarks, added, "I hope he does not forget to tell Marcos to lift martial law."[6] This remark elicited loud and long applause that had the feel of spontaneity.

Before the convention, Phil Vera Cruz had decided to resign his position as second vice president, and arrangements had been made to fill the vacancy with Eliseo Medina. When the time came for Vera Cruz to make his resignation public, he made it clear that he was resigning and not retiring. He also indirectly referred to the suppression of differing points of view in the union by arguing that a diversity of ideas in a union was natural and its growth and development could not be guaranteed without it. He criticized the praise given at the convention for the Marcos dictatorship. But true to his word, he made no mention of his sharp differences with César Chávez or disagreement with other union policies.

Cal Coastal and Baseball

It was late summer, and Interharvest's lettuce ground crews were not working very much. There were rumors floating about that more production was being switched over to lettuce-wrap machines, in response to market pressures. This created additional anxieties on the crews. I was on crew number 7, the low-seniority crew. We were laid off for a time, and there was no indication when work might start up again. Luckily I managed to get a dispatch for Cal Coastal. Coastal workers had voted to join the UFW during the election campaign in 1975, and the company finally signed a contract in May of 1976. I worked at Coastal the rest of the Salinas harvest and prepared to meet the crew in Calexico for the winter harvest.

The Cal Coastal crew was young and speedy. I thought if there were ever an Olympic lettuce-cutting event, this bunch might have a run at the gold. It took all I had to keep up with them.

There were a couple of really fast workers on my trio. We would switch off cutting and packing, and when I packed it was always full tilt. My already bruised hands and fingernails got a beating in my furious efforts to keep up with my cutters. Years later a former crew member claimed that one of my trio partners was taking some kind of over-the-counter remedy to kill the pain, which helped his speed. I don't know if that was true; they weren't doing drug testing in those days, which was good, because otherwise the company might have made us all take them—drugs, that is.

As my pride was at stake, nothing satisfied me more than packing behind my cutters' heels and dashing to the stitcher truck to grab our boxes and still keep up. But this was rare, and more often than not one of the cutters would turn down the row and pack boxes to bring me up to speed. I was an average packer at best on this crew, but my cutters were among the best on any crew I'd ever been on.

We had a closer named Ronco. Every time he spoke or laughed, it was obvious where his nickname came from; he had a voice that sounded like gravel. Ronco was a cheerleader among workers, appropriate on a crew that always seemed to be in a race against itself. With Ronco around, the crew was never in short supply of humorous put-downs and colorful exhortations. But Ronco had a good heart, and his spirit was never tainted with meanness toward anyone.

When I think about this crew, the image that comes to mind is my favorite baseball team, the Dodgers, in their early days in Los Angeles when they were a run-and-hit team, with Maury Wills as their scrappy lead-off hitter, Junior Gilliam and Charlie Neal hitting behind him, speeding him along the bases on ground balls that "had eyes," as they say. Small, scrappy, and fast. This baseball imagery is appropriate, because this crew was full of baseball fanatics.

Professional baseball had come to Mexicali just the year before, in 1976, with the formation of the Mexicali Aguilas of La Liga Mexicana del Pacífico. The Aguilas were one of the crew's passions, taking a back seat only to its first passion, *playing* the game. Because the crew was so fast, we'd often finish the *pedido*—the day's quota—early so that even though it was winter, we were sometimes able to get to the diamond and get a game going before dark. The company cooperated and supplied the crew with bats, balls, and gloves.

Even though Mexicali was expanding fast, parcels of ground remained empty, and these became fair game for a young, baseball-hungry population. It seemed that where there was a suitable (defined flexibly!) large flat open area, someone would put up a simple backstop and lay down some base lines. These were unadorned fields, without names, without fences, without grass, without bases except some cast-off sweatshirt or jacket thrown down before the game; with maybe a bench or two for a primitive dugout.

The field we played on was such a patch of ground not far from the Infonovit, a public housing project of tiny cinder-block dwellings squished up against each other, to save its residents from any wasteful open space! We would arrive in the late afternoon, sometimes straight from work or after a quick stop to change clothes, pick up equipment, and get the beverage that was a central feature of these games—beer. In describing what we did on those afternoons it's hard to say whether we drank beer while play-ing baseball, or played baseball to accompany beer drinking.

When the team captains selected their players, I was a popular choice because, unlike my crewmates, relative newcomers, and recent converts to the game, I had played it when I was younger. But maybe more than my experience was the fact that I drank less than the others and stayed sober longer. This made me an asset for those that might, in those early, sober moments, consider winning something worth considering. While win-ning might have been a motivation at the beginning of the game, it faded more quickly than even the weak sunlight of those winter afternoons. The game generally started out well enough, with people keeping track of the score and hitting in some kind of organized order. Fielders were atten-tive and pursued the ball when put in play. But after a few innings came telltale signs of disintegration: balls passing through the legs of infielders; outfielders running in on balls hit over their heads; pitchers getting a bit wilder. As the game wore on, you might see a batter swing at the ball before it was pitched; a pitcher falling off the mound—staggering might be a better description—before or after throwing; easy fly balls dropping in as hits while the outfielder attended to his bladder; ground balls turn-ing into home runs as infielders chased grossly overthrown tosses. The point of the game gradually began to disappear altogether amid the flow of beer and insults.

If I held my own in baseball terms, I was out of my league in the exercise of insults, put-downs, and deprecating jokes. Though seven years into my course in Spanish I had made progress, but when it came to intense, rapid-fire group conversations, plays on words, digs and asper-sions, I was strictly bush league. I contented myself with observing the scene around me, happy to stay out of the way of derision as much as the wild throws of late-inning pitchers.

This was not slow-pitch softball. We used baseballs, and the pitchers threw relatively fast. That no one was seriously injured was perhaps the most miraculous part of the game, which ended when the beer ran out or dark shadows overran the field.

Sharpening Lines

When I got back to Salinas after the winter harvest, I learned that rela-tions between those of us at the *Worker* and the UFW staff had become tenser. Farmworkers were being told at meetings that they should not buy or read the paper, that it was "communist" and "against the union." Some of this was getting rather strange. If someone was selling the paper and there was a union staff person in the vicinity, he or she would try to corral workers and move them away from the paper. If these tactics intimidated some people, they angered others and motivated some to get the paper if for no other reason than to show that they were not going to be told what to do and what to read.

Carla, who worked with the paper, was the union rep on an Interharvest thinning crew. One morning a representative from the union office showed up at the spot the crew gathered to catch their bus and announced that union officials had decided to appoint another person to be the crew's representative. This was met with a hostile response. "You can't replace the rep, because it's our decision who represents this crew, not yours!" was the message from the crew. After work some of the workers showed up at the union office, and one of the women from the crew confronted Roberto, the field office head. She said to him loudly, so others could hear, "You don't like the *Worker* people because they're communists. Well, we like them because they are!" In general, the anti-communist tactics employed by the union staff were not serving them well, and they alienated the workers even further.

Fired Again

It was now the spring of 1978. I went back to work with the Cal Coastal crew in Salinas as the harvest got under way, but I had my eye on the Interharvest ground crew, waiting for the number 7 crew to start up. I had every intention of returning there.

We were in the first weeks of the harvest season at Coastal, working down the valley around Gonzales or Soledad. It was getting deep into the afternoon, and we were close to finishing the *pedido*, which was a relief because it was a warm day, and I was pretty wiped out.

I'd been packing most of the day and thought everything was going well when a supervisor came over to my row and began looking into the finished boxes. After a few minutes he called me over to one of the boxes I'd packed and said to me that I would have to do better than this. I was irritated at his tone and for being singled out. I said I thought the pack was good; maybe it could be better, but it was the end of the day and there is such a thing as being tired. "Well, you can just go to the bus, then," he said to me. I was a bit shocked by that. "Are you firing me?" I asked. "Just go to the bus, we'll talk about it later." "No," I said, "I want to know now if you are firing me." "Ya," he said, "you're fired, now get to the bus!" I was angry. "Ah, fuck you anyway," I said and walked away. As I headed for the bus, some of the workers called after me, "Donde vas, güero?" I said, "Me corrieron los pinches cabrones culeros" (Those assholes just fired me), no longer feeling any need for politeness. Before getting to the bus, I decided to talk to the crew's union rep and asked him to take a look at the boxes I'd packed. I wanted a witness that I was doing a passable job. I had a few more thoughts I was interested in conveying to the company man, but the union rep counseled me to hold off. After looking at the boxes, he assured me that there would be a grievance from the union. At that, I went to the bus to wait for the crew to finish up.

About a week later I got a visit at my cottage on Central Avenue from a union staff person by the name of Frank Ortiz. I had seen him before, during the mobilization in Coachella in 1973, but I knew little about him. Ortiz asked if he could come in, and I offered him some coffee. No thanks, he said, he didn't plan to stay long. He wanted to talk about the situation at Cal Coastal. He didn't ask me what happened, what I thought about it, nor what I wanted to do. He said the union had decided not to fight the firing. No explanation. It was the union's decision and that was that.

I didn't have a long time to think about what to do about this. I was able to return to Interharvest to join the number 7 crew within a short time. I put the Cal Coastal matter behind me.

Disaffection

The mood among the workers at Interharvest (now Sun Harvest) was pretty tense. Unhappiness with the situation was rising and boiling to the surface. This was a remarkable change from several years before when Interharvest workers voted 1,167 UFW to 28 Teamsters in the most lop-sided of ALRA elections. The inflation rate in the country was rising, and wages had fallen behind. (The situation was mitigated somewhat by the collapse of the peso in Mexico, which, though it made life there more precarious, made those earning dollars feel as if they were, at least comparatively, better off.) There were more and more complaints about the union's medical plan. The Teamsters had bowed out of the fields the previous year, leaving the UFW with a clear field. There was no common enemy to rally against. However, Chávez had painted a vision of the American Dream prosperity that lay ahead, and now work was getting slower, and it didn't feel like we were moving in that direction.

The Cal Coastal workers had voted for the union, but they had a more distant relationship with the union than the Sun Harvest workers. Perhaps this was because they were mainly young and had not experienced the oppressive bracero years and did not appreciate the kind of empowerment the union movement had brought to the fields. On the other hand, the sense of bitterness felt by workers at Sun Harvest was far sharper than at Cal Coastal. This was probably because Sun Harvest workers had been for a decade the solid heart of the union. They had tasted that elixir that a movement of people can bring to the mouth. They had sacrificed for this and had higher expectations, which gave rise to greater disappointments. Not that the union movement had not accomplished anything. It had resulted in the end of *el cortito*— the short-handle hoe; it had succeeded by the mid-1970s in gaining unemployment insurance; there were health benefits, no matter how imperfect; there was less arbitrariness in hiring and firing; sanitation in the fields had improved; there was a reduction in the overall abuse by labor contractors; and wages had risen in times of strikes and other battles in the fields. Farmworkers had stood up and achieved a level of empowerment that never existed before. But to the extent that this seemed to be slipping from their fingers, it was galling.

There had long been some tension internally in the union around a number of different issues. One was the boycott versus the strike. There was a long-running argument about which aspect of the movement was more central to its success. The boycott advocates viewed the strike as an important background to the success of the boycott, but an inferior weapon in the movement. The boycotters often saw their role as bringing urban liberals, religious communities, progressive organizations, and unions to the cause but saw the workers as humble and meek, in need of rescue from predatory powers. They used this image to arouse sympathy from those liberal supporters. The lettuce workers, with their militant struggles and aggressive image, seemed, if anything, a detriment to this goal as they did not fit the sympathetic image. To the workers, the boycotters' attitude was condescending. And they were not interested in condescending saviors. Although the grape boycott became emblematic of the whole union cause, it was in the coastal valleys where the most powerful strikes, wildcats, and job actions of all kinds had taken place, where the union had, without a doubt, its most solid and powerful base. This glaring contradiction was a source of tension in the union. It would soon become much more so.

Religion was another source of tension. Religious symbolism and religious alliances had been central elements of union culture from the beginning. But this did not necessarily accord with the sentiments of a lot of workers, who considered themselves more secular than the popular image of the union might imply.

But mainly the tension was heightened by the ever more autocratic character of the union leadership. There had always been a top-down structure, but in earlier days there had been a great deal of initiative from below that tended to drive things forward. Union leaders on the local level generally welcomed this upsurge, and there existed a relatively vibrant democratic character. Now the initiative from below was less assertive, owing to the ebb in the social movement, and there was overt suppression of initiative as the union now sought to prove it could control things and create the businesslike calm that powerful sectors of the country were expecting and demanding.

There was suspicion growing on either side of the equation. A culture of mistrust was taking hold. The leadership began viewing the workers with their demands and complaints as though they were an obstacle to the advance of the union. The workers viewed the "movement" now as lobbying, alliances with "friendly politicians," and making deals while they rotted in the fields.

UFW leaders early in the union's history had put emphasis on a ranch committee structure at the grassroots level. This made sense, because workers, unlike their counterparts in industry, are scattered about the countryside in different ranches. An elected committee on each ranch could handle work problems and union issues related to each company. But there were no union locals as such. Rather there were field offices, appendages of the center, with no autonomy. There was no structure by which the workers could exercise their will on a local level. There were two levels of democracy, the executive board, which made all the important decisions for the union, and the ranch committees, which were confined to issues involved in contract bargaining and contract enforcing. As a result, as questions and unrest began to mount about issues affecting the union more broadly, there was no regular or official forum for raising them. As unresolved issues mounted, so did the anger.

At Interharvest the head of the ranch committee was Armando Ruiz, a tall, medium-built man in his late thirties, with a large mustache and comically friendly face, a loader for one of the seniority crews. He was elected to the ranch committee at a time of widespread support and enthusiasm for the union, as one of the most loyal "Chavistas." As time went on and things changed, his popularity eroded. His defense of anything and everything from the union leadership began to turn into its opposite. The workers were beginning to look at Armando as a yes-man, a flunky. He possessed neither a deep intelligence nor a fast tongue. And he had little to say about things beyond what he had absorbed from the union leadership. When criticisms were raised at meetings, he got defensive and attacked the people raising the questions or criticisms, trying to humiliate them. While some were intimidated, others were enraged, and when sentiments began to shift even further toward disillusionment, Armando became the focal point of a lot of anger.

There were other things that rankled people about Armando. He had a big van, a twelve-passenger, and because a lot of the workers didn't have cars, they relied on others for rides to Mexicali to visit their families. Armando became notorious for charging premium rates for rides to the border. Some of the workers thought it wrong in principle for workers to make money this way off other workers. There were also rumors flying fast and thick that Armando's position as ranch committee head was being used for more than altruistic purposes. I don't know what this might have involved, but it was grist for the mill of a lot of unhappy discussions.

In Mexico at the time, there was a growing movement inside the unions against leaders who were using posts to their own advantage and doing the bidding of the employers or the government. These leaders were called *charros*. The word *charro* began to be used in reference to Armando.

With alienation growing, democratic avenues closed off, and a ranch committee headed by a man many vocal Interharvest workers considered, in their most generous moments, a chump, there seemed to be no way out. There was only one avenue of protest and expression for these sentiments, the CPD.

The CPD Rebellion

The Citizens Participation Day (CPD) was negotiated in union contracts beginning in 1975. It was a paid holiday, but workers were expected to turn over money they received from the company to the union to finance political campaigns, such as fighting anti-union laws, backing certain friendly politicians, paying for lobbying costs, sponsoring initiatives, such as Proposition 14, and so on. It was a political fund not unlike the AFL-CIO's Committee on Political Education (COPE) fund. In the first few years of CPD, there wasn't much controversy around it. Here and there a worker might object to signing over the funds to the union for personal reasons or selfish reasons, but this was minor. But as discontent in the union grew, more and more people refused to sign over their CPD checks to the union. The union characterized this as selfishness or ignorance. But that was not the essence of the problem.

Among the more politically conscious workers there was dissatisfaction with the union's embrace of the Democratic Party. It was hard for some of these workers to get excited about Democrats and other "friendly" politicians. From the point of view of people historically victimized by colonialism, invading armies sent by Democratic governments or Republican ones did not seem all that different. Nor did immigration policies seem to vary greatly from one party to the other. Sure, the Democrats came and spoke at the rallies and they made speeches at the conventions praising the union and pledging support to the struggle, but in Mexico that was the politicians' stock-in-trade. The politically conscious workers had no reason to believe it was any different here. When workers used the expression, "*puro conveniencia*," most accurately translated into English as "pure self-interest" but more akin to "pure bullshit," to describe the behavior of certain leaders and politicians, it was based on painful historical experience. In the United States, politicians might lie about their true intentions some or most of the time. In Mexico, they lied *and* sold the country out to foreign interests, lining their pockets and their nests with the proceeds.

A resolution in the union's convention of 1977 made paying CPD mandatory, under pain of expulsion from the union. However, it allowed people who opposed using the funds for political lobbying and such the option of earmarking their holiday pay for other union purposes. Nevertheless, CPD continued to be a point of struggle, because other avenues of redress were blocked to workers.

Frank Ortiz, who'd delivered the news about my union grievance, was spending a lot of time in Salinas. It became apparent that he'd been sent by La Paz to look into the discontent and presumably try to ameliorate it or suppress it. The dissatisfaction with the union was becoming so serious that there were stories of workers on crews telling union staff people they were not welcome in the fields. Growers were getting wind of this. There was even some talk in some areas of decertifying the union.

Ortiz called a meeting of Interharvest lechugueros at Sherwood School late that summer of 1978 to try to deal with the CPD rebellion and other issues. One of the goals of the meetings was to come to agreement on the election of ranch committees. A ranch committee election was going to come up in Sun Harvest, and it was an issue at other companies. The union leadership was proposing a system by which the union's executive board would either appoint the ranch committee members or have the power of veto over elections by the rank and file. The rank and file soundly rejected both suggestions and insisted on their right to elect or reject ranch committee members. The vehemence was a reflection of just how dearly the rank and file understood the need for a democratic voice in the union. The meeting turned into a fiasco as the workers, faced with criticism about their refusal to sign over their CPD checks, unleashed a torrent of indignant grievances mainly centered on the poor operation of the medical plan. People had to wait months to be reimbursed for medical payments or to have their bills paid. Particularly rankling were stories from workers in other, non-union ranches that their health plan worked better. On some ranches, like Hansen Farms, growers had eluded the union by staying one step ahead on wages and benefits. That the workers in these places enjoyed slight advantages was totally due to the union struggle. Nevertheless, the fact that non-union health plans seemed to serve the workers better than the union's plan was a source of stinging irritation.

To add to the general picture, there was confusion about things taking place in La Paz, whose very remoteness from the fields was the subject of some discord. The union's legal staff had quit over a dispute about compensation for their work. Longtime union staff were being driven out of the union, accused of disloyalty. There was an anti-leftist purge going on. People with views deemed inimical to the union leadership were being publicly humiliated and shown rudely to the door. There were rumors of union staff being obligated to participate in the Synanon game, which Chávez had learned from Synanon founder Charles Dederich, where staff members were subject to humiliating criticisms.[7] There was a mean-spiritedness in it all, and a frantic effort to impose loyalty. The spirit of struggle for justice, a better world, however people saw this, which had brought people together in a common cause, was coming to an end. The union leadership was demanding loyalty, but loyalty to what? It sounded more like unquestioned obedience.

All this was swirling in the ether.

Inquisition

The union's contracts in the vegetables were due to expire at the beginning of 1979, and word was out that the union hiring hall was going to be eliminated from future contracts. The hiring hall, perhaps more than any other aspect of the union, represented the rebellion of the workers against their unfair treatment in the fields, the favoritism of the bosses, the extortion of favors, the arbitrary firing. It was unpopular with many workers, and there were rumors of corruption and the selling of dispatches, and a host of other issues, but the hiring hall, when properly run, sheltered the worker from one of the one biggest clubs the contractor or grower held over the worker—the power to withhold or grant work. The Worker published an article on the union's intention to dump the hiring hall in a late-summer issue and strongly criticized the proposal as a step backwards.

After the first, unsuccessful meeting Ortiz had with Sun Harvest workers, the union decided to call another one. I arrived at the Sherwood

310 / LETTUCE WARS

School to attend the meeting and distribute papers outside the auditorium. The head of the Sun Harvest Ranch Committee, Armando, was at the door as I reached the top of the steps. His arms were folded, and he told me that I could not come to the meeting. A decision had been made that no one associated with *The Worker* would be allowed inside. A decision? By whom? As Armando was telling me this, I felt hands grabbing me on both sides. Before I had time to think about it, I was pushed forward up the stairs and past Armando, who gave way. "He's coming into this meeting," the voices behind me said, "he's one of us, OK? OK, Armando?" This was not so much a question as an assertion. There was a group of about a half-dozen lechugueros around me. There was little Armando could do.

It quickly became apparent why I was to be kept from the meeting. I was one of the items on the agenda. I suppose I should have felt honored to be placed in the center of such attention, but it wasn't the kind of attention most people would crave. And what was said about me, perhaps a bit more nervously by Frank Oritz, since I was actually *there*, was something to the effect that this guy's a communist, and he's an agent of the growers, someone who has snuck into the union in order to undermine it. Ortiz told the gathering of lechugueros that the union had done an investigation into my family (I found out later that it was the FBI that had been snooping around my parents' neighborhood) and "discovered" I was from a wealthy family (my father was a small businessman). Presumably my family wealth made me sympathetic to the growers and motivated me to devote my life to undermining the union cause. That was the extent of the case laid out against me.

But this accusation was part of a larger picture Ortiz asserted at length. The union was under siege by forces, the growers, the Republicans, who were hell-bent to destroy it. The growers had done their best to sabotage the ALRA; they were using every tactic to subvert the will of the workers expressed in the elections; they were working to undermine the morale of the workers and confidence in the union. The union was fighting for its life, and at this crucial juncture discontent and protest within the union was playing into the hands of the enemy. Presumably, since the *Worker* newspaper had published articles questioning the union's policies, it was contributing to this destructive dissent.

It's not that what Ortiz said did not have any resonance among the workers. But what Ortiz set out was a pretty hard sell. And at this point people did not seem in the mood for buying. Still, a seed had been planted, and under the right conditions seeds can grow.

At one point, I got up to speak. I was both nervous and outraged. The torrent of words that poured from me was, if anything, more impressive in volume than in cogency or eloquence, but I did my best. I remember bits and pieces of what I said. Accusations of being an agent of the growers was so absurd, it didn't merit a response. Anyway, it wasn't my idea to give up the hiring hall in the coming contract. People had the right to protest CPD because it represented taking the struggle out of the hands of the workers and putting the workers' fate into the hands of the Democrats, who were allies of the union but were really enemies and represented the very system that lives from the exploitation of the farmworkers. I defended communists by saying that communists have always fought for and defended the struggles of the workers and unions, as they did during the big wave of unionization in the 1930s. This was a limited view of communists, but it was what came to mind at the moment.

I defended myself, but, as I realized later, this was really beside the point. Ortiz's strategy was to establish the idea that the growers were counting on internal dissent to kill the union. I was being singled out as the dissenter, but the workers knew that dissent sprang from many quarters. If I could be tainted with the brush of grower complicity, wouldn't this taint any other worker who expressed unhappiness? It was discontent itself and the temerity to express it that were being targeted. Dissent was undermining the union; therefore dissenters, consciously or not, were traitors to the union. This was dangerous ground. Not only could it create conditions for internal repression, but it could also lead to demoralization or rebellion that could tear the entire union apart. For if there was no outlet for discontent in the union, then what?

As I was leaving the meeting, several workers came up to me and asked if I would join them for a beer at a place just around the corner on Alisal, a short walk from the union hall. We ordered beer and sat in the otherwise quiet place and talked over the meeting. How did I feel? OK, I said. Maybe I'm just surprised at how contentious things are getting to be. Don't feel bad, said one of them; I think he was a loader, I'd seen him around but didn't know him well. I've seen this kind of thing before in Mexico, he said. They try to kill off dissent in the unions by singling out people as troublemakers so as to intimidate everyone. Then he said something like, don't think we aren't sympathetic to the things you believe. But we're guests in this country, and there's not much we can do here but try to protect ourselves, to make a living. We appreciate you putting your voice out there. You say things that we can't. Don't take our silence to be opposition.

I felt like saying, you have as much right as anyone here to raise hell and fight for something better; you're part of this society. Don't you produce the food that sustains it? Don't let the system deny you your voice because you're from a different country. Imperialists don't respect anyone else's place. Don't they overthrow any government that they find unsuitable to their interests? Don't they send their armies into any country when they feel their interests threatened? Shouldn't we oppose the borders and other lines that nations have imposed to divide people? We have a right to fight for a better world no matter where we live. We can't allow those national differences to divide us or hold us back. But I didn't say any of this. Perhaps the conservatism of the times was affecting me also. Revolutionary spirit was on the wane, so I thought about all the obstacles that immigrants face here and how these can limit what people do. I said, "I understand what you're saying. I don't think it should be this way and we need to change that."

This talk with the lechugueros moved me. In some ways it disturbed me more than Ortiz's accusations. I suddenly felt, in addition to anger and disgust, a huge weight of responsibility not to back down from defending what I understood to be right: the right of people to rebel against their oppression.

I tried to make sense of what was going on. What analysis corresponded to this reality? What were the threads that led here? Now that the Teamsters were out of the picture, there was no common enemy to rally against. Inflation and other economic factors, outside the control of the union, were creating pressures. The tangible arena of struggle in the fields where the "enemies," be they growers, goons, scabs, or police, had moved to a new, ephemeral venue where the "enemies" lurked in courtrooms and came in the form of legal documents, backroom deals, and invisible manipulations in government offices. A growing union was bogged down with the challenge of servicing new union contracts and administering benefits funds. Workers' aspirations were being frustrated by a reality outside anyone's control, and the diminution of social movements, worldwide, was affecting the mood of the people, in and out of the fields. Reality is complex, and there were many different factors to this equation. But one central fact remained dominant: this is an exploiting society, and there is class conflict. No union, no matter how militant and organized, can override that basic fact, which is the root source of much of the misery and anger and rebellion in human affairs. Without taking that into account, you could not understand, let alone find a solution to, the thorny contradictions that bedevil human existence in modern society. In the larger picture of a world torn by conflicts that had their source in the system of exploitation, farmworkers and the struggles in the fields were but a tiny part. *But they were a part.*

A few days after the meeting at Sherwood, another meeting of Sun Harvest lechugueros was held at a vegetable packers' hall on Alisal Street. I hardly slept the night before, going over the ideas I wanted to express there. When I saw the chance, I got up to speak. At that time, Nicaragua was in upheaval. The Sandinistas, a front of various sectors of society led by political forces allied with the Soviet Union—though that connection was not clear to me then—were leading a rebellion against the pro-U.S. Somoza regime. It was a popular rebellion, focusing on the accumulated frustrations of years of corrupt rule, big-power domination, and aspirations for a more just society, coalescing in an armed conflict. I tried to link the struggle against the U.S.-backed Somoza regime with the struggle inside the United States; both involved the same system, the one that can only live through exploitation of people and countries. I said that I stood for the struggle to rid the world of imperialism, here and everywhere else. I'd come into the fields at a time of upheaval and shared aspirations for a better future. I was inspired by the struggle to stay and become part of it. The struggle farmworkers had waged over the years influenced others, inspired students, workers, people in many walks of life. Who knows, maybe the people in Nicaragua were also encouraged by what went on in the fields here. For myself, I was reaffirming why I was in the fields, what had and continued to motivate me, that there was something better than what existed for people.

Those remarks got a warm reception from lechugueros, and Frank Ortiz and Armando Ruiz, who were chairing the meeting, did not seem happy about it.

After I spoke, another worker got up to speak. I didn't know him well, but I had talked with him a few times and regarded him as an honest and sincere person. He began his remarks by saying that Sun Harvest workers had gone through a lot together over the years, had accomplished some things and had done so by sticking together and supporting each other. This, he said, was what they needed to do in face of new problems. He did not raise criticisms of anything that anyone had said. While he professed grave doubts about the direction of the union, he posed things to the gathered meeting this way: "I think we have to stick with Chávez." He acknowledged that there were serious questions about the direction things were going in the struggle and the union, but he felt that there was no other reasonable way forward to protect the workers or fight for their interests. He reminded them that though a lot had been accomplished in the previous years, they could not in the future take things for granted, leave things up to others. They could not just go along with clever slogans. In his remarks there was none of the cheerleader-like acclamation that so often accompanied union rallies. Such hype would get nowhere with this group. This was practical-minded analysis that focused on the issues that most of the workers felt at hand. It argued for them to take more responsibility for their future. It was a call for them not to give up on the union, but not to be slavish to whatever dictates came down from above. But it was also a call for people to focus on the issues affecting them in the fields and not the broader world around them. That's the way I took what this brother was saying. He also received strong applause for his remarks.

After the meeting, I went to the front of the room to talk to Frank Ortiz. I said, "Maybe we could sit down and see if there's any room to work some of these issues out." He said, "You do what you have to do. I'll do what I have to do." His comment came accompanied by an icy stare.

Prelude to a New Chapter

The Sun Harvest contract was due to expire the following January of 1979. I was of the opinion, given all that I had heard and seen in Sun Harvest and among other workers, that the union would seek a strike. There was no way that the growers were going to negotiate a decent contract without one. Clearly, the only way the union could begin to recoup falling morale was to rally workers around a struggle. My trust of the union leadership, of its good intentions and its scruples, was near zero. I felt a strong bond with the workers, and my belief in their basic integrity and spirit was not shaken. But I also sensed that what lay ahead was not going to be all sweetness and light. The world of the fields was governed by harsh realities, and I saw no reason to believe that much other than these were in store.

As the harvest season wound down, I prepared to trek off to the Imperial Valley once again, to witness and participate in the strike that seemed likely to occur.

9. A LETTUCE STRIKE

INTERNAL DISSENT was not only based on disappointment and frustration with the union's tendency toward autocracy, its turn away from and against its progressive side, or the overall decline in rebellious spirit. It also had a basic material element. Despite the union wage gains, high inflation had undermined wages, so that by 1978 farmworkers' real wages, non-union and union, were below those of 1970. The union realigned its message, putting greater weight on economic gain alone, yet it was proving deficient on this score as well. In fact, in comparison to other workers in agriculture, farmworker wages were becoming proportionately lower.

The UFW made public its study of wage rates, and the results were revealing. From 1970 to 1975 farmworkers' base wages rose from $2 to $2.43. In the election campaign in summer of 1975 they jumped to $2.95. Something similar happened in 1976 just before the elections were to resume, when they rose another 45 cents to $3.40. Some of this was clearly attributable to grower efforts to undermine support for the union by making non-union wage rates more attractive. Still, wages barely ran ahead of inflation. In 1970, ground-crew cutters and packers were making 40½ cents per box. By 1978 the rate was 57 cents per box. In real dollars it was a loss of 4 cents after eight years.[1]

The inflation rate was rising through the 1970s, far faster than during the long post–Second World War boom of the 1950s and 1960s. This, and a slower growth rate in the economy as a whole after the oil shock of 1973, brought an erosion of wages and greater resistance to wage increases.

Relative to other workers, farmworkers were falling further behind. Workers who ran the vacuum coolers where lettuce boxes were prepared for shipping made $3.50 per hour in 1970 and were earning $8.28

by 1978, an increase of $4.78. Teamster agricultural truck drivers were making $4.30 in 1975 and $7.10 an hour in 1978. Cooler workers were getting five times more than farmworkers in their medical plan, six times more for their pensions, and making three times more in wages. This reflected the degree to which farmworkers were squeezed as a source of profit, another illustration of how important national oppression is to the functioning of the system. So much for the prospect of farmworkers rising into the ranks of the worker elite!

It must have occurred to the union leadership that a strike might well accord them an opportunity to win back support from the rank and file, *and* change the dynamic within the union, silencing forces unhappy with the direction things were going.

By the fall of 1978 the union was holding meetings to lay out the plan for the strike. As the winter harvest was about to begin in the Imperial Valley, César Chávez and Marshall Ganz took the stage at a Calexico school auditorium to explain that the growers had rejected their proposal for a 40 percent wage increase and had instead proposed 7 percent, which was below the inflation rate of 1978 alone. Using diagrams on a large easel, they laid out the plan for a strike that would build by degrees, spreading to more and more companies as conditions warranted. By not striking all the growers at once, the union reasoned it could divide the growers and concentrate the union's forces. It hoped to force some companies to give in to demands and use the leverage thus gained to defeat the rest.

Meetings were held at the ranches to discuss the strike proposals. I attended a meeting called by the Sun Harvest ranch committee in a schoolroom in Calexico. Here the proposal for a big wage increase and a substantial increase in the per box rate for contract work was presented. This was something that naturally drew the interest of the workers. As the proposals were laid out, you could feel a change in the atmosphere; a sense of solidification in the face of the task ahead was palpable.

Several controversial proposals were put on the negotiating table at Sun Harvest. One was for a change to the system of crew rotation that had prevailed at Sun Harvest since 1970. A policy of equalization of work among the lettuce ground crews was to be replaced by a system strictly along seniority lines. Under the new proposal, if work slowed down, the crews would be laid off in order of seniority. The higher seniority crews would be virtually guaranteed continuous work, whereas in slow periods lower-seniority crews would be relegated to part-time work at best. Needless to say, this was a proposal that had more appeal to the higher seniority crews. I saw this as a system more likely to foster division in the company and demoralization among the low-seniority workers. But the ranch committee supported it, and the majority of the workers at the meeting went along with it.

Tony and I disagreed on this new policy proposal. We argued about this in a restaurant in Mexicali after the meeting. As a top seniority worker, Tony felt that he was entitled to more steady work. Tony was in his forties, and he didn't believe he had that many years of piece-rate work left in him. He felt the urgency to make the best of what he had. He also argued vigorously from the point of view of the right of seniority. Seniority is an established principle, and I had no qualms about that. My argument with Tony was that privileging seniority in this way would drive a wedge between the workers, weaken unity, and lead to bad things in the long run. The low-seniority workers would feel they had little stake in the strike if, at the end of it, they barely had work.

The second controversial proposal was a plan to have the company pay union ranch committee leaders wages equivalent to workers on their ranches. Union reps had always volunteered their services. It was argued that paid reps, freed from having to work in the fields, would be more effective in representing the workers on issues that arose on the ranches and thus would be more professional. Though I thought that would be a positive aspect, I feared it could create a level of bureaucracy that might choke off the one avenue of democratic input open to the rank and file. I was thinking about the bad experience with Armando Ruiz, and I was suspicious of the motives behind the proposed change. The rank and file had fought doggedly to retain the right to elect their crew and ranch committee reps. Was this a move to control the reps, by buying them off, to make them more pliant to the whims of the leadership? Looking back, even if I was right about the motives behind this proposal, in terms of actual outcome, I could hardly have been more wrong.

Warnings

The strike began on the morning of January 19, with a calmness that belied the storm that would soon break over the valley. On the first afternoon of the strike I was at the union hall, a few blocks from the Calexico-Mexicali border. Small groups of workers were milling in front of the hall, raking over the little bits of news of that morning's events like campers poking a fire searching for embers that might kick up a flame. The walkout at Cal Coastal had been complete, the workers had all gone out, and the company was shut down. There seemed little news beyond that.

While I was talking with one group, I saw a figure standing in the doorway of the office surveying the scene. I did not know Jose Luna well, but he was someone close to the inner circle of the union leadership and one of the leaders of the so-called night squad. You'll recall that this was an arm of the union that carried out actions the union did not want to be publicly associated with, a clandestine service, if you will. Jose's presence would have been uneventful to me if not for the fact that he seemed to be staring at me for what seemed like an uncomfortably long time.

Having exhausted our conversations, people began drifting away from the hall, some moving toward the border crossing a few blocks away. I drifted off with them, intending to stop at a store on the Calexico side before heading to my hotel in Mexicali. I was a block or so from the border and about to turn toward a store's open door when three young men leaped on me, knocking me to the ground. One of them landed a punch as I fell, but it was not a punch that had much force behind it. In fact, the whole assault was done with such gentleness that I felt no pain whatsoever after it ended. One second I was on the ground, the next I was on my feet looking to see where the youths had gone. They disappeared as quickly as they'd appeared.

There were several lettuce workers from Sun Harvest walking a block or so behind me, and when they saw what happened they ran to where I was. By the time they caught up to me, I was standing, unhurt. What was that all about? I didn't know, but I had an inkling it was not a random attack. One image immediately stood out in my mind, that of Luna standing and staring from the doorway of the union hall.

While I suffered no physical damage from this assault, it was not something that I could easily forget. It put me on guard, and I began to feel a tension and distrust that was soon to grow more pronounced.

Sun Harvest had not been called out on strike, but the strike was proceeding and spreading, and with it general tension in the valley was growing. I was coming off the bus at El Hoyo one afternoon as the winter light was beginning to fade into an early winter darkness. Buses filled with workers were turning into the lot, clanking passed the leaning posts of the surrounding chain-link fence, tires crunching on the gravel as they rolled into the large lot.

I heard Tony call my name and saw him walking toward me from the direction of the employment office; his baseball cap clung to the side of his head, revealing the dark, curly hair. It made him look off balance, accenting a face that looked too tired to care about appearances. He carried a worn jacket draped over his shoulder. "Hola, Bruch," he said. "I need to talk to you." His voice was weary and worried.

"This morning by the garrita, after crossing, I was distributing the paper. Carlos was with me." I could see perspiration on his nose and a thin streak of dirt clinging to sweat on one side of his face below his curly sideburn. "A couple of guys came up to us: I don't know who they were, I'd never seen them. Nos dijeron que nos iban a joder!" "Because of the paper?" I said. "Ya. They said that they would fuck us up; actually, they said they'd kill us if we distributed the paper. One of them tried to knock the papers out of my hand. Then one of them put his finger under his throat." I looked at Tony and felt what his eyes betrayed. It felt like the spirit inside me was shrinking, wobbly and vulnerable, a vulnerability that seemed magnified down here by the border. I tried to fight this feeling and regain perspective. It would do no good to let fear guide thinking. But there needed to be time to reflect and discuss this. "Somebody's feeling threatened by the paper," I said. "We'll have to talk about this." Tony nodded. "I'll see you here in the morning."

The paper we were distributing was no longer *The Worker from the Salinas and Pajaro Valleys*; it was the *Revolutionary Worker*, and it was being published out of Chicago. The big issue in the paper at that time was the visit to the United States by China's new leader, Deng Xiao Ping. For the first few years after Mao's death in 1976 and the change in government that took place, Deng, well known as the leader of the capitalist group within the Chinese Communist Party denounced during the Cultural Revolution, kept a low profile while the capitalists went about consolidating their power. By 1979 they were firmly enough in control to bring Deng out into open leadership. He was now making his way to the United States to meet with Jimmy Carter. It was appropriate for a man who stood for making China into a new superpower to meet with the leader of the reigning superpower.

There was a demonstration in Washington on the occasion of Deng's visit, denouncing him and upholding Mao. The police fiercely attacked that demonstration, and many people were hurt and arrested. Especially targeted was the Revolutionary Communist Party's chairman, Bob Avakian, who faced a long string of trumped-up charges, with the potential of decades in prison. Carter and Deng had to wipe tears from their eyes as the tear gas used on the demonstrators wafted in the direction of their White House press conference.

Several mornings after Tony's encounter, Mickey and I were near the border crossing selling the paper. I was up the street going to stores to leave off papers. When I got back to Mickey, he said matter-of-factly that someone had come up to him and grabbed the papers trying to pull them out of his hands. "I kicked him and started to yell and he took off." He laughed nervously. We decided after these encounters that if we were going to sell the paper on the street, we'd do it as a group.

A Field Strike

It wasn't long before strike tension began to build. The growers were beginning to play their cat-and-mouse game with the strikers. Some of this involved bringing in convoys of buses, their windows covered in plywood, accompanied by company pickups and sheriff's department or even CHP patrol cars. It was impossible to tell whether there were strikebreakers in the buses or how many were in the fields a good distance from the public road. But by observing the trucks bringing lettuce out of the field, it seemed in those first few weeks that little work was being done at the struck ranches.

The grower convoys drew the anger of the strikers, who mobilized to stop them. A strike in a field is a different matter than a strike in other industries. The work is usually spread out over many square miles, and its location can change from day to day. The strikers, who never know for sure where a crew might be brought, must be constantly on guard. To deal with this logistical problem, the workers and the union developed a scheme of roving patrols and mobile picket lines. A system of paved and dirt roads crisscrosses the valley to give access to the fields. Workers familiar with the area set up relay spots at key intersections where the patrols could leave and pick up information. From early hours in the morning, groups of pickets began setting up small "bases" at these intersections. The Imperial Valley in winter can be really cold at night and below freezing in the mornings. To deal with the cold, striking workers huddled around trashcan fires. Here they exchanged information on the strike while awaiting word from the roving squads. This was in the days before cell phones, and it worked reasonably well.

These moving squads searched out signs of strikebreaking activity. Sometimes this meant looking out for company supervisors or foremen who scouted fields prior to bringing in crews, or looking out for caravans of strikebreakers, which were, in these flat open fields, fairly visible. The trick was to spot them and then mobilize strikers quickly to mass at a field entrance before the company could get its strikebreakers there. Striking patrols, once they spotted a likely field, would fan out to inform the groups of workers scattered throughout the area. This method of striking was very effective in the beginning of the strike and a lot of pressure was put on the struck companies and the sheriff's deputies who had the job of escorting and protecting scab buses.

Sun Harvest on Strike

On January 22, three days after Cal Coastal's walkout, Sun Harvest was
called out on strike. Our small army of strikers headed out of El Hoyo in
a convoy of cars and pickups toward the group of large fields we'd been
harvesting the day before. There we set up our picket line and prepared
for whatever might come. But when Sun Harvest made no effort to bring
in strikebreakers, the picket line soon broke down into a kind of army
encampment, we "soldiers" lounging, playing cards, and shooting the
breeze while we waited for signs of battle.

Late one morning a roving picket pulled up to the field. A group
of picketers gathered around the driver's side of the car. Within a few
moments the workers were racing toward their cars. "Holtville, vámonos!
Al rancho de Maggio!" Soon a whole caravan of Sun Harvest cars was
racing toward a field at the Maggio ranch a few miles away where some
kind of action was taking place.

When we arrived at the field, signs of a battle were apparent. Cars and
vans were lined up on both sides of the road, parked haphazardly. A bus
sat just off the road near the entranceway, streaks of black on its hood,
as though a smoky fire had puffed out from the cracks where the hood
and body met. The windshield was broken, as were some side windows.
A wave of strikers was charging down a road to a field that lay below the
level of the street. We followed.

When we reached the field, we saw another field partially hidden by
a ridge that jutted out between them. As we ran toward it, we saw a large
group of workers who were already beginning to scatter, leaving behind
a broccoli machine sitting helpless on its side, its craning neck partly
buried in dirt.

A skirmish line of sheriff's deputies, their faces covered with plastic shields, was marching up the field toward the machine behind the
retreating workers. Tear gas canisters began arcing in the sky, the wind
blowing the smoke from their tubes when they landed. Rocks flew in the
opposite direction.

As we retreated, a helicopter made a pass over the field and then,
incredibly, dipped low over a group of retreating workers, knocking one
into the dirt. Strikers rushed toward their fallen *compañero*, lifting him
and carrying him forward, his legs hanging limply below him.

More tear gas canisters, more rocks. The deputies' line advanced and
retreated, but its movement overall was forward, taking advantage of protective equipment and superior firepower. The crowd was being pushed
up the entrance road to the road. Young workers were on the front lines
pumping rocks at the approaching police. The barrage threw the police

advance back several times. I saw police, their faces shielded in Plexi-glas, grab a worker and hold him while they placed cuffs on him. Then I saw a rock flying toward the police hit the worker in the head. As the police pushed forward, the worker in their grasp, I saw the blood streak-ing down his face and his head wobble weakly back and forth.

A California Highway Patrol car raced up the road, passing the line of retreating workers. Like a large moving magnet, it drew a barrage of rocks. The windshield and a side window cracked. Rocks thudded off the passenger door and rear panel. The car skidded to a stop along the road, sending a small shower of dust and dirt flying. A young lechuguero from Cal Coastal stood on the side of the road near the CHP car as it came to a halt. He backed away as a patrolman appeared from an open door. The patrolman moved to the front of his squad car grasping a shotgun. He reached the front of his car, swung around and at the same time worked the pump action on the shotgun. In an instant, the large barrel was aimed directly at the young lettuce worker, just turned nineteen. As the patrol-man squeezed the trigger, the youth instinctively grabbed his stomach, as if to say, "This is the way I'm going to die." But there was only a loud click. When the youth looked down at his hands, there was nothing. The shotgun wasn't loaded. He ran in shock. It was his last day in the strike.[2]

The police advance ended at the roadway. People drifted back to their cars, as the police set their skirmish line at the entrance to the field.

In strikes things can change quickly, and momentum can pass from one side to another in a matter of days. It seemed as though the Holtville battle was the high point in the first period of the strike.

After Holtville, orders were issued for strikers to stay at their ranch picket lines. The strike headed into a period of calm, a calm like the sur-face of a balloon as it slowly expands toward the bursting point. As the weeks unfolded, word came that strikebreakers were beginning to appear in growing numbers on other ranches.

At the Sun Harvest field where our strike camp was set up, there was little to do but sit and watch the lettuce mature, sprout flowers, shrivel, and rot. Sometimes it felt like our moods went through the same cycle.

The strike was hit by court injunctions limiting picketing, and the union responded by clamping down on the strike to avoid brushes with the law. In 1973 the grape strikes faced injunctions aimed at breaking the strikes, but the union responded with mass picketing in defiance of the law. The strikes were lost, but the movement emerged in many ways stronger than before. This time, in 1979, in the face of injunctions, the union acted quite differently.

Tensions

One evening during the first weeks of the strike, Mickey and I were in a nightclub in Mexicali listening to music and sharing drinks. We had just ordered a couple of beers from the bar and placed them down on a table to one side of the dance floor. It was dark and music was blaring loudly. A young man asked me for a match for his cigarette. I strained to hear his request. "Cerrillos, tienes cerrillos," he shouted above the din. I started to pat my breast pocket to see if there might be matches there when I felt a sharp pain in my jaw. The next second I was down on the ground and the room was swaying. And at that it ended. Whoever hit me, for whatever reason, did not stick around to explain. Coincidence or another warning? It was hard to believe that this was another random attack. Like the others, it made me feel vulnerable. Suddenly both sides of the border felt like dangerous ground. I began carrying a small cast-iron pipe as protection in the pocket of a jacket or inside my sleeve.

I was on strike with Sun Harvest, but Bruce Church was still working, so Mickey was going to work every day. So was Richard, who'd come to Mexicali for the harvest and possible strike. But then Richard fell into a funk. He no longer just drank his usual quotient of beer. Now he was "medicating" himself with tequila, and, almost unheard of for him, missing work. It was a rarity now to see him sober, and it was painful to see him sinking. Mickey and I sat with him in his room, a layer of smoke sitting above our heads, ashtrays lying atop his cracked wooden dresser, the butts spilling over onto the dresser top and the floor. Work clothes hung forlornly from the dresser drawers, and Richard sat, a bottle of tequila between his legs. We tried to coax the tequila out of his hand. We lectured him, swore at him, badgered him. We resorted to stealing his bottles, but this did no good, since he bribed people around the hotel to make liquor runs for him when he was too smashed to leave his room. His funk only got deeper.

Rufino Contreras

It was midday when a union courier skidded to a stop by the quiet field where we Sun Harvest workers had our strike encampment. "Everyone, come to El Hoyo!" He said little more, but the rumors had already begun to make the rounds of our strike encampment. A striker had been shot.

By the time we reached El Hoyo, a large crowd was milling about. For the first time I heard the name Rufino Contreras. A story was making the rounds. Rufino was with a group of picketers at a Mario Saikhon field.

According to the story being told, the sheriff's deputies had suddenly and uncharacteristically disappeared, leaving the field unguarded. It was not hard to predict what would happen next. The strikers, frustrated by the days of watching strikebreakers work under the protection of the police, needed no coaxing. They ran for the field yelling angrily. Shots rang out. As the picketers retreated, one fell facedown in the lettuce field. Rufino had been shot in the head and died instantly. A foreman, it was believed, had shot him down! No one was allowed to retrieve his body for a long time. A striker murdered for fighting for his rights, that was the word people were passing from group to group. And one word arose above all the others: this was a setup!

It wasn't hard to find angry words among the knots of people in El Hoyo, recounting what they'd heard, adding their bits of knowledge or speculation. A worker from one of the Sun Harvest ground crews spoke bitterly. "If they want to bring guns into this, we can too! Las balas pueden volar en más de una dirección!" (Bullets can fly in more than one direction!).

Crews getting off work thickened the crowd until there were several thousand gathered. The shadows of afternoon lengthened. Agitation, anger, and worries filled the voids between words. A flatbed truck took its place in front of the covered area just to the side of the farm labor office. The sound of an amplifier whining and screeching, then the tap, tap on the mike. "Compañeros, compañeras, nuestro compañero César viene. No salgas, espera. Viene desde Los Angeles." No one was to leave. No one felt like leaving. Chávez was coming in and would be there by early evening. (I heard later Chávez was in negotiations with Sun Harvest when the word of the shooting arrived.) People talked more quietly now, searching for some deeper message, some overarching meaning to the moment.

When Chávez arrived, the knots of conversation and debate melted into a broad mass facing the flatbed. Light was fading as he climbed up on the truck platform and grabbed a microphone, his other hand clutching a sheaf of papers.

Chávez's first words were meant to validate the anger and then direct it. He spoke of his own anger and grief. But then he set about explaining his central message. "Confia," confide. The ultimate message was unmistakable. In my own mind I made a note. Anger would not accomplish anything; people had to have faith, faith and confidence, most of all in the courts and in God. It was time to control anger. There's a legal system, a system that may not be perfect, but it is the system that we need to respect. We need to await the outcome of the courts to punish the villain or villains who shot down brother Rufino. Confide. (You can be sure there were many in the crowd like myself who found such words less than reassuring.)

Then he called for action. Turn Rufino's death into determination to win the strike. The next day no one would work, a general strike in honor of Rufino. Come in the morning and call on everyone to stop work out of respect to Rufino and the strike.

Then the crowd faded, even as the light faded, obscuring the wooden line no more than fifty yards from where we stood—that line demarcating two worlds, worlds apart yet interwoven with economic and political relationships.

The Green Banner

The word of Rufino's murder spread rapidly. I got a call that a reporter from the *Revolutionary Worker* in L.A. was coming to Calexico, and could I show him around? He arrived late that night. In the morning we came across the border together. It was still dark when we arrived at El Hoyo, but a table stood at the end where the flatbed truck had been the night before. On the table and around it were candles, flowers, and a picture of Rufino—a memorial altar. The picture caught my eye; he was a young man of twenty-eight, a father of three children. Then I saw the banner displayed above the altar. It was white with green letters. I stood a few feet from the altar and the banner. I read it several times over. Perhaps I was reading it wrong, maybe the meaning in Spanish was not what it seemed. Because the words had an unexpected electricity. "Rufino Contreras vivió con los Ideales de Flores Magon!" I knew little about Flores Magón, other than that he was considered the most radical voice of the Mexican Revolution and had been imprisoned in the United States and died at the federal penitentiary in Leavenworth, Kansas. I did not know about his connection to Mexicali, of the aborted uprising that he directed from Los Angeles in the hope of influencing the revolution that had caught fire in the lower states. I looked around to see if others were close by, but we were alone. Where had this banner come from? I looked closer. The banner was carefully made, the letters neatly drawn. But after the word "Magón" were the words "y César Chávez." This "César Chávez" appeared to be something added to the banner. It was written in a different hand in a different color. I didn't know what to make of the banner, but I had a feeling it would not be well received by some in the union.

We were standing in front of the altar for Rufino, looking at his picture, the candles, the flowers, and contemplating the significance of the banner with its neatly printed green letters when we heard shouting behind us. A group of workers were standing in a circle, listening to someone in the center of that circle speaking loudly and excitedly. The reporter and I went to see what was going on. We stood at the edge of the crowd and then tried moving in. There were perhaps thirty to forty people in the group.

And as we edged our way in, we saw a slight-looking man. His face was unshaven and his hair was disheveled. He was wearing work clothes. His most prominent feature was an apparent intense anger. He was talking loudly, and his closed fist was beating the air as though it were pounding an invisible drum to the beat of his words. I was trying to catch the drift of his message when I saw Frank Ortiz roughly push his way into the crowd. He, too, was angry, and I was taken by his insensitivity as he pushed his way into the circle toward the angry man. "Cállete mentiroso!" screamed Ortiz, his face red with rage. "Cállete, vete a la chingada! Pura pendejadas hablas! Pinche borracho mentiroso!" He grabbed the slight man, who he'd accused of being a drunken liar and shook him and then pushed him out of the group. "Son puras mentiras," said Ortiz, now addressing the crowd, "No lo hagas caso!" (Don't pay attention to this liar!).

I turned to a woman next to me, a short woman with a broad, dark face, wearing a scarf over her head as though she'd come over the border to work. "Qué dijo el hombre?" I asked, pointing to the man that Ortiz had screamed at. "El señor dice que el mayordomo de Saikhon que mató a Rufino ya esta libre, que el juez le dejó libre." The man said a judge had cut free Rufino's alleged murderer, a Saikon foreman. Was that true?

Ortiz was counseling the crowd that remained. "Chase them out, don't let them spread their rumors; we need discipline." As he turned, he saw my reporter friend and me. Then he repeated to the crowd, "A los mentirosos, no les creen—corréeles para afuera!" (Don't believe the liars; throw them out!). Ortiz was in a tizzy. The knot of people dissipated. The man in the middle was gone. I didn't see where he went. But there was reason to be concerned because the courts that César Chávez had counseled the people to confide in had allowed Rufino's alleged murderer to walk free on bail without even a night in jail.

Behind the scenes, the death of Rufino and the potential for things to break out of control created a crisis in the leadership. Marshall Ganz, a liberal who was more inclined to put value on the initiative of the rank and file, was about to be replaced as strike coordinator by Frank Ortiz, a conservative, if not outright reactionary, who feared and distrusted rank-and-file workers.

More people were coming into El Hoyo. A rising tension gripped my shoulders and neck. I didn't smoke much, but I ached for a cigarette at that moment, thinking that it would relieve the tightness. But my reporter partner didn't smoke.

In front of the altar for Rufino, I saw a small group of union officials, with a group of people I didn't recognize. Marshall Ganz was there with several men in corduroy jackets in what looked like serious conversation. I saw Marshall turn toward me, and I saw his finger point in my direction. The men in the corduroy jackets also looked toward the reporter and me. I had a feeling this was not a positive development, and I was not being hailed for my lettuce-cutting skills.

We headed out of El Hoyo toward the border where strikers were gathering to call on workers coming over the border to stop work for the day. As we made our way toward the road that skirts El Hoyo, I saw the corduroy jackets walking briskly in our direction. When we reached the opening in the fence, one of the corduroy jacket guys said loudly, "Bruce, can I speak to you?" I turned and saw a wallet flop open and a badge flash into view. "I'm _____ from the Riverside Sheriff's." He was a stocky man of medium height, probably in his mid- to late thirties. He seemed self-confident and he spoke forcefully, "I Just want you to know Bruce, that we will be watching you." His smile looked cold enough to freeze water.

If I'd been in a less tense mood, I might have mustered the levity to have said, Well, you'll just have to get in line. But I wasn't in such a mood. No such thoughts could loosen themselves. I felt a strong pressure pushing in on me, as though my brain were in a clamp, my thoughts trapped between walls thick enough to corner and stifle any creative thought. I tried to answer as calmly and nonchalantly as I could, "Thanks for the information."

It was still dark when we made our way up the street toward the border crossing. In the tug of war between the emerging light on the horizon and the lingering darkness of the night, day was getting the upper hand. A crowd of strikers gathered at the doors where workers emerged from the Mexican side, having passed the booths of skeptical Immigration cops, their tired questions, their flat, deadpan gaze, to the small open plaza. Some strikers were passing out leaflets, others calling out to the arriving workers, "Coopera con la huelga! No trabajamos! Huelga general! Mataron nuestro hermano Rufino Contreras. Paro total, paro general!" (They've killed our brother Rufino Contreras, general strike!)

The reporter and I stood at the entrance, shouting "Huelga!" with the rest. But it was hard to be in that time, one that called for denunciation, for condemnation of a system that heaps indignity and criminality on top of injustice, hard to stay with that thought, when the gaze of hostile eyes, all the more piercing for being not quite visible, penetrated the moment.

As we stood in the plaza, I felt movement around us, like some subtle stalking. Frank Ortiz joined the crowd at the border entrance and gradually and casually moved his way toward where we were standing. It was daylight by then. I caught sight of reporters jostling around César Chávez up a ways from the Plaza. I pointed this out to the reporter. We moved to another spot in the plaza further away. I did not want to be anywhere close to Chávez. The fear of a setup was in my blood.

Frank Ortiz made his way down the line until he was standing next to the reporter. He stood there for a time and said nothing. I had just turned in his direction when I caught sight of his arm swinging with a motion like someone tossing a discus. His arm then slammed into the body of the reporter, who fell back and then tripped on the curb and dropped down backwards. "I don't like what you're saying to the workers, you prick!" Ortiz screamed, his face repeating the color and contortions from El Hoyo. The whole thing happened very quickly, and just as quickly a group surrounded us. I reached to grab the reporter to help him to his feet when a body bumped into mine, and a face appeared, serious and threatening. It was Roberto Garcia. "You need to get out of here."

Other figures were moving around us. Among the crowd at the border there were some who were looking our way and Roberto seemed nervous. "Out of here!" he said quietly but menacingly. It was a moment to make a decision, and we made the wrong one. Instead of staying and denouncing the group that was positioned around us, which would likely have forced them to back off and, at least, alert the people around the border crossing as to what was going on, we moved out, away from the crowds. Roberto and his crew were following, but kept their distance.

When we got to my car, and away from the crowd at the border, they rushed and jumped us. I got hit with a fist with a ring, which cut me under my eye. The reporter was shoved down on to the pavement and kicked. In the end we were shaken, but not badly hurt.

Several days after the general strike, Rufino was brought to a cemetery in Calexico. Thousands accompanied his casket, carrying special black and white flags in place of the usual black and red. California's governor, Jerry Brown, was in the procession.

The general strike had been largely successful, but it was only one day, and soon we were back at the Sun Harvest ranch, once again watching the lettuce decay. There was residual anger in the air, but no one defied the order to stay put at the ranch. As the days wore on, the mood seemed glum.

The cut under my eye opened up some avenues of conversation. When I explained how events had gone down the day of the general strike, I got little reaction. When I told them who had hit me and how, I got a lot of shaking heads, but little comment. There was in this some of the distance that had opened up between me and others on the crew, fanned by what the union leadership had promoted and continued to promote. Workers like Tony and Carlos, who clearly understood the implications of it all, were themselves feeling on the defensive.

There was fear and growing despair. The companies were not budging. There were strikebreakers in some fields, and it seemed their ranks were growing. The growers were losing a lot of their crop but seemed unmoved. It was not clear why. Everyone was aware that lettuce prices were up and that some companies were doing quite well.

The union's strategy had counted on shutting down some companies, while allowing others to work unmolested. It was believed that divisions would grow between companies losing their crops and others that were making a killing selling the scarcer and higher-priced lettuce. Would the struck companies seek to sign to minimize their losses? Or would the companies stand firm or even share the windfall of higher prices among them? This was unknown.[3]

The end of the harvest season was only weeks away. There was no contract in sight. Sun Harvest gave up on its Imperial Valley fields, and 3,000 acres went to seed, or would have if they hadn't been disked under first. There were rumors that the company had strikebreakers in Yuma and elsewhere and were conducting harvesting. We were not kept well informed about things going on in other ranches, about what the company and union were saying to each other. But I was purposely being kept out of the loop.

The prospect of actually losing the strike was frightening. It would mean loss of seniority, stagnating wages, and a general decline. Whatever people may have felt about the union leadership, it was the only game in town. It seemed at the moment that there was little to do but ride out the strike, even if it felt at times like it was leading nowhere.

Trapped

I was leaving the strike encampment with a fellow striker when a Calexico cop put his lights on me and pulled me over. "You were weaving on the road," he said. He demanded my driver's license and ordered me out of the car. "Walk over to the side of the road. Now walk in a straight line." When I did all that, he started asking questions. "Where do you live?" "It's on the license." "This license has a Salinas address, where do you live here?" "How is that any business of yours?" "You can make this easy on yourself and just give me your local address, or you can go the hard route and make me take you down to the station." "Under what charge?" "I don't need a charge, you're refusing to identify yourself properly." "I live in Mexicali," I said, and then regretted the words. "Where in Mexicali?" Thinking he probably had no idea of what was over there, I told him a name that came to mind at that moment. "The Frontier Hotel." As far as I knew, there was no such place. But when I went to get in the car, the passenger was upset. "Why did you say the Frontier?" he said. "It's what came to me, why?" "Because I live in the Hotel Frontera!" "Frontera" means border, but it is close to "frontier." Since the cop got my passenger's name, he was afraid he'd get harassed.

Several days later, at the Sun Harvest encampment, the worker who'd been in the car when we were stopped came up to me. "The judicial [something like the political police or FBI here] stopped me the other day on the street in Mexicali," he said. "They were looking for you. They asked me where you were. I told them I didn't know."

One evening, around that same time, I was crossing the border to Mexicali when I saw Manuel Chávez crossing in the other direction. Manuel, César Chávez's primo hermano, was active in the union from its earliest days. He was an experienced agitator and often sent to hot spots to rouse action. He was also known to be the leader of the night squad crew. As I saw him walking past me, a hat pulled down as though he would just as soon not be recognized, it appeared as though he'd given me a long second look. Was I just getting paranoid? Though I had never met him formally and only saw him at union functions, I was sure that he knew me and what I looked like. His close ties with the Mexicali chief of police were the subject of discussion among the workers. If this was paranoia, it was not without justification.

I have great respect for those brave fighters who dare to defy authorities in places where repression is widespread and more vicious than is normally true in the United States. This is often the case in oppressed countries where conditions are more desperate and where volatility gives rise to greater brutality by authorities, ever vigilant to crush nascent movements that might prove dangerous to their interests. This is also the situation in oppressed communities in the United States, where activists are much more likely to be jailed, beaten, and killed. Those weeks on the border, living in a state of alert for danger, were a difficult time and a small taste of what activists in other countries and communities have to deal with. I don't know how people can stand it for long. It sapped me. It messed with my nerves. It wore me down. It felt like walls were closing in.

We had lost our political initiative. It didn't seem like there was much to do about it. I talked it over with Mickey. He was on strike with Bruce Church but didn't feel threatened. We'd stopped distributing the paper in the mornings some weeks before.

I decided to leave the area. The end of the harvest was approaching. The strike would be heading north and resume in Salinas within a month or so. When Mickey and Tony agreed with my plan, I decided to go.

It took me a day of driving to get back to Salinas. The evening after arriving, I got a call from Mickey. "Guess what," he said. "The Mexicali judicial were at the San Antonio Hotel yesterday. They came looking for you, buddy, came straight to your door!" "I'm sorry I disappointed them," I said. "If you see them again tell them I'll look them up next time I'm in town." I felt fortunate that I was not in my room to greet them. It likely would not have been a pleasant visit.

My Own Private Union Goon

Not long after the Sun Harvest crews returned to Salinas, there was a plan to mobilize a trip to Sacramento to pressure the ALRA to take action on stalled issues. I planned to go with the crews. But the night before, I received a call from Tony. He sounded worried. "Be careful," he said on the phone. He was talking in a low voice, and it seemed apparent that he was calling from the camp. "I've heard talk at the camp that if you show up to go to Sacramento that there's going to be trouble." From whom? "There are some guys here that are pretty stirred up. They're talking about messing you up."

The atmosphere among the workers was sullen and less friendly than in the past, but I'd never felt threatened among them before. I was not going to be driven away from the crews if I could help it. I was hoping to get a chance to talk to some of the workers I hadn't seen in a while.

I showed up early at the Sun Street camp where the strikers were living. As I was standing outside, waiting for the bus, people started filing out of the mess hall to the street. One of them was a fellow I had only seen once before, a water sprayer on one of the ground crews. Water spraying to keep the lettuce fresh was an hourly job that didn't require a lot of physical stress. Still, I had never, in my years in the fields, seen anyone like him. He was not tall, maybe slightly taller than I was, but he was huge, at least 300 pounds. As he came out of the mess hall, slamming the screen door behind him, he headed straight toward me with a stick in his hand. As he approached, I saw his lips moving, but I couldn't hear what he was saying. It did not look at all like a friendly greeting, and I started looking around for something to defend myself with—a stick, anything. There was nothing.

Before he got within head-bashing range, Cleofas Guzman, the new ranch committee head, put himself between me and a beating. Cleofas was smaller than I, but he had been elected by the workers to replace the discredited Armando Ruiz. He was very well thought of, someone who was honest and a fighter for the interests of the rank and file. The stick

332 / LETTUCE WARS

wielder was not going to defy Cleofas, so when he was told to back off, he did. Then Cleofas turned to me and said, "You'd better get out of here. If you don't there's going to be trouble." I wanted to ask Cleofas who the stick wielder was, but it didn't seem like an appropriate moment.

Tony came over to where I was standing, and we walked out of the area together. Tony was nervous, and I felt he was taking a chance just walking with me, but he insisted. Tony told me that things were very uptight at the camp, and a lot of people were feeling intimidated by what they felt were threatening conditions.

"Who is this guy?" I asked Tony. He laughed, a bit nervously. "Well, I guess he's your own private union goon," said Tony. "I mean, he talks about you a lot. I never saw the guy before he got hired on as a waterboy before the strike. He only worked a short while before the strike began. I don't know where he's from. But don't feel too bad, he seems to dislike a lot of us in the camp. It's just that you're his favorite." Tony did not want to talk much more. I thanked him for taking the risk to walk with me. "I'll be all right," he said. "I don't think they would attack me openly. A lot of people don't like what is going on but they don't feel they have much choice right now. I hope you understand that."

Picnic Fight

Maybe I'm just stubborn, but I didn't want to give up on the situation. The problem was that it was difficult to go anywhere around the union without the fear of some kind of assault.[4]

Sun Harvest workers were having a picnic at Sherwood Park near the rodeo grounds. I decided to go. Tony had told me that a lot of people were fed up with the intimidation, and I didn't want to leave the impression that I was intimidated by the threats. I was afraid, but not so much by the fear of physical violence as the sense of political isolation from the workers.

When I showed up at the park, the workers were sitting and talking at picnic tables. As I approached, things got tense and quiet. I tried to act natural. I went to sit at one of the tables and share a beer. I had just settled on a bench, trying to think of some light remark to break the tension, when the fat waterboy showed up and came to where I was sitting. I got up from the bench, since I didn't want to be grabbed from behind. I could see that, in addition to his angry demeanor, he was also drunk, so much so that he could hardly talk. Up to that point I hadn't heard him say anything I could understand. Now he was woozy and uncommunicative. "Qué quieres, cuál es tu problema?" (What's your problem?), I yelled at him. But he said nothing. "Qué sabes de mi?" (What do you know about me?). Still nothing. He tried grabbing my head, and I pulled away. As he was coming at me, I took a swing and hit him square in the face, several times. It didn't faze him. I took a few more punches at the lumbering body and bobbing face, both of which seemed incapable of moving with any agility or speed. But since my punches did not seem to have a noticeable effect, I reached for his leg and upended him. He fell hard on the ground and seemed content to kind of roll around there, grunting.

While that was going on, and as the strikers looked on in silence, another worker came up and lunged at me. To the outside observer it might have seemed bizarre, this absurd ballet of uncoordination, because as the other fellow, who was also well along in his drinking, swung at me, he not only missed but fell forward on the ground. I must have seemed a pretty accomplished fighter, standing over two people so much larger. But in reality, both of my opponents were stone drunk and would have found it challenging to stay on their feet even without a fight.

The prospects at the picnic did not seem promising. My presence was only creating more tension, so I decided to call it quits and left. It was the last time I would be around the Sun Harvest strikers for the duration of the strike.

I was not the only one who was being pressured and forced out of the strike. Angelina, a friend of one of the *Worker* staff and from a family that had been in the thick of the union since the big strike in 1970, was refused strike benefits and also decided to leave the strike.

A Puppet and a Pickup Truck

In mid-July the Somoza regime in Nicaragua was overthrown. The Somoza family had ruled Nicaragua since the 1930s, and Anastacio Somoza Debayle, the last of the family line to rule, had held power since 1967. Anger against his corrupt and despotic regime—the Somoza family controlled much of the country's wealth, and his brutality had been endorsed by the United States for years—boiled over in the years following a devastating earthquake that struck in 1972 when it became known that the regime had siphoned off funds meant for earthquake relief.

When Somoza fled, Nicaraguans celebrated in the streets. This also sent shock waves throughout the region and the world. In solidarity with such earth-shaking events, we thought it would be appropriate to join the celebration in Salinas somehow.

We got a pickup truck and made a banner, "Ya Calló El Titre, Somoza. Falta su Amo" (The puppet Somoza has fallen. His boss remains to go).

By boss we meant his imperial backer, supporter, and arms suppliers—
the United States. We drove the pickup around the barrios, and we went
to the different labor camps. It created a stir. The largest and most interesting rally took place at Bud Antle's camp on Natividad Road. Antle
workers were not on strike, but the strike and the agitated atmosphere
in the valley had aroused them and there was talk of joining the strike.
At the Antle camp people climbed up on the truck to speak, some about
events in Central America and Mexico, and some about their immediate
situation and desires.

Spreckels

I might have worked in the fields for some time to come. But that choice
was no longer mine. No one was going to give me a job in the fields.
I tried some of the companies that were not on strike. In one place, a
labor contractor, who may have heard about Anglo "troublemakers," just
laughed at me. Fat chance of a job.

I figured even if the workers at Sun Harvest won the strike and I
somehow got my job back, the tension was such that returning might
not be much to look forward to. I was also on the low-seniority crew, and
given the changes in rotation rules, long-term prospects for work were
not good. And if the strike were lost, there's no way I could have gotten a
job at Sun Harvest.

They were hiring at the Spreckels sugar plant. They were *always* hiring
there. It was not a lucrative job. What it lacked in good working conditions, it made up in low pay. But it was a job.

The massive construct of Adolf Spreckels, once the largest sugar mill
in the world, was an aging and decaying edifice moving headlong toward
obsolescence. I got a job that must have been the starting point for many
new hires down through the years, poking hot lime from the tall heating kiln. Lime is one of the main minerals used in sugar beet processing.
The lime was dropped into a large vertical funnel and heated as it moved
down the funnel. The red-hot lime gradually made its way down to where
I stood with a long metal poker to loosen the chunks so they'd drop into a
pit. Where it went from there, I don't know. But hydrated lime was used to
extract impurities from the sludgy raw juice that's extracted from the beet.

On the night shift, I worked near a young crew whose job was to drop
the lime from a crane into the heating funnel. They dealt with the tedium
of the job by getting stoned whenever possible, which was nearly all the
time. They were good guys, and I liked them, but in my short stay at
Spreckels, I never got close to them socially.

I worked a rotating shift, going from day shift to swing shift to grave-yard. Graveyard was the hardest because I found it difficult to get good sleep during the day. I was sleep-deprived most of the time. To relax I started swimming at the college pool across from Central Park near where I lived. It was an outdoor pool, and I used it in the mornings after my graveyard shift. I nearly always had that large pool to myself. Swim-ming after work helped me feel relaxed and cleansed of the chemical dust of the factory.

Leaving

I worked at the Spreckels sugar factory until late fall. By that time, the strike that began in January in the Imperial Valley had ended. The grow-ers finally agreed to terms in late August. They gave in to the demands of the strike, pushing farm wages up toward $5.50 an hour and lettuce piece rate to 75 cents a box. This was a victory, a major triumph. The workers, in their relief and joy, celebrated. But the celebration, regrettably, was not to last.

I liked Salinas and would not have minded staying there. But things had changed. My discomfort with a world of vast injustice had not abated. Nor did my belief in the need for fundamental social changes. But the revolutionary upsurge had come to an end, and any immediate prospect for its renewal did not exist. "Where there's oppression, there's resistance" would always hold true and would give rise to new struggles and move-ments. But new understanding would be required to sum up the lessons of the previous stage and lay the basis for success in movements to come. In the meantime, I was ready to begin a new phase in my own life and view the world from another angle. I bid good-bye to Salinas.

10. VICTORY FROM DEFEAT, DEFEAT FROM VICTORY

BY MID-FEBRUARY 1979 Sun Harvest, the largest of the struck companies, had given up any effort to cut the remainder of its lettuce crop in the Imperial Valley, writing off 3,000 acres, half of its normal lettuce acreage. It was not alone in walking away from a crop it would have had great difficulty harvesting. Still, the Imperial Valley strike proved indecisive. Sun Harvest did not give in quickly, as some in the union leadership suspected or hoped they might.[1]

There were objective difficulties in applying more pressure. Sun Harvest and Bruce Church had fields in the Yuma area on Indian reservation land, and the union was denied permission by the Tribal Council to picket there. At harvesting locations off the reservation, Sun Harvest was granted a court injunction, restricting the strike to twenty-five pickets each quarter-mile. The strike in the Yuma was therefore ineffective and the harvest there largely unaffected.

The strike in the Imperial Valley significantly reduced the harvest. This drove up the price of lettuce. Through much of the winter harvest a box of lettuce was going for $10 to $12, which gave a hefty profit, considering that according to growers' figures $3.50 represented the "break-even" cost. A study of the Imperial Valley strike several years later would confirm that reduced production caused a spike in prices 400 percent above normal. The net result was that, as a whole, growers doubled their income, even while their crops were cut in half. Some growers lost a lot; newspapers at the time quoted $20 million in losses. Others made windfall profits. These growers passed some of their profits on to the struck ranches, allowing them to recoup their production costs. By spring 1979 the Western Growers Association expanded this "sharing program" to create an insurance fund to blunt the effects of a strike.[2]

When the harvest ended in the Imperial Valley, none of the companies had broken away from the pack to come to terms with the union. They all publicly held firm to their insistence that the union's proposals were unrealistic and even illegal. In response to high inflation, the Jimmy Carter administration had proposed guidelines for limiting wage increases to 7 percent. The growers stuck to that figure, claiming anything else would violate the guidelines. They also gave wildly inflated figures to the press regarding the union's proposals, painting them as so extreme that they would likely lead to the demise of any grower foolish enough to agree to them. Growers raised the specter of industry bankruptcy should they give in to these excessive demands.[3]

In the waning weeks of the Imperial Valley strike, while hope had faded that any growers would come to terms, rank-and-file leaders led by Mario Bustamente convinced Frank Ortiz, the union's strike coordinator, to allow for another day of mass strike action. Their objective was to revive the flagging spirit of the strikers. On February 21 strikers fanned out on Calexico streets appealing to workers to stay out of the fields for a day. A caravan of cars with several thousand workers wound its way across valley roads and engaged in field invasions and fights with local police. It was a day of battle that revealed the anger and frustration of the strikers, and it demonstrated that though lettuce strikers might have been down, they were far from defeated.[4]

The corrida, or harvest cycle, as it moved north after the Imperial winter season to such places as Blythe and Huron, was largely unaffected by the strike. This gave the struck companies space to pull together strikebreaking crews in anticipation of the Salinas harvest.

Striking workers also moved north from the Imperial Valley, following the strike as they'd followed the harvest in other years. The strikers were, in the recollection of some workers, in a state of demoralization. The clampdown on their strike activities by the union after the murder of Rufino Contreras had put them in a passive position. There was grumbling discontent, a sense of defeatism, and a sense that things were going wrong. Morale was so low that Marshall Ganz was reinstated as strike coordinator. Frank Ortiz, who had replaced Ganz after the murder of Rufino Contreras, was relieved of his command of the strike.

Strike activity began in the Salinas Valley as early as late January, but, with little work going on in the fields, it was largely limited to picketing company offices. One of the first outbreaks in Salinas occurred the third week in February when 300 strikers massed at a field near Chualar and fought with Monterey County sheriffs who tried to prevent them from rushing a Sun Harvest field where strikebreakers were harvesting cauliflower.[5]

By March, Sun Harvest made public its intention to harvest its 9,000-acre Salinas Valley lettuce crop with scab workers. The fence surrounding Sun Harvest's Toro camp on Hitchcock Road and the fences at its other camps around Salinas were topped with layers of barbed wire. Private security guards were brought in to secure the camps. A company spokesman in Salinas announced plans to hire and, if necessary, house 1,500 strikebreakers. The company sent out letters to striking workers in mid-March stating, "This is to notify you that effective today you have been permanently replaced and are no longer an employee of Sun Harvest."

Strike and "Guerilla Actions"

By March, there were one-day walkouts at non-struck ranches, and roving caravans of strikers appeared in the Valley, occasionally carrying out hit-and-run raids of fields where scabs were working.[6] As in nearly every strike in the fields there were strikebreakers recruited from among the desperate, the unknowing, and others who just didn't care but needed the money. Raids in the fields could discourage strikebreakers and make the job of recruitment more difficult, but, with grower resources and contacts throughout the region, strikebreakers were an inevitable part of the battle.

By the beginning of spring, twelve growers were being struck by nearly 5,000 workers. Only about half of those growers were in Salinas, but it included two of the three largest Salinas lettuce companies: Sun Harvest and Bruce Church. People began asking themselves, is the strike going to spread?

Strike incidents began to multiply. In early April strikers confronted scabs, and a fight erupted at a Sun Harvest plant on Abbott Street. When a cop tried to arrest a striker, he was surrounded by forty to fifty people. As the officer began spraying the group with Mace, a woman striker, using her picket sign, clubbed the policeman and the striker was able to slip the cop's grasp and dash away into the crowd. A few days later, in the early morning hours, hundreds of strikers, tipped off by a roving strike patrol, surrounded a bus parked near downtown Salinas. It was attempting to pick up strikebreakers for the JJ Crosetti Company, a struck vegetable grower from Watsonville. A fight broke out as forty police were rushed in to protect the bus and its passengers.

In mid-May hundreds of broccoli workers in their yellow rain gear streamed out of the fields of three companies to demonstrate their impatience over the growers' refusal to meet the demands of the strike. A few weeks later, scores of strikers charged through a broccoli field of a union company and drove out the non-union workers who'd been brought to harvest there. The following day, much to the satisfaction of union activists like Raphael Lemus and Mario Bustamente, all 600 workers walked out in protest from two union companies, Harden and Green Valley Produce. These companies were not being struck. The one-day protest was meant as a show of solidarity and a warning to the growers.

By early June, the first summer harvest was reaching its peak. In a show of force, over a thousand workers walked off non-struck ranches and joined picket lines. The emboldened workers invaded fields from King City and Greenfield, to Salinas and Watsonville. They especially hit the larger companies, smashing the windows of company cars and trucks, overturning and dumping boxes of lettuce harvested by scab crews, and chasing crews out of the fields to the refuge of grower buses. Police and sheriffs were mobilized throughout the area from King City to Marina and Santa Cruz to protect company lands. John, on strike from Sun Harvest, described incidents near Chualar during the strike mobilizations: "I was in a group of strikers off on one side of a field. The sheriffs were staying between the scabs and us and we nearly succeeded in tipping over a bus. We were pushing it from one side and would have tipped it over but we forgot to disconnect the *baño* [portable toilet] first. I always felt like that was a valuable life lesson—always disconnect the *baño* before you try to tip over a bus."[7]

At another field a melee erupted that took on the look of a big soccer match, with the Monterey County tactical squad huffing and puffing in pursuit of the fast-moving strikers as they ran back and forth across the fields. "The women were definitely more militant than the men," said several people recounting the actions. "Where the guys would go into the field and talk to the scabs *por la buena,* the woman might run in, take the guy's hoe away from him and hit him over the head with it."

Caravans of police vehicles raced through the area to keep up with mobile strikers, and there were some pitched battles and a growing number of arrests as the anger among the workers intensified and their impatience with the measured pace of the strike was wearing thin.

The union once again turned to its tactic of pressuring the INS to raid fields and loudly blamed the use of undocumented strikebreakers for the difficulties of the strike. In early May, the local Salinas paper reported, "Striking farmworkers cheered at the sight of Border Patrol agents raiding Salinas Valley fields" and commented, "It was an unprecedented experience for agents who are used to being heckled, jeered or worse."[8] The INS claimed it had brought in additional migra agents and stepped up its enforcement of immigration laws in response to pressure, claiming they were arresting 100 undocumented workers on some days, far above the "average" rate of twenty to thirty deported in "normal" times. Raids had also been reported at a Sun Harvest labor camp in Huron and at Grower Exchange fields. The growers, as might be expected, expressed surprise that any undocumented workers had been found in their fields and pledged to "continue to try hiring only legal workers."[9]

Once again the issue of the union's tactic of calling in the migra flared into prominence. A civil rights group from Arizona that worked with the undocumented sent a letter to the UFW criticizing its tactics and called on the union to organize undocumented strikebreakers. Marshall Ganz denounced the group publicly as "students and do-gooders" who could criticize because their jobs were not on the line. Whether the group was made up of students was not certain, but the fact that being a student would disqualify someone's opinion in this matter was interesting.

While some workers did cheer the migra as they led the strikebreakers away, for those listening carefully to the rumblings among the striking workers, the broad and growing sentiment was for not pressuring the migra but widening the strike.

As the summer months progressed, this sentiment expressed itself in the enthusiastic response to the job actions, such as the one-day walk-outs of non-struck companies and a growing fierceness on the part of the strikers, especially the women, when confronted with scabs and sheriffs. It expressed itself in the response at rallies at the mention of a more generalized strike. It expressed itself in the willingness of non-striking workers to sacrifice days of work to aid those on strike.

What began to take shape was a contradictory direction to the strike. Statements from the union's headquarters in La Paz put emphasis on a potential boycott, while in Salinas public references to broadening the strike were coming from Marshall Ganz, the union's strike coordinator.

The Salinas lettuce crop has two main harvest periods. One peaks around the latter part of June, the second in late August. As the June harvest passed and the relative lull between the two peaks progressed, tension built. A strike not decided by late August would continue into the following winter with very unpredictable and not optimistic prospects.

As the fat part of the harvest season approached, plans at union headquarters in La Paz were being made to greatly scale back the scope of the strike. A letter sent by Chávez on July 27 to boycotters and union supporters declared, "On August 13, 1979, hundreds of lettuce strikers will leave California and go to the cities of America to tell the story of their struggle and to seek support for the boycott of Chiquita bananas and non-union lettuce. Other strikers and their families will stay behind to continue the picket lines and to keep the pressure on the growers and the strikebreakers."[10] (Chiquita bananas was the label and principal product of Sun Harvest's parent company, United Brands.) Chávez felt the strike, which in the minds of some had hardly been fought, would be a failure, but the boycott would keep the union struggle alive.

In the lead-up to the August harvest, a march through the Salinas Valley was proposed. A number of people in the union were advocating this, including, especially, the elected rank-and-file union representatives. They argued for a march from San Ardo at the southern end of the Salinas Valley through the farming towns north on the road to Salinas. They saw the march as a means to arouse and mobilize the workers and farmworker communities along the way. Chávez and his allies on the executive board agreed to a march, but their vision was quite different. Looking ahead to a boycott, they proposed a march from San Francisco to Salinas that would garner national publicity. In the end, both marches were organized.

For a week in August a march of striking farmworkers made its way from San Ardo in the southern tip of the Salinas Valley north, through King City, Greenfield, Soledad, Gonzales, and Chualar, rallying people at each stop with an expression of determination to press ahead and broaden the strike. One former striker recalled the march as "a great renewal of the spirit of struggle," an action that bolstered the morale and the sense of strength in the strikers with its clear expression of support from the farmworker communities in the area.

On August 11, the march from San Ardo entered Salinas and met up with the march that originated in San Francisco, arriving in Salinas via Watsonville and Castroville to the north. The march around Salinas that day of farmworkers and supporters numbered in the neighborhood of 20,000 people, perhaps the largest march of its kind in the fifteen-year history of the farmworker movement, and surely the largest march in Central California since the march on Fort Ord at the height of the Vietnam War nine years before.

If the march measured a favorable mood for pressing ahead and broadening the strike, there were other indications as well that a broader strike could succeed. In July, Bud Antle, the largest lettuce grower in the valley, part of the Dole Corporation, raised the base farmworker wage to $4.60 an hour, the highest in the Valley. But this 35 percent increase in base wage was not greeted with satisfaction but disappointment and anger among Antle workers, and it set off a struggle within Teamsters Local 890, with a faction lead by Roy Mendoza challenging that contract and denouncing the local's head, Jose Charles, as a sellout. Into this mix a rank-and-file group of Antle workers, sympathetic to the UFW, joined in protesting the Teamster contract. Work stoppages put pressure on Antle and threatened to overturn the Antle-Teamster alliance. Mickey, who was working at Antle at the time, recalled a large angry meeting at the Antle camp. He was among a group calling for Antle workers to join the ongoing UFW strike and adopt its demands. In the face of such discontent and agitation, Antle's management quickly "negotiated" a new base wage of $5 an hour and declared their resolve to pay 25 cents an hour above *any* wage agreed to by *any* grower with the UFW. [11]

The UFW's national convention was timed to begin in Salinas's Hartnell College a day after the convergence of the marches. It was Chávez's intention to present the boycott proposal there. Confident of winning approval from the delegates, he was prepared to make public the plans he had set in motion for a new lettuce boycott to be launched from Salinas, spearheaded by strikers from the Salinas and Pajaro Valleys.

There was a hitch in this plan, however. It had never been discussed with the rank and file. The union representatives, reflecting the sentiment of broad numbers of workers, were troubled by a strike strategy that seemed too cautious. They had organized successful one-day walkouts. They had witnessed successful field actions to drive out strikebreakers. They had been encouraged by the solidarity of workers in non-struck ranches who gave up days of work to help out those on strike. They had been encouraged by the support given by San Francisco longshoremen, who arranged for strikers to work temporary jobs on the docks to supplement strike benefits. All this bolstered confidence that a broader, more powerful strike was possible. Many of these rank-and-file leaders were wary of César Chávez and were certainly not ready to rubber-stamp his decision that was made without consulting them.

The night before the Hartnell convention, union representatives such as Hermilo Mojica from Harden Farms, Mario Bustamante from Green Valley, Cleofas Guzman and Sabino Lopez from Sun Harvest, Aristeo Zambrano from Associated Produce, Chava Bustamante from Cal Coastal, and Rigoberto Perez from Mann Packing, met with César Chávez, Dolores Huerta, David Martinez, Marshall Ganz, and other top union officials. Tension pervaded the meeting as it became clear that there were two strikingly different views on the future of the strike.[12]

When the rank-and-file leaders stated their determination to continue the strike, Chávez countered by saying that the union had already spent nearly $3 million on the strike and funds were nearly exhausted. The response to this was later summed up by one of the reps present at the meeting: "We thought, we'll eat beans if we have to, but we're going to win or lose this strike here, in the fields of Salinas."[13]

Sentiment was strong against going on a lettuce boycott. The reps saw the boycott, at best, as a long drawn-out affair with unclear prospects for a favorable outcome. A boycott would take the initiative out of the workers' hands. Nor did they believe that the strike had been lost—far from it. In fact, it was a broadly felt sentiment that the strike had lost momentum because it had failed to boldly call on the workers to shut the fields down. The workers were tired, not of striking, but of striking halfway. Significantly, there was also a split on the union's Executive Board on this issue. Marshall Ganz sided with the union reps but tried to take a neutral stand in the meeting to avoid a break with Chávez.

The meeting went on until the early hours of the morning, one rep recalled. In the end, a compromise was reached, or so it was thought. A resolution would be presented to the convention delegates advocating for a continuation of the strike and a lettuce boycott.

The rank-and-file union representatives were not naïve about the union leadership, nor ignorant of manipulations at union conventions in the past. But they were not prepared for what they encountered just hours later at the convention. Mario Bustamante, head of the Green Valley ranch committee and a member of the convention resolution committee, read the "compromise" resolution and found *no mention* of the strike.

For the rank-and-file reps, the struggle now hung in the balance. They strongly believed that if the strike were abandoned, the union movement in Salinas would lose momentum and be pushed back. The taste of the workers' determination was in their mouths. It was up to them to find a way to give it expression. But they had little time to act and obstacles to overcome.

Gilberto Padilla, one of the founding members of the UFW, sat on the union's Executive Board. That day he also sat on the Resolutions Committee and was charged with responsibility to ensure that no resolution unsupported by the union leadership—that is, César Chávez—be allowed to reach the floor. Bustamante questioned the resolution and told Padilla that it betrayed the agreement between the workers and the union leadership reached the previous night. Bustamante told Padilla he intended to rewrite the resolution. Padilla told him that if the rank-and-file field reps could get their resolution written in the proper language, he would not block it. For Padilla, as for the reps, it was to be a day of fateful decisions. The rewritten resolution called upon the delegates to approve a plan to prolong and expand the strike.

Around the time this strike resolution was being written, word came through that Meyers Tomatoes, a company in King City, had agreed in principle to the strike's demands and was preparing to negotiate. Resolve for a broader strike was further solidified.

Then a key moment arrived at the convention. Resolution 10, written by the UFW top leadership to rally the convention to the boycott, was to be read on the floor. Mario Bustamante rose and walked to the microphone. When the section of the resolution on expanding the strike was read, the convention erupted. What had been a quiet, almost nonchalant meeting up to that point, broke into shouts, foot stomping, and raised fists, a loud and emotional approval of the resolution. Chávez, chairing the meeting, quietly declared the resolution's unanimous approval.

One can speak in general terms of political forces that lay behind important movements and events, and in the strategic sense, these are key, the necessities that face empires and systems that compel human behavior along certain trajectories. But there are the interventions of fateful events and decisions based on the complexities of history, personality, and psychology that enter at crucial moments, that can nudge the asteroid onto one trajectory or another, that make prediction a fool's game. When César Chávez heard the shouts of "Huelga!" from assembled delegates and looked out across the crowd, their fists pumping the air, he did not celebrate with them this burst of rank-and-file initiative and leadership from the fields, but instead felt the internal heat of defeat, of walls closing in, of air being suddenly sucked from the room. Nor was the joy of the delegates to the call to break through the deadlock of the strike his joy. Rather their cheers were insults, sharp and painful.

It is tempting to see in this moment the makings of a Shakespearean tragedy, with Chávez seemingly about to undo what he had taken a good part of his life to do. Who can unwind the political, social, cultural, historical, and psychological threads that wove their way through time to arrive at this critical juncture, this precipice from which one flies or falls?

It's also tempting to assign what came next to an overarching ego, to a personality too long protected from criticism by fawning supporters and confidants too timid to confront him with the truth. Or to the paranoia of an aging leader who saw disloyalty in every contrary opinion, and who now believed that this dispute was nothing but an effort to undermine his authority. Many have advanced this psychological view, and no doubt there is some truth here. But there were political underpinnings to this moment and the trajectory that brought things to this point.

Chávez had, over time, become a gatekeeper for the very system, in the larger sense, of which farmworkers were the victims. He had internalized the concerns of those with whom he had allied himself and the union, especially the Democrats, the liberal wing of imperialism. In so doing, he had, to an increasing degree, taken on their political outlook and sentiments. Among those sentiments were fear and hostility toward any initiative from the people that could repolarize the atmosphere in favor of resistance from below, or inspire other sectors of the population to do so, and certainly any action that threatened or targeted the system itself.

The union movement in the fields arose during the 1960s, when upheaval of unprecedented proportions emerged from a confluence of forces and shook the United States and much of the capitalist world. Much of what occupied the political establishment in the post-1960s was the effort to crush, blunt, undermine, divide, and discredit independent, radical political impulses. The farmworker movement, part of that larger movement, was both energized by it, and in turn, influenced it. The farmworker union struggle was also a movement of people, exploited as workers, and oppressed and marginalized as a nationality and a lower caste.

Chávez had spent the latter years of the 1970s driving the 1960s influence out of the union. If this was paranoia, it was paranoia with a clear political agenda. It was in sync with the increasing conservatism in the country, of a ruling establishment on the lip of the Reagan years, when unabashed and undisguised imperialist politics would once again take center stage. It's true that the union's leaders saw themselves as victims of this conservatism in such things as the changes within the ALRB under right-wing California governor George Deukmejian, but these were rather like skirmishes within the larger scheme of things. The union leadership did not try to fight the trend as much as accommodate the new reality as an acceptable element of it, and the anti-communist and anti-progressive purges fit in with this.

This is not to say that the rank-and-file leaders who now were taking the stage were guided by a radical or revolutionary agenda. However, they did have their feet planted among the rank and file. They were determined to mobilize the workers to carry out a struggle for greater organized power, and they were not particularly oriented toward alliances with the political establishment. When people take up large-scale struggle against an aspect of the system, especially when this comes from the most oppressed people, there is the *potential* for it to take political form beyond what is considered *acceptable*.[14]

There were moments in the course of the lettuce strike that reflected a fear of the out-of-bounds action of the people. The panic in the wake of the shooting of Rufino Contreras and the clampdown on the strike that followed reflected such a fear, especially as it was playing out on the volatile U.S.-Mexico border.

The quid pro quo that in 1975 exchanged peace in the fields for legal "guarantees" of unionization depended a great deal on Chávez's authority. This was now being challenged. What would it mean if he lost control?

Some have suggested that Chávez's actions during the strike and after were a response to a challenge to his leadership from within, and that he thought Ganz, in league with rank-and-file union reps, was conspiring to seize the reins of leadership. Perhaps. But it should be noted that had he recognized the will of the strikers rather than covertly trying to subvert it, there would have been no such challenge.

Consider, too, that the UFW was, to put it crudely, "valuable property." It enjoyed widespread goodwill with the public; it was a marketable name. Key leaders in the union were members of Chávez's family through blood or marriage. In fact, it has been argued that Chávez actually wrote off the rank and file because he no longer needed them, since the union was taking in more money from outside sources than from union dues. Chávez's struggle to control this asset has been suggested as the key element that explains subsequent events.

Perhaps all the above were factors. The fact is a decision was made, a turning point was at hand and the implications of this decision would stretch decades into the future. Indeed, it still resonates in the lives of those most immediately affected and in the conditions in the fields today.

General Strike

The decision to broaden the strike created a furor in the union that would reverberate for a long time. But for the time being, the Hartnell convention's call moved workers across the valley to join a general offensive to bring the growers to the bargaining table around the demands of the strike.

An immediate result of the convention's strike resolution was the decision by workers at West Coast Farms, a Watsonville lettuce company, to walk out on strike without authorization or consultation with the union. Within a week or so of that walkout, West Coast officials sought out UFW negotiators and asked for a settlement. The result was a 67 percent hike in the minimum hourly wage of general field labor, up to $6.20 an hour by July 15, 1981, a 50 percent increase for piece-rate workers, from 50 to 75 cents a box. The UFW retained the right to strike if mechanization at West Coast displaced 20 percent of the workers in any category. Half the new wages were retroactive to December 2, 1978.

In the wake of the West Coast settlement, walkouts, marches, and sit-down strikes rippled across the valley in union and non-union companies. Some non-union companies did not wait for walkouts but immediately raised wages. Within a few days Sun Harvest indicated it was ready to come to terms as well and negotiated a contract that included a first of its kind cost-of-living clause and increased medical benefits. Some non-union companies announced wage and benefit increases above those at

Sun Harvest. The wage demands that Robert Thornton, executive vice president of Grower-Shipper Association, had said a few months before "would put us out of business" were now being adopted as the new base rate of the industry.

This was a significant victory for the workers and the union. In one stroke, the hourly wage in the vegetable crops, which had risen from roughly $1.90 to $3.40 over the previous decade, now jumped to $5 an hour. Contract wage rates rose proportionately higher. There were raises in health benefits and holiday pay. The growers agreed to pay the wages of union representatives. Through all its years in California, in terms of material gains, this was the most resounding victory the farmworkers' union movement had ever achieved.

This was cause for celebration. Happy and relieved farmworkers toasted their victory and once again, for a moment, felt their strength. The happiness around Salinas and Watsonville was palpable, but not exactly shared in La Paz. Chávez tried to sabotage the strike by cutting off union strike funds after the Hartnell convention. As the new union contracts were being signed in Salinas, he chose to remain at union headquarters, barely acknowledging the breakthrough.

Torn Apart

It was a heady time. Workers returned to work with their spirits high and their heads up. They had held together for many months, and, in the end, they had rallied across the valley and brought growers to a compromise they had declared they would never make.

But the party was not destined to last long. The sudden jump in wages and benefits was startling, but you had to step back and realize that much of the rush of growers to raise wages and benefits was motivated by the desire to avoid unionization. When the dust settled after the strike, the UFW still had less than 40 percent of the Salinas lettuce industry under contract. This was an area of vulnerability. It was not clear whether Chávez was committed to doing much about this. Soon after the strike, he spoke out against putting too much emphasis on the wage and benefit increases. "What is a union?" he said to a meeting of union staff. "It is not the wages and benefits and protections. The wages are the fruit, the union is the tree." But not everyone was in agreement about what constituted a healthy tree.

With the success of the 1979 strike behind them, the union reps who had led the strike came together to spearhead organizing at other ranches in the Central California area.

In the words of one of the union representatives, Aristeo Zambrano:

> When we were elected as representatives we began a campaign to organize all the ranches we could. Marshall Ganz, who believed that if we did not continue organizing and broadening the organization, we would be vulnerable to the growers' counterattack, spurred us on in this work. And we continued, bringing more companies into the union, as many as possible. We worked hard to represent the workers at our ranches and at the same time put in the time and effort necessary to organize from King City to Gilroy. We worked in Greenfield, Soledad, Gonzales, the Salinas area, Watsonville, Castroville, as far as San Juan Batista, Hollister, and Gilroy—especially during the time of the garlic harvest. We won elections at many ranches. But then the conflict in the union heated up. We were ordered by Chávez to stop organizing. We were told the union did not see Salinas as important. There were other areas considered more important. They wanted no more organizing there for the time being.[15]

The rift between Chávez and the people allied with him on the union's Executive Board and the rank-and-file union representatives, which had broken into the open during the strike, was widening. The union's top leadership continued to insist that elected union reps, now paid representatives under the terms of the 1979 contract, were beholden to them, subject to their approval and dismissal. But the rank and file had consistently rejected that interpretation, insisting that electing and changing union representatives was their prerogative.

Tensions in the union continued to mount. In 1980, when union reps were asked to go to La Paz to assist the union with administering the medical plan, they resisted. They saw this as a tactic to pull them away from the rank and file and weaken their ties with the base. Thirty elected reps from ranches across the Salinas and Pajaro Valleys held a meeting in Watsonville that summer. They debated what to do in the face of policies from the Executive Board that they believed were neither beneficial to the rank and file nor to the union. They broadly agreed that in conflicts between the interests of the rank and file and the interests or wishes of the union leadership, their obligation was to the rank and file. This was the overwhelming sentiment of the gathering. They agreed to oppose the leadership's call.

The discontent that had hung like a chilly fog around the fields of Salinas was now coalescing into an opposition group coming directly from the grass roots. It was further influenced by splits within the leadership. Marshall Ganz, Gilberto Padilla, and Jessica Govea, all longtime union leaders, were leaving the union as a result of disagreements related to the tensions in Salinas.

There were two centers of leadership clearly emerging, one in La Paz, led by Chávez, Dolores Huerta, Frank Ortiz, David Martinez, and others, and the rank-and-file leadership in the Salinas area. There had been long standing cracks within the union that could perhaps be traced back to Chávez's Oxnard days when his vision of organizing farmworkers first emerged and found its bearings in the conflict between braceros and locals over field jobs. Among some leaders of the union there was a long standing attitude toward Salinas that it was too militant, too independent, and, as strange and contradictory as it may seem, too *Mexican*.

In fact, some rank-and-file leaders in Salinas took the hostility they felt toward them as a form of discrimination against Mexican immigrants by a mainly Mexican-American Executive Committee. Some began to interpret Chávez's rage at having been defied in Salinas as an anti-Mexican immigrant prejudice. And they criticized the Executive Committee for being out of touch with the rank and file because it did not reflect the composition of the union's rank and file. They made a decision to challenge that.

Their chance would come in the next union convention, due to be held in Fresno in 1981. According to Aristeo Zambrano, one of the key organizers of the rank-and-file initiative:

> As the union's convention in Fresno approached we began to discuss the idea of getting people from the fields on the union's board of directors in order to fulfill the principles that had been laid down for the union constitution's first article—this union is of farmworkers, paid for by farmworkers, and should be led by farmworkers. We took this seriously and began to look for men and women from the fields who could take this responsibility—people who had experience working in the fields, who had suffered there, that knew what it was like to strike and negotiate contracts, who knew about the life of the farmworker. We had an active core of union representatives. We visited St. Helena, Oxnard, Coachella, Modesto, and other places. We took on the task of visiting these ranches to build a consensus and to prepare a platform for the convention in Fresno. We were conscious that the time had arrived for the farmworkers to take leadership in their union, the union built through their efforts, their work, through their strikes and picket lines, and the days of going hungry and losing jobs and all that went into the struggle. And yet, when the struggle was over and the contracts were signed, they were the ones who were forgotten.[16]

Convention, Threats, and a Walkout: 1981

Rank-and-file leaders from the Salinas area came to the 1981 UFW convention in Fresno prepared to challenge the union's leadership with their own slate of candidates. Their goals were quite modest. They were not asking to replace the current board, but to seat one or several of their candidates on it. They chose three farmworkers, Rosario Pelayo, a longtime union activist and well-respected worker from the Imperial Valley area and the San Joaquin grape fields, Jose Rentaria, a union leader from Salinas who had once headed the union hiring hall, and a farmworker from the grape fields of the Central Valley. The Salinas group had developed some contacts across the state, but their strength was overwhelmingly in the Salinas-Watsonville area. They were prepared to wage a struggle that they saw as critical for the future of the union movement.

Anticipating a challenge to their leadership, Chávez and the Executive Board had taken measures to protect their exclusive hold on power. First, they tried to prevent any of the paid union reps from Salinas from being elected delegates to the convention. When that failed, they passed a rule that if as few as 7 percent of the workers at a ranch signed a petition supporting a convention slate of candidates, any convention delegate chosen from that ranch would be obligated to vote for that slate. They then went about gathering signatures at the ranches for the Executive Board's slate.

When the Salinas delegates arrived in Fresno, they were confronted with the rule that now bound them to support the Executive Board's slate. According to the 7 percent rule, they could not even vote for their own candidate! From there, things turned uglier.

Once again Aristeo: "When we arrived at Fresno they began to harass us. There was a guy with a gun. He was trying to intimidate us with his pistol, showing it to us," by allowing his jacket to open revealing the pistol in his waistband. "His name was Orozco. He was taken out of the union hall area without ever showing his pistol to the room full of delegates." The union reps from Salinas challenged the 7 percent rule and asked for a vote from the delegates. "When the vote was taken César said, 'It looks too close to call.' And he said, 'Let's close this until after we've eaten.' And during this time when we went to eat they began passing out leaflets to the convention, leaflets prepared beforehand, and it said something like, 'Mario Bustamente is out to destroy the union and Aristeo Zambrano is a communist and he's out to destabilize the union. Don't believe anything they say.' And we could see that there was a lot of distancing going on, a lot of effort among the delegates to trash us and turn people against us. We saw this harassment going on against us and we thought, if we stay here tonight we'll run the risk of one of us being killed. So we made the decision to leave the convention."

The Salinas delegation walked out of the convention that afternoon, bringing with them the delegates from the Salinas area and a few others. From outside the convention hall they held a press conference denouncing what had happened inside.

When the representatives returned to Salinas, they convened meetings of all the ranches they were representing to explain what had happened at the convention. Within a few days, members of the union's Executive Board, Dolores Huerta, David Martinez, and Frank Ortiz, showed up in Salinas. They visited fields and convened meetings of their own to condemn the Salinas convention delegates and demand that they be expelled from their jobs as union representatives. They tried to get petitions signed by 20 percent of the rank and file at each ranch to hold new elections. They failed at all the ranches. Frequently, they were themselves condemned by the assembled workers.

From an article from the *Salinas Californian*, September 9, 1981: "Then, at a ranch committee meeting Thursday night Dolores Huerta handed [Mario] Bustamante a letter from César Chávez informing him that he had been suspended as union representative at Green Valley and replaced by someone more to the executive board's liking. Union bylaws require that committee vice president Jose Garcia take over, Bustamante maintains. But because Garcia like Bustamante was part of the eighty-member Salinas delegation that stalked out of the Fresno convention to protest a union rule binding delegates to vote for particular executive board nominees, he too was shunted aside."

The union reps appealed their removal to the ALRB. But in a ruling several years after the firing, the ALRB stated what some might find paradoxical: "As long as the rights of union members aren't violated . . . the UFW can select its representatives by whatever means it chooses."[17]

The reps filed a suit against the union in court demanding reinstatement, claiming that Chávez had no power to strip them of their jobs as rank-and-file elected union representatives. The judge agreed. The union retaliated by filing a suit against the reps demanding a huge sum in damages, claiming they had defamed the union's reputation.

As the period of Citizen's Participation Day approached, Aristeo, along with other union reps, decided that, as a protest of the repression and of how the CPD funds were being used, they would refuse to pay the funds. This meant risking being fired from their field jobs under the 1977 convention resolution making CPD a mandatory obligation. Despite the risk, many refused to pay the CPD and indeed lost their jobs.

But that was not all, nor the worst of what happened to those who dared to stand up for their rights in the union. Mario Bustamante was jumped and beaten up at a union office in the Imperial Valley. A near fatal accident on a road near the border between Mexicali and San Luis, Arizona, left Cleofas Guzman, the head of the Sun Harvest ranch committee, partially paralyzed. The circumstances of the accident left many familiar with its details convinced that this event was anything but accidental.[18]

Defeat Out of Victory

Andrew Church, a lawyer acting on behalf of the Sun Harvest company, argued before the ALRB that the move was "brought about by economic necessity, not by anti-union feelings." The move was the transfer of some of Sun Harvest's growing and shipping operations for broccoli, cauliflower, lettuce, and other products to other non-union companies. The transfers affected about 600 jobs. The UFW challenged the transfers in front of the Executive Board. The lawyer for Sun Harvest expressed confidence that the ALRB would rule in Sun Harvest's favor but vowed to "fight the issue in court" if it didn't. ALRB attorneys vowed to seek out experts in "corporate formation, reorganization and economics" in considering their decision.[19] It was mid-December 1981, and the legal death dance of farm unionization was under way.

By mid-August 1983, Sun Harvest publicly announced it was shutting down all operations the following January 1 "because of economic considerations." The 800 UFW members who still worked for Sun Harvest would have to fend for themselves, their seniority, guaranteed wages, and benefits all evaporating like summer fog. Yet they were luckier than some. Other companies followed in the wake of Sun Harvest and dissolved so suddenly that workers only found their employers had "disappeared" the morning they showed up for work.

I got my first direct glimpse of what this meant in 1985. I'd gone down to Salinas to visit friends and find out how things were going. It was an early July morning in a donut shop on the edge of a farmworker pickup spot in front of Safeway on Alisal Street. I sat with my Styrofoam cup of 35-cent coffee across from Jorge, a veteran lettuce worker I'd known from my time on the ground crew at Sun Harvest. Slowly stirring his coffee, he said:

I was there, for the "negotiations" when Sun Harvest dissolved in 1984. The whole meeting lasted eight minutes! A company official threw the papers on the table kind of rudely. "Read them carefully," he said.

Chávez was there. He said, "This is a serious matter that needs more discussion." But the company said, "If you have any questions about it call one of our lawyers." That was it. Fourteen years of contracts. That was it. After Sun Harvest "went under" a lot of other growers "went bankrupt." Mainly, they just painted their buses a different color and started up again a week later with the same supervisors under a different name, with different workers, naturally, and lower wages. We know which companies work which fields. Sometimes now you get hired on by a contractor to work the same field you worked before. Only now they pay $2 an hour less. We lost all our benefits, all our seniority, everything we thought we had. Two years ago I made over $20,000 in the lettuce. Last year I made $10,000 and this year just $5,000 so far. I took my daughter out of high school so she's working at Kentucky Fried Chicken making $3.35 an hour. It's a shame, but we can't make it without her now.

The dumping of union contracts did not come all at once, but as one company after another disappeared and reemerged in a different form, the whole landscape was transformed.

There were three factors that the growers were able to use to their advantage to achieve this. One, the key rank-and-file leaders that had developed over the decade of the 1970s, through all the twists and turns in the movement, were driven from their positions as representatives and in many cases, fired from the companies under pressure from the union. This left workers leaderless and demoralized. Two, the organizing drive that Chávez had ordered stopped around 1980 left the vegetable fields still mainly non-union, a base from which growers could expand. With organizing in the fields at a standstill, the only defense for the union was through the ALRB. And three, unfair labor practice complaints from the workers in the fields piled up in the Labor Board's ample files, moldering in legal limbo while the conditions that led to the grievances in the first place changed. Even a favorable ruling, so long delayed, often melted into irrelevance.[20]

The UFW argued vigorously that the Deukmejian regime, which followed Jerry Brown's governorship of California, was pro-grower and destroyed the effectiveness of the ALRB. But the fact is, even when the majority of the Agricultural Labor Relations Board was sympathetic to the union, growers had found ways to undermine, delay, and subvert union efforts.

The New Order

With the disappearance of union companies, the growers imposed a new order. Lettuce crews that had worked together for many years and formed the backbone of the movement in the fields since before 1970 were broken up, their members scattered in the fragmented work units of newly formed companies and labor contractors. Pickup spots, which once concentrated many workers in particular areas, were dispersed across the city. Some of this was surely a conscious effort to make any organizing and resistance more difficult. Some of this was also spontaneous, as large companies broke up their operations into smaller, separated units.

Labor camps, which despite their austerity and frequent shabbiness, did offer a reliable living place for migrants during the harvest season and allowed for a greater coherence among the workers, were closed and torn down. Their former occupants now had to seek housing among the aging apartments, shacks, motel rooms, and garages of the Alisal.

Union workers were driven from their companies and their crews and put at the mercy of foremen and labor contractors who had previously been their adversaries. Some were forced to leave the area to find work. Others found work with contractors who realized they no longer constituted a threat.

Raphael Lemus had played a key role in organizing at D'Arrigo in 1970, and later, after returning from the lettuce boycott, turned a Harden Company celery crew into a corps for organizing the UFW at that company. He did not take part in the rebellion of union reps after 1979. In 1986, with the death of Harden's owner and the disappearance of Harden Farms as a corporate entity, with its union contract nullified, its operations divided among disparate units, Lemus found himself without work. At that, Lemus considered himself lucky as he got hired on as foreman for a labor contractor, working there until his retirement six years later.

As to what happened to the other workers mentioned in this book, I only know of a few, as I lost contact with most of them after leaving the fields. For the sake of their privacy, I shall restrain from any mention of that here.

By the late 1980s, the farmworker union had largely disappeared. In the Salinas Valley and the surrounding areas where it had found its strongest base, only a handful of contracts remained. The union hall on Wood Street, which under the influence of Chávez's "business union" model had been transformed—its once ample open meeting space reduced to a space that had all the appeal of a dentist's waiting room—fell silent and was closed down.

Apartheid Broadening

If the 1970s had given rise to hope for a new kind of relationship in the fields, for a movement that would sweep away an apartheid-like system that held sway there, then the 1980s might well have swept away any illusions that such a thing was possible. In fact, far from ending, the caste-like system of labor relations in the fields broadened into the larger economy. Under pressures of a more competitive and parasitic world capitalist system, areas of the economy such as the service sector, light industry, meatpacking, and construction gradually found the abundance of cheap labor available across the border too tempting to pass up. As they had in the case of the fields, immigration agencies fashioned their policies to fit the needs of capital. There was no new green card program to "legalize" labor, and so undocumented workers came into the country in large numbers to fulfill the corporate hunger for cheap, vulnerable labor.

As the braceros-turned-green-carders retired or moved on, in their place came undocumented workers lured to the fields by whatever means labor contractors and growers could offer them. But the situation in the fields was dismal. Wages were falling, benefits were disappearing, and working conditions were deteriorating. As jobs in the cities and in other industries opened up for immigrants, they attracted workers from the fields. There were concerns among the growers of obtaining a sufficient supply of low-wage workers to fill their needs.

As the number of undocumented people increased, anxiety grew among the political establishment. There was now a mass of people who were uncontrolled, unregistered, and largely underground in cities throughout California, the West, and beyond. In an effort to gain control of the border, an amnesty proposal, the Simpson-Rodino Bill, was passed in 1986. Under the amnesty bill, immigrants who could prove they were in the country prior to January 1982, after passing through a civics and English course (a program I was very much involved in as a teacher), could legalize their status. A special provision of the bill, the Special Agricultural Workers (SAW) section, was included specifically to aid the growers with their supply of labor. It allowed farmworkers to legalize under less stringent conditions. Under the SAW provision, perhaps a million workers were given legal residence, providing growers with a large supply of workers. They used this to drive wages down further.

But the growers were taking no chances, and they constantly sought out new supply. For years, farmers from the poorest sections of Mexico, indigenous people from Oaxaca, Chiapas, Puebla, Veracruz, and Guerrero, had traveled to the northern states of Mexico as an internal migrant workforce. Beginning around 1986, workers and farmers from these southern states, especially Oaxaca, began crossing the U.S. border, recruited by labor contractors and lured by the promise of pay, which even in the highly depressed wages of the late 1980s was considerably higher than those paid in Mexican fields or what farmers, plagued with depressed prices for such things as coffee, corn, and beans, could make. Oaxacans soon became a critical part of the workforce in the fruit and vegetable crops in California and elsewhere.

And so the cycle continues. As it had with the Chinese brought in and driven out; with the Japanese hired and then barred from owning land; with the Filipinos welcomed then marginalized and isolated; with the Mexicans contracted and then hounded by the migra; through the rebellion, organization, and aspirations of the 1960s and 1970s to the defeat and demoralization of the 1980s, it continued. And it continues today in those same fields, under that same sun so often obscured by morning fog, within view of the hills whose lush colors change, chameleon-like, with the seasons. I still drive through that valley and pause sometimes, awed as always by the vast fields spread over hundreds of square miles of fertile lands, from which much of a huge nation is fed, and over which pass the thinners and weeders, irrigators and tractor drivers, cutters and packers and loaders, massed around the hum of an ever greater variety of harvest machines. The women still work with their scarves shielding them from the sun, the men with their *cachuchas* and *fuldas* sticking from their back pockets. They work far from the supermarkets, warehouse stores, supermarts, and corner stores where we buy our food—perhaps not so far in distance as in recognition—with many people having little more than the slightest notion of those who plant, cultivate, and harvest the food we buy there and depend on.

EPILOGUE

THE FIELDS TODAY

THERE ARE MORE THAN TWO MILLION year-round and seasonal farmworkers in the United States, including 100,000 children. One in ten farmworkers in the United States is a U.S. citizen.

About 684,000 farmworkers work for California growers. California has 44 percent of the country's fruit, vegetable and horticultural workers. 95 percent of those workers are immigrants, the vast majority, 93 percent, are Latinos from Mexico. An estimated 85 percent are workers who have been deprived of legal documents.

In the year 2000 Monterey County farmers employed 86,941 farmworkers, including 46,687 migrant workers. Another 20,000 farmworkers were employed in nearby Santa Cruz County. Estimates of the number of women in California fields varies from 20 percent to 50 percent depending on the crop.[1] The crops requiring most labor are lettuce, strawberries, grapes, broccoli, and cauliflower.

The national average annual output per farm employee in 2010 was $43,177. The average agricultural output per employee in Monterey County was $183,331 in 2010. The mean annual wage of a Salinas agricultural worker in 2011 was $19,350.[2]

Salinas, late August 2009

It was still dark at 5 a.m., and I was making visits to places I'd known well thirty years before. I was under a covered walkway at the edge of a large parking lot on Alisal Street, the largest of a number of Salinas farmworker shape-ups. Workers in hooded sweatshirts and jackets, head scarves, and wool caps looked like dark shadows in the doorways of closed shops. Others drifted in and out of a restaurant that serves coffee and pastries in the early morning.

The crowd on the walkway was growing. Buses and vans were turning in the lot, rolling slowly, their headlights illuminating a fine mist, drawing the shadows toward them. Small groups of workers waited, their attention now drawn to the slowly filling parking lot. I was heading toward one of these groups when I heard someone call out, "Hola, no me recuerdas?" A hand reached out in my direction and behind it the broadly smiling face of a hatless man. "Hola," I said as I grabbed, by instinct, for his hand. "Trabajamos juntos con la Norton, en el valle, por la frontera. No recuerdas, verdad?" (We worked on the ground crew together in the Imperial Valley. Remember that?). I looked at the man before me dressed in a green, buttoned shirt and a tan suede jacket, clothes that betrayed him as other than a down-on-the-ground lettuce worker. No memory surfaced to match the face: a light complexion, a large mustache and side-burns tinged gray, and a hairline in radical recession. But then, he was referring to thirty-five years ago,

"Well," I said, searching for common ground to land a memory, "then you remember that camp in Blythe, the raunchy one that had those show-ers with a horrible sulfur smell?" He looked at me smiling. "Blythe . . . " This time his face was searching. "And that wildcat in the Imperial when the loaders refused to work because the field was wet, they were afraid of hurting their backs? They were fired and we stopped work in solidarity with them." All the hours I'd spent writing about such past events came in handy. The hatless man pulled his head back, perhaps straining for a vision. "Oh, ya. We won them their jobs back, yes?" he said, but without enthusiasm. At that moment a vision came to my mind. I saw a young man sitting on lettuce box in the fields, his long hair flowing from behind a blue or red bandana, his fist in the air, along with a group of other young workers. I tried to compare the face before me with my mental image of that photo of a moment in an El Centro lettuce field that I still had at home. "Well, I'm Israel," he said. "You probably don't remember my name. I'm a foreman for this company." He pointed to the bus in front of us, "The Growers Company," it said. "I'm Bruce," I replied. "Of course, I remember," he grinned, displaying a memory that put mine to shame.

To answer the question I saw lurking on his face, I said, "I'm here to see about the fields, to write something about the history of those years and about what's happening today. Things are pretty messed up now, seems a lot worse now in the fields than before," anticipating an assent to a proposition that seemed obvious to most everyone I'd talked to around

Salinas. "Oh, no," said Israel, shaking his head. "No es así. Está mejor que en aquel tiempo" (Things are better for the people today). "Then, we had no protection. But now the government protects the people. When there are problems now the people can get the government to defend them—not at all like before." "Really?" I said; "I hear that if you have papers many contractors don't want you. They just want people without papers, people they can fuck over more easily." Even as I spoke these words, I questioned the wisdom of speaking so bluntly. Israel winced slightly. He looked over the lot and then back at me. "Sorry, Bruce, but I have to get to the bus now." We shook hands again and he left. His friend, a somewhat younger man in a cowboy hat, a foreman as well, picked up on the conversation. "Actually, everyone has papers. And we have to see them before we hire them." He sounded defensive, but I knew where he was coming from. I took it as an official dissimulation meant for public consumption. He had no time, or perhaps desire, to elaborate. He too had to get to his bus as a hint of light beyond the shops lining Alisal Street evoked the day and work.

A short distance down the walkway, a group of men were waiting for work. One of them, thin with straight brown hair shooting out from his baseball cap, was standing next to a cluster of benches. He was close enough that I thought he might have heard a little of the conversation with the foremen. He looked at me and the little notebook I was holding and came over to talk. Without introduction, I said, "That foreman back there said that things are pretty good for the workers here now, that the people are protected by the government." "Well," said the man, who introduced himself as Jorge and looked to be in his mid-forties, "I don't see it that way. Last season we were out in the field when our lettuce machine broke down. We sat around for hours before the repair guy could get the machine running. When it finally started up I asked the foreman, 'Are we going to get paid for the time waiting here in the field?' And the foreman said, 'We can't pay you because you didn't work.' And I said, 'That was no fault of ours.' So I began to talk to the crew. I said, 'We should get paid for at least some of this time we lost. They should pay us at least an hour.' And the people agreed. When the foreman refused to even consider this we decided to walk out. And then a supervisor came and threatened to fire and replace us all. Soon after that I was laid off. I couldn't get a job again with the Los Garcias, that was the contractor. Every time I asked for a job with them it was always the same: 'No openings.' But I knew better. I'd been marked as an agitator."

Jorge looked out across the parking lot, suddenly bathed in the pale diffuse light of an overcast early morning. "You can go to the Labor Commission and make a complaint. Ya, they're sympathetic. But how many people want to run the risk of putting in a complaint and get known as a troublemaker? The government has agencies to protect the workers and all that. I've seen the inspectors come out to check the fields. When the foreman sees them coming he gives a signal to the machine driver." Jorge raises his hand and with a thumb, index, and middle finger makes a twisting motion. "And the driver slows the machine down. As soon as the inspector leaves, the machine speeds back up. It's even worse for us when they come out because as soon as the government man leaves the foreman'll tell the machine operator, 'OK, let's get moving, we've got to make up for lost time!' Casi siempre las maquinas vienen en madriza!" (The machines are nearly always running fast as hell!).

Machines on Speed

It's another morning in the same labor pickup area. In a darkened space shielded from Alisal's streetlights by the large Casa de Lavandería Laundromat, clusters of workers from the Baja Fresh Company stand waiting by dark, silent buses. A young man, his hooded head making his face barely visible, explains he's been five years in the lettuce. He speaks emphatically to my question about work. "Nos tienen corriendo, allí (They've got us running out there). "Nos sentimos mareado todo el dia" (We're like all dizzy). It's all day, cut and throw, cut and throw. You have to work real fast to keep up. You run like crazy and can't think straight." The women around him nod in agreement. One of the women has a white scarf that covers her head and most of her face. She has a plastic tote bag and a large, wide-brimmed straw hat in her hand. Only her eyes are visible. She moves a few steps toward me and speaks in a voice so low and I have to move close to hear her. "I worked for six years at T and A [Tanimura Antle]." Her voice wavered. "I was a packer on the machine. And they kept speeding us up more and more. I got to a point where I was forcing myself to keep the pace and I started getting very anxious on the job. The strain got to me. I had some kind of breakdown and I left work. I couldn't work for months. It took a long time before I could recover." And now, I asked? "We get pushed, and it's hard, but I try not to let it get to me like before. Besides," she looks over at a bus whose door has just opened, "I have to work, I have to eat."

It's 5:45 AM. I'm at Kristy's donut shop at the edge of the large parking lot that is the morning pickup spot for many contractors and smaller farm companies. Inside the small brightly lit shop, workers wait in line to buy coffee and sweet pastries from the friendly Chinese couple that runs the place. Outside, at one edge of the building, four men are standing together talking. Two are young, another, middle-aged. The older worker among them I recognize as a coffee grower from Puebla I'd spoken with before. As I approach, I sense a feeling of trepidation. The younger workers seem especially uncomfortable as I enter their circle to introduce myself. The middle-aged worker, who indicates he's from Oaxaca, is the first to answer my question about how things are in the fields. "El pago es muy bajo" (The pay is low). I ask, "About $8.50?" I already know the answer, but you have to start a conversation somewhere. He nods. "A little more than they paid back about thirty years ago," I say. "I was working here until about 1979. I worked in the lettuce, hardest work I've ever seen." I feel the wall between us begin to crack slightly. One of the youths, who's from El Salvador, quiet and looking sullen until then, speaks up. "We work long hours at times, twelve, thirteen hours and we get paid straight hourly pay. Is that legal?" I profess I'm not sure of the law, but I tell him I will check. "In California," I tell him, "for workers outside the fields, the law requires time and a half after eight hours a day, or forty hours for the week. That's the law. Any employer who doesn't pay it is committing a crime." (Only later at California Rural Legal Assistance—CRLA—do I find out that time and a half in the fields is mandatory by law after *ten* hours, *sixty* hours a week, something I'd forgotten.) The taller youth, who's from Mexico, begins to speak. "They have us working really fast; it's full tilt. Trailer after trailer leaves the field, but they never pay the contract rate like they're supposed to." The youth from El Salvador comments: "If we all stopped we could change things. If one person acts alone they'll just get rid of you, but if the whole crew acted they couldn't do that." He is more emotional now. "We were working in a field with a few machines that were making contract wages. We were getting paid hourly, but we were moving faster than the other machines making contract! The machine is going too fast and sometimes lettuce is left behind uncut because people can't keep up. One time this was happening and someone said, 'Slow down the machine, it's too fast to keep up,' and the foreman barked at him, 'If you can't make it leave the field, we'll find someone to take your place.'" I'm about to ask what companies they were talking about, but someone calls out, "Ya viene, vámonos," and they move out to the bus that has just pulled into the lot. They get on a plain white bus, "Sam Andrews Company" written in small black letters on its side.

The Bud Antle Company set a pattern in 1962 when they first put the awkward new machines in the lettuce fields with a crew of cutters, wrappers, and packers to send cellophane-wrapped heads of lettuce to market. The machines were worked by hourly crews with a contract incentive, a bonus above hourly pay per box after a certain threshold of production.

The system worked reasonably well; that is, the company got more production from the crew and the workers got a bonus corresponding to their increased production. But the system was always subject to company cheating. The farmworker movement in the 1970s took aim at this corruption, and the workers brought greater vigilance and organization to protect themselves.

"The problem is," Jorge, the worker mentioned earlier, told me, drawing from his twenty years' experience in the lettuce, "no matter how fast the work, the premium rate never seems to kick in." He offered this explanation: "On one of the crews I became sort of friendly with the foreman. A few times we went out after work for beer. And this one time, after we'd been drinking a bit, he started getting chummy and he showed me his checks. He had a bonus check for extra work he'd gotten out of us that week. I didn't say anything to him, but I took note of that. The *foreman* got a bonus for extra production, while the crew got *nothing*. Everyone along the line gets a cut from squeezing the blood out of us."

Invasion of the Labor Contractors

I first met Baltazar one chilly morning in front of Kristy's. He wore a heavy blue jacket. Thick brown hair with hints of gray bulged out below his blue and gold trimmed baseball cap. In a short time our conversation became animated as we exchanged names of people and companies we knew and worked in common. Baltazar began working in the Salinas Valley fields in 1969. He worked with Merrill, Interharvest, and later Hansen Farms. He'd been at Hansen for some years when the company metamorphosed in the early 1980s. He vividly recalled the scene one morning at the Hansen ranch at the southern edge of town when company buses appeared in the lot, their colors transformed, and the Hansen name replaced with another. A former Hansen supervisor brusquely announced that the Hansen company was dead, and a new company had arisen, as it were, from its grave. All the workers present, some with thirty or more years on the job, were told they could apply to the new outfit, but all seniority, benefits, and so on accrued at Hansen were no longer in effect.

Baltazar was set adrift among the growing ranks of workers vying for jobs with one or another of the contractors who were sprouting like weeds in the valley. Baltazar had not been an activist and didn't have to deal with the blacklist that dogged other workers. But having made as much as $800 a week in the lettuce at Hansen, he was in shock when his first full week's check netted him less than $200. Any sense of security from built-up seniority was replaced by the realization that his livelihood depended on staying in good stead with his boss. He went into depression mode for a while, but he persevered. For a time in the 1990s he got hired as a foreman for a small contractor. When I met him he was out beating the bushes again for a job, ready to take just about whatever came along, though he was hoping to catch another foreman job, which was easier on his body and his income.

In 1972 there were twenty-two registered labor contractors in the Salinas Valley. The head of the Salinas California State farm labor office had seen the numbers of contractors dwindle in the years following the 1970 strike and concluded, "I don't doubt that labor contractors are a vanishing breed."[3] Unionization and conglomeration in the fields appeared destined to make the labor contractor a relic of a bygone era. Yet, by the 1990s, the number of farm labor contractors in the valley had risen to at least fifty-nine and was still growing into the new millennium. A few growers, D'Arrigo, Tanimura Antle, and Bud Antle among them, still employed workers directly under their own auspices. But even these companies were jobbing more and more of their work out to contractors. Today, in the Salinas Valley, crews working under a large number of seemingly unconnected small operators do most of the fieldwork. The labor contractor has returned with a vengeance.

There is little independent about independent labor contractors. Their existence depends on the grower-shipper companies. Many contractors are former company foremen or supervisors. One of the largest contractors, Richard Escamilla, had as many as 3,000 workers on his crews. Escamilla got his start from his father, Domingo, a longtime supervisor for Bud Antle. People close to this history say Antle bankrolled Domingo. Contractors serve the growers and provide a vital function. They recruit labor in normal times and strikebreakers during periods of resistance. They reduce the cost of labor and have served as a "legal" way to ditch union contracts. Their effectiveness in squeezing more labor for less cost from the workforce is the key to their popularity.

Hairnets and E. coli

While we're talking, Baltazar pulls out a hairnet he has stashed in a pocket and with a grin slips off his *cachucha* and pulls the net neatly over his thick hair. A hairnet was unseen in the old days, but has now become standard issue on lettuce and other machines. Baltazar is ironic when talking about the origin of the hairnet and other sanitary measures, recalling how disdainfully the growers and contractors once treated issues related to workers' health and safety.

Baltazar points to the buses pulling into the lot hauling three port-a-potties and what at first glance looked like some portable medical unit—special sinks with tubes attached to containers of disinfectant, hand soap dispensers, and paper towel containers. He details the rituals workers are now exhorted to perform: hand and glove washing, lettuce knives kept in disinfectant liquids, plastic aprons and hairnets, even nets to cover beards. All this is a revelation to someone like me, a long time away from the fields.

It's not hard to find veteran workers with stories of having worked on crews where "toilet facilities" came with a full panoramic view of the valley. This was especially tough for women, who would take toilet breaks as a group so that they could shield each other and provide something resembling "privacy" behind a large bus tire or squatting on the sloping edge of a canal or ditch. Such a practice was common enough to engender a special name, *canaliar*, relieving oneself by a canal. The upsurge of the 1970s brought a spate of laws and regulations mandating clean water, toilet facilities, and so on in the fields. And conditions did change. Toilets and clean drinking water became more common.

When labor contractors surged back into the Salinas Valley of the 1980s, the growers washed their hands, so to speak, of working conditions, and disregard for the sanitary needs of workers was often a result. A CRLA worker familiar with field conditions in the San Joaquin Valley in the early 1990s disdainfully called sanitary regulations "beautiful . . . but a fantasy" because they were so widely ignored.[4]

Yet there was no doubting that a major effort to put sanitary facilities on the factory farm had now taken place. These facilities began appearing around the year 2000, after a number of well-publicized incidents of illness and death were traced to bacteria found in lettuce and spinach from the Salinas Valley. These problems began surfacing after a major shift in lettuce and vegetable production. The story begins in the 1990s with a growing public interest in non-processed, fresh "natural foods." Vegetable growers took note. The Taylor Company, a spinoff of the old Bruce Church Company, took a leap into the production of ready-to-eat, pre-washed veggies.

Through the 1990s, marginal sideline crops like romaine, green leaf, red leaf, and butter lettuce, escarole, endive, radicchio, chard, arugula, and spinach grew in popularity. In 1984, 6,000 acres of leafy varieties of lettuce planted by Salinas growers were dwarfed by 56,000 acres of the iceberg (head lettuce) variety. But by 2004, 69,000 acres of leaf lettuce surpassed old King Iceberg in both acreage and market value.[5] By late in the first decade of the 2000s, production of spinach had risen 1,000 percent from the 1970s level.[6]

Once numerous "naked pack" ground crews all but disappeared, field machines in many new configurations came to rule the day. Most machines still required lots of human labor, but one machine, like a huge lawn mower, cuts its leafy product into bins for the shed, using only a few workers. Bagged lettuce, with many fancy mixes, colorful labels, and upscale prices, were remaking the industry—in the markets, in kitchens, and in the fields. The industry that had once turned almost exclusively to field-packed lettuce was now hauling a lot of its greens from the fields into huge new packing sheds. Between 1997 and 2005, pre-washed packaged salad sales nearly tripled, creating a rapidly expanding $3 billion-a-year industry.[7]

Then came a nasty surprise. In August 1993, fifty-three people reported getting sick after eating from a Washington State salad bar. Nearly every succeeding year more outbreaks of illness occurred traced to lettuce and spinach from Salinas Valley fields. A bacteria of the E. coli family, known as E. coli 0157:H7, once thought to be only a danger in undercooked meat, turned out to be the cause.[8] Beginning around 1991, outbreaks of illness traced to the E. coli virus O157:H7 were reported in such products as melons, grapes, coleslaw, sprouts, and unpasteurized apple juice.

E. coli 0157:H7 is one of millions of kinds of bacteria, but unlike its benign brethren that nestle helpfully in human intestinal tracts, this one is more inclined to kill or gravely injure the host than partake of some mutually beneficial symbiosis. E. coli 0157:H7 was found to be lurking in the lettuce and other vegetables grown and harvested in the Salinas area.[9]

Large recalls of bagged vegetables and warnings to consumers, mandated by the Food and Drug Administration (FDA), sent the industry scurrying to protect itself. The growers and contractors rushed to clean up their act with a passion for enforcing stringent sanitary conditions unheard of when it was only the workers' health at risk. By the year 2000, new port-a-potties, sinks, and the like were common throughout the fields as the growers declared to the world their intent to stop further outbreaks by making sure their workers kept clean.

But after years of measures such as multiple toilets, portable sinks, disinfectant soaps, plastic aprons, and hairnets, E. coli continued to find its way into salad bars and spinach salads, and from there into people's digestive tracts, secreting potent toxins, attacking intestinal cells, causing bloody diarrhea, and renal failure—debilitating and even killing the very young and the very old.

The strain of E. coli that has been making people sick has been traced to the guts of cows, not people. Those studying the matter pointed to irrigation water contaminated by cattle dung as a likely culprit. The bacteria

368 / LETTUCE WARS

was found to be able to survive in many different environments outside a cow's colon—for 77 days in lettuce, on carrots for at least 175 days, and on onions for at least 85 days.[9] A September 2006 outbreak that sickened hundreds across the country and caused five deaths was traced to a spinach field in San Juan Batista, just over the hill from Salinas, and to feces from a cattle field near that field thought to have been brought in by wild boar.[10] The case against farmworkers as the source of bacterial illness was not supported by the facts.

In the 1990s Jesus Lopez from the Salinas office of the California Rural Legal Assistance could go out in the field in any given week and find thirty contractors who were violating state law by not providing toilets, clean water, and so on. Now, in the E. coli 0157:H7 era, it is rare to find contractors or companies that don't provide the facilities, and, in general, the facilities are much cleaner and there are often three toilets. But, Lopez said, you can still find some who don't have toilet facilities. Jesus, sitting at his desk in Salinas, leaned forward toward me. "What do you say about a system that can't or won't provide for one of life's most basic needs? Aren't toilet facilities right up there with breathing and eating?"

As to hairnets on field-workers, it's hard to see how this is anything but a cosmetic effort to create the image of an industry cleaning up its act. The real problem is clearly deeper and more difficult (and costly) to resolve. But, hey, why not put it on the workers? Hairnets are cheap.

Triumphs of the Free Market

I. CLEARING THE PATH

The 1970s was a bad decade for growers, with control over their key commodity was disrupted. I'm not referring to their vegetables, but the *labor power* of their workers. By 1979, some workers were hearing growers talk aggressively of vengeance to come.[11] By the mid-1980s, with the farmworker movement defeated and union organization shattered, growers moved to recapture lost ground. With the farmworker movement and the larger social upsurge a thing of the past, the market was "free" to move the cost of workers' labor power to the level dictated by supply and demand, with the growers pushing hard on the supply side. The bad days were over; "peace" was restored to the fields.

Labor contractors became the fortress standing guard over the newly reconquered terrain. By using contractors the growers created a downward pressure on wages and conditions through competition among the contractors; distanced themselves from blame for worsening working conditions; and made collective action by farmworkers to defend themselves extremely difficult. The results were evident: wages dropped dramatically and then stagnated; benefits deteriorated or disappeared; working conditions declined. Around the mid-1980s, growers began to dismantle the labor camps, reaping the benefits of rising real estate prices while dispersing the workers even more and ratcheting up the debilitating struggle for survival.

By the time Jacinto, a lettuce and broccoli cutter with thick calloused hands and a ready laugh, came north from Oaxaca in the mid-1990s, part of a new wave of tens of thousands of workers recruited or lured to fruit orchards, melon fields, grape vineyards, and vegetable farms of California, his starting wage was around $3.50 an hour, a disastrous drop from a decade before. Wages inched up in the years following Jacinto's arrival, but never enough to compensate for rising rents and other costs.

As we sipped hot coffee to warm ourselves in the damp morning wind, Jacinto spoke of his struggle to wrest a living from fieldwork and help his family in Mexico, without a hint of any options but those of unrelenting hard work and a wrenching struggle for survival. "Resistance movement," "union movement": these were uprooted from his and the collective vocabulary, consigned to the war stories of aging veterans.

II. "AMNESTY"

The federal government in 1986 passed the Simpson-Rodino Act, known broadly as "La amnistía." The Simpson-Rodino Act aimed at getting information on and control over the millions of undocumented workers. By employing and popularizing (propagandizing) the concept of "amnesty," the government built into the immigration process the concept of criminalization. Forced from their native lands by the rape of their homeland economies, immigrants are labeled as criminals, for which designation, they must atone and ask forgiveness. Thus, even the word *amnesty* reinforces a prejudiced view among the population.

During the 1950s, when the U.S. government carried out a militarized ethnic cleansing campaign called "Operation Wetback," it first moved to ensure growers an adequate supply of labor.[12] The Simpson-Rodino Act also came with a provision to meet grower needs through the SAW (Special Agricultural Workers) provision. The Immigration Service accepted special letters written by growers on behalf of workers as proof of qualification. Growers wrote a lot of letters. A growers' group opened offices in Mexico to help people apply for the SAW program, adding an interesting new wrinkle to the concept of amnesty, since these workers were offered amnesty *before* they had committed their "crime"![13] A million "legalized" workers (so-called Rodinos) came into the fields this way, adding leverage to the downward push on wages and conditions.[14]

III. OAXAQUEÑOS

Oaxaca, located in the southern part of Mexico, is the second poorest Mexican state in per capita income. Its 40 percent indigenous population suffers from a long history of exploitation, discrimination, and abuse stretching back to La Conquista, more than 500 years ago. Desperate conditions among Oaxacan farmers drove many to become internal migrants to Mexico's large capitalist farms. The collapse of coffee prices in the late 1970s drove an initial wave of Oaxacans to sugarcane fields in Veracruz and later to the vegetable fields of the northern Mexican states of Sinaloa and Baja California. Northern Mexican growers sent buses to transport Oaxacans north, where they worked the fields for about $5 a day.[15]

Communities of Mistec, Zapotec, and Triquis-speaking people grew in places like Ensenada, San Quintin, and Tijuana in Baja California. In the 1990s, Oaxacan farmworkers began moving north of the border into California, likely encouraged, if not directly recruited, by labor contractors. For many Oaxacans, Spanish was their second language, and plenty spoke little or no Spanish at all. Growers were quick to see the advantage of workers culturally and linguistically isolated from other sections of workers. As the historian Carey McWilliams noted in the 1940s, "When it comes to conjuring up new sources of cheap labor, California growers are unexcelled; they are probably the world's most resourceful labor recruiters." And, he added, "The farm labor problem has become encysted, i.e., embedded, in the very structure of the state's agriculture economy." And to the very structure of the imperialist global economy.[16]

IV. COFFEE AND LETTUCE

It was dark and early in the parking lot near El Pueblo market when I approached two older workers wearing broad-brimmed hats. After my initial introduction and a nervous beginning, they spoke quietly of the conditions that brought them north. They were coffee growers from Puebla, Mexico, unable to survive on the prices paid for their crops. Coffee plants require three years to bring up their yield. The coffee they were harvesting now was yielding them 3 pesos, 50 centavos, a kilo at the bodega where they brought their beans for drying and processing—about U.S. 30 cents for a little less than two pounds, barely enough to justify the investment in fertilizer and other inputs, to say nothing of the labor, cleaning, and pruning prior to harvesting the crop. The irony strikes me as we talk. Their wives and children are left to harvest the coffee, corn, and beans on their small plots, while they come north to make money to subsidize their income: cheap coffee on one end, and labor for cheap lettuce on the other.

I'd taken out my notebook to jot down the information they were giving me, but I sensed their discomfort and they soon began drifting off. As I turned, I saw that their bus had now arrived and it struck me that they probably didn't want to be seen giving me information. Despite my old crewmate Israel's assurances that the workers are now protected, these workers did not feel protected at all.

V. HURON

It was late morning and Baltazar had given up finding work. We were outside Kristy's again, leaning against his car. I was agitated by the conversations I'd had that morning with the farmers from Puebla. But Baltazar had something pressing to say. The news was reporting a critical situation in Huron, a fruit and vegetable growing area in the West San Joaquin and 100 miles south of Salinas. "You'll find lots of people from Oaxaca there and Salvadorans and Guatemalans. I think you'll find something there worth writing about." Baltazar, as he had before, was urging me to talk to the Oaxaqueños.

I decided to make a trip to Huron. "It's going to be very hot there," said Baltazar as I was getting into my car to leave, "just so you know what to expect."

I took Highway 101 south through the Salinas Valley. The car thermometer reached the high 90s by the time I hit San Lucas and kept climbing as I headed west along Highway 198 through brown, rolling, and somehow calming, hills. When the thermometer hit 110, somewhere west of Coalinga, I rolled down the windows, shut off the air conditioning to feel what 110 F felt like. Hot.

As I passed Highway 5, large signs set up in dry, brown fields announced, or denounced, the "New Dustbowl." Several years of low rainfall, historical circumstances, and a host of complex issues related to California water policies, led to severe water restrictions for farmers in this area of the West San Joaquin Valley. They were hurting and angry. These farmers stuck the blame for all this squarely on the Democrats, especially House Majority Leader Nancy Pelosi, as indicated by their angry signs. Well, I thought, at least this time immigrants weren't in the crosshairs of criticism, and I imagined some idiot talk-show type ranting, "These people come north across our border to drink all our water!" The conservative West San Joaquin farmers, unlike the immigrant-bashing right-wing know-nothings so vocal in the first decade of the twenty-first century, are not ready to join the "drive out the immigrants" bandwagon, as they understand that without immigrants the "great San Joaquin" would be little more than one big dusty valley, drought year or no.

Huron is a rectangular patch of a town in the flat turf of the West San Joaquin Valley. You could likely travel to the heartland of Mexico and not find a town with a larger percentage of Mexicans than Huron. Officially Huron is 98.6 percent Latino, a percentage that undoubtedly rises when its year-round population of 6,000 balloons to 15,000 as grapes, melons, and tree fruit ripen in the blistering summer sun. Autumn lettuce brings another harvest time and draws another large working crowd.

Lassen Avenue, Huron's commercial heart, beats with that harvest rhythm. In the pre-dawn summer mornings before the first rosy hint of day, as the air anticipates the coming heat, thousands of workers emerge from crowded residential blocks and converge on street corners and parking lots, surrounding waiting vans and buses sometimes lobbying contractors for work. The tide returns to afternoon streets, but more gradually. By early evening, restaurants and stores spring to life, catering to the workers' hungers and needs.

It's early afternoon when I arrive at Lassen Avenue, and vans and buses are discharging workers into the streets. As I leave my car, I feel overwhelmed by the brightness of the day. If it were possible to drown in light, this is where it would happen. It's scalding hot, but groups of women emerge from vans, bundled up in long-sleeve shirts and jackets. Looking at them gives me a sensation of suffocating. I want to talk to them, but they melt into the surrounding residential streets or disappear into corner stores before I can reach them. It's men I find hanging out after work along the streets, sitting on benches or lingering in doorways.

Notebook in hand, I begin making the rounds: to a tractor driver who quietly explains a dramatic reduction in fields plowed and planted in lettuce, foretelling a hardship in scarce harvest work to come; to an older harvest worker and year-round resident who shrugs and talks about a really bad year, matter-of-factly, as one might talk about a bad night's sleep; to a group of very young workers who have traveled a long distance looking for work and who have just arrived in Huron without any assurances they will find any here. Nearly everyone I talk to lectures on recession and water rationing and the math of income falling below the cost of basic needs. There's a worried edge to the conversations, an edge that I can only imagine, because in my life I have never faced the prospect of hunger.

As I make my way up the street talking to the willing, I notice a short, wiry man in his thirties who takes an interest in a conversation I have with several young workers. Before I can turn to him, he walks across the street. I see him later coming out of a small grocery store. Though he has several bags of goods, he sets them down on the hot asphalt and readily stops to talk. He is Filemon, from the southern part of Oaxaca.

He worked a family plot of corn and beans before braving the trip north eight years ago. I wonder whether he is one of the hundreds of thousands of NAFTA refugees kicked over the economic edge by the millions of tons of cheap subsidized U.S. corn that pushed Mexican corn prices below the survival line. To this speculation he gives me no definitive answer. Rather he describes the impact in his town of people returning from working in the United States. Tractors and pickup trucks paid for by dollars brought south draw the greatest interest. Filemon has staked everything on making enough money up north to return home and make a living with his family. But his plan is in danger of unraveling. Recession and water problems have slowed down the work.

"We're thinking of going back," he says, explaining that he and his compatriots are getting restive. "How many of you are thinking this way?" I ask, expecting him to tell me about he and few of his friends. "About three thousand," he says, and he's not kidding. There is growing sentiment that living up north is no longer worth the cost to be here, and he knows the sentiment from discussions in some of the big gatherings of Oaxacans earlier in the summer.

"Work is down to six or seven hours a day," says Filemon. How many hours do you need, I ask. "Thirteen to fourteen, a day." For the past eight years he's been working those long days, seven days a week during the melon and tree fruit season. I've been around the fields, and I've known about hard work, but this is on another level—fourteen hours a day and in this heat! Filemon smiles at my reaction and shrugs. Yes, it's hard, he says, because there's barely time to eat, to prepare food for the next day, to clean clothes, or take care of other chores. He has no time for anything else, like listening to the news or watching TV.

Filemon and his *compañeros* have studied their options carefully. They sift through information that comes by way of informal networks in their community, and by way of workers who come from other parts of the country, passing through Huron following rumors or advice in their own searches for work. They report on prospects in places as far away as the Midwest, the East Coast, and the South of the United States. This is a mobile community with its own channels of communication, including programs in Mayan dialects on the Radio Bilingüe network. From Filemon, I begin to get a sense of this force that now forms the backbone of the fruit and vegetable crops. If Filemon is any measure, they are tough, experienced, resourceful workers with a strong sense of community and clear objectives in mind.

What I cannot judge is just how realistic their goals are for some stable life in the homeland. Given my sense of how things are unraveling socially in this globalized economy, I have my doubts.

From my conversations with Filemon and others I met in farmworker gatherings in Greenfield and crews around the Salinas area, I have a sense of Oaxacan workers as a subculture within a culture, and a crucial link in the food chain, people most of us have no idea about but whose work sustains the life we know.

VI. BACKACHES AND BAGGED LETTUCE

When I left Salinas in 1980, lettuce cutters were making pretty good money, for an incredible amount of work. A ground-crew cutter/packer on a regular day could harvest about 5,000 heads of lettuce. At 75 cents per box of 24 heads, each worker got about 3 cents per head. Fast-forward thirty years to the modern lettuce machines where a typical cutter may harvest 3,300 heads of lettuce or more in a ten-hour shift. At $8.25 an hour this works out to about 2.5 cents per head, *less than the 1980 rate*.[17] On the ground crews, cutters work bent over for long periods of time, standing up to get boxes or to stretch. Lettuce machine cutters bend down to cut and stand up to place the head on the machine, rising and bending thousands of times a day. Today's lettuce, cut up and packaged, yields a much higher price per weight than in the past. It requires more processing than field-harvested lettuce, but it is hard to avoid the conclusion that farmworkers now are more exploited than those in the 1970s.

Maintaining this level of intense exploitation is only possible under a regime of national and racial oppression backed by the armed power of the state. In the 1970s farmworkers faced immigration and police repression, housing discrimination, social segregation, poor schools, and other indignities. But in the new millennium, by many measures, their situation is worse. They face all the indignities of the past with the added insult of being denied the legal right to drive, of facing a militarized and deadly border, and a growing number of laws, like Arizona's 1070 and the federal "Secure Communities" law, which make the life of working immigrants ever more precarious and dangerous.[18]

Overtime

In July 2010, a bill crossed California governor Arnold Schwarzenegger's desk for his signature to become law. It mandated that farmworkers be paid overtime after eight hours, as other workers are entitled to by law. Schwarzenegger vetoed the bill, claiming he had the well-being of farmworkers themselves in mind! Schwarzenegger reasoned that if the eight-hour bill passed, growers would cut back on farmworkers' hours and hire more workers to avoid paying overtime. He claimed that special circumstances in agriculture would put "burdens on California businesses." All this sounded suspiciously like grower logic. Sighting "special circumstances" to justify rotten conditions is just policy as usual. During the Great Depression, the U.S. Congress debated measures to extend overtime pay to most workers. Southern planters won an exemption for farmworkers, contending that the measure would "destroy the plantation system." A Florida congressman named James Wilcox put it bluntly: "You cannot put the Negro and the white man on the same basis and get away with it." It's Jim Crow logic applied to farmworkers *everywhere*.

In 1941, the year Mexican braceros began working the fields and rail yards, California's legislature reiterated national policy and voted to exclude farmworkers from overtime pay. This held until 1976, when, as a result of the farmworker movement, California farmworkers were granted the right to overtime after ten hours a day or sixty hours a week.[19]

One afternoon in August 2010 at the Farmworker Appreciation Day in Greenfield, I spoke with Sylvia, a veteran of thirty-plus years in the fields who sarcastically referred to overtime pay in the fields as "an unconfirmed rumor." A woman who worked years on a labor contract crew in the 1990s told me that she and a group of women crew members kept careful track of the hours every day and never received a check for the full amount they were owed. She could not recall ever receiving overtime, regardless of the hours worked.

Labor contractors and foremen are adept at extracting unpaid hours. They simply begin the *paid* part of the day later than work actually begins, or end it sooner than it actually ends. Finding farmworkers familiar with such tricks is not difficult at all.

Midnight Shift: Fresh Leaves and Restless Sleep

It's past midnight and I'm drinking coffee to stay awake as I wait by a bus in a dark, quiet parking lot of El Pueblo market. I have Baltazar to thank for this adventure in sleep deprivation. He urged me to find out about the night fieldwork that began with the advent of delicate bagged salad mixes, which demand harvesting in cool, damp weather. The streets are pretty quiet, but I see other buses making their way up Alisal to other gathering spots. A stream of workers wearing high rubber rain boots and clutching lunch bags makes its way across the lot to where the bus idles. "Why do you work at night?" I ask a few who've made it to the bus and stand quietly by the open door. Necessity, they almost all say, matter-of-factly. A few talk about avoiding the heat of the day. A thin older worker from Veracruz, with a wispy beard and a well-worn baseball cap, stands outside the bus marked "Custom Harvesting." He's in the mood to talk and goes on about picking coffee and lemons in his hometown. There he made $8 a day, about 10 percent of what he can make here. He has four teenage children back home, reason enough for him to sacrifice. He works nights because he hasn't had success getting steady work during the day. The cold and wet of night gets into his bones. But most aggravating is the sleep problem. When he gets off work he showers, eats a taco, and goes to bed, but he lives with a lot of people and when work is slow, or school is out, it's noisy. He rarely gets more than four or five hours of restless sleep. "How do you deal with that?" "You try to get used to it," he says with a shrug. He reaches down for his bag; the bus is about to leave.

Mary Zischke of the Research Lettuce Board, from behind her Growers Association office desk, explains, "Night work takes place for spinach and leaf lettuce used for spring mix to preserve freshness and keep it from being damaged by the heat of the day. About ten percent of the valley's leafy greens fall into this category." And the workers? "They get used to it."

Social Insecurities

Baltazar has been in the fields for forty years. He came north from Guanajuato with his father in 1965, attended high school in Salinas, but dropped out to work in the fields to help his family. He's pushing sixty now but not sure about retirement. "Most of us were foolish," he says. "We worked for companies and contractors and never checked to see if they were really paying money into Social Security." He'd worked a long time for Hansen, but when the company disbanded his retirement fund there disappeared, or so he thinks.

Stories of farmworkers being cheated out of Social Security are as common as breezes off the bay. One morning in Calexico I sat in the lobby of the old De Anza Hotel, now a farmworker retirement residence, and listened to retirees talk at length about such matters. "The contractors promised to do right by us if we stayed clear of all that union stuff," said one tall retiree, with a large gray mustache and hair to match. "But the *sin verguenzas* [shameless ones] were pocketing the Social Security funds all along!" And he spoke sadly of short funds and housing fears. There's reason to believe this situation is even worse today.

A study by a group of University of California researchers in 2000 concluded that "two-thirds of the growers using contractors were paying contractor fees so low that workers and the government could not be receiving contributions to mandatory benefits such as Social Security, workers' compensation or unemployment insurance—unless, that is, the workers were being paid substantially less than the minimum wage or the contractors were independently wealthy and in the business for the purpose of losing money." The study indicates that the contractor system does not just *allow* for widespread filching of workers' pay and Social Security, it *requires it*.[20]

"There's a story behind this," says Jesus Lopez as he sits at his desk waving a copy of a paycheck, "and I can say it's a typical one, if you want to know." Jesus, a CRLA investigator, has been around the fields for decades. He worked in them in the 1970s, and his outrage at the injustice he sees has not cooled with the years. He's telling me of an older woman worker who'd recently come to see him. "Her lettuce crew worked a long, hard week of twelve-hour days at a piece-rate pace. The foreman assured the workers they'd be paid accordingly. After twelve hours of work Friday the foreman announced the crew was moving to yet another field. They were exhausted and most of the workers did not want to go. Three of the workers spoke up, saying they were tired from the long week. You can leave if you want, the foreman told them matter-of-factly. When they showed up for work the next week they were told they no longer had jobs. As far as the contractor was concerned they'd quit." "I did the math," says Jesus, holding up the week's paycheck of one of the fired workers. "I calculated the hours and rate of pay and found that the piece-rate bonus for the *entire week* of twelve-hour days at contract speed came out to $12! Here's the proof," says Jesus, "here's how the workers are tricked and cheated. And this is nothing special. It's business as usual."

In 2005, the California Institute for Rural Studies found that 70 percent of farmworkers were without health insurance, and the numbers were growing. Eighty-three percent of undocumented farmworkers were uninsured. Only 16.5 percent of farmworkers worked for growers who offered health insurance, and one-third of those workers could not afford premiums or co-pays. In that study, 32 percent of male farmworkers said they'd never been to a doctor or clinic. A larger percentage had never been to a dentist.[21]

The lack of health insurance stands out starkly in an industry that has proven hazardous to health. Here it's worth quoting from the excellent book, *The Farmworkers' Journey*, by Ann Aurelia Lopez. "The National Safety Council (2002) reported farmwork as the most hazardous U.S. industry of 2001 with 700 deaths and 130,000 disabling injuries reported. In 2002 the death rate for agriculture was almost six times greater than that for all other industries, with a death ratio of 21 per 100,000 workers (National Safety Council 2003)." And further, "No state is deadlier than California. . . . Farmwork is California's second-most dangerous industry after construction. In 1999, seventy-six California agriculture employees were killed on the job, according to the California division of Occupational Safety and Health Administration. The figure represents a 33 percent increase over agriculture's 1995 fatality figure of fifty-seven. During the same period industrial deaths (nationally) dropped by 8 percent from 646 to 591."[22]

The push for more production adds to dangers in the fields, as for example, when machine drivers are taken off tractors to do other jobs, leaving a machine running without a driver capable of reacting if something goes wrong. This is a common practice and has resulted in deaths and injuries when workers cutting in front of the machines have slipped and are unable to move quickly enough to get out of the way of a moving machine. Piece-rate work (according to one study, about 30 percent of farmwork in California) also adds to the dangers. In early July 2010 Rodolfo Ceballos Carrillo, fifty-four, died while loading grape boxes at Sunview Vineyards. At the time, Ceballos was working by piece rate in temperatures somewhere between 96 and 103 degrees. He was the fourth farmworker to die in a month from heat in California fields. At least sixteen farmworkers have died the last few years while toiling in hot California fields and orchards. As one researcher put it, "Evidence suggests that some employers who hire Mexican workers for the most perilous work regard Mexican workers as disposable human beings."[23]

In early October 2012, Governor Jerry Brown of California vetoed a bill called the Farmworker Safety Act, which would have allowed workers to enforce the state's heat regulations by suing employers who repeatedly violate the law. The same week as the veto, a lettuce worker in the Salinas Valley collapsed and died while harvesting lettuce in 94-degree heat. [24] Contrary to the popular narrative, denying minimal rights and benefits to farmworkers, and immigrants in general, is a bipartisan affair in California.

Accidents are not the only health issues farmworkers face. There is great irony in the fact, confirmed by various studies, that farmworkers suffer from "food insecurity" and hunger at a far greater rate than the general population and suffer high rates of diabetes and even obesity associated with poor diets high in fat and calories, problems related to low incomes and limited choices.

I was near a pickup spot on Sanborne Road early one morning when I saw a group of a half-dozen men on the porch of house. They looked nervous as I walked by, and I tried to appear as uninterested in them as I could. But it was impossible not to notice the well-lit living room behind them and a floor filled with mattresses.

Some Salinas neighborhoods are notoriously high-density places. The destruction of thousands of seasonal housing units (labor camps) since the 1970s, the increase in housing prices, and the decline and stagnation in wages have forced families to double and triple up in apartments and houses.

"In the city's poorest neighborhoods, the shortage forces families to triple or even quadruple up in apartments with nowhere for children to play but a parking lot. A 2000 estimate indicated that some Salinas neighborhoods housed as many as 22,000 people per single square mile."[25] Anna Caballero, then mayor of Salinas, claimed that there were 31,000 to 34,000 people per square mile in Census Tract 7 in the area of Del Monte Avenue, with 30 percent of households with seven or more people.[26] By comparison, San Francisco, the second-most densely populated large city in the United States, has about 17,000 per square mile.[27]

Not only is the overcrowding in Salinas shocking but it's so much worse than it was in the1970s, when the housing was often poor but (with the exception of single men's camps) not nearly so overcrowded as today.[28]

On a Calexico Street

One August morning at a Salinas pickup spot, I met Raymundo, a young worker with a friendly outgoing manner. "I'm just up here from Mexicali," he said energetically. "I get unemployment there now, but to make it I came here to work." He's not at all contrite about working the system this way. "I can't make it otherwise," he says, "and I work hard. Work is fast here, sometimes we make contract rate, usually not. Sometimes we start at 6:30 but the foreman will put down 7:00 and because we've worked an hour and a half and they're counting only an hour, we'll qualify for contract rate. So we actually get cheated a half an hour but they placate us with giving us a little more in piece rate. Lately we work fast but never seem to get that rate, so I guess we're getting cheated."

"What's it like in Mexicali these days?" I ask. "I get up at 3:30 down there, it's worse than here in some ways. It's cheaper to live in Mexicali, but the wait at the border in the morning is 1½ to 2 hours to cross. The line is like a snake, you've got thousands of people waiting to cross and only a few agents checking people's papers. Sometimes we'll pay a *raitero*, someone who get ups real early like 1:30 or something and gets in line and we'll get in the car when it's near the *garrita* [border crossing] but a ride costs us $3 or $4 a piece. Otherwise we'll have to wait that long time to cross. Then once across we wait until light, maybe 6:30, unless the lettuce is frozen. We might start at 7, 8, 9 or even later. It gets dark early. So all that time for a few hours of work." Raymundo sees the door of the bus closing and takes off with a friendly good-bye. And I make a note, check out Mexicali this winter.

It isn't until February that I finally make it to Calexico on the border opposite the expanding city of Mexicali. I arrive in downtown Calexico after a twelve-hour marathon ride on the Greyhound line from San Francisco.

My second morning in town I'm up before four because the first morning I got up at 4:30 and I barely had a chance to talk to some workers before they headed off to the fields. Even so, 4 a.m. is nothing here. Many of the workers are up at 2 a.m. and even earlier to cross the border, waiting in long lines of cars or of pedestrians that move in agonizing slowness toward the spartan building that houses the immigration inspectors. Most people I talk to take this inconvenience for granted, but it makes me angry, as I can't see this as anything but an insult to the people who harvest this country's food. In the 1970s I lived in Mexicali and crossed the border each morning to work. There were many inconveniences to this arrangement, but I never had to wait more than a few minutes to cross the border on foot.

I wander around the well-lit corner of 3rd and Paulin Street, crowded with workers, and go into a corner coffee shop. Every table is filled with people drinking coffee and eating pan dulces and donuts. I grab a cup of coffee and a plain old-fashioned donut and head out to the street. On this morning I'm determined to talk to some of the women workers. In Salinas I found it far easier to engage with the men, who were out on the streets longer. When I did engage with women, a different narrative began to unfold, including a side of work and life in the fields to which men are often oblivious.

One of the first people I talk to is a woman who crosses every day at midnight so as to avoid the early-morning line of cars along the road next to the border and the insanely slow crawl over dozens of blocks to the crossing. Crossing at midnight, she sleeps in her car, warily, and not well, fearful of missing the bus and a day's work she can't afford to lose.

I approach a group of women waiting in front of a parking lot across from the coffee shop and ask them about work. Most seem shy or reluctant to talk, but Margarita, a woman in her forties with reddish hair visible on the edges of her blue and white bandana, is anxious to tell a story of a day on a melon crew the previous May. "It was a very hot day. By afternoon the crew was suffering from the heat and also lack of water." Margarita was among four melon workers who led a protest over the lack of adequate drinking water. They finally got their water, but the protest leaders, three women and one man, were fired. They appealed the firing to the Labor Commission. After many months of waiting, they received their reply. "The Commission found there was 'no basis' for our protest," says Margarita indignantly. "What a farce!" Margarita continues about the fields, this time it's about "*acoso sexual*" (sexual harassment and abuse). It's everywhere, she says, and describes the situation on a melon crew and the pressure put on women to provide sexual favors, or risk losing their jobs. She describes favoritism given younger women by foremen angling for sexual favors, and the casual insults to older women who are shunted aside or trampled on by foremen or labor contractors seeking some favor to toss to their sexual prey. Her story is cut off, practically in mid-sentence, as she heads off to a van about to leave. I don't have time to arrange some way to continue the conversation.

This was not the first time I'd heard this kind of story and the frequency of these stories is quite stark.[29] In the 1980s, a group of women working under a Teamster contract got together and began an organization they called "Las Pañolistas"—after the *pañuelo* or scarf women in the fields wear over their faces as protection from the sun. Las Pañolistas organized house meetings and pickets that denounced the sexual harassment in the fields and encouraged women to speak up about it. It was the only case of any kind of organized resistance to sexual exploitation that I'd heard about in the fields.

I wander over to the coffee shop, and I find Mayta and Catalina standing in front of the large picture window. Catalina is a mother of four in her late thirties; Mayta, single, is in her twenties. Catalina begins answering my question about life in the fields by describing her farmworker mother's long illness and death and the afflictions her mother suffered like "*rheumas*" and strange skin problems Catalina attributes to farm chemicals.

It soon becomes clear that, such tragic aspects notwithstanding, Catalina and Mayta have a penchant for joking around. When I ask about work and who they work for, Mayta replies with a shy grin, "Oh, trabajamos con un caballero, Sr. Matagente." "Matagente?" (Killer of people?), I repeat. At that both almost fall over laughing. "That's what we all call him," says Mayta, "when he's not around. Don't think we're not respectful. We never forget to call him Señor." They go on to describe their foremen, one they call "Quitacueros" (he who skins you alive) and the other "El Látigo" (the whip). "We wouldn't think of calling them anything else," says Mayta, referring to themselves and their crewmates. "I mean, what do you call a shoe but a shoe, no?" And once again they laugh. Then Mayta and Catalina describe their job on the lettuce machine, and the frequent eleven- or twelve-hour days, but emphasize the joking and kidding on the crew. "We are like family," says Catalina, who has worked in the fields thirteen years since the breakup of her marriage left her the sole support for four children. "We help each other, take care of each other, and we play around because it's how we make the work and our days endurable."

Moving from group to group, I find there's plenty of anger and anxiety over border hassles, inadequate wages, and especially now, slack work. I meet a number of workers who are legal U.S. residents but are unable to survive living on the U.S. side and so have moved to Mexicali where rents are lower, though the cost of everything else is not that much cheaper, and in some cases even more expensive. It occurs to me that with so many workers living on the Mexican side, Mexico is *subsidizing* the United States by providing the cheap labor and absorbing the social costs of workers' families. It's a great big giveaway by Mexico, one that you'll *never* hear mentioned by the Glenn Becks or Jan Brewers, or even the Nancy Pelosis or Barack Obamas for that matter.

Wanderers

A group of men are sitting at the edge of the parking lot in Salinas, waiting. It's morning, already light, but they're hoping against odds that someone will come and offer them a job. I stand near them, staring out on the now quiet parking lot. One of the men is middle-aged, with a mustache and a three-day beard in transit from blond to gray wearing a straw hat pulled down low covering his eyes. As he looks up I can see his light blue eyes, "What are you waiting for?" he asks me. "I'm waiting for a job on a lettuce ground crew," I say, as seriously as I can. He and the others looked surprised. Then there's a murmur of disbelief. "Actually I'm here to learn about what's going on in the fields," I explain a little. "And you, waiting for a job in lettuce?" I ask. "Oh ya. But it's hard to get on; they just want young people," and he pushes back his straw hat. "And where are you from?" I ask. Costa Rica, he says. And now it's my turn to look surprised. I find out his name is José. He's been in the United States twenty-six years, eight in Salinas. He got his green card in the amnesty of 1986. Where else has he lived? In Alaska, where he worked the fish canneries; New York where he did gardening; Seattle where he picked apples. Now Salinas in the lettuce, but work is slow. He blames this on the preference the contractors have for young workers. "Somos maltratados, humillados, nos tratan peor que burros" (They treat us worse than donkeys).

Another José, who has just come from Merced where he worked in the "limpia de tomates," weeding tomato plants, joins the conversation. "One day we were in the field and the foreman called for a lunch break. It was very hot. We were halfway through the break when the contractor came out and asked why we weren't working. The foreman said that it was lunchtime. They got into an argument about whether the break was fifteen or thirty minutes. The foreman said people need a break, especially in the heat. But the contractor said, 'To hell with that. Sometimes people have to die to get things done.' Can you believe that? Like he could care if we lived or died. The work was not that hard in general, but his attitude!"

The Costa Rican José talks about a young pregnant woman who died in the grapes the previous year from the heat. José from Merced is surprised at that. Really? He hasn't seen anyone die. But he recalls a young Oaxacan on a melon crew near Phoenix. "The poor guy passed out from the heat. When he woke up he felt really bad, he was physically in pain, but also distressed because he thought he'd lose his job."

I tell him I've heard from others that the immigration police are more active on the border. José nods. "Well, I don't have to worry, I've got papers." His laugh reveals he's joking. He tells a story about working in Yuma. "One day the contractor told us, 'Tomorrow we're working at such and such a place. It's right near the border and we're going to see immigration there. But I don't want anyone running. If you run that'll attract the immigration and everyone will get busted. So if anyone feels they can't be near the migra without running, don't come to work tomorrow.' So the next day we go to this field and, sure enough the immigration is there, but no one runs. One guy, who managed to sneak across the border that day, comes to the field and joins in the crew. He's pretending to work on the crew to avoid the migra, but the foreman kicks him off the crew, because he's afraid a migra has seen him and will come and get them all in trouble."

Both Josés are single. Neither has children. "I'm like the bird who wanders from here to there," says the José from Costa Rica. "I'm tired of being exploited. I'm tired of being treated with no respect at all. I'm tired of the way all of us who work, especially in the fields, get treated. I'd say, overall, the fields are the worst I've seen of the different places." The other José says, "The workers are the basis for everything, where all the wealth comes from." And I answer, "There's a fellow by the name of Carlos Marx, have you heard of him?" "No," says José. "Well, he said what you just said. He called it the dirty little secret of capitalism, that exploitation is where all social wealth comes from. It's a relationship that is largely hidden from people, but understanding this really allows us to understand something very fundamental about this society and the root of injustice. To talk about ending injustice without talking about ending the exploitation at the heart of this system is futile." And I try to explain what I understand of this and what it would mean to end the exploitation of some humans by others and all the relationships and ideas that flow from this exploitation.

José from Costa Rica says, "A lot of people don't want to work anymore because they're sick and tired of so much exploitation. People call them lazy, but that's not it. It's just that you get sick and tired. It's really just slavery." But then he adds, "It's never going to end because, for one thing, we're not from here. We're outsiders, what say do we have? What power do we have? What rights do we have?" "You've been here twenty-six years and you have papers and you don't have a right to speak up?" I ask. And I think back to these same sentiments, expressed by others. "I don't think the exploiters, the Europeans, the United States and so on, ever had a second thought about invading, taking over countries, changing governments whenever they felt it in their interests. But you, crossing a border to get work, are criminals and have no rights?" "Ya," they say, "but it will never change." I explain my resolve not to use that word *never*. "El nunca va usar la palabra never," says the Costa Rican José, and we all laugh.

Another day, it's late morning, and hope for work for the day is fading faster than the sliver of a moon that's heading for the horizon. Once again I'm at the edge of the large parking lot of the Salinas shopping mall. This time there's a group of five young Guatemalans in their late teens or early twenties. One just arrived weeks before from New York where he'd spent the previous three years working construction, making about $18 an hour. He learned many different skills there, but work dried up and his sister said that there was work in Salinas. Another youth came from Las Vegas where he'd worked the previous three years in restaurants. Two others are up from Los Angeles. One worked in demolition, the other had two jobs until the crisis. Because of the dangers of the migra at Greyhound stations, they came up with a *raitero,* a ride provider. They paid $80 each for the ride. A friend told him that there was work in the greenhouses, but this turned out not to be true. They're all from the same town in Guatemala, and knew each other back home.

All of them had tried to find work in grapes, then lettuce. They finally copped some work in the *mora,* blackberries, in Watsonville. Piece-rate pay, $3 for a small bucket. After working all day, from morning to late afternoon, they were able to pick ten buckets. They worked two weeks, making around $150 a week. From this they had to pay their way to and from Watsonville. Several of them talked of returning to Guatemala if the conditions don't improve. They'd heard of an anti-immigrant group, the Minutemen, active at the border, and they wondered about how dangerous they really were.

Teamsters Revisited

When the Teamsters signed a contract with Bud Antle in 1962, it was a good business deal for both parties. Antle got a loan for $2.5 million, and the Teamsters got a contract covering 3,500 workers, dues, paycheck deductions to the union's retirement fund, and so on. When the farmworker movement erupted in the 1960s and 1970s, the growers put up the Teamsters barrier to protect themselves from the movement's onslaught.

The Teamsters were more barrier than union, but with Antle, as always the innovator out in front of the pack, including in wages and benefits, workers did as well on the economic front as any other farmworkers.

In 1979, Antle once again set the trend for the industry when it stopped hiring its own thinning and weeding crews and passed these jobs on to labor contractors. Money saved on benefits and "cut corners" caught industry attention. When internal turmoil overtook the UFW and Chávez decided to cash in on his fame, the way was open for the industry to once again follow Antle's lead, this time into the labor contractor era.

Antle kept its Teamster contracts, allowing the workers hired under its name to retain benefits other workers in the industry had lost or were losing. But Antle also followed the tide it helped set in motion, whittling down benefits and wages, speeding up work, eliminating camps, and whatever else would lower costs. In 1986, Antle workers fought back. They struck for fifteen days in defiance of their union. They lost the strike and some lost their jobs. By 2010, Antle wages were roughly the same pathetic level as the rest of the industry. Health benefits were greatly eroded, and of the 3,750 workers Antle had once employed directly, only 750 remained. The rest were pushed out to labor contractors, some cultivated in Antle's own company managerial greenhouse. In all this, the Teamsters union had done nothing but, as they say, provide the vaseline.

A group inside the Teamsters in Salinas, and farmworkers under Teamster contract, tried to build some kind of resistance to the implosion of wages, benefits, and working conditions. One of them, Froilan Medina, whose activism hailed from the1970s, quit his job as a Teamster organizer in protest over corruption and collusion. He joined ranks with a worker activist, Guillermina Garnica, with forty-four years at the Dole Company but fired after she suffered an accident to her back, and Roy Mendoza, a former Teamster organizer from back in the day. Together they sought to stem the downward plunge by supporting reform candidates. Their efforts proved unsuccessful, as the needed upsurge from below never materialized. The Teamsters' farmworker local proved itself impervious to reforms.

Braceros, Again

If social progress could be measured in names, then an argument might be made that things are moving forward. We've gone from "wetback" to "illegal" to "undocumented," and from bracero to the nice twenty-first century moniker "guest worker." Guest worker, such a welcoming name. "Come in, you're our guest. You're welcome . . . just as long as you leave when you're no longer wanted!"

According to the U.S. Labor Department, as of 2009 there were 86,000 H-2a (guest) workers in the United States, and growers have made it clear they would like more. Those in government who advocate expanding the contract-a-slave, guest worker program, are generally on the liberal side of the ledger, while the right generally opposes it, not in principle, but still miffed, because during the Bracero Program of 1941 to 1964, there was a large increase in the size of Latino communities, something the bracero system was supposed to prevent.

Toro camp near Salinas is an old bracero camp that became an Inter-harvest and Sun Harvest lettuce crew camp in the 1980s. Later it became one of the few remaining camps for workers making the migratory circuit through the 1990s. Today, it has returned to its roots, a camp for workers brought in to the fields under the Labor Department H-2a (guest worker) program. I used to spend time here when it was the main camp for Sun Harvest ground crews more than three decades ago. The camp looks a little cleaner now, but it's essentially the same, with fewer cars. Modern updates include closed-circuit cameras. There was more vigilance at the bracero camp than I had seen previously. One day I was stopped going in and told, for the first time, that I needed permission to enter.

On another occasion I was able to get in without a problem. I found Celestino, a man in his early thirties standing in the doorway of one of the barracks, looking out on the adjacent fields. He was friendly and open and talked at length about his village in the Sierra Sur de Oaxaca, its problems, and the allure of possibilities that drew him north.

He was one of 140 H2a workers at the camp working for Fresh Harvest Company. In his first year, he made $9.72 an hour working on a lettuce machine where lettuce is cut and cored and dumped in bins for the shed and the salad shredder. But the wage dropped the following year to $9, which he attributed to the recession. Ten dollars a day was subtracted for camp room and board.

As a contracted worker, Celestino spent six months in Salinas and then four or five months in the Yuma area. The contract had to be renewed in Nogales every six months. Celestino was happy with his arrangement because it allowed him a month in Mexico with his family without risking his life crossing the border. Celestino thought he never would have come north had it not been for the H2a program. Ten people from his Oaxacan village disappeared at the U.S-Mexico border in recent years, and there were plenty of stories of hardships and abuse. He was especially incensed at the mistreatment of young women from his village, many of whom were raped in the course of the perilous journey, some as young as fifteen.

Celestino has two young children. He wants them to study, and this is much of what pushed him to this sacrifice of living apart from his family.

Growers can qualify for H2a workers if they can prove that they are unable to find workers they need in the United States. There are far more such contracted workers in the border area, especially Arizona, because of immigration raids. It is the migra that guarantee that the growers qualify for "guest workers." And so the dance of U.S. immigration continues, in many ways, like always.

Bud Antle and the Dole Company are among the large-scale exploiters of bracero labor. Antle has 750 bracero/guest workers, mainly in the Yuma, Arizona, area. To qualify for contracted workers, growers must supply a certain amount of worker housing, but growers are trying to get rid of the housing provision.[30]

Many people I spoke with around Salinas were surprised about the existence of the bracero camp. Some farmworkers expressed envy that these braceros can go home and return without risking their lives, and without spending thousands on payments to "coyotes" to bring them across. I've even heard progressive, pro-immigrant rights people like actress Eva Longoria call for an expanded guest worker program. I take this as a sign of just how much things have deteriorated.

Labor Commissions and Revealing Admissions

Remembering what Israel, my old crewmate and now foreman, had told me, I went to the Labor Commission office on North Main Street in Salinas to see for myself how well this government agency protects the rights of workers. I introduced myself to the commissioner at the complaints window. She expressed frustration as she related a recent case against a labor contractor who was paying in cash and pocketing money deducted for Social Security. Her witness, a single mother, told the commissioner she would not testify against the contractor for fear of the consequences for her and her children. According to the commissioner, this was a fairly typical situation.

When several young workers came in looking for help, I moved back to give them space at the window. I overheard the labor commissioner

talking to them. One of the workers had been fired from a lettuce contractors crew, accused of stealing something from the company. "I didn't
steal anything," he insisted. He demanded proof from the contractor but
was offered none. He wanted to know how he could fight the accusation and get his job back. The commissioner was sympathetic, and took
time to hear the young man's explanation. Finally she said, "You know,
the fact is, the company can fire you without any cause whatever. They
don't even have to have an excuse, so there is really no way you can fight
this." Then, perhaps to soften the blow, she added, "But you know, you
can quit too, without any excuse or explanation at all." At that, I had to
stop myself from laughing. The Labor Commission woman had just sum-
marized about as succinctly as one can the logic of justice that lies at the
heart of this "democracy": "We can take away your livelihood without
cause or recourse. But you can quit, take away your own livelihood, also
without cause." Here is the logic of a system based on the exploitation of
labor, and engaged in constant warfare to protect or expand that exploitation: "We reserve the right to kill you, but you can also commit suicide."
Human (though I prefer to call it inhuman) exploitation demands the
suffering of some as the prerequisite for the sustenance of others, and for
the ceaseless drive to accumulate capital. It is the injustice at the base of
all injustice, the foundation of the whole capitalist edifice and the monstrous roadblock to human progress.

No matter how wired (or wireless) we become, how advanced our
forms of transportation or communication, how fine our instruments of
discovery, how vast our ability to produce, so long as we humans live off
the suffering of one another, so long as our social system rests on such
relations of exploitation, we will remain stunted, primitive and barbaric,
violent, destructive, and unjust. So foundational to this system are these
relations of exploitation that they are usually equated with human nature
itself. We may continue, almost oblivious to their historically limited role
in our suffering, until that time when we no longer can . . .

NOTES

1. A THINNING CREW, OR "*LOS AGACHADOS*"

1. Some thirty ROTC buildings nationwide were bombed or burned in the days of student uprisings that followed the Cambodian invasion. Millions of college and high school students took part in strikes and mobilizations. National Guard troops were mobilized at twenty-one campuses in sixteen states. On May 4, 1970, four students were killed by Guard troops at Kent State, Ohio, and on May 14, two students at Jackson State in Mississippi were killed and eighteen wounded by police in actions related to the nationwide student protests.

2. Thomas McCann, *An American Company: The Tragedy of United Fruit* (New York: Crown, 1976), 232. Black's efforts were rather awkward and unsuccessful. He created resentment among the old hands who were used to a more unabashed and unapologetic approach to corporate success, and the company's fortunes declined under his directorship. In 1975 Black committed suicide by leaping from the 44th floor of United Brands' office in New York. A bribery scandal involving Black and the president of Honduras had just begun to emerge.

3. *Salinas Californian*, October 2, 1974: "The red baiting and vigilantism came to a climax September 22, 1934, when a labor camp near Chualar owned by Filipino labor leader Rufo Canete burned to the ground following a raiding party firing upon the building with shotguns and rifles in an effort to intimidate the 60 occupants."

4. "Salinas Lettuce Strike of 1936," *The Worker*, July 1972, 6–7: "The *Monterey Herald* ridiculed the hysteria rattling nearby Salinas Valley and reported on an exasperated director of the state traffic court lamenting the disappearance of red flags used to mark out future work on the highway near Salinas."

2. FALL AND WINTER

1. Katsuichi was held at Lordsburg Internment Camp in New Mexico and later in a prison in Santa Fe. Meanwhile, his family was in an internment

camp in Poston, Arizona. There the family pleaded repeatedly to the authorities to allow Katsuichi to join his wife and children. These requests were denied, and family members were accused of disloyalty for their pleas on his behalf. Meanwhile, Katsuichi's health deteriorated and he was hospitalized for several months. Finally, in September 1943, he was allowed to join his family in the internment camp in Arizona. But his health had been shattered. He died in January 1944.

2. "As the workers scrambled off their ladders and dove for cover, they saw Romulo standing there clutching his hand and the patrolman still holding his .357-magnum revolver on Romulo at point-blank range. Within a minute the officer fired again. The second shot struck Romulo in the chest and he crumpled to the ground mortally wounded. . . . Romulo's brothers . . . were prevented from getting near his body. None of the workers were allowed close enough to administer first aid or religious rites. When Jose Reyes, the local UFWOC Representative, arrived at the field, he could see Romulo's body still lying where he had died." UFWOC, "How Romulo Avalos Died," February 1972, UFW Research Collection, Box 47, folder 21, Wayne State University, Reuther Library.

3. The Merced grand jury later ruled the shooting justified.

3. THE WINDS KEEP BLOWING, 1972

1. Mae Sakasegawa, *The Issei of the Salinas Valley: Japanese Pioneer Families* (Salinas, CA: Salinas Valley JACL Senior, 2010), 145. One of the most successful lettuce growers was a Nisei farmer named Takeo Yuki. He is credited, along with his partner Tom Bunn, for initiating year-round lettuce farming with a winter harvest in Yuma. In 1942 he was interned along with his family. While he was being held at the Salinas rodeo grounds the *Saturday Evening Post* interviewed him. The same article quotes the secretary of the Salinas Vegetable Grower-Shipping Association, Austin Anson: "We're charged with wanting to get rid of the Japs for selfish reasons. We might as well be honest. We do. They came into this valley to work and they stayed to take over. If all the Japs were removed tomorrow, we'd never miss them in two weeks, because the white farmers can take over and produce everything the Jap grows. And we don't want them back when the war ends either." *Saturday Evening Post*, May 9, 1942. In fact, an atmosphere of racist hatred kept many Japanese Americans from returning to Salinas following the Second World War.

2. John C. Hammerback and Richard J. Jensen, *Rhetorical Career of César Chávez* (College Station: Texas A & M University Press, 1998), 113.

3. "It is a story that does not deny or forget that it was due to this revolution that the average life expectancy of the majority of Chinese increased from 35 in 1949 to 63 by 1975, that it was a revolution that brought unity and stability to a nation tortured for so long by disunity and instability. . . . It is a story about a revolution 'of the people' that enabled land reform, that promoted women's status, that improved popular literacy and health care, and that eventually transformed Chinese society beyond recognition from its parlous state prior to the Revolution." Mobo Gao, *The Battle for China's Past: Mao and the Cultural Revolution* (London: Pluto Press, 2008), 10.

4.   Hammerback and Jensen, *Rhetorical Career of César Chávez*, 102.

5.   Ibid. Author's emphasis.

6.   Bai Di, Xueping Zhong, and Wang Zheng, *Chinese Women Growing Up in the Mao Era* (Camden, NJ: Rutgers University Press, 2001), 1. There were 16.23 million urban youths who went to the countryside during China's Cultural Revolution (1966–76).

7.   "By the standard of the currently dominant discourse of liberal democracy shangshan xiaxiang [sending the educated youth to the mountain and the countryside] was a violation of human rights. This identification with the globally dominant value means that it is irrelevant that most, if not all, educated youth, at least at the initial stage, volunteered to take part in the movement. . . . It is also irrelevant that for all intents and purposes educated youth 'suffered' only from an urban perspective and to large extent only from hindsight. From the perspectives of the rural residents, the educated youth had a good life. They did not have to work as hard as the local farmers and they had state and family subsidies. They would frequently go back to visit their parents in the cities and they had money to spend and wore fashionable clothes. They would bring food in cans and tins that the rural people had never seen." Gao, *The Battle for China's Past*, 35–36.

8.   Ibid., 128. The dominant narrative on the Cultural Revolution skirts the issue of why it was initiated and what it sought to accomplish. "The intellectual consensus all over the world seems to be that not only should the Russian and Chinese Revolutions be jettisoned but that the idea of revolution should be buried. This global intellectual climate change has been so convincingly persuasive that the two-line struggle thesis that was offered as the rationale for the origin of the Cultural Revolution has been considered largely discredited. The dispute between Liu (Shao Shi) and Mao is seen as largely a personal power struggle." Mobo Gao subsequently discusses the growing criticism of that view being debated within China and the evidence that is being published that, in fact, the Cultural Revolution was no mere power struggle but a "two-line struggle" over which path Chinese society would take, socialist/Communist or capitalist. To use an analogy, reducing the Cultural Revolution to a personal rivalry between Mao and other leaders in Chinese society is like consigning the U.S. Civil War to a personal rivalry between Abraham Lincoln and Jefferson Davis. In that light, the Civil War would indeed seem like a brutal and pointless slaughter and Lincoln a demagogue guilty of grave and pointless injury to the people of the United States. To advance such a thesis would be historically inaccurate, intellectually lazy, and outright dishonest. This is no less the case with regard to the Cultural Revolution in China. If the fate of the United States—slave or free, that is, based on the system of wage labor—was decided in the Civil War, the Cultural Revolution was over matters no less weighty.

9.   "I was not sent to [the countryside]. I volunteered . . . I always felt that I was a revolutionary. I was about making a change in society. So I was graduating from middle school, I was 15 years old, that was in 1971. The state had a policy at that point that you could stay in the city . . . but I always thought I should go to the countryside because the educated youth were sent down to the countryside in order to receive a re-education from the

peasants. Mao's idea was that the youth, especially from the urban areas, they had a very limited understanding of society. They were privileged and didn't understand 80% of the population, the peasants. So you should go there to understand the reality of China. That started in 1964 before the Cultural Revolution. But then the mass of educated youth would go to the countryside starting in 1968. When my time came I said I wanted to go to the countryside. . . . That was the most memorable time of my life. . . . We worked 10 hours in the field but we were singing songs. We felt with our own hands we were making something. " Bai Di, co-editor of *Some of Us: Chinese Women Growing Up in the Mao Era*, interview with Michael Slate, KPFK, November 11, 2009.

10. We were naïve in underestimating the complicated and protracted process this entailed. A lot of us underestimated the intensity of the struggle inside China even though Mao warned repeatedly that capitalism could return to power. We were unaware of some of the Maoist policies themselves that contributed to these problems of continuing on the socialist road. For an in-depth discussion on these matters see Bob Avakian, "The Cultural Revolution in China . . . Art and Culture . . . Dissent and Ferment . . . and Carrying Forward the Revolution Toward Communism," *Revolution* #260, February 19, 2012.

11. There were within the revolutionary movement competing ideas about how to bring about radical change, even among and within organizations that sided with and raised the banner of Mao. The struggle over various ideas raged with great passion in the movement of those days and within all the groups and individuals who were part of it.

12. Burton Anderson, *The Salinas Valley: A History of America's Lettuce Bowl* (Monterey, CA: Monterey County Historical Society, 2000).

13. Sandy Lydon, *Chinese Gold: The Chinese in the Monterey Bay Region* (Capitola CA: Capitola Book Company, 1985), 72.

14. Ron Takaki, *A Different Mirror: A History of Multicultural America* (New York: Little, Brown, 1993), 199. "In the Salinas Valley, Chinese laborers dug six miles of ditches to drain the land, cutting peat soil with huge knife-like spades and pitching it out with steel forks and hooks." Their work boosted the value of the land from $28 per acre in 1875 to $100 two years later.

15. Carey McWilliams, *Factories in the Fields: The Story of Migratory Farm Labor in California* (Santa Barbara, CA: Peregrine Press, 1971), 1–3.

16. Jennie Verardo and Denzil Verardo, *The Salinas Valley: An Illustrated History* (Northridge, CA: Windsor Publications, 1989). Sugar beet production around Castroville, north of Salinas, gave way in the 1920s to artichokes.

17. "The harvest from each acre [of sugar beets] produced 17,036 pounds of sugar—enough to sweeten 175,000 12-ounce bottles of soda water or 27,155 gallons of ice cream." *Monterey Herald Weekend Magazine*, September 15, 1973.

18. Fragging was a violent form of protest involving the use of fragmentation grenades tossed into the sleeping quarters of unit officers. In 1970 in Vietnam, 209 incidents of fragging were reported. Dave Zirin, in *A People's History of Sports* (New York: New Press, 2008), 182, says that "U.S. troops

carried out an estimated eight hundred to one thousand fragging attempts against their commanding officers." Hundreds of officers were killed or wounded in these attacks.

19. An 18-hole round of golf at the Pebble Beach course in 2010 would cost roughly 62 hours of backbreaking labor in a Salinas lettuce field, excluding cart fees.

20. The idea that anyone can rise above a life of poverty and exploitation is logically absurd. This same idea was expressed quite dramatically by Bob Avakian in his book, *Basics* (Chicago: RCP Publications, 2011): "Determination decides who makes it out of the ghetto—now there is a tired old cliché, at its worst, on every level. This is like looking at millions of people being put through a meatgrinder and instead of focusing on the fact that the great majority are chewed to pieces, concentrating instead on the few who slip through in one piece and then on top of it all, using this to say that 'the meatgrinder works'!" (8).

21. *Apodos* were a convenient and acceptable way to address someone whose name you might have forgotten or never knew. Among fieldworkers one encountered many had nicknames taken from physical characteristics: Chino, curly; Flaco, skinny; Gordo, fatty; Chato, bulldog-nosed; Bonito, pretty. Animal nicknames were also common: Gato, cat; Chivo, goat; Culebre, snake; and many others.

22. From interviews conducted by the author with Rafael Lemus, Salinas, September 2009.

23. The NFWA and UWOC merged in September 1966 to form the United Farmworkers Organizing Committee. The Executive Committee formed from the merger included the founders of NFWA and the Filipino leaders from UWOC, Larry Itliong and Phil Vera Cruz.

24. From interviews conducted by the author with Jose Perez, veteran farmworker activist, Salinas, July 2009.

25. "Several years later Cal Watkins, the personnel manager for Interharvest, filed a sworn affidavit testifying that he attended a meeting of the Grower Shipper Vegetable Association negotiating committee on July 23, 1970 when it was decided to get powers of attorney from members to 'feel out the Teamsters and explore the prospects of negotiating an agreement for agricultural workers.' On the next day, his affidavit said, 'The committee reported that the Teamsters were interested and receptive' and 29 firms signed a recognition agreement. On July 25 they started negotiating with the Teamsters. 'The union did not claim to represent any agriculture employees at this time,' Watkins said." Jacques Levy, *Autobiography of La Causa* (New York: W. W. Norton, 1975), 403.

26. From interviews conducted by the author with residents of Toro Camp, McFadden Road, Salinas, July 2008.

27. *El Obrero del Valle de Salinas,* June 1972.

28. *Salinas Californian*, December 6, 1972.

4. THE BATTLE LINES SHARPEN, SPRING 1973

1. "The most recent recession of the lake probably occurred between 1400 and 1500 AD, only a few generations before Alarcon sailed into the mouth

of the Colorado with the royal banner of Spain flapping from his mast. The desiccation of the lake may have forced lake dependent bands to compete for territory on the already occupied banks of the Colorado which might partly account for the enduring hostility among river tribes that Alarcon and every European who followed him observed." William deBuys and Joan Myers, *Salt Dreams, Land and Water in Low Down California* (Albuquerque: University of New Mexico Press, 1999), 58.

2. From a conversation with Sid Valledor, historian and former assistant to Larry Itliong, Oakland, CA, September 8, 2012.

3. Marshall Ganz, *Why David Sometimes Wins* (New York: Oxford University Press, 2009), 111.

4. Different numbers have been cited by different sources as to the actual offer from the growers. One source told me that César Chávez recalled it was $1 an hour, whereas Ronald Taylor, a journalist who was actively reporting on field issues in the period and is author of *Chávez and the Farmworkers* (Boston: Beacon Press, 1975), quoted the figure at $1.20 an hour. Sid Valledor, Filipino farmworker, historian, and author of *The Original Writings of Philip Vera Cruz* (Indianapolis: Dog Ear Publishing, 2006), also cited the $1.20 an hour figure to me.

5. "On September 8, 1965, at the Filipino Hall at 1457 Glenwood St. in Delano, the Filipino members of AWOC held a mass meeting to discuss and decide whether to go on strike or accept the reduced wages proposed by the growers. The decision was to strike and it became one of the most significant and famous decisions ever made in the entire history of farmworkers' labor struggles in California. It was like an incendiary bomb, exploding out the strike message to the workers in the vineyards, telling them to have sit-ins in the labor camps and set up picket lines at every growers ranch. There had been small strikes in Delano before but this was the first major strike." Craig Scharlin and Lilia V. Villanueva, *Philip Vera Cruz: A Personal History of Filipino Immigrants and the Farmworkers Movement* (Los Angeles: UCLA Labor Center, Institute of Industrial Relations & UCLA Asian American Studies Center, 1992), 30.

6. The dream of a white California accompanied the western migration for the Gold Rush of 1849 and the Mexican War. Southern slave owners lost their bid to make California a slave state, but the vision of a white California was never seriously contested. Thus when the waves of immigrants from Asia and south of the border were brought in to do the hard labor in California's fields, laws were imposed to restrict their rights, and recruitment alternated with spasms of racist pogroms and campaigns of mass deportation—a schizoid dance of immigration. The battle to prevent the establishment of large communities of "color" was lost long ago, but the dance continues to this day, now on a national scale.

7. "The virus of McCarthyism had spread to infect virtually all of American life. By the beginning of the fall semester of 1951, after nearly two years of McCarthyism, fears of Communism were imposing a crippling conformity on American campuses. 'Misguided zealots shout "communist" at every college professor who ventures a new idea or selects a different text book,' Jazzes H. Halsey, the president of the University of Bridgeport, told his stu-

dents and faculty in that fall's convocation. 'Pressure groups issue blanket condemnations of new curriculum developments, and State Legislatures conduct investigations about subversive campus activities. These are days of crisis and on every hand we see numerous evidences of attempts to curb freedom of thought and freedom of expression.'" Haynes Johnson, *The Age of Anxiety: From McCarthyism to Terrorism* (New York: Harcourt Inc. 2005), 231.

8. Literally, *zángano* is the male drone that aids the queen bee in reproduction but does no gathering of honey. From this comes its colloquial meaning, "lazybones." In Mexico it is used to refer to men who live off women, or workers in any group who hang back and let others do the bulk of the work. Because the word sounds like the Spanish word *sangre*, blood, for a long time I assumed *zángano* was a bloodsucking insect and meant "bloodsuckers." In fact, zángano's insult value is more potent than the literal meaning, "drone," in English, would imply.

9. "At the highest level, labor operations congenial to the Agency are supported through George Meany, President of the AFL; Jay Lovestone Foreign Affairs Chief of the AFL; and Irving Brown, AFL representative—all of whom were described to us as effective spokesmen for positions in accordance with the Agency's needs." Philip Agee, *Inside the Company, CIA Diary* (New York: Farrar, Straus and Giroux, 1975), 75.

10. A sharp ideological debate in the early 1960s first came to light in a series of letters between the Communist parties of the Soviet Union and China. China accused the Soviet Union of abandoning revolution in pursuit of a policy of imperialist expansion. The Soviet Union accused the Chinese Communists of adventurism and recklessness in the face of a nuclear-armed world. In 1959 the Cuban Revolution overthrew the U.S.-backed Batista dictatorship and began a process of radical social reform, welcomed by progressive people across the world. When Cuba allied with the Soviet Union in the early 1960s, it provoked debate. Some saw this as a necessary step to defend Cuba from U.S. threats, regarding the Soviet Union as an uninspiring but genuine socialist regime. Others, myself included, saw in the Soviet Union a restored capitalist society pursuing an imperialist agenda behind the facade of socialism, using Cuba as a cover for the pursuit of its own imperial interests.

11. Ojo Negro, *Lettuce: From Seed to Supermarket: A report about the lettuce industry from the 1970's*. Prepared for the United Farmworkers Organizing Committee, May 1972.

12. Ibid. The 1970 break-even costs for lettuce growers were about $1.90 per box for "naked pack" lettuce. The price to consumers averaged about $6.35 a box. Out of that, the cost of farmworkers' labor, from thinning and hoeing, irrigating, tractor driving, and harvesting, came to about 2.4 cents a head or about 29 cents a box; 2.4 cents equaled about 9 percent of the cost of a head of lettuce as sold by a grower-shipper, but only about 3 to 4 percent of the price to the public.

13. Ibid. "The industry is constantly going from feast to famine and back again. The classic example of famine is the 1966–67 winter deal. The Salinas district had completed a prosperous season that summer and when Central

Arizona opened on November 1 prices were quoted at $3.75. By the time Yuma opened on Nov 22, FOB was down to $1.63. The Imperial Valley deal started on Dec. 7 at $1.25. Only when ice formed on the lettuce in the fields in mid January did the shortened supply kick the price up to $3, but a week later it was down to $1.38. By mid-Feb. the FOB had reached a rock-bottom $1. The result was 2,000 acres of lettuce left uncut, representing 5 to 8 million cartons left in the fields. Losses were estimated to be $30 million."

14.   I was unable to find a reliable figure for the life span of a California farmworker. In a 1984 speech to the San Francisco Commonwealth Club, César Chávez states that a farmworker's life span was forty-nine compared to the national average of seventy-three. The forty-nine figure was quoted in the 2010 publication by Gabriel Thompson, *Working in the Shadows: A Year of Doing the Jobs Most Americans Won't Do* (New York: Nation Books, 2010), 74, and attributed it to the National Migrant Resources Program. But some, including Gil Padilla in an interview with Frank Bardacke, questioned this statistic.

15.   If several conditions are present at the same time, a person's body temperature may rise above safe limits. The body loses large amounts of body water and salt in perspiration. Perspiration is one of the body's defenses against heat: the body releases water to cool the skin. Most people suffer only muscle pain as a result of heat stress. The pain is a warning that the body is becoming too hot. Doctors say those suffering muscle pain should stop all activity and rest in a cool place. That they should also drink cool liquids and not to return to physical activity for a few hours because more serious conditions could develop.

16.   "After all it was Chávez's own people who went to work behind the picket lines in Coachella, and that didn't indicate much support from the workers for Chávez . . . that situation in Coachella was almost a disaster." Taylor, *Chávez and the Farmworkers*, 317.

17.   Francisco Balderrama and Raymond Rodriguez, *Decade of Betrayal: Mexican Repatriation in the 1930s* (Albuquerque: University of New Mexico Press, 2006), 82: "After the advent of the New Deal administration of Franklin D. Roosevelt, deportation proceedings assumed a more humane aspect." The authors point out, however, that this was not due to a change in administration. Rather, "immigration to the United States decreased dramatically from previous years. From 1925 to 1929, 2,474,500 immigrants entered the country, whereas from 1930 to 1934 only 1,216,396 entries were recorded. Most of them were legal immigrants admitted under quota to join families already in the United States. The lack of employment opportunities discouraged many would-be illegal aliens from entering the country. . . . This did not mean the end of the deportation terror [under Roosevelt], but after 1934 the number of Mexicans being deported fell dramatically by approximately 50%."

18.   "Once hired, blacks found themselves placed in the least desirable jobs, disproportionately in unskilled and semiskilled sectors, usually in the dirtiest and most dangerous parts of the plant. Some employers based hiring decisions on straightforward racial antipathy. One auto company official hired blacks to work in the dangerous paint room. He explained his ratio-

nale: 'Yes, some jobs white folks will not do, so they have to take n_____ in, particularly in duct work, spraying paint on car bodies. This soon kills a white man.' Asked if it killed blacks, he responded, 'It shortens their lives, it cuts them down but they're just n_____. . . . As a result of discrimination at the hiring gate, blacks remained overrepresented in unskilled occupations, were most susceptible to layoffs, and most vulnerable to replacement when plants automated." Thomas J. Sugrue, *Origins of the Urban Crisis* (Princeton: Princeton University Press, 1996), 99–100.

19.   "One important report did appear in 1973. Called the *Health Research Group of Disease among Workers in the Auto Industry*, it was based on figures compiled by the National Institute for Occupational Safety and Health and was written by two medical doctors, Janette Sherman and Sidney Wolfe. The report estimated sixty-five on-the-job deaths *per day* among auto workers, for a total of some 16,000 annually. Approximately half these deaths were from heart attacks. There were also some 63,000 cases of disabling diseases and about 1,700,000 cases of lost or impaired hearing. These statistics did not include many long-term illnesses endemic to foundry workers and others exposed to poisonous chemicals and gases, nor did they include deaths and injuries by accident. Even these limited figures made it clear that more auto workers were killed and injured each year on the job than soldiers were killed and injured during any year of the war in Vietnam." Dan Georgakas and Marvin Surkin, *Detroit: I Do Mind Dying* (Boston: South End Press, 1998), 88.

20.   In August, a more serious wildcat hit another Chrysler plant that produced crankshafts, pinions, and torsion bars. It followed six months of seven-day weeks and a series of accidents that crippled several workers. When the company fired sixteen workers for publicly exposing health and safety violations, the 1,100 workers at the plant shut it down for six days. Later in August a third major wildcat shut down another Chrysler plant. This time, the UAW, along with local police, helped break the strike. The conflict within the UAW was at the center of a much bigger controversy. The wildcats were taking place because of brutal conditions in Detroit auto plants. And these were part of larger changes unfolding in these years—speed-ups, plant closings, runaway shops, especially in the southern United States. A new phenomenon was making its appearance in twentieth-century America—the Rust Belt and inner-city devastation that would cause enormous suffering, especially to the African American population.

21.   Ellen Hawkes, *Blood and Wine: The Unauthorized Story of the Gallo Wine Empire* (New York: Simon and Schuster, 1993), 190.

22.   Ross was a close associate of the social activist Saul Alinsky, who described himself as a radical community organizer (his most famous book is *Reveille for Radicals*) to distinguish his views from the liberals he scorned. Alinsky sought greater social justice through mass action. On a deeper level, Alinsky's differences with liberals were more tactical than strategic. Alinsky's politics could be described as radical reformism, using the leverage of various kinds of pressure to wrench reforms from the established structure of industry and government. His aims were never to challenge the basis of that power or any of the underlying structures of exploitation.

23. The quote is from Leo Chávez, *Shadowed Lives: Undocumented Immigrants in American Society* (Fort Worth, TX: Harcourt Brace Jovanovich, 1992).

24. Wages, working, and living conditions of contracted braceros were established through agreements between the United States and Mexican authorities. Literature on the Bracero Program is filled with accounts of violations of established wages and conditions. To cite just one example, a researcher from the U.S. Bishops Committee for the Spanish Speaking documented how record books were cooked so that braceros he knew "were all working 12 hours a day and who were being credited and paid for 6 or 7 hours of work." Cited in Juan Ramon Garcia, *Operation Wetback: The Mass Deportation of Mexican Undocumented Workers in 1954* (Westport, CT: Greenwood Press, 1980), 51.

25. Frank Bardacke, *Trampling Out the Vintage: César Chávez and the Two Souls of the United Farmworkers* (New York: Verso, 2011), 160.

26. Ibid., 392.

5. FIRES STILL BURNING

1. Manuel Chávez, César's first cousin, was part of the original core that initiated the National Farmworkers Association. He developed a reputation within the close circle of the UFW as a scoundrel, someone given to exaggeration and outright lying at times. Manuel was given free rein, especially around the strike wave of 1974, to organize job actions and for a number of years was active among Central Valley melon workers, and credited with bringing them out on strike. Manuel became closely associated with what became known as the "night crew." In less neutral language, union goons.

2. "Nixon had long engaged in similar illegalities against anti-war groups and dissidents." Nixon's fatal mistake was to use these illegal tactics on the liberal class itself. Once the Democratic Party and the liberal class became targets of Nixon's illegalities, the media were empowered to expose abuses they had previously ignored (258). Chris Hedges, *Death of the Liberal Class* (New York: Nation Books, 2010), 169.

3. UFW, "Fresno County Illegals Campaign—1974 to October 12," UFW Research Collection, Box 7, folder 5, Walter P. Reuther Library, Wayne State University. The report outlines the extensive campaign of documentation, aimed at pressuring government authorities and public opinion, launched in Fresno County, which the UFW leadership chose as the focus of the campaign. Among the efforts outlined is the following passage from p. 2:

> In an attempt to discourage local residents from contributing to the illegals problem by housing the aliens, our office wrote a form letter to more than 175 of such people who had been reported to our office. . . . Of the ones that arrived at the correct address, many brought rapid and decisive replies. More than a few of the addressees telephoned the office saying that their illegals were going to go.
>
> As it states in the letter to harborers, all of their names and addresses were turned over to the Internal Revenue Service and the U.S. Border Patrol. The Border Patrol has not to my knowledge arrested any of the harborers to date, but the IRS at least gave us a call in an effort to determine the more serious offenders. We have not

yet sent the list of the tax evaders that we consider to be the "big offenders," but the option is still open.

4. Frank Bardacke, *Trampling Out the Vintage: César Chávez and the Two Souls of the United Farmworkers* (New York: Verso, 2011). Bardacke's detailed history of the UFW has a fairly extensive account of brutal actions carried out by Manuel Chávez's squad on the Arizona border, including this on p. 501:

> The fullest account of violence on the wet line comes from an article written by Tom Barry for *Mother Jones* in 1978 but never published . . . . Salvador Sandoval Yala, the city attorney of Ciudad Morales, who headed a Mexican federal investigation into the San Luis strike, told Barry that "wet line patrollers had beaten, stripped and robbed undocumented workers." An unnamed Mexican labor official said, "There were many, many beatings during the strike, especially right along the border. The men were stripped, beaten, and sent back across. I saw two men who had been beaten with chains, and I know of one worker who had his fingers crushed with a brick." A reporter from *El Malcriado* who asked not to be identified said, "There were many cases of atrocities, including one man who had a knife stuck up his nose and ripped out just like in the movie *Chinatown*."

6. NEW LAW, 1975

1. One dramatic example of this was the rapid rise in the U.S. prison population that began in the mid-1970s, related to efforts to prevent the kind of radical upheaval in the black community that helped spark the 1960s and give it its radical character. Drug laws were used to incarcerate millions of young African Americans and Latinos with the intent of suppressing radical leadership from within before it could develop. Michelle Alexander called this policy "the new Jim Crow." See Michelle Alexander, *The New Jim Crow: Mass Incarceration in the Age of Colorblindness* (New York: New Press, 2010).

2. Frank Bardacke, *Trampling Out the Vintage* (New York: Verso, 2011), 512. Growers, under advice of anti-union law firms, "challenged certain provisions of the law procedurally and simply ignored others. They would play the ALRB as industry played the NLRB where employers violated the law with impunity."

   Roy Mendoza, a longtime Teamster farmworker official, recalled a general confidence among growers that the ALRA could be used to work in their favor; for example, Andrew Church, a prominent grower attorney, confided that the ALRA would be used to advance grower interests. Roy Mendoza, conversation with author, Salinas, 2010.

3. "The apparition of the Virgin of Guadalupe was the cornerstone of the evangelization of Mexico and Latin America . . . just as the silver lodes of Zacatecas would soon generate incalculable wealth for the secular kings, the Guadalupana reaped bonanza of souls for the Lords of the Church. In 1536, five million Indians were converted from heathen idolatry to the Roman Catholic version of Christianity, five times the harvest of the previous

15 years of conquest and annexation." John Ross, *The Annexation of Mexico: From the Aztecs to the IMF* (Monroe, ME: Common Courage Press, 1998), 17.

4. The White Rose story was more interwoven with my family than I realized at the time. Years later, while traveling in Munich, I saw a granite monument commemorating the White Rose. In the spring of 1942 my grandfather Benno and my grandmother Anna had been picked up by the Gestapo after three desperate years trying to leave Germany. Benno was taken to Berlin, put on trial, accused of sending anti-Nazi propaganda through the mail, and executed in late summer 1942 at the Plotzonsee prison, in a death house used to execute resisters. In the summer of 1942 White Rose activists from Munich's Catholic University began printing leaflets and distributing them on the college campus and anonymously through the mail. For many months the authorities were unable to discover the resisters behind these acts. Some of the core activists of the White Rose were discovered in 1943 and executed in Munich.

5. *Salinas Californian*, October 14, 1975.

6. Bardacke, *Trampling Out the Vintage*, 515–16. The UFW's successes came mainly in the vegetable-growing areas and in some of the areas where strike battles erupted in 1974. The UFW did poorly in the grape-growing areas, winning only a small minority of elections in Coachella and the Delano area.

7. *Fayuca* is the name workers used for the food trucks that were on streets in the early morning, and sometimes came to the fields. *Fayuca* means contraband or black market. According to one source in the 1950's smugglers around the U.S.–Mexico border areas brought *U.S. goods into Mexico* and sold them from trucks. Such trucks were called fayucas and their owners, fayuqueros. Workers coming over the border then brought the habit of calling vending trucks fayucas with them.

8. Miriam Pawel, *The Union of Their Dreams* (Bloomsbury Press, 2009), 149. "When Jerry (UFW attorney Jerry Cohen) called Chávez to tell him about the victory (passage of the ALRA through the California Assembly) Chávez reacted with resignation, not joy. He knew a law would fundamentally change the rules of the game."

9. Dorothy P. Kerig, *El Valle de Mexicali y la Colorado River Land Company, 1902-1946* (Mexicali: Universidad Autónoma de Baja California, 2001), 28–29.

10. William De Buys and Joan Myers, *Salt Dreams: Land and Dreams in Low-Down California* (Albuquerque: University of New Mexico Press, 1999), 144–45.

11. The population of Mexicali in 2005 was more than 900,000.

7. 1976

1. *U.S. News and World Report*, July 5, 1976, 343.

2. John Ross, *The Annexation of Mexico: From the Aztecs to the IMF* (Monroe, ME: Common Courage Press, 1998), 74–77. General John J. Pershing led a U.S. force that grew to 10,000 soldiers to capture or kill Villa in punishment for a cross-border raid on Columbus, New Mexico. Villa's raid was

intended to provoke such a reaction and put the United States in conflict with Mexico's Carranza government, which had previously worked with the United States to attack and destroy Villa and his "Division del Norte." Pershing's expedition, which began March 14, 1916, ended unsuccessfully in February 1917.

3.   The contrast between conditions and policies in China's factories in the socialist period, especially during the Cultural Revolution, and today could hardly be more dramatic. Then, emphasis was on developing collective leadership and expanding participation of workers in factory affairs *and* affairs of the state. Slogans urged workers to become the masters of society, to take up the reins of responsibility in all spheres of society including governing. Chinese factories today, like Foxconn, are hellholes where workers are kept locked down, work long hours, and live in poor conditions, such that suicide among them has become a growing occurrence. The role of workers in China today is that of wage slaves.

4.   One of the earliest and most powerful critiques of the new regime came from Bob Avakian. In 1978 the Revolutionary Communist Party (RCP) published his pamphlet, "The Loss in China and the Revolutionary Legacy of Mao Tse Tung." In his speaking and writing Avakian analyzed changes in China and the reasons behind them while defending principles Mao had fought for. His works on the situation in China, the causes of the loss of socialism, its implications and lessons for the struggle to achieve socialism and communism, is part of a body of work being called the new synthesis.

5.   "It has been said that 'one of everything' has been found in the waters of the New River: all three types of polio virus, several of hepatitis, and the agents for a full gamut of gastrointestinal illnesses. The bacteria responsible for infectious diseases such as cholera, tuberculosis, and typhoid have also been found in the New River, as have salmonella bacteria and a medley of carcinogens. . . . Health officials have repeatedly measured coliform in the river at levels several thousand times that which triggers beach closings in San Diego." William DeBuys and Joan Myers, *Salt Dreams: Land and Dreams in Low-Down California* (Albuquerque: University of New Mexico Press, 1999), 236.

8. DISCONTENT

1.   "The INS had originally established the commuter status by administration fiat, and perpetuated the practice despite a number of legislative attempts to end it. . . . Senate Immigration Subcommittee Chair Senator Ralph Yarborough of Texas agreed, 'This represents an executive suspension of the immigration laws . . . this green card is something outside the law.'" Kitty Calavita, *Inside the State: The Bracero Program, Immigration and the INS* (New York: Routledge, 1992), 156–57.

2.   The views of those of us at *The Worker* on socialism and on how to get there were primitive and naïve. Fundamentally different views of socialism were not clearly delineated in our thinking. One vision was of a kind of radically reformed capitalism, which left intact many of the essential underpinnings of class society but with greater emphasis on social welfare programs, schools, health care, and the like. The other was the socialism envisioned by

Marx and carried forward most consciously by Mao: socialism as a transition to a classless society. In the latter vision, socialism is a transition period full of struggle, debate, and wrangling to bring about new relationships among people and the eventual elimination of the state, national borders, and the achievement of the Four Alls envisioned by Marx: "The abolition of class distinctions generally; the abolition of all the relations of production on which they rest; the abolition of all the social relations that correspond to these relations of production, and the revolutionizing of all the ideas that result from these social relations." The end result would be a social order of freely associating human beings all over the world. The Four Alls formulation is part of the work *Class Struggles in France*, written by Karl Marx, January–October 1850, for the *Neue Rheinische Zeitung Revue*, published in book form by Friedrich Engels, 1895.

3.   There was another "disconnect" embedded in this vision, which was impossible to resolve, against which all the mightiest efforts to reform this kind of society must crash. Even if one could imagine lifting the oppressive weight of white supremacy and national oppression, peeling away one foundational element upon which society as a whole and California agriculture in particular rests, even if this were possible, one would be left with an irresolvable dilemma: The American Dream is only possible because the American Nightmare exists elsewhere, and perhaps nowhere more destructively than in Mexico. Mexican workers in the United States could only prosper in this system by getting a greater share of the spoils of the exploitation of people on the other side of that line drawn by expansionist violence. This contradiction, purposely obscured, lies at the heart of an explosive issue with the potential to shatter all illusions of fundamental change coming by way of reform.

4.   César Chávez, "Union Business and Purpose," July 13, 1977, UFW President Collection, Box 18, folder 14, Wayne State University, Reuther Library.

5.   "The conventions were manipulated to give the union members a certain impression. Everything was planned ahead of time, but when you are there, and if you don't know what's going on, you think that things just happen on their own spontaneously. . . . There was no real substance of Filipino rank-and-file support for what César was doing. The only Filipinos he was impressing besides Andy [Andy Imutan, a conservative Filipino organizer who was close to the UFW leadership] were those from the Philippines, the Marcos supporters." Craig Scharlin and Lilia V. Villanueva, *Philip Vera Cruz: A Personal History of Filipino Immigrants and the Farmworkers' Movement* (Los Angeles: UCLA Labor Center, Institute of Industrial Relations & UCLA Asian American Studies Center, 1992), 117.

6.   Ibid., 118.

7.   Michael D. Yates, "The Rise and Fall of the United Farmworkers," review of Miriam Pawel, *The Union of Their Dreams* (New York: Bloomsbury Press, 2009), *Monthly Review*, May 2010: "Chávez began taking his inner circle to Synanon for training, and made 'The Game' a centerpiece of union activities. Right after the lost initiative campaign, Chávez had begun to purge some key personnel, charging them with disloyalty, complicity with the growers, and communism." Chávez argued that the vicious personal at-

tacks The Game encouraged was a way of fostering community. In fact, it destroyed what little progressive community remained in the union.

9. A LETTUCE STRIKE

1. According to union figures, the Salinas lettuce crop was worth $69 million in 1970 and $210 million by 1978. Profits from lettuce were $6.6 million in 1970. By 1978, they had grown to $71 million. Some of this increase was due to inflation. But the statistics were dramatic. At the same time as wages had risen 80 percent, profits were said to have increased more than 1,000 percent.

2. Author's interview with Tony Gonzales, Salinas, July 2010.

3. "Our results show that lettuce prices, as well as short-term profits to certain growers, increased substantially as a result of the strike. We demonstrate that if a union is to strike against the entire industry (i.e., all growers simultaneously), it must reduce output substantially below competitive levels in order to reduce industry profits so that growers will have an economic incentive to negotiate with union leaders. This is largely because of the number of lettuce producers and shippers and the relative abundance of farmworkers available in the Imperial Valley during the winter season." *Western Journal of Agricultural Economics* 6/1 (July 1981).

4. In Miriam Pawal's *A Union of their Dreams* (New York: Bloomsbury Press, 2010), Sandy Nathan, who worked in the UFW legal department, related the following: "Good enemies had always been central to Chávez's strategy. His union did not depend on contracts or money to be strong, he often said. . . . 'When we had a visible opponent,' Chávez reminded the board members now, 'we had unity, a real purpose. It was like a religious war'" (218–19). Chávez used anti-communism as an internal bond. It also served to cement ties with the Democrats and the establishment in general. I think this, in part, explains his fanatical, out-of-proportion preoccupation with leftists in the union.

10. VICTORY FROM DEFEAT, DEFEAT FROM VICTORY

1. *Salinas Californian*, February 20, 1979.

2. "Lettuce Strike Increased Grower Profits, Study Finds," *Los Angeles Times*, January 15, 1982.

3. *Salinas Californian*, February 3, 1979.

4. Frank Bardacke, *Trampling Out the Vintage: César Chávez and Two Souls of the United Farmworkers* (New York: Verso, 2011), 613.

5. *Salinas Californian*, February 21, 1979.

6. *Salinas Californian*, March 8, 1979.

7. John Dury, email to author, September 2008.

8. *Salinas Californian*, May 3, 1979.

9. Ibid.

10. César Chávez, "Solidarity Booklet for the Farmworkers Strike and Boycott of 1979," letter of July 27, 1979, UFW/Ganz Box 3, folder 21, Wayne State, Reuther Library.

11. *Salinas Californian*, August 4, 1979.

12. Author's interview with Aristeo Zambrano, Oakland, CA, April 2009.

13. Ibid.

14. In *Mexico Unconquered* (San Francisco: City Lights Books, 2009), John Gibler observed that there is a tendency for resistance movements among oppressed people, especially in countries dominated by imperialism, to "take on an anti-colonial dimension that challenges and threatens the legitimacy of the fundamental tenets of the state and leads to bold, creative, massive and energetic social participation" (18). Dangerous political movements are also to be found in the United States in the 1960s, when black youths began to break beyond the call for civil rights reforms and took up the perspective of Black Liberation, inspiring other oppressed groups and youth in general to do the same.

15. Author's interview with Aristeo Zambrano.

16. Ibid.

17. *Salinas Californian*, November 3, 1983.

18. Author's discussion with Mario Bustamente, El Centro, CA, January 2010.

19. *Salinas Californian*, December 18, 1981.

20. A *Salinas Californian* article in 2007 noted that of the 468 election victories of the UFW over the years, only about 140 were ever certified. Companies like Bruce Church and D'Arrigo were able to tie up negotiations for decades.

EPILOGUE: THE FIELDS TODAY

1. Ann Aurelia Lopez, *The Farmworkers' Journey* (Berkeley: University of California Press, 2007), 110–111.

2. U.S. Bureau of Labor Statistics, *Monterey County: DRI-WEFA,* quoted in Monterey County Farm Bureau 2012 report and U.S. Bureau of Labor Statistics, May 2011, Occupational Employment Statistics for Salinas, CA.

3. *Salinas Californian*, October 10, 1972.

4. Carol Sabin, *Mixtec Migrant Farmworkers in California Agriculture: A Dialogue among Mixtec Leaders, Researchers and Farm Labor Advocates* (Davis, CA: California Institute for Rural Studies, 1992), 32.

5. Major Crops, 1984–2004, Monterey County, *Salinas Californian*, May 11, 2005.

6. *Newsweek*, October 2, 2006, 43.

7. Josie Glausiusz, "Toxic Salad: What Are Fecal Bacteria Doing on Our Leafy Greens?" *Discover Magazine*, April 17, 2007.

8. E. coli stands for Escherichia coli, named after Theodor Escherich, a German-Austrian pediatrician who discovered the bacteria in the late 1800s. It's a rod-shaped bacterium that is commonly found in the lower intestine of warm-blooded organisms. Most E. coli strains, called commensal organisms because they can coexist with warm-blooded organisms, are harmless and helpful in breaking down cellulose and assisting in the absorption of vitamin K, the blood-clotting vitamin, for example. But some, like serotype 0157:H7, can cause serious illness.

9. Glausiusz, "Toxic Salad."

10. Cary Blake, "Growers, Shippers Germinate Leafy Greens Marketing Agreement in Arizona," *Western Shipper and Grower,* October 31, 2007. Vegetable growers claimed $1 billion in losses from the fallout of the deaths and illnesses.

11. Author's interview with Sylvia, veteran farmworker, Greenfield, CA, August 28, 2010.

12. In July 1954, the U.S. government launched "Operation Wetback," a tightly planned military-style operation headed by a veteran of General Pershing's 1916 invasion of Mexico, Lt. General Joseph Swing. The INS claimed it deported or drove out more than a million immigrants. Two measures preceded the actual deportation campaign. First was a massive media campaign to demonize immigrants. For example, the U.S. attorney general warned, "Wetback smuggling has mushroomed into a grave social problem involving murder, prostitution, robbery, and a gigantic narcotics infiltration . . . a malignant threat to the growth of our society." Second were measures to ensure the growers an adequate supply of bracero labor. Undocumented immigrants—"wetbacks" in the racist terminology—were "dried out," signed up as braceros, and people lured north across the border by radio advertising were also contracted. The scope of the INS operation and the intensity of the media campaign that accompanied it speak to its ambition of terrorizing the entire Latino community.

13. Carol Zabin: "We have to remember that there were grower associations from the San Joaquin that opened offices in Mexico to help people enter the United States if they wanted to apply for amnesty."

14. Don Villarejo, PhD, and Marc Schenker, MD, MPH, "Environmental Health Policy and California's Farm Labor Housing," report prepared for the John Muir Institute on the Environment (Davis: University of California, October 1, 2006): "The 1986 Immigration Reform and Control Act (IRCA) . . . granted permanent legal residence status through the Seasonal Agricultural Worker (SAW) visa program to more than 1.1 million agriculture workers, all of whom claimed to have previously worked in the U.S. without authorization. Hundreds of thousands of additional workers followed in their footsteps contributing to a substantial farm labor surplus throughout the 1990s."

15. Ibid. "The most significant development within the California farm labor market in recent times is the sharply increased flow of indigenous migrants from the southern Mexican states of Chiapas, Oaxaca, Guerrero, Puebla and Veracruz. . . . All observers agree that indigenous migrants are the fastest-growing component of the state's farm labor force."

16. Carey McWilliams, *California: The Great Exception* (Berkeley and Los Angeles: University of California Press, 1949), 155.

17. Gabriel Thompson, *Working in the Shadows: A Year of Doing Jobs Most Americans Won't Do* (New York: Nation Books, 2010). Thompson spent several months on a lettuce machine for Dole Company in Yuma, Arizona, where he cites these statistics about daily lettuce production. It should be pointed out that the Dole Company had a Teamsters union contract and conditions that were at least marginally better than those found on many contractor crews, so the 3,300 might be a low average for daily lettuce cutting.

18. Secure Communities, or SCOMM, requires local law enforcement to submit fingerprints of anyone they arrest who might be undocumented to ICE (Immigration and Customs Enforcement). The policy began in late 2008 but was expanded under Obama. It has been used to deport thousands of immigrants

and created fear in immigrant communities. It has generated widespread opposition. In October 2012, California governor Jerry Brown vetoed a bill that would have limited SCOMM to people arrested for serious crimes.

19. U.S. Agriculture and Food Law Policy blog (http://www.agandfoodlaw. com): "The bill, SB 1121, passed in the California Assembly earlier this month would have reversed a 1941 state law exempting agricultural employees from being paid 1.5 times their normal hourly rate for working over 8 hours in a day. The 1941 exemption was modified in 1976 when the Industrial Welfare Commission ordered overtime pay after 10 hours on the job and for all work on the seventh day of a week after putting in six straight days of 10 hours or more."

20. Suzanne Vaupel, "Growers' Decisions to Hire Farm Labor Contractors and Custom Harvesters,"CRLA Report of Farm Labor Contractor Abuses in California (Berkeley: Cooperative Extension, University of California, Division of Agriculture and Natural Resources, 2000), available at http://are. berkeley.edu/APMP/pubs/flc/grower-decisions.pdf.

21. Lopez, *The Farmworkers' Journey*, 143.

22. Ibid., 128.

23. Ibid.

24. Annenberg TV News, October 2, 2012; *Salinas Californian*, October 3, 2012.

25. Lopez, *The Farmworkers' Journey*, 152.

26. Ibid., 152; author's interview with Mayor Caballero, October 19, 2001.

27. Jason Clarke, "Environmental Factors for Violence," master's thesis, Naval Post Graduate School, December 2009: "The economic boom in the late 1990s and mid-2000s led to skyrocketing home prices in California, including Salinas. The median home price in Salinas in 2000 was $245,377; by 2007, it soared to $531,170. In the same time frame, median household income in Salinas went from $43,720 to $52,560. Low-income residents of Salinas were also hit hard by high unemployment and low paying jobs contributing to high population density in some areas of Salinas, forcing families to share inadequate spaces."

28. Villarejo and Schenker, "Environmental Health Policy": "A study of stressors associated with symptoms of anxiety and depression finds that poor housing conditions identified by farm laborers were associated with significant elevated levels of anxiety and depression."

29. A report by Human Rights Watch released May 16, 2012, asserts: "Our research confirms what farmworker advocates across the country believe: sexual violence and sexual harassment experienced by farmworkers is common enough that some farmworker women see these abuses as an unavoidable condition of agricultural work." *San Francisco Chronicle*, May 17, 2012.

30. Thompson, *Working in the Shadows*, 50: "Dole began using guest workers in 2005. In order to qualify they had to prove that there was not a sufficient number of American workers willing to do the work, and to show the government that they have the ability to house their workers—regardless of whether or not anyone would take them up on the offer. As a result, the town of Dateland, about 75 miles east of Yuma, has enough housing for the 293 guest workers the company employs during the year."

INDEX

Page numbers in italics refer to photos and their captions."